DARE NOT LINGER

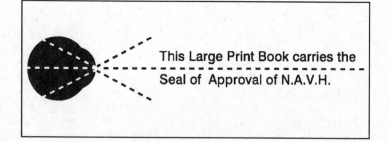

This Large Print Book carries the
Seal of Approval of N.A.V.H.

DARE NOT LINGER

THE PRESIDENTIAL YEARS

NELSON MANDELA
AND MANDLA LANGA

With a prologue by Graça Machel

THORNDIKE PRESS
A part of Gale, a Cengage Company

Farmington Hills, Mich • San Francisco • New York • Waterville, Maine
Meriden, Conn • Mason, Ohio • Chicago

LIBRARY OF CONGRESS CIP DATA ON FILE.
CATALOGUING IN PUBLICATION FOR THIS BOOK
IS AVAILABLE FROM THE LIBRARY OF CONGRESS

ISBN-13: 978-1-4328-4793-7 (hardcover)
ISBN-10: 1-4328-4793-7 (hardcover)

Published in 2018 by arrangement with Farrar, Straus and Giroux

Printed in the United States of America
1 2 3 4 5 6 7 22 21 20 19 18

The truth is that we are not yet free; we have merely achieved the freedom to be free, the right not to be oppressed. We have not taken the final step of our journey, but the first step on a longer and even more difficult road. For to be free is not merely to cast off one's chains, but to live in a way that respects and enhances the freedom of others. The true test of our devotion to freedom is just beginning.

I have walked that long road to freedom. I have tried not to falter; I have made missteps along the way. But I have discovered the secret that after climbing a great hill, one only finds that there are many more hills to climb. I have taken a moment here to rest, to steal a view of the glorious vista that surrounds me, to look back on the distance I have come. But I can rest only for a moment, for with freedom come responsibilities, and I dare not linger, for my long walk is not yet ended.

— Nelson Mandela, *Long Walk to Freedom*

4

I have to be bossy and establish that I obeyed.

The subpoena out of strength and not weakness.

These two examples clearly demonstrates

that in the new South Africa there is nobody, not

even the President, is above the law, that the rule of

law generally, and in particular the independence

of the judiciary should be respected.

landmarks in our turbulent history.

The world, aware of the turbulent formidable

challenges facing the first democratically

elected government, hailed us as a miracle

nation, and threw wide open its previously

closed doors to all South Africans, irrespective of

their ethnicity and background

This was the day for which a succession of

CONTENTS

PROLOGUE

It was three months after Madiba and I married that he sat down to write the first chapter of what he intended to be the sequel to his autobiography *Long Walk to Freedom*.

A sense of duty to his political organisation and the broader struggle for liberation in southern Africa informed his decision to write *Long Walk*. And it was a sense of duty to South Africans and to global citizens that energised him as he began the work which has now become *Dare Not Linger*.

He wanted to tell the story of his years as the first president of a democratic South Africa, reflect on the issues that had occupied him and his government, and explore the principles and the strategies they had sought to apply in addressing the innumerable challenges the new democracy faced. More than anything, he wanted to write about laying the foundations of a democratic system in South Africa.

For about four years the project loomed

large in his life and in the lives of those close to him. He wrote painstakingly, with his fountain pen or his ballpoint, awaited comments from trusted associates, then rewrote and rewrote until he felt he could move on to the next chapter or section. Every step was marked by a commitment to consultation. I am particularly grateful to Prof Jakes Gerwel and Madiba's personal assistant Zelda la Grange, who gave him every encouragement and supported the project in multiple ways in this period.

The demands the world placed on him, distractions of many kinds and his advancing years complicated the project. He lost momentum, and eventually the manuscript lay dormant. Through the last years of his life he talked about it often — worried about work started but not finished.

This book represents a collective effort to complete the project for Madiba. It presents the story he wanted to share with the world. Completed and narrated by South African writer Mandla Langa, with Madiba's ten original chapters and his other writing and thoughts from the period elegantly interwoven, the story has his voice ringing clearly throughout.

Mandla has done an extraordinary job of listening to Madiba and responding to his voice authorially. Joel Netshitenzhe and Tony Trew, trusted advisers and members of Madiba's staff during the presidential years, provided comprehensive and richly mediated research, analysis and preliminary narrativisation, and the Nelson Mandela Foundation anchored our endeavour institutionally. I am grateful to all of them, and to our publishing partners, for enabling us to bring Madiba's dream to fruition.

My wish is that every reader will feel challenged by Madiba's story and be inspired to work toward sustainable solutions to the world's multiple intractable problems. The title of the book is drawn from the final passage of *Long Walk,* where Madiba speaks of reaching the summit of a great hill and resting briefly before continuing his long walk. May we all find places of rest but never linger too long on the journeys we are called to.

— Graça Machel

A NOTE TO THE READER

A significant proportion of the words in this book are from Nelson Mandela's own writings, encompassing text from his unfinished memoir on his presidential years as well as personal notes, and speeches made in Parliament, at political rallies or on the international stage in his capacity as a revered advocate for human rights.

The unfinished memoir, 'The Presidential Years', consists of ten draft chapters, most of which include several versions, as well as notes toward further chapters. The sequence of chapter versions is not always clear from the archival evidence. Text for this book has been extracted across chapter versions and note accumulations.

In an effort to retain the historical integrity of Mandela's writing, we have made very few editorial interventions to his extracted text, apart from standardising quotation marks, italicising titles of books or newspapers and occasionally inserting a comma for sense or correcting the rare occurrence of a misspelt name. Editorial interpolations to provide further information to the reader appear in square brackets. We have retained Mandela's characteristic style of capitalising professional titles and have also preserved inconsistencies, such as his occasional capitalisation of terms such as 'Blacks' and 'Whites'. Quoted material from interviews where Mandela was speaking without notes has been standardised to be consistent with the editorial style of the narrative.

To assist the reader, we have included a comprehensive glossary of significant people, places and events mentioned in the book on page 609, along with a list of abbreviations for organisations, a map of South Africa and an abridged timeline of the period of Mandela's life ranging from his release from prison in 1990 until the inauguration of his successor, Thabo Mbeki, in 1999.

PREFACE

For many South Africans, in 1997 the public holiday of 16 December was remembered more as an important milestone in Nelson Mandela's long journey than for its poignant provenance, which simultaneously commemorates the victory of the Voortrekkers over amaZulu armies in 1838 and marks the establishment of Umkhonto weSizwe (MK), the military wing of the African National Congress (ANC), in 1961.* Having gone through various name changes, the day was finally renamed the Day of Reconciliation in 1994.

On this Tuesday afternoon, when the temperatures in the North West provincial town of Mafikeng were already in the upper thirties, the more than three thousand ANC delegates gathered for the Fiftieth National Conference of the ANC sat in rapt silence

* African National Congress (ANC); Umkhonto weSizwe (MK) — see People, Places and Events.

17

waiting for President Mandela to deliver his political report. Minutes earlier he had sat on the dais among the leadership of the outgoing National Executive Committee (NEC), a small smile on his face as he listened to the spirited singing of liberation songs, which was punctuated by rapturous applause as he stepped towards the podium.

Unlike most tall people, Mandela was unconscious of his height, standing erect as he read from the report, his delivery flat and matter-of-fact. He believed in the import of his words and therefore saw little use for rhetorical devices much favoured by some of his compatriots. The new South Africa, ushered in with joy and celebration by the first democratic elections of 1994, was already experiencing the traumatic aftermath of a difficult birth.

On the ANC's role as the governing party, Mandela said, 'During these past three years, it has been a basic tenet of our approach that despite our people's achievements in stabilising the democratic settlement, we are still involved in a delicate process of nursing the newborn baby into a state of adulthood.'

If the future was certain, the past was proving unpredictable. Violent crime — a legacy of previous iniquities and inequalities — was making headlines every day. Unemployment, which the government sought to confront through pro-growth policies and affirmative action, caused a measure of disaffection among the majority; this was exploited by opposition political parties, especially the National Party. Once the ruling party of the apartheid state, the National Party had withdrawn from the Government of National Unity (GNU) in 1996, citing its inability to influence government policy.*

'The more honest among its members,' Mandela said of the National Party's politicians, 'who occupied executive positions and were driven by the desire to protect the interests of both the Afrikaners and the rest of the population, did not support the decision to pull out of the GNU.'

As Mandela spoke in December 1997, there was a sense of expectation. The dramatic events of the previous year in South Africa, such as the expulsion of General Bantu Holomisa from the ANC and the formation of a breakaway political party, the United Democratic Movement, must have conjured up the trauma of the schism that gave birth to the Pan Africanist Congress of Azania (PAC) in 1959.† Once a favoured son, with a reputation for speaking his mind, Holomisa was also credited with the rise of populist tendencies

---

* Government of National Unity (GNU) — see People, Places and Events.
† Bantu Holomisa; Pan Africanist Congress of Azania (PAC) — see People, Places and Events.

within the ANC, equally fostered by Winnie Madikizela-Mandela and Peter Mokaba, the outspoken president of the ANC Youth League (ANCYL).*

Then there was the question of succession. Mandela had already voiced his intention to step down as ANC president at this conference. In a televised broadcast on Sunday, 7 July 1996, Mandela confirmed the rumours that he wouldn't be available for elections in 1999. In keeping with his promise when sworn in as the country's first democratic president in 1994, he felt that, although he could have served two terms as stipulated by the Constitution, one term was enough as he had already laid the foundation for a better future for all.†

Editorials and analysts presented the conference as an arena in which a trusted hero would be handing over the baton. The question of who would succeed him, Thabo Mbeki or Cyril Ramaphosa, had already been settled.‡ They both had sterling struggle credentials. Ramaphosa excelled in the Mul-

* Winnie Madikizela-Mandela; Peter Mokaba; African National Congress Youth League (ANCYL) — see People, Places and Events.
† Constitution of the Republic of South Africa — see People, Places and Events.
‡ Thabo Mbeki; Cyril Ramaphosa — see People, Places and Events.

tiparty Negotiating Forum of the Convention for a Democratic South Africa (CODESA), which started in October 1991 and ended in 1993, and which culminated in the adoption of the Constitution on 8 May 1996.* Mbeki was widely hailed for his stewardship of the country's affairs as Mandela's deputy.

Anxious to dispel the widely held criticism that the isiXhosa language group dominated the ANC, Mandela had in 1994 suggested Ramaphosa while broaching the question of succession to the remaining three senior ANC officials, Walter Sisulu, Thomas Nkobi and Jacob Zuma.† He was advised instead to anoint Mbeki. Mbeki was ultimately elected ANC president in 1997, thus putting him in line for the country's presidency ahead of Ramaphosa.

A piquant flavouring to the drama of the five-day conference came from the elections for the top positions in the ANC, with only two of the six being contested. Mbeki was elected unopposed as ANC president and Jacob Zuma became deputy president. Winnie Madikizela-Mandela had considered running for the deputy presidency against Zuma, but she could not muster enough support from

* Convention for a Democratic South Africa (CODESA) — see People, Places and Events.
† Walter Sisulu; Thomas Nkobi; Jacob Zuma — see People, Places and Events.

delegates to second her nomination and was forced to stand down. Many felt that her dalliance with populist causes and barbed comments about government shortcomings, which sometimes smacked of defiance towards her erstwhile husband, had alienated the membership and led to her humiliation. Kgalema Motlanthe, one-time trade unionist and, like Mandela and Jacob Zuma, a Robben Island alumnus, was elected secretary general, with Mendi Msimang taking over as treasurer general from Arnold Stofile.* Of the two contested positions of national chairman and deputy secretary general, Mosiuoa 'Terror' Lekota trounced one-time fellow inmate on Robben Island Steve Tshwete for the position of national chairman; and Thenjiwe Mtintso won narrowly against Mavivi Myakayaka-Manzini for the position of deputy secretary general.†

At the close of the conference, it was again a sombre Mandela who gave his farewell speech on the afternoon of 20 December 1997. Hands clasped in front of him, he departed from his written script to speak from the heart. Without naming names, he cautioned the incoming leader against surrounding himself or herself with yes-men and -women.

* Robben Island — see People, Places and Events.
† Steve Tshwete — see People, Places and Events.

'A leader, especially with such a heavy responsibility, who has been returned unopposed, his first duty is to allay the concerns of his colleagues in the leadership for them to be able to discuss freely, without fear within the internal structures of the movement.'

Waiting for the applause to die down, he elaborated on the contradiction that faced a leader who had to unite the organisation while allowing internal dissent and freedom of expression.

'People should even be able to criticise the leader without fear or favour, only in that case are you likely to keep your colleagues together. There are many examples of this — allowing differences of opinion as long as those don't put the organisation in disrepute.'

As an illustration, Mandela cited a critic of Mao Zedong's policies during the Chinese revolution. The Chinese leadership 'examined whether he had said anything outside the structures of the movement, which put the movement in disrepute'. Satisfied that this was not the case, the critic was brought into the central committee as president of the Chinese Chamber of Workers — the trade union movement.

They 'gave him responsibility for which he had to account,' Mandela said to gales of laughter, 'and he was forced to talk less and to be more accountable.'

He went on, 'Fortunately, I know that our president understands this issue. One thing I know is that in his work he has taken criticism in a comradely spirit and I have not the slightest doubt that he is not . . . going to sideline anybody, because he knows that [it's important] to surround yourself with strong and independent persons who can within the structures of the movement criticise you and improve your own contribution, so that when you go outside your policy your decisions are foolproof and they cannot be criticised by anybody successfully. Nobody in this organisation understands that principle better than my president, comrade Thabo Mbeki.'

Mandela went on, reading from his speech, to reiterate how leaders' association with 'powerful and influential individuals who have far more resources than all of us put together' could lead to their forgetting 'those who were with us when we were all alone during difficult times'.

Following another round of applause, Mandela went on to justify the ANC's continued relationships with countries such as Cuba, Libya and Iran. This was against the advice of governments and heads of state that had supported the apartheid state. To the foreign guests present in the hall, from all those shunned countries and the anti-apartheid movement worldwide, Mandela conveyed his gratitude. They 'made it possible for us to win. Our victory is their victory.'

Towards the end of his address, Mandela took a moment to admit to the vulnerability of the struggle and its gains. While there had been signal successes, there had also been setbacks.

'It is not because we were infallible,' he said, departing from his written speech. 'We have had difficulties in the past, like any other organisations.

'We had a leader who also was returned unopposed, but then we were arrested together with him.* But he was wealthy by the standards of those days and we were very poor. And the security police went to him with a copy of the Suppression of Communism Act, and they say: "Now look here, you've got farms. Here is a provision that if you are found guilty you'll lose those properties. Your associates here are poor people, they have nothing to lose."† The leader then opted

---

* Mandela is referring to Dr James Moroka (see People, Places and Events), a conservative former president of the ANC, who denounced Mandela and others arrested during the Defiance Campaign Against Unjust Laws in 1952. Later, Mandela forgave him and made him godfather to his grandchild.

† Suppression of Communism Act, No. 44, 1950 — see People, Places and Events.

to have his own lawyers and refused to be defended with the rest of the accused. Then the lawyer leading his witness told the court that there were many documents where the accused were demanding equality with the whites: what did his witness believe? What was his opinion?

'The leader,' Mandela continued, with a small chuckle at the memory, 'said, "There will never be anything like that." And the lawyer said, "But do you and your colleagues here accept that?" ' The leader 'was beginning to point towards Walter Sisulu when the judge says, "No, no, no, no, no, you speak for yourself." But that experience of being arrested was too much for him.' He paused, reflecting. 'Now we nevertheless appreciated the role that he had played, during the days before we were arrested. He had done very well.'

Not pausing to explain the ambiguity of the last statement, which elicited great hilarity — was 'doing well' an appreciation of the leader's service to the organisation or a barbed comment aimed at his material wealth? — Mandela wound up his off-script commentary.

'I'm saying this,' he concluded with a mischievous glint in his eye, 'because if one day I myself should cave in and say, "I have been misled by these young chaps", just remember I was once your colleague.'

Returning to the script, he said that the time had come to hand over the baton. 'And,' he went on, 'I personally relish the moment when my fellow veterans, whom you have seen here, and I shall be able to observe from near and judge from afar. As 1999 approaches, I will endeavour as State President to delegate more and more responsibility so as to ensure a smooth transition to the new presidency.

'Thus I will be able to have that opportunity in my last years to spoil my grandchildren and try in various ways to assist all South African children, especially those who have been the hapless victims of a system that did not care. I will also have more time to continue the debates with Tyopho, that is Walter Sisulu, Uncle Govan (Govan Mbeki) and others,* which the 20 years of *umrabulo* [intense political debate for educational purposes] on the Island could not resolve.†

'Let me assure you . . . that, in my humble way, I shall continue to be of service to transformation, and to the ANC, the only movement that is capable of bringing about that transformation. As an ordinary member of the ANC I suppose that I will also have many privileges that I have been deprived of over the years: to be as critical as I can be; to

* Govan Mbeki — see People, Places and Events.
† Tyopho was the clan name of Walter Sisulu.

challenge any signs of autocracy from Shell House and to lobby for my preferred candidates from the branch level upwards.*

'On a more serious note though, I wish to reiterate that I will remain a disciplined member of the ANC; and in my last months in government office, I will always be guided by the ANC's policies, and [will] find mechanisms that will allow you to rap me over the knuckles for any indiscretions . . .

'Our generation traversed a century that was characterised by conflict, bloodshed, hatred and intolerance; a century which tried but could not fully resolve the problems of disparity between the rich and the poor, between developing and developed countries.

'I hope that our endeavours as the ANC have contributed and will continue to contribute to this search for a just world order.

'Today marks the completion of one more lap in that relay race — still to continue for many more decades — when we take leave so that the competent generation of lawyers, computer experts, economists, financiers, industrialists, doctors, engineers and, above all, ordinary workers and peasants can take the ANC into the new millennium.

'I look forward to that period when I will be able to wake up with the sun; to walk the

* Shell House was the ANC's headquarters from 1990 until 1997.

hills and valleys of my country village, Qunu, in peace and tranquillity.* And I am confident that this will certainly be the case, because, as I do so, and see the smiles on the faces of children which reflect the sunshine in their hearts, I will know, comrade Thabo and your team, that you are on the right track; you are succeeding.

'I will know that the ANC lives — it continues to lead!'[1]

As one, the conference delegates and invited guests rose to their feet and started singing, clapping and swaying to a medley of songs before settling on one that was both a valediction to a unique son and a sad admission that, whatever happened, South Africa would never be the same again.

'Nelson Mandela,' the song went, 'there's no other like him.'

* Qunu — see People, Places and Events.

CHAPTER ONE:
THE CHALLENGE OF FREEDOM

Nelson Mandela had heard this freedom song and its many variations long before his release from Victor Verster Prison in 1990.* The concerted efforts of the state security apparatus and the prison authorities to isolate him from the unfolding drama of struggle — and its evocative soundtrack — could not stop the flow of information between the prized prisoner and his many interlocutors. The influx into prisons, including Robben Island, in the late 1980s of newcomers who were mainly young people from various political formations — preceded in 1976 by the flood of student activists following the upheavals in Soweto and elsewhere — marked the escalation of the struggle and brought with it new songs, each verse a coded commentary on progress or setback, tragedy or comedy, unfolding on the streets. The recurring refrain of the songs was that the South

* Victor Verster Prison — see People, Places and Events.

31

African regime was on the wrong side of history.

Like most people who accept that history has carved for them a special place, and probably being familiar with Emerson's mordant dictum — 'to be great is to be misunderstood'[1] — Mandela knew that his own legacy depended on the course he had championed: the talks between the government and the ANC. These had started five years prior to his release, when fresh from a check-up at Volks Hospital where he was visited by Kobie Coetsee, the minister of justice, Mandela had broached the question of talks between the ANC and the government.* Coetsee's presence was a glimmer of hope in an otherwise unrelieved darkness. The year 1985 marked the bloodiest period of the struggle, a time characterised by an irreversibility of intent and a hardening of attitudes among the warring sides that stared at each other from across a great gulf.

Oliver Tambo, the ANC president and Mandela's compatriot, had just called on South Africans to render the country ungovernable.†[2] Mandela, however, realised that the toll would be heavier on the unarmed masses facing an enemy using the panoply of state power. But he was a prisoner, a political

* Kobie Coetsee — see People, Places and Events.
† Oliver Tambo — see People, Places and Events.

32

prisoner, who, like a prisoner of war, has only one obligation — and that is to escape. Only, his escape from his immediate confinement was irreversibly intertwined with the need for the broader escape, or liberation, of the people of South Africa from the shackles of an unjust order. Having long studied his enemy and having read up on its literature on history, jurisprudence, philosophy, language and culture, Mandela had come to the understanding that white people were fated to discover that they were as damaged by racism as were black people. The system based on lies that had given them a false sense of superiority would prove poisonous to them and to future generations, rendering them unsuited to the larger world.

Separated from his prison comrades on his return from hospital to Pollsmoor Prison, a period Mandela called his 'splendid isolation', it was brought home to him that something had to give.* He concluded that 'it simply did not make sense for both sides to lose thousands if not millions of lives in a conflict that was unnecessary'.[3] It was time to talk.

Conscious of the repercussions of his actions to the liberation struggle in general and the ANC in particular, he was resigned to his fate: if things went awry, he reasoned, the ANC could still save face by ascribing his ac-

* Pollsmoor Prison — see People, Places and Events.

tions to the erratic frolic of an isolated individual, not its representative.

'Great men make history,' C. L. R. James, the influential Afro-Trinidadian historian writes, 'but only such history as it is possible for them to make. Their freedom of achievement is limited by the necessities of their environment.'[4]

In almost three decades of incarceration, Mandela had devoted time to analysing the country he was destined to lead. In those moments of waiting for word from his captors or for a clandestine signal from his compatriots, he mulled over the nature of society, its saints and its monsters. Although in prison — his freedom of achievement limited by the necessities of his environment — he gradually gained access to the highest councils of apartheid power, finally meeting with an ailing President P. W. Botha, and later his successor, F. W. de Klerk.*

Outside, deaths multiplied and death squads thrived; more funerals gave rise to more cycles of killings and assassinations, including of academics. A new language evolved on the streets, and people became inured to self-defence units and grislier methods of execution, such as the brutal 'necklace', being used on those seen as apart-

* P. W. Botha; F. W. de Klerk — see People, Places and Events.

34

heid collaborators.*

In all the meetings Mandela held with government representatives what was paramount in his mind was a solution to the South African tragedy. From De Klerk down to the nineteen-year-old policeman clad in body armour, trying to push away angry crowds, these were men and women of flesh and blood, who, like a child playing with a hand grenade, seemed unaware of the fact that they were careening towards destruction — and taking countless millions down with them.

Mandela hoped that sense would prevail before it was too late. Nearing seventy, he was aware of his own mortality. Perhaps it was in a whimsical mood that he wrote, much later, what amounted to a prophecy:

'Men and women all over the world, right down the centuries, come and go. Some leave nothing behind, not even their names. It would seem that they never existed at all. Others do leave something behind: the haunting memory of the evil deeds they committed against other human beings; the abuse of power by a tiny white minority against a black majority of Africans, Coloureds and Indians, the denial of basic human rights to that

* Necklacing is a torturous method of execution where a tyre filled with petrol is placed around a victim's neck and then set alight.

majority, rabid racism in all spheres of life, detention without trial, torture, brutal assaults inside and outside prison, the breaking up of families, forcing people into exile, underground and throwing them into prisons for long periods.'[5]

Like almost all black South Africans, Mandela either had first-hand experience of each violation he cited, or knew of people close to him who had suffered hideously in the hands of the authorities. This was the period of sudden death, where the incidents were reminiscent of titles of B-grade American movies: The Gugulethu Seven. The Cradock Four. The Trojan Horse Massacre.* In all of these instances, where young community leaders and activists were killed brutally at the height of state clampdowns in the mid-1980s, the

* The Gugulethu Seven were seven young anti-apartheid activists who were shot dead by police on 3 March 1986 in Gugulethu, near Cape Town; the Cradock Four were four anti-apartheid activists travelling from Port Elizabeth to Cradock, in the Eastern Cape, on 27 June 1985, when they were kidnapped by security police, then tortured and murdered; the Trojan Horse Massacre took place on 15 October 1985, when security police in Athlone, Cape Town, hid behind wooden crates on a South African Railways truck, then stood up and opened fire on an anti-apartheid demonstration, killing three youths, including an eleven-year-old.

state security agencies either denied complicity or claimed to have been under attack.

Remembering Sharpeville and other massacres perpetrated by the apartheid security forces where scores of people had been maimed or killed through police action, Mandela evokes disturbing images of a 'trigger-happy police force that massacred thousands of innocent and defenceless people', and which blasphemes, using 'the name of God . . . to justify the commission of evil against the majority.* In their daily lives these men and women, whose regime committed these unparalleled atrocities, wore expensive outfits and went regularly to church. In actual fact, they represented everything for which the devil stood. Notwithstanding all their claims to be a community of devout worshippers, their policies were denounced by almost the entire civilised world as a crime against humanity. They were suspended from the United Nations and from a host of other world and regional organisations . . . [and] became the polecats of the world.'[6]

The fall of the Berlin Wall in November 1989 was an international story that almost overshadowed a major domestic development that had occurred a month earlier. On 15

* Sharpeville Massacre — see People, Places and Events.

October 1989, Walter Sisulu was released from prison together with Raymond Mhlaba, Wilton Mkwayi, Oscar Mpetha, Ahmed Kathrada, Andrew Mlangeni and Elias Motsoaledi.* Five of them, alongside Mandela, had been among the ten accused in the Rivonia Trial of 1963–4,† and were his closest comrades.‡ Jafta Kgalabi Masemola, co-founder with Robert Sobukwe of the PAC, was also released.§ Six months later, Masemola died in a car crash, which some PAC members still regard as suspicious.

Mandela had prevailed on the authorities to release the men in Pollsmoor and on Robben Island as a demonstration of good intent. The negotiations for their release had started with Mandela and Botha, and had stalled when, according to Niël Barnard, former head of the National Intelligence Service (NIS), due to 'strong antagonisms in the SSC [State Security Council] these plans [to

* For biographical notes on these individuals, see People, Places and Events.

† Rivonia Trial — see People, Places and Events.

‡ Wilton Mkwayi and Oscar Mpetha were not accused in the Rivonia Trial. Mkwayi was sentenced to life imprisonment in January 1965 and Oscar Mpetha was sentenced to five years' imprisonment in 1983.

§ Jafta Masemola; Robert Sobukwe — see People, Places and Events.

release Sisulu in March 1989] were put on the back burner'.*[7] The release left Mandela with mixed emotions: elation at the freeing of his compatriots and sadness at his own solitude. But he knew that his turn was coming in a few months.

Kathrada recalled how the last time 'prisoner Kathrada' saw 'prisoner Mandela' was at Victor Verster Prison on 10 October 1989, when he and other comrades had visited Mandela in the house where he was held for the final fourteen months of his imprisonment.

Mandela said to the group, 'Chaps, this is goodbye,' and Kathrada et al. said they'd 'believe it when it happens'. Mandela insisted that he had just been with two cabinet ministers who assured him that his comrades would be freed. That evening, they were given supper in the Victor Verster Prison dining hall instead of being returned to Pollsmoor. And then, just in time for the evening news, a television was brought in and an announcement was made that President F. W. de Klerk had decided to release the eight prisoners: Kathrada, Sisulu, Mhlaba, Mlangeni, Motsoaledi, Mkwayi, Mpetha and Masemola.

The men were returned to Pollsmoor Prison and three days later they were transferred. Kathrada, Sisulu, Mlangeni, Motsoaledi,

* Niël Barnard — see People, Places and Events.

Mkwayi and Masemola were flown to Johannesburg where they were held at Johannesburg Prison. Mhlaba went to his home town of Port Elizabeth, and Mpetha, who was from Cape Town, remained at Groote Schuur Hospital where he had been held under armed guard while being treated. Then, on the night of Saturday, 14 October, the commanding officer of Johannesburg Prison approached the prisoners and said, 'We've just received a fax from prison headquarters that you are going to be released tomorrow.'

'What's a fax?' Kathrada asked. He had then been in prison for over twenty-six years.[8]

On 2 February 1990, F. W. de Klerk stood up in Parliament and announced the unbanning of the ANC, the PAC, the South African Communist Party (SACP) and about thirty other outlawed political organisations.* He further announced the release of political prisoners jailed for non-violent offences, the suspension of capital punishment and the abrogation of myriad proscriptions under the State of Emergency.† For many South Africans who had writhed under the jackboot of apartheid rule, this was the proverbial first day of the rest of their lives.

* South African Communist Party (SACP) — see People, Places and Events.
† State of Emergency, 1960 — see People, Places and Events.

40

Like almost all political prisoners who would be required by history to service a broader humanity, among them Mahatma Gandhi, Antonio Gramsci, Václav Havel and Milovan Djilas, Mandela was able to impose his will on himself and, to a certain extent, on his captors. He had read everything available to him about the devastating patience of leaders such as Ahmed Ben Bella, Jomo Kenyatta and Sékou Touré, who had persevered through the hardships imposed by colonial administrators and emerged strong — stronger perhaps, given that they had proven that prison could not break their spirit. But Mandela was aware of the changes wrought by the reality of life outside prison. The seduction of office and the invincible allure of power. He had seen it happen in his lifetime, in certain cases with people with whom he had rubbed shoulders, of whom he writes:

'There were also those who once commanded invincible liberation armies, who suffered untold hardships, yet ultimately succeeded, not only in freeing their people, but also in improving their living conditions. They attracted respect and admiration far and wide, and inspired millions in all continents to rise against oppression and exploitation.'

For Mandela, it was saddening to see some of these leaders, former freedom fighters, going astray. In critiquing their disastrous hubris, he tried to convey the magnitude of the resultant betrayal of the cause. He could also have been expressing his own inner fear of what might happen, when he writes about situations where 'freedom and the installation of a democratic government bring erstwhile liberators from the bush to the corridors of power, where they now rub shoulders with the rich and mighty'.

He continues that it is 'in situations of this nature that some former freedom fighters run the risk of forgetting principles and those who are paralysed by poverty, ignorance and diseases; some then start aspiring to the lifestyle of the oppressors they once detested and overthrew'.[9]

The genesis of these observations can be seen in Mandela's own life, where discipline was his watchword. He followed a strict regimen of exercise and kept himself in good physical shape. He was used to doing things for himself and continued to do so after his release, on one occasion astounding the cook assigned to him, Warrant Officer Swart, by insisting that he would do the washing up and cook his own meals.

Mandela writes: 'One day, after a delicious meal prepared by Mr Swart, I went into the kitchen to wash the dishes. "No," he said, "that is my duty. You must return to the sitting room." I insisted that I had to do something, and that if he cooked, it was only fair for me to do the dishes. Mr Swart protested, but finally gave in. He also objected to the fact that I would make my bed in the morning, saying it was his responsibility to do so. But I had been making my bed for so long that it had become a reflex.'[10]

To a large degree, Mandela had observed a soldier's code of conduct long before his own arrest in 1962. He expected his confrères, members of a select fellowship of committed fighters, to be beyond reproach; the apartheid machinery was rigid and regimented and would need an equally disciplined force to resist and finally overthrow it.

'Unless their political organisation remains strong and principled, exercising strict discipline on leaders as well as ordinary members alike, [and] inspires its membership, apart from government programmes, to develop social initiatives to uplift the community, the temptation to abandon the poor and to start amassing enormous wealth for themselves becomes irresistible.'[11]

From inside prison, Mandela had been monitoring world affairs, noting with dismay that not a few of the leaders on the African continent were in the grip of megalomania. From the northernmost point down to the tip of the continent, self-appointed leaders, their uniforms bristling with medals, inflicted untold misery on their subjects in countries where plunder of state resources was the order of the day. The people became prey to famine, violence, pestilence and extreme penury. About this, Mandela says: 'They come to believe that they are indispensable leaders. In cases where the constitution allows it, they become life presidents. In those cases where a country's constitution imposes limitations, they generally amend the constitution to enable themselves to cling to power for eternity.'[12]

Questions about how he was going to lead roiled in his head when the moment of his release came. The larger world promised to introduce complications more daunting than the negotiations he had conducted with his captors, including when he prevailed over the prison authorities about the time and place in which he was to be released. De Klerk's government had wanted to release him much earlier, and certainly without fanfare, to his home in Soweto, but Mandela had baulked. He wanted to be released in Cape Town where he could thank the people of the city before going home:

'I was saying that I want to be released at the gate of Victor Verster. From there I'll look after myself. You have no right to say I should be taken to Johannesburg. I want to be released here. And so eventually they agreed to release me at the gate of Victor Verster.' In addition, Mandela asked for his release to be postponed by seven days for the people 'to prepare'.[13]

It was in prison that Mandela perfected what would later become one of his greatest strengths, the ability to appreciate that a person in front of him, friend or foe, was a complex human being with many facets to his or her personality. One of his regrets, while cameras clicked and the crowds were in rhapsodies over his release on the afternoon of 11 February 1990, was that he had not been able to say goodbye to the prison staff. To him they were more than an assemblage of uniformed functionaries at the sharp end of an unjust regime; they were people with families, who, like everyone else, had anxieties about life.

This, of course, did not mean that Mandela would let evil off the hook, nor was he wilfully oblivious to the excesses of the white apartheid regime. In his single-minded preparation for the future, which had started with the closing of the prison gates behind him, he knew he had to unburden himself of the clutter of resentment and concentrate on what lay ahead. Even if he had started his sentence as an individual, Mandela had been part of a committed fellowship called upon by the exigency of struggle to sacrifice the best years of their lives for a greater good.

Going out alone, with the rest of the Rivonia defendants and fellow prisoners having been released earlier, he knew there would be millions of eyes looking to see what he had become. For months Mandela had been meeting and conducting telephone conversations with a number of people from the ANC and the United Democratic Front (UDF), an umbrella organisation with a broad range of affiliates, including hundreds of youth organisations, scores of civic associations and student organisations. Hours before the actual release, he had consulted with members of the National Reception Committee,* a selection of battle-hardened activists and leaders of the mass democratic movement, which included Cyril Ramaphosa, Valli Moosa, Jay Naidoo and Trevor Manuel, all of whom would play important roles in the future government.† Almost all long-term prisoners have a heightened perception for situations and read them more quickly than others for the simple reason that their survival depends on it. Therefore, while excited at the prospect of being released, Mandela picked up on the anxiety of the ANC representatives who had received very little notice of the change in his release venue from Soweto to

* The National Reception Committee of four hundred prominent anti-apartheid activists was established to prepare for and run Nelson Mandela's release from prison and the consequent activities.
† Valli Moosa; Jay Naidoo; Trevor Manuel — see People, Places and Events.

46

Cape Town.

'The notice was less than twenty-four hours,' said Valli Moosa. 'We were quite shocked but none of us gave in to the temptation to ask that he be kept in any longer, though we wanted to ask that.'[14]

Mandela understood the dilemma that his release posed for both the government and the ANC as a measure of the complexity of the road ahead. On the journey out of Victor Verster he had already told himself that his life's mission was 'to liberate the oppressed and the oppressor both'.[15] This meant that he would have to try and straddle the gulf between the oppressor, represented by the government that had jailed him, and the oppressed: the majority of the people of South Africa in all their diversity. He had already accepted what it would take to achieve that goal. It was a goal that destiny had set for him.

'The real test of a man,' Václav Havel writes, 'is not when he plays the role that he wants for himself but when he plays the role destiny has for him.'[16]

Much later, Barbara Masekela, a renowned writer and diplomat who was chief of staff in Mandela's office, echoed this sentiment.* 'Mandela,' she said, 'knew that being presi-

* Barbara Masekela — see People, Places and Events.

47

dent was playing a role — and he was determined to play it well.'[17]

Playing it well was far from easy, however, and Mandela's preparations had begun a long time before. In the mid-1980s Mandela had grasped the nettle and explored the possibility of initiating talks between the ANC and the National Party government of De Klerk's predecessor, President P. W. Botha.* A cartoonist's favourite, whose scowling countenance and finger-wagging admonishment graced national newspapers, President Botha was one of the last hard men, a hawk nicknamed 'Die Groot Krokodil' (The Big Crocodile) for his hard-line stance, who saw brute force as the answer to conflict. But even Botha had learnt from some of his most hawkish generals that the resolution of the South African nightmare could not be achieved through military force alone.

Mandela knew that the cycle of violence was taking its toll on the poorest and most marginalised sections of the population. The restive black majority had its expectations. The benefactors of the apartheid regime — many of them armed and possessed of a formidable capacity to wreak havoc — were also waiting with bated breath for a significant threat to the status quo.

In all this, Mandela had to signal that F. W.

* National Party — see People, Places and Events.

de Klerk was a man of integrity, if only to disarm the hardliners who would have chortled with glee if the South African president were further weakened by the ex-prisoner's rejection. According to the right-wingers' so-called logic, it was one thing for De Klerk to release the terrorist, and another for the self-same terrorist to call the shots while spurning the hand of his liberator.

For Mandela, conducting the dialogue with the Pretoria regime was like negotiating a route through volatile traffic. He had to act as a buffer between the group of negotiators led by De Klerk and two vehicles coming from different directions — one driven by the expectations of a black majority who would wait no longer, and the other by the right-wing hardliners, influenced by fear and a misplaced sense of righteousness. For Mandela, the derailment of the negotiations before they even started would have been the greatest tragedy. In this regard, he went against the counsel of the representatives of his own organisations, who were uncomfortable about his intention to call De Klerk a man of integrity. When his colleagues bristled at his accommodation of De Klerk he always insisted that he would continue to accept De Klerk as a man of integrity until he was presented with facts to the contrary. Until then, De Klerk was going to be his future negotiating partner.

Mandela was able to see and make a distinction between F. W. de Klerk the man and De Klerk the representative, if not the victim, of a repressive and all-powerful state machine. Perhaps Mandela's one wish was to work on his political counterpart and wean him from the influence of the political party that espoused apartheid as a policy, a stance he found wholly repugnant.

On this, he would comment later: 'The apartheid regime, even during the period of negotiations . . . still believed that they could save white supremacy with black consent. Although the apartheid negotiators tried to be subtle, it was clear right from the start of the talks that the overriding idea was to prevent us from governing the country, even if we won in a democratic election.'

He'd had a foretaste of this stance when he first met President de Klerk while still a prisoner at Victor Verster, on 13 December 1989. He writes:

'Shortly before that meeting, I had read an article written by the editor of *Die Burger*, then the official mouthpiece of the National Party, under the pen name of Dawie in which he sharply criticised the concept of Group Rights which was being peddled by that Party as the best solution for the country's problems. This meant that each population group after the first democratic elections would retain permanently the rights and privileges

50

it had enjoyed before such elections, no matter which political party had won.'

This deception would mean that the 'white minority would continue to monopolise all the important rights of citizenship. The revolutionary changes demanded by the liberation movement, and for which martyrs across the centuries had paid the highest price, would be stifled. The new government would be unable to provide shelter for the people and quality education for their children. Poverty, unemployment, hunger, illiteracy and disease would be rampant. *Die Burger* criticised this pseudo policy as introducing apartheid through the back door.'

Mandela pointed out to De Klerk that 'if their own mouthpiece condemned this idea, he could well imagine what we thought of it. We would reject it out of hand.'[18]

'It was at this point that the president impressed me,' Mandela writes. 'He conceded that if our movement would not even consider the idea, he would scrap it. I immediately sent a message to the ANC leadership in Zambia in which I described the President as a man of integrity with whom we could do business.'[19]

Mandela might have been impressed with De Klerk, but it was another matter to sell the proposition to the ANC. The ANC, as has been noted countless times, is another animal altogether, at once a broad church, a liberation movement and a way of life for millions of South Africans. It has been in certain families for generations, passed down from one generation to the next like a family heirloom. Such an organisation inevitably becomes hidebound to tradition, viewing any innovation with suspicion. In its seventy-seven years of existence at the moment when the talks between Mandela and apartheid presidents reached their acme in 1989, the issue of negotiations had never been detailed in its policy. But in exile, the ANC had had to make a realistic appraisal of the situation and the balance of forces. The relentless assault by the South African military machine against Frontline States, an alliance of southern African countries united in opposing apartheid from 1960 to early 1990, for harbouring the ANC, changed the geopolitical character of the region.

More crucial was the ANC's forced removal from various strategic zones, the most important being Mozambique after President Samora Machel signed the non-aggression pact with South Africa, the Nkomati Accord, on 16 March 1984. This meant that the ANC had to pursue its armed struggle without the benefit of bases in neighbouring states. This put pressure on the leadership to start thinking about what to do with the thousands of displaced cadres in Zambia and Tanzania. In that same year, a mutiny that broke out in the MK camps in Angola shook the leadership, especially as its raison d'être was impatience on the part of MK soldiers who wanted to return home to fight the enemy, instead of being embroiled in the domestic conflict between Movimento Popular de Libertação de Angola ('The People's Movement for the Liberation of Angola') (MPLA) troops and the União Nacional para a Independência Total de Angola (National Union for the Total Independence of Angola) (UNITA)) bandits, who were backed by South Africa.[*] Similar pressure had forced the ANC to assign the Luthuli Detachment of MK into the Wankie and Sipolilo campaigns in what was then Rhodesia from 1967.[†] In the camps, in most areas where there was a significant com-

[*] The MPLA gave the ANC military training facilities for MK. During the civil war following the MPLA's ascendance to power in 1975, the South African Defence Force (SADF) shored up UNITA in its campaign to destabilise Angola and forestall Namibian independence.

[†] The Wankie Campaign of 1967 was the first joint military operation between MK (through its Luthuli Detachment unit) and Zimbabwe People's Revolutionary Army forces to infiltrate fighters into South Africa from what was then Rhodesia. Another MK unit called Sipolilo was then sent into Rhodesia to attack from the east, towards Sipolilo, to open up a second route.

munity of exiles, people sang songs invoking a pantheon of heroes and martyrs, including the names of Nelson Mandela or Oliver Tambo. They sang to dedicate themselves to the struggle and of how they were going to march on Pretoria. Sometimes the revolutionary songs were about the perfidy of agents of the South African regime, some of them one-time comrades who had crossed to the other side. But the most reviled figures, looming large in the collective imagination of the fervent singers, were the succession of apartheid leaders, especially Botha and De Klerk.*

Even before Mandela had actual contact with Botha and De Klerk, rumours of the talks and Mandela's imminent release had been doing the rounds. In early July 1989, a group of exiled ANC writers on their way to meet with Afrikaner writers and academics at

* On 16 June 1976 police opened fire on a crowd of between 10,000 and 20,000 schoolchildren in Soweto as they marched to a rally at Orlando Stadium to protest the Afrikaans Medium Decree, which required all black schools to use a fifty-fifty mix of Afrikaans and English in their lessons, and some subjects to be taught solely in Afrikaans. This marked the beginning of the Soweto Uprising, which went on for several months in many parts of the country until the government reversed the decree, and during which time it is estimated that up to seven hundred students were killed.

the Victoria Falls stumbled on a whole battery of red-eyed South African and international journalists and TV crews camped outside the Pamodzi Hotel in Lusaka. Acting on what was obviously gross misinformation, the media were keeping vigil outside the airport and at the gates of the ANC headquarters on Chachacha Road downtown, on the off-chance that they would get a scoop if Nelson Mandela were released into the custody of the ANC in Zambia as they had been told. More disturbing, however, were the charges from some youthful firebrands at home and in exile that 'the old man had sold out'. There was even talk of threats on Mandela's life.

Notwithstanding this, however, the ANC has consistently possessed an unerring political instinct, seeking, through the years, to find a solution to its problems. Even the men and women under arms, in camps or operating in the underground inside the country, were guided by political principles. There were members of the NEC, the highest decision-making body between conferences, who were hugely uncomfortable with the possibility of a rapprochement with Pretoria. But there was Oliver Tambo, the president, whose credo was decision-making by consensus, who insisted that each aspect of a difficult problem be discussed and analysed, no matter how long it took, until an agreement was reached.

Inevitably, any liberation movement comes to a crossroads where crucial decisions that have a bearing on people's lives have to be made. OR, as Tambo was affectionately called, made them. Untiring and scrupulous to a fault, he consulted leaders in his own party as well as ensuring that leaders of the Frontline States were briefed on the developments.

Ultimately, it was quite clear to all that talking with the enemy was an idea whose time had come. To strengthen this, representatives of various trade unions and political and civic organisations flew into Lusaka to confer with the ANC and to start mapping out strategies for dealing with the unfolding scenario. The arrival in Lusaka of the grand old men — Walter Sisulu, Govan Mbeki (who had been released two years earlier), Wilton Mkwayi, Raymond Mhlaba, Elias Motsoaledi and Ahmed Kathrada — and their interaction with the membership, made everything real. It also acted as an escape valve for the pent-up emotions of MK comrades, mainly members of Special Operations working underground, who had grievances about the heightened casualty rate among MK members infiltrating inside the country. It was Walter Sisulu who told the ANC members congregated in Mulungushi Hall, Lusaka, that they should get ready to go home.[20]

CHAPTER TWO:
NEGOTIATING DEMOCRACY

On 11 February 1990 it was at last time for Nelson Mandela to go home. A sizeable percentage of the world community watched live that afternoon as Mandela stepped out of the gates of Victor Verster Prison.

Almost two years earlier, on 11 June 1988, an estimated television audience of 600 million people from sixty-seven countries had watched a concert broadcast, a popular-music tribute to Mandela's seventieth birthday at Wembley Stadium in London. Described by the BBC presenter Robin Denselow, in 1989, as the 'biggest and most spectacular pop-political event of all time', it was organised by the British Anti-Apartheid Movement (AAM) under the guidance of its president, Archbishop Trevor Huddleston.[1] The concert once again proved how present Mandela could be by his very absence.

But now, here he was, a living embodiment of the failure of prison and of the apartheid regime, walking into the Western Cape sunshine, now and then saluting the crowds, smiling.

Being part of the new, emergent South Africa meant that Mandela had to enter into the bustle and hustle — and confusion — of the country and the people he meant to lead. Mandela's journey from the prison gates to Cape Town's Grand Parade, where thousands of supporters stood waiting to hear him speak, was marked by detours and trepidation, auguries, perhaps, of the twists and turns the country was fated to take on its journey towards democracy. There was a little drama when Mandela's driver, intimidated by the throngs lining the road close to the City Hall, first drove to the nearby suburb of Rondebosch, where the convoy waited in a quiet street. There, Mandela saw a woman with her two babies and he asked to hold them. After that, one of the activists present, Saleem Mowzer, suggested his house in Rondebosch East. Later, a concerned Archbishop Desmond Tutu tracked them down and urged Mandela's party to head to the City Hall, or there would be a riot.*

Eventually, in the early evening, Mandela was able to speak to the people. He greeted the expectant multitude in the name of peace, democracy and freedom for all:

* Archbishop Desmond Tutu — see People, Places and Events.

'I stand here before you not as a prophet but as a humble servant of you, the people,' he said. 'Your tireless and heroic sacrifices have made it possible for me to be here today. I, therefore, place the remaining years of my life in your hands.'[2]

Writing in the *New Yorker,* Zoë Wicomb captures the moment well: 'Mandela looked nothing like the artists' renderings of an aging boxer, which had been circulating. That day, a tall, handsome stranger strode into the world. His face had been transfigured into sculpted planes that spoke of bygone Xhosa-Khoi relations, and the awkward hair parting was gone. Supermodels and philosophers sighed alike.'[3]

Even though Mandela was still first among equals, he was now as aware of danger as everyone else. He was also conscious of the violence that was wrecking the country. Every province had its tale of woe, with Natal bearing the brunt of brutality. This is where the Inkatha Freedom Party (IFP), backed by covert elements within the South African Police Force, waged war on the ANC and its supporters.* The Natal Midlands and many parts of urban Natal became no-go zones both for law enforcement and the ANC.

One of the memorable, chastening mo-

---

* Inkatha and Inkatha Freedom Party (IFP) — see People, Places and Events.

ments for Mandela came two weeks after his release, during an intense period of fighting in Natal, when he addressed a crowd of more than a hundred thousand people at Durban's Kings Park Stadium.

'Take your guns, your knives and your *pangas,* and throw them into the sea!'* Mandela pleaded. A low rumble of disapproval started off somewhere in the crowd and rose into a crescendo of catcalls. Stoically, Mandela continued; he had to deliver his message. 'Close down the death factories. End this war now!'[4]

The war that didn't end with Mandela's plea had its roots in the past and sought to frustrate the emergence of the future. Slowly, ineluctably, Mandela's dream towards a democratic South Africa was being realised. The last few stumbling blocks were being knocked aside like skittles. A notable development was the return, on 13 December 1990, of Oliver Tambo, who had left South Africa in 1960 on a secret mission to rebuild the banned ANC in exile. Returning to a tumultuous welcome after three decades as external leader of the liberation movement, the seventy-three-year-old ANC president seemed frail but happy as he acknowledged the greetings of a throng of ANC leaders, foreign ambassadors and miscellaneous

* A *panga* is an African machete.

dignitaries. Standing with his one-time law partner, Nelson Mandela, Tambo waved from the balcony of the Jan Smuts International Airport, near Johannesburg, to some five thousand supporters, who cheered and sang and danced. Nelson Mandela, then the ANC deputy president, told the crowd: 'We welcome him with open arms as one of the greatest heroes of Africa.'[5] Then the two men disappeared into a sedan as their motorcade departed with a police escort.

Two days later, the ANC held its first national consultative conference at Nasrec, near Soweto. It was an emotional moment when Tambo gave his report, effectively handing the ANC back to the people of South Africa. The singing was electrifying, the songs from exile in counterpoint to ditties and dirges and chants of mainly young people who would be manning the barricades in restless townships of the East Rand before the night of the following day. A carnival spirit among the delegates intermittently leavened the solemnity of the occasion. Comrades fresh from prison, some toting prison-issue duffel bags, were meeting relatives and friends after long years of separation. Someone, pointing to the concentration of many echelons of ANC leadership — from Mandela and Tambo and the old men from Robben Island, hoary-haired luminaries, veterans and NEC members down to the *kursanti* (rookies) in faux-battledress attire — quipped that the whole consultative conference idea had been hatched up by the enemy to eliminate the ANC with one powerful bomb.

One part of the proceedings that had even some of the battle-hardened delegates weeping openly was the parading of a dozen men who had returned from Zimbabwean prisons. They had been in jail since the valiant though ill-advised joint Zimbabwe African People's Union–ANC campaigns in Wankie and Sipolilo, in 1967 and 1969 respectively, where they had been captured after skirmishes with Rhodesian prime minister Ian Smith's British South Africa Police and South African security forces. Each of the inmates had been on death row awaiting execution before being reprieved when Robert Mugabe's Zimbabwe African National Union–Patriotic Front took power in April 1980.

The conference took place at a time of great violence, almost approximating a low-intensity war. It was therefore not surprising that the delegates called for the establishment of self-defence units.

Significantly, two days later, on 18 December, the government finally gazetted legislation, publicising a long-awaited law to allow exiles to return to South Africa. This was a measure to satisfy one of the remaining obstacles to negotiation. Asked by the media two or three days after his release if he would agree to De Klerk's terms on lifting the State of Emergency, Mandela had said, 'The attitude of the ANC is perfectly clear. No negotiation will take place until the government has met all those preconditions because to get a mandate from our people is impossible with these conditions, without the State of Emergency being lifted and without political prisoners being released and without exiles being given the assurance that if they return they will be doing so under an amnesty and none will be prosecuted.'[6]

The liveliness and diversity of the more than 'fifteen hundred delegates from forty-five regions, from home and abroad' gave Mandela a glimpse into the crazy-quilt make-up of the ANC community.[7] A significant percentage of the delegates were the returned exiles, many of whom were part of the ANC's diplomatic mission. The fact that these individuals had helped to ensure, as Mandela expressed it, that 'almost every country in the world in due course shunned South Africa, and [ensured that] apartheid [was] condemned as a crime against humanity, was a measure of the success of their historic campaign. Those who lived in exile crisscrossed the five continents to brief heads of state and governments on our situation, attending world and regional gatherings, flooding the world with material that exposed the inhumanity of apartheid. It was this worldwide campaign, which made the ANC and its leaders, inside and outside the country, one of the most well-known liberation movements of the world.'[8]

Mandela had already met with the general ANC membership in Lusaka, Zambia, earlier in March, but this was the first time such a meeting took place on home soil. The reality of the South African situation, the threat of violence hanging in the air, meant that the state had to keep an eye on the unexpected and, by implication, on its own over-exuberant zealots who might take issue with the ANC holding its conference in Nasrec. As a result, the venue's perimeter bristled with antennae on official-looking sedans housing hard-faced security men; and, now and then, an armoured police car trundled along the street, its headlights, protected behind steel wire, probing the shadows cast by the late-afternoon sun. Standing in twos and threes a short distance from the tent, the ANC security detail kept its own vigil. Indoors, there were just too many people whose loss would plunge the country into turmoil; they were the lynchpins of the new dispensation currently being hatched.

It was here, under the marquees on the sports ground and outside during breaks in proceedings, that Mandela saw the interaction of the delegates with the leadership, notably members of MK and their commanders. As a founding member of MK, his high regard for its members shines through.

'The fighters of Umkhonto weSizwe (MK) displayed exceptional courage and infiltrated the country on many occasions, attacked government installations, clashed now and again with the apartheid forces, and in several engagements put them to flight. Other freedom fighters worked inside the country, either above or underground, urging the masses to rise and resist all forms of oppression and exploitation. They braved the brutality of the regime regardless of what happened to themselves. For their liberation they were prepared to pay the highest price. Still others languished in apartheid jails fearlessly asserting their right to be treated as human beings in their own fatherland. They literally dug themselves in [in] the lion's den, demonstrating once again the universal principle that evil men cannot smother the freedom flame. Some of these courageous fighters are still alive, helping to address national problems, and they now enjoy the fruits of their labour at last. Although many of them are old, frail and jobless, they become animated when we remind them of their historic achievement. Others have passed on, never to return. We acknowledge them all as men and women who have made [a] decisive contribution to our liberation.'[9]

■ ■ ■ ■

The year ended but the violence continued. This, however, did not stop the first phases of negotiations towards a democratic outcome despite the serious attempts of the right wing to sabotage the process. Sydney Mufamadi, one-time general secretary of the General and Allied Workers Union and later on the ANC executive, remembers the earlier efforts at instigating a lasting peace in a country that was increasingly spiralling into uncontrollable violence.* He says:

Now, before, the release of our senior political leaders, culminating in the release of Madiba, the UDF and COSATU [Congress of South African Trade Unions] started to reach out to Inkatha . . . for ways of ending the violence, particularly in Pietermaritzburg . . . where the violence was at its most intense. We . . . took trips to Lusaka to discuss that initiative because our interlocutors in Inkatha — Dr Mdlalose, Dr Madide and Dr Dhlomo — the three doctors, had an express instruction from [the president of the IFP, Chief Mangosuthu] Buthelezi to say to us [that] they will continue to deal with us if . . . our dealings with them have the sup-

* Sydney Mufamadi — see People, Places and Events.

66

port of Lusaka . . . [which] wouldn't oppose any move that was intended to bring about peace.*[10]

But, angry 'at this brutalisation that was taking place', activists on the ground 'were not keen to negotiate'. If Lusaka was to be involved at all it had to be 'by way of arming them to fight back. So we had all these difficulties of having to persuade our own people about the merits of negotiations.'[11] The confusion was deepened by the release from prison of the ANC leadership, especially the legendary, fiery and uncompromising Harry Gwala, aptly nicknamed 'The Lion of the Midlands', who 'was not convinced about the usefulness of negotiations'.†[12] Gwala regarded any meeting between the ANC and Buthelezi and King Goodwill Zwelithini, the head of the Royal Zulu Family, as an anathema.‡ (In those sentiments, Gwala was not alone. Mandela later told Richard Stengel, with whom he collaborated on *Long Walk to Freedom,* how when he visited Pietermaritzburg in 1990, the people wanted to 'choke'

* Mangosuthu Buthelezi — see People, Places and Events.
† Harry Gwala — see People, Places and Events.
‡ King Goodwill Zwelithini kaBhekuzulu — see People, Places and Events.

him when he mentioned Buthelezi.*[13])

'That,' says Mufamadi, 'did not help because we had made some progress on the ground in persuading the younger comrades,' and this success was being jeopardised by 'a comrade who is senior to all of us'. Madiba came out and 'made a call on the people of KwaZulu-Natal to lay down arms . . . Initially there was some resistance, which we had to work to overcome.'[14]

With more and more revelations of covert state involvement, which forced the state to take action, there was a marked decline in some of the more horrific violence, such as attacks on commuters on trains. These attacks had done much to disrupt and intimidate mass support for the ANC. The capacity of the growing right-wing parties to thwart progress by political means was diluted in 1992 when De Klerk called a referendum of white voters to endorse 'continued negotiations' and got a big majority voting 'yes', nearly 69 per cent of the voters. Smarting from this defeat, right-wing parties substituted their resistance for terrorism and mobilised for armed revolt. Different strands of the Afrikaner right wing yearned for a separate state and there was much sabre rattling.

In a 1992 interview with Irish peacemaker

* Richard Stengel — see People, Places and Events.

Padraig O'Malley, Conservative Party (CP) leader Ferdinand Hartzenberg said that the CP would help other parties by not participating 'because [Mandela] wants us to participate and to admit that we will accept the outcome of the negotiations — and that we are not prepared to do.* We say if we get an ANC government in this country we will do the same that we have done at the beginning of this century when Britain tried to rule this country. We will resist.'[15]

Three months after the referendum, on Thursday, 17 June 1992, in Boipatong, south of Johannesburg, Zulu-speaking men from a nearby hostel killed forty-five, and seriously injured twenty-seven, men, women and children in a cowardly massacre, using AK47s and their *assegais* (throwing spear). There was something especially chilling about the murders: twenty-four of the victims were women, one of them pregnant, and a nine-month-old baby was also killed. In the aftermath the police made few arrests. As happened in many such cases where the victims were ANC supporters, the investigation was botched, spluttering to an inconclusive end that yielded no significant arrests. Responding to writer John Carlin's question about the massacre, Jessie Duarte, Mandela's

* Ferdinand Hartzenberg — see People, Places and Events.

former personal assistant and now an ANC politician, recounted Mandela's reaction: 'I will never forget his face . . . He was a man who was deeply shocked by the fact that people will do this to each other . . . I had the view that Madiba hadn't actually ever confronted the cold face of the violence during the twenty-seven years of his incarceration.'*[16]

Following a muted response from President F. W. de Klerk about steps taken to curb violence and bring the perpetrators to book, Mandela announced the ANC's decision to suspend the talks. The violence was leading to a growing sense of mass disillusionment with the ANC's stance on negotiations. At a rally in Boipatong to mourn the deaths, angry people sang, 'Mandela, you are leading us like lambs to the slaughter'.

At Mandela's insistence, the ANC took the issue to the United Nations in spite of a previous position that there would be no international involvement in the negotiations.

Nonetheless, negotiations were resumed a few months later, mediated by a Record of Understanding fleshed out by a backchannel — a low-profile line of communication to avoid crises established between Cyril Ramaphosa and his counterpart from the National Party, Roelf Meyer — and encouraged by

* Jessie Duarte — see People, Places and Events.

Tanzanian president Julius Nyerere. When Mandela explained that the ANC's withdrawal from the talks was due to the orchestration of violence by the apartheid state, Nyerere reminded him that the South African freedom fighters had always contended that the apartheid state was inherently violent. How, he asked, could it be cogently argued that violence would be totally eliminated before the apartheid state itself was abolished?

The quibbling, wrangling, horse-trading and compromises among the negotiating parties came to an abrupt stop with the assassination of Chris Hani, undoubtedly one of South Africa's most popular leaders,* on 10 April 1993, by a right-wing Polish immigrant, Janusz Waluś, at the behest of a Conservative Party member of Parliament, Clive Derby-Lewis.†

Mandela writes that the killing of Hani, a man 'who could have easily risen to the highest position in government', almost precipitated a calamitous crisis.[17] Hani's popular

---

* Chris Hani — see People, Places and Events.
† To date, there is discontent with the way that only Waluś and Derby-Lewis were charged with the crime, as it is said that the gun came from a state military armoury, which points to a chain of events involving a number of other people which eventuated in the Hani killing.

following was outraged. Tens of thousands spontaneously poured out into streets throughout the country. Wide ranges of other South Africans were numbed with shock.

'As the country teetered, [I] was given airtime on SATV [South African TV] to broadcast to the nation, appealing for discipline, and to avoid giving way to provocation. Many commentators of our negotiated transition were later to observe that the effective transfer of power from the National Party of De Klerk to the ANC occurred not with the elections in April 1994, but in this critical week one year earlier.'[18]

South Africa does not lack for examples when it has had to pull back from the brink of self-destruction. Among them would be Sharpeville on 21 March 1960; Soweto, Nyanga, Langa and Gugulethu after June 1976; and, of course, the countless instances of insanity under the cloak of a succession of States of Emergency. At no time, however, had the collective rage — and despair — been so concentrated that all it needed was a spark for the powder keg to blow up as in the aftermath of the fateful Easter weekend of Hani's assassination.

The spark was dampened by Mandela's timely intervention on television on 13 April 1993. His tone carrying exactly the right mixture of indignation and moral strength, he addressed the South African people:

72

'Tonight I am reaching out to every single South African, black and white, from the very depths of my being.

'A white man, full of prejudice and hate, came to our country and committed a deed so foul that our whole nation now teeters on the brink of disaster.

'A white woman, of Afrikaner origin, risked her life so that we may know, and bring to justice, this assassin.*

'The cold-blooded murder of Chris Hani has sent shock waves throughout the country and the world. Our grief and anger is tearing us apart.

'What has happened is a national tragedy that has touched millions of people, across the political and colour divide.

'Our shared grief and legitimate anger will find expression in nationwide commemorations that coincide with the funeral service.

'Tomorrow, in many towns and villages, there will be memorial services to pay homage to one of the greatest revolutionaries this country has ever known. Every service will open a Memorial Book for Freedom, in which all who want peace and democracy pledge their commitment.

'Now is the time for all South Africans to

* Mandela is referring to Hani's neighbour, who recorded Waluś's licence-plate number and called the police.

stand together against those who, from any quarter, wish to destroy what Chris Hani gave his life for — the freedom of all of us.

'Now is the time for our white compatriots, from whom messages of condolence continue to pour in, to reach out with an understanding of the grievous loss to our nation, to join in the memorial services and the funeral commemorations.

'Now is the time for the police to act with sensitivity and restraint, to be real community policemen and women who serve the population as a whole. There must be no further loss of life at this tragic time.

'This is a watershed moment for all of us. Our decisions and actions will determine whether we use our pain, our grief and our outrage to move forward to what is the only lasting solution for our country — an elected government of the people, by the people and for the people.

'We must not let the men who worship war, and who lust after blood, precipitate actions that will plunge our country into another Angola.

'Chris Hani was a soldier. He believed in iron discipline. He carried out instructions to the letter. He practised what he preached.

'Any lack of discipline is trampling on the values that Chris Hani stood for. Those who commit such acts serve only the interests of the assassins, and desecrate his memory.

'When we, as one people, act together decisively, with discipline and determination, nothing can stop us.

'Let us honour this soldier for peace in a fitting manner. Let us rededicate ourselves to bringing about the democracy he fought for all his life; democracy that will bring real, tangible changes in the lives of the working people, the poor, the jobless, the landless.

'Chris Hani is irreplaceable in the heart of our nation and people. When he first returned to South Africa after three decades in exile, he said: "I have lived with death most of my life. I want to live in a free South Africa even if I have to lay down my life for it." The body of Chris Hani will lie in State at the FNB Stadium, Soweto, from twelve noon on Sunday 18 April until the start of the vigil at 6 p.m. The funeral service will commence at 9 a.m. on Monday, 19th April. The cortege will leave for Boksburg Cemetery, where the burial is scheduled for 1 p.m.

'These funeral service and rallies must be conducted with dignity. We will give disciplined expression to our emotions at our pickets, prayer meetings and gatherings, in our homes, our churches and our schools. We will not be provoked into any rash actions.

'We are a nation in mourning. To the youth of South Africa we have a special message: you have lost a great hero. You have repeatedly shown that your love of freedom is greater than that most precious gift, life itself. But you are the leaders of tomorrow. Your country, your people, your organisation need you to act with wisdom. A particular responsibility rests on your shoulders.

'We pay tribute to all our people for the courage and restraint they have shown in the face of such extreme provocation. We are sure this same indomitable spirit will carry us through the difficult days ahead.

'Chris Hani has made the supreme sacrifice. The greatest tribute we can pay to his life's work is to ensure we win that freedom for all our people.'[19]

Hani's fifteen-year-old daughter, Nomakhwezi, had witnessed the incident. The full horror of Hani's murder, which could easily have changed the history of South Africa, was counterpoised by the quick action of Retha Harmse, Hani's Afrikaans neighbour, who rang the police with Waluś's licence plate number, helping the police capture Waluś with the weapon still in his possession.

Mandela had a special regard for Chris Hani. Some will say it was due to the younger man's exemplary leadership, which endeared him to the membership, especially of MK, who sought to emulate him as much as possible. He was brave and charismatic, and leading from the front he was as unafraid to lead MK cadres infiltrating inside South Africa as he was of ANC authority when he penned his famous memorandum to the ANC leadership.

Impatiently cooling his heels while based in the Tanzanian camps of the ANC, Hani had excoriated its leadership in exile, accusing it of relinquishing its mission towards liberation and wallowing in corruption, which weakened the prospect of MK returning to fight inside South Africa. He and his co-signatories to the memorandum were charged with treason and sentenced to death. It was only through Oliver Tambo's intervention that they were reprieved. Hani's action contributed to the ANC's Luthuli Detachment's campaign in Wankie and Sipolilo.

Similarly, more than two decades earlier in 1944, Mandela was among the pioneers of the ANC's Youth League — the erstwhile Young Lions — who challenged orthodox views in order to re-energise the ANC. One of the veterans of Wankie, Major General Wilson Ngqose (Ret.), remembers Hani at a camp called Kongwa in Tanzania in the late sixties, which the ANC shared with the MPLA, Frente de Libertação de Moçambique (Mozambique Liberation Front (FRELIMO)) and the South West Africa People's Organisation (SWAPO). The MPLA already enjoyed liberated zones in Portuguese-occupied Angola. It was in Kongwa, he says, that MPLA leader Dr Agostinho Neto invited Oliver Tambo to send trainees to the camps, seeing that the ANC was facing problems in Tanzania.[20] Already a celebrated poet, Neto's ringing call to arms in a poem titled 'Haste' could have informed Hani's impatience with the slothful leadership of the time. It also speaks to the fighting spirit that imbued Mandela and his colleagues in the Youth League to challenge the ANC leadership, which believed in petitions and appeals to the consciences of a heartless regime.

I am impatient in this historical tepidness
of delays and lentitude
when with haste the just are murdered
when the prisons are bursting with youths
crushed to death against the wall of
    violence

Let us end this tepidness of words and
    gestures
and smiles hidden behind book covers
and the resigned biblical gesture
of turning the other cheek

Start action vigorous male intelligent
which answers tooth for tooth eye for eye
man for man
come vigorous action
of the people's army for the liberation of
    men
come whirlwinds to shatter this
    passiveness.[21]

Much later, Mandela would acknowledge the debt of gratitude that democratic South Africa owed to the people of Angola. In his 1998 address to the Angolan National Assembly in Luanda, he said that Angola's solidarity with South Africans 'struggling for their liberation was of heroic proportions'.

'Before your own freedom was secure,' he said, 'and within the reach of our ruthless enemy, you dared to act upon the principle that freedom in southern Africa was indivisible. Led by the founder of liberated Angola, that great African patriot and internationalist, Agostinho Neto, you insisted that all of Africa's children must be freed from bondage.'[22]

Of the young hero, Chris Hani, Mandela continues writing: 'In 1959 Hani enrolled at Fort Hare University [Mandela's own alma mater] and attracted the attention of Govan Mbeki, the father of Thabo Mbeki. Govan played a formative role in Hani's development. It was here that Hani encountered Marxist ideas and joined the already illegal Communist Party of South Africa. He always emphasised that his conversion to Marxism also deepened his non-racial perspective.

'Hani was a bold and forthright young man and did not hesitate to criticise even his own organisation when he felt it was failing to give correct leadership. He recalled that: "Those of us in the camps in the sixties did not have a profound understanding of the problems. Most of us were very young — in our twenties. We were impatient to get into action. 'Don't tell us there are no routes,' we used to say. We must be deployed to find routes. That's what we trained for."[23]

'Hani became the leading spokesperson for MK soldiers who felt that the leadership was too complacent. After writing a formal petition, Hani found himself in hot water with the camp leadership and he was detained a while by his own organisation. He was, however, released when his plight came to the attention of the more senior ANC leaders, notably Oliver Tambo and Joe Slovo.[*]

'Hani returned to South Africa in August 1990, a hero to a great majority of South Africans. Several opinion polls at the time showed that he was easily the second most popular politician in the country.[24] In December 1991, he became general secretary of the SACP.

'Hani [spent] the last years of his life tirelessly addressing meetings throughout the length and breadth of South Africa, in village gatherings, shop stewards' [meetings], councils and street committee [meetings]. He lent all his authority and military prestige to defend negotiations, often speaking patiently to very sceptical youths or communities suf-

[*] Joe Slovo — see People, Places and Events.

fering the brunt of Third Force violence.*

'In their amnesty application to the Truth and Reconciliation Commission, the two convicted killers of Hani — Janusz Waluś and Clive Derby-Lewis — admitted that they had hoped to derail negotiations by unleashing a wave of race hatred and civil war.† It is a tribute to the maturity of South Africans of all persuasions, and it is a tribute to the memory of Hani in particular, that his death, tragically but factually, finally brought focus and urgency to our negotiated settlement.'[25]

If the steps taken to hammer out an agreement about the date of elections had been onerous and strewn with casualties, the attainment of a negotiated settlement was proving to be an even thornier issue. In 1993, as the elections approached, the possibility of a dangerous, armed right-wing revolt was taking shape. Although huge obstacles had been removed, the potential for renewed violence and disruption of the election was only too real. The fragile conditions for an election of a legitimate Government of National Unity (GNU) had only just been put in place and

* Mandela and other ANC leaders believed there was a 'third force', a clandestine force responsible for a surge in violence.
† Truth and Reconciliation Commission (TRC) — see People, Places and Events.

needed consolidating.

The situation was of great concern for Mandela, who writes: 'A dark cloud was hanging over South Africa, which threatened to block and even reverse all the gains South Africans had made in regard to the country's peaceful transformation.'[26]

Chris Hani's body was barely cold in his grave when, almost a month after his killing, four former generals of the South African Defence Force (SADF), including the widely respected former army chief Constand Viljoen, established a committee of generals, the Afrikaner Volksfront (AVF).* This could have been a reaction to the widespread damage in the wake of Hani's murder, where media reported that there were some white victims among the more than fifteen people killed on the day of the funeral. The generals' stated intention was to unify Afrikaner elements disillusioned with De Klerk's National Party and agitate for a *volkstaat,* an Afrikaner homeland. Most of the press, more volubly the *Weekly Mail,* saw this initiative as part of a route towards secession.[27]

Mandela was receiving intelligence reports 'to the effect that the right-wing Afrikaners had decided to stop the forthcoming elec-

* Afrikaner Volksfront — see People, Places and Events; Constand Viljoen — see People, Places and Events.

tions by violence. To be on the safe side, the president of an organisation must carefully check the accuracy of such reports. I did so, and when I discovered that they were accurate, I decided to act.'[28]

According to the historian Hermann Giliomee, Mandela had learnt that 'Viljoen planned to disrupt the elections, have De Klerk removed as leader and restart the negotiations.'[29] Some believed that he could raise 50,000 men from the Active Citizen Force or reservists and also some defence force units. In his book *The Afrikaners,* Giliomee describes how two important generals debated the implications of armed resistance:

In a briefing, General Georg Meiring, Chief of the Defence Force, warned the government and the ANC of the ghastly consequences of Viljoen's opposing the election.* To dissuade Viljoen, for whom he had 'the highest regard', Meiring had several meetings with him. At one of them Viljoen said: 'You and I and our men can take this country in an afternoon,' to which Meiring replied: 'Yes, that is so, but what do we do in the morning after the coup?' The white–black demographic balance, the internal foreign pressures and all the intractable problems would still be there.[30]

* Georg Meiring — see People, Places and Events.

Mandela knew better than to underestimate an opponent hell-bent on wreaking havoc, especially one that perceived itself to be on a just crusade to preserve vanishing glories. In his quest for a solution he might have been thinking of some of the stalwarts, like Chief Albert Luthuli, the Nobel peace laureate whose stewardship of the ANC had been at a most difficult time in the 1960s.* What would he have made of this situation? Or Oliver Tambo, his friend and comrade who died on 24 April, barely two weeks after Chris Hani's burial — what course of action would he have advocated? In making his decision, however, Mandela must have been hearing echoes of Martin Luther King, Jr's lecture on receiving the Nobel Peace Prize in 1964.

'Violence as a way of achieving racial justice is both impractical and immoral,' Dr King said. 'I am not unmindful of the fact that violence often brings about momentary results. Nations have frequently won their independence in battle. But in spite of temporary victories, violence never brings permanent peace. It solves no social problem: it merely creates new and more complicated ones. Violence is impractical because it is a descending spiral ending in destruction for all.'[31]

In forestalling this destruction, Mandela

* Albert Luthuli — see People, Places and Events.

knew he had to enlist the help of someone whom the right-wingers held in high esteem. In the townships, it was practice to negotiate with the bully's big brother to get some respite.

'I flew down to the Wilderness,' he writes, 'the retirement home of the former President P. W. Botha, [and] reminded him of the communiqué we jointly issued when I was still in prison in July 1989. In that communiqué we pledged to work together for peace in our country.'[32]

The twenty-five-minute drive from George Airport to Wilderness is a beautiful journey. There are beaches, passes, pristine rivers and the famous arched railway bridge that traverses the Kaaimans River, which washes into the sea at Wilderness. This scenic view is interrupted by the sudden appearance of informal housing, which spreads along the N2 highway. It being a Saturday afternoon, Mandela would have seen the people milling around and the traffic on the road.

P. W. Botha's retirement home, called Die Anker (The Anchor), is on farmland almost contiguous with valuable, protected wetland and overlooks the lakes that stretch from Wilderness all the way to Sedgefield. This, Mandela must have thought, is exactly the kind of privilege that the right wing wishes to hold on to, and will fight tooth and nail to keep as the sole preserve of the volk. But he had work to do. He had his meeting with P. W. Botha.

Mandela writes: 'I informed him that the peace was now threatened by the right wing and asked him to intervene. He was co-operative and confirmed that Afrikaners were determined to stop the elections. But he added that he did not want to discuss the matter with me alone, and suggested that I bring President F. W. de Klerk, Ferdi Hartzenberg and the General.

'I proposed that we should also include the leader of the extreme Afrikaner right wing, Eugene Terre'Blanche, on the grounds that he was a reckless demagogue who at that time could attract larger crowds than President De Klerk. On this issue, the former president was so negative that I dropped the subject.'*[33]

Mandela's meeting with P. W. Botha in the latter's own backyard could not have been without disagreements on specific issues. However, the cordiality reported in the press, which had characterised the two-hour meeting, had as much to do with realpolitik as with culture, where the two septuagenarians were closer in age and had a shared if divergent grasp of South Africa's history. Mandela was also aware that P. W. Botha had himself taken on the mantle of reformer at the begin-

* Eugene Terre'Blanche — see People, Places and Events.

ning of his presidency, when he made his famous call to his recalcitrant followers that they must adapt or die.[34] In time his stance had hardened when his ill-advised tricameral parliament gave rise to resistance and the birth of the UDF. By then he had cast himself as an irascible and obdurate old man.

Reacting to his meeting with Mandela, commentators recognised that 'while Mr Botha might have some residual influence with the far right, his far greater influence lies with the SADF, over which he presided with extravagant indulgence for many years and some of whose generals, past and present, reportedly maintain affectionate contact with him'.[35]

'I returned to Johannesburg,' Mandela writes, 'and immediately telephoned President de Klerk and informed him of Botha's invitation. He was as hostile to the whole idea of us meeting the former president as the latter was towards Terre'Blanche. I then approached the progressive Afrikaner theologian, Professor Johan Heyns, to bring together the General, Hartzenberg, Terre'Blanche and myself. Terre'Blanche was uncompromising and rejected any meeting with me, a communist, as he said.'[36]

Mandela was alive to the irony of an ex-prisoner mediating not only between the restive black majority and the government, but also between De Klerk and the bellicose right wing, which seemed prepared to set the whole country ablaze. The National Party's backward policies throughout the decades had been a shrill dog whistle to which the dogs of hate were now responding in Ventersdorp, Terre'Blanche's home town. Mandela had heard the rhetoric of scorn spewed by Terre'Blanche and his Afrikaner Weerstandsbeweging (AWB). He had seen how, in mid-1993, they had stormed the World Trade Centre in Kempton Park, Gauteng, smashing through the glass doors in an armoured car to disrupt the talks.

Notwithstanding his acceptance of De Klerk as a negotiating partner, Mandela was somewhat unimpressed with his handling of the right-wing threat. In a prescient interview with *TIME* magazine five days after his release from prison in February 1990, when asked if President de Klerk's fears of the threat of the right wing were justified, he stated emphatically that they were overblown. While the threat was real, he argued, De Klerk viewed it from the perspective of white South Africa, the Afrikaners in particular. If he would only embrace a non-racial South Africa and begin viewing challenges from black perspectives, then his fears would diminish.[37]

There is an expression much favoured in political mobilisation among black people of South Africa, which is used by almost all the language groups: Nguni, Sesotho and Xitsonga. In the Nguni version people say, *'Si-hamba nabahambayo'*, which simply means in isiZulu 'We take along with us those who are ready for the journey.' *'Ha e duma eyatsamaya'* (When the engine starts roaring, this vehicle is leaving) goes the refrain of a traditional song in Setswana — advice for ditherers to get on with it. For Mandela, the time had come for movement.

He had already identified the people to take on his journey. He was favourably disposed towards General Constand Viljoen. This was also based on practicalities because Mandela knew of Viljoen's track record and the role he had played in the destabilisation of neighbouring states, especially against SWAPO, the Namibian national liberation movement and sister organisation of the ANC; Mandela was aware of the massacre of Namibian refugees by the SADF in Kassinga, Angola, on 4 May 1978.*

But, in line with his attitude towards De

---

* Also known as the Battle of Cassinga, the Kassinga Massacre of 1978 was a major assault by the South African military against Namibian refugees and freedom fighters in Angola. The South African Air Force first bombed a camp of the SWAPO and its military wing, the People's Liberation Army of Namibia (PLAN). After the air raid hundreds of paratroopers were dropped to complete the attack. More than six hundred Namibians were killed.

Klerk, Mandela saw the general as an ex-soldier who was also in search of a solution.

Mandela writes: 'A meeting facilitated by the general's twin brother, Braam, and stockbroker Jürgen Kögl took place between the general and his colleagues on the one hand, and Joe Nhlanhla, Penuell Maduna, Jacob Zuma and Thabo Mbeki for the ANC, on the other. In this regard, these ANC leaders had a vision far ahead of their comrades. They fully grasped the disastrous repercussions of the impending disaster.'[38]

There were numerous such bilateral meetings between the ANC and Viljoen's delegation of retired generals and others, which included Ferdi Hartzenberg, Tienie Groenewald and Kobus Visser, operating under the umbrella of the AVF. Some meetings were facilitated by Mandela himself, others by Mbeki and the leadership of the ANC, including Joe Modise.* In the meeting with the AVF at his home in the leafy suburb of Houghton, Mandela played the genial host, pouring the men tea and charming General Viljoen by speaking to him in Afrikaans, the general's mother tongue.

Mandela asked generals Viljoen and Hartzenberg 'whether it was true that they were preparing to stop the elections by violent means. The General [Viljoen] was

* Joe Modise — see People, Places and Events.

90

frank and admitted that this was correct, and that Afrikaners were arming, and that a bloody civil war was facing the country. I was shaken, but pretended that I was supremely confident of the victory of the liberation movement.

'I told them,' Mandela continues, 'that they would give us a hard time since they were better trained militarily than us, commanded more devastating weaponry and, because of their resources, knew the country better than us. But I warned that at the end of that reckless gamble, they would be crushed. We were then on the verge of a historic victory after we inflicted a mortal blow to white supremacy. I pointed out this was not due to their consent; it was in spite of their opposition.'[39]

Mandela told the generals that the people of South Africa 'had a just cause, numbers and the support of the international community. They had none of these. I appealed to them to stop their plans and to join the negotiations at the World Trade Centre. I spent some time persuading them, but they were adamant and I could not move them at all. Finally, when I was about to give up, the general softened a bit and said he could not approach his people with empty hands at such an advanced stage of their preparations.'[40]

Mandela had spent a great deal of time in

prison thinking about the dilemma in which South Africa found itself. Much more, he saw his incarceration as a chance to know himself. In a letter dated 1 February 1975, he wrote to his wife, Winnie, who was then in Kroonstad Prison, telling her that prison was an ideal place to get to know oneself. 'The cell,' he wrote, 'gives you the opportunity to look daily into your entire conduct, to overcome the bad and develop whatever is good in you.'[41] It was here, too, that he had immersed himself in understanding the salient aspects of Afrikaner history and culture. He practised his Afrikaans in exchanges with prison officials, although, years later, he still couldn't quite flatten the broad isiXhosa inflection in speech, which was as much a source of amusement for apartheid functionaries as for ANC members. It is a universally known fact that people love being addressed in their own language — and Mandela had grasped that long before it became a necessity.

What did the generals know of this black man who had survived them and who now parleyed with them? They must have known of the power he represented and the people behind him, but what did they know of him? That he was amiable, avuncular and smiled a lot — knowledge that might have been muddled up in their own memory of his origins and his championing of the armed struggle. It is also a truism that black people end up knowing more about white people than the other way round. Mandela realised that the generals represented, in the main, a demographic steeped in tradition, with a respect for authority, law and order — a Calvinist dogma — whose overwhelming majority consisted of members of the middle class; family men and women who simply wanted to be left alone. A good percentage had already embraced some form of reform, looking beyond the present and seeking solutions for a liveable future (witness their support of De Klerk's options in the referendum). Conformity with societal mores and respect for law and order were ingrained in young Afrikaners, a view supported by Niël Barnard, who writes:

'At school and in the hostel, as in the home environment, there were standards; there was order, discipline: bells rang when it was time to rise and shine . . . there were prayer meetings . . . and traditional folk games and dancing. We walked in single file to school, and for anything that looked the least bit like a serious transgression the cane was brought out . . . All those who were in positions of authority were respected; their word was law.'[42]

That De Klerk's — and, to a large extent, Mandela's — word was law had been accepted, albeit grudgingly, by a significant section of Afrikaners. The exceptions, such as

Eugene Terre'Blanche, who operated outside the accepted code of conduct — as determined by Afrikaner authorities — were in many instances a source of embarrassment rather than of pride. Were these people ready to relinquish the comfort of their factories, businesses, homes, farms and schools to take up arms in defence of . . . what?

Notwithstanding all these considerations, Mandela had read enough about the history of conflict to know that language, culture and nationhood had been the source of devastating conflicts across the globe. The fall of the Berlin Wall and the break-up of the old Soviet Union had already opened up a Pandora's box of ethnic resurgences in Eastern Europe. The general's conciliatory tone about his reluctance to go back to his people 'with empty hands' on the question of a *volkstaat* struck a chord with Mandela. He knew that, however right he might have been, it was supremely unwise to swell the numbers of opponents to him or to the envisaged democratic republic.

'Up to that moment,' Mandela writes, 'I had insisted that as long as I was President of the ANC, there would never be a *Volkstaat* in this country. A *Volkstaat* was a separate, autonomous area for the Afrikaner. But now, faced with such a formidable challenge, I decided to retreat but in such a way that they would find it far from easy to realise their demand.'[43]

More than thirty years earlier, while operating underground and on the run, Mandela had lived in SACP activist Wolfie Kodesh's flat. Kodesh introduced him to Carl von Clausewitz's classic, *On War*.[44] In dealing with the right wing as he did, Mandela put into practice the Prussian general's theory of war and conflict.

In his essay 'Mandela on War', Jonathan Hyslop concludes that '[in] understanding that South Africa could not avoid violent conflict but that the prosecution of conflict without limit was a danger to any possibility of creating a viable future society, Mandela charted an intelligent and principled course. And this can also be understood as a notably Clausewitzian way of thinking: Mandela grasped that responsible leadership requires a recognition of the conditions of real war, of the limits of what it can achieve, and of the problems that flow from it rather than the pursuit of the chimera of absolute war.'[45]

Mandela informed generals Viljoen and Hartzenberg that he would approach the ANC and ask that it 'review its attitude to the *Volkstaat* on three conditions. The two of them, plus Terre'Blanche, claimed that they represented the majority of Afrikaners who wanted a *Volkstaat*. On the other hand, President de Klerk insisted that only he represented the majority of Afrikaners, all of whom rejected the demand.

'The first condition was, therefore, that Afrikaners should have a referendum to determine whether or not they wanted a *Volkstaat*. Second, the result of the referendum would not necessarily bind the ANC, but would be an important factor to take into account when considering their demand. Finally, they should answer the question: Who was an Afrikaner? Was it a white person who spoke Afrikaans? Or was it any person — [including] black, that is African, Coloured or Indian — who spoke the language? On compliance with these conditions, I would then report to my organisation, leaving it to its members to review the matter as they deemed fit.

'The general,' Mandela writes, 'was satisfied that I had given him something to present to his force, but Hartzenberg sharply differed and insisted that I should there and then make an unequivocal undertaking that I would give them the *Volkstaat*. I told him that I was a mere servant of the ANC, subject to their authority and discipline; that if I acted unilaterally on a principle of such fundamental importance the organisation would summarily dismiss me, rendering me useless to the right wing. He retorted quite firmly that if I did not accept his demand, the plan would be carried out. I said: "So be it," and that was the end of our discussion.

'That same day, I telephoned former President Botha and briefed him on the General's decision. I requested the former president to persuade the General to join the negotiations at the World Trade Centre.

'A few days later,' Mandela continues, 'the General [Viljoen] pulled out of the conspiracy of the right wing and joined the negotiating parties. His colleagues heavily vilified him for saving South Africa from such a calamity. Hartzenberg did not have any military capacity at all, and Terre'Blanche relied on a collection of undisciplined amateurs who had no idea whatsoever of what war involved.'[46]

General Viljoen, who knew exactly what war entailed, reached an agreement with the ANC negotiators on 12 April 1994, having registered his own newly formed political party, the Freedom Front, on 4 March 1994. But Mandela's signature was still needed to secure the Freedom Front's participation in the forthcoming elections. As days passed, a restive Viljoen decided to act. He knew that war was not actually an option, but he believed he could mobilise enough people to seriously disrupt the elections, and resolved to do so. Before taking the final decision, however, he confided his plans to the US ambassador, Princeton Lyman, who had maintained contact with Viljoen since late 1993, and with Mandela.[47] The latter had phoned President Bill Clinton in February

1994, asking him to persuade Viljoen and others to take part in the elections.[48] Lyman informed the ANC of the situation, and the Afrikaner Accord on Self-Determination was signed on 23 April 1994, three days before the start of the elections, by the Freedom Front, ANC and the National Party. It was an agreement for the parties 'to address, through a process of negotiations, the idea of Afrikaner self-determination, including the concept of a *Volkstaat*.'[49]

The rejection of the right-wingers' demands precipitated mayhem. Mandela writes that 'on the eve of the elections, bombs exploded, especially in Johannesburg, and killed about twenty innocent civilians. It was a matter for police action, and the culprits were arrested and convicted. The situation would have imposed formidable difficulties if Viljoen was still part of the plot.'[50]

The media at home and abroad, which had been watching the unfolding drama with interest, reported how the elements of the right wing made good on their threat to try to disrupt the elections. The explosions, according to Bill Keller in the *New York Times:*

most minor, but ominous in their message, led some panicky residents to stockpile household goods but seemed only to harden the resolve of black voters to exercise their first franchise.

Bolstered by the united condemnation of politicians and by their own lifetimes of being denied, even blacks in the line of fire said they would not be frightened from voting.

'Someone is trying to scare us away from the election,' said Zole Msenti, who was sitting in his baby-blue minibus chatting with a friend when the Germiston blast suddenly lofted his vehicle into the air and smashed all the windows. Scores of vehicles gather each morning at suburban taxi parks to bring commuters into the city to work.

Bandaged but unbowed, he returned from the hospital to retrieve his taxi and accept the condolences of whites who stopped to commiserate.

'They are wasting their time,' he said of the spoilers. 'We are going.'[51]

Mr Msenti's three words — 'we are going' — almost certainly meant that he, his colleagues and their families were going to vote, come hell or high water. A few decades earlier, such determination might not even have been there, but now that the resistance had gained a foothold in every corner of the country, it had started to become a reality. As a taxi driver he might have ferried thousands of passengers and heard their tales of woe, which reflected the reality of what he and his peers had endured. And then one day, change began to seem possible. In 1976, the youth in schools had revolted against the imposition of Afrikaans as a language of instruction; in response the regime had tightened its choke-hold around the necks of the people and declared States of Emergency. To many this was a sign that the apartheid government was losing its grip. In the words of American writer James Baldwin on the decline of a kingdom, 'Force does not work the way its advocates seem to think it does. It does not, for example, reveal to the victim the strength of his adversary. On the contrary, it reveals the weakness, even the panic of his adversary, and this revelation invests the victim with patience. Furthermore, it is ultimately fatal to create too many victims.'[52]

When eight men were released from prison on 15 October 1989, it heralded the end of a system that had led to so much pain, and signalled that the walls were coming down. The hour of the victim had come. And then, on 11 February 1990, almost 120 days later, Mandela stepped out and it all became real. At last, it was happening. All the songs that people had sung in churches, at the lips of open graves and in the camps thousands of miles from home, all transmuted into an affirmation: 'We are going to cast our vote.' Seven simple words whose import had eluded

the architects of apartheid for decades.
The Afrikaner right wing had failed.

CHAPTER THREE:
A FREE AND FAIR ELECTION

With the immediate roadblocks removed, the way was open for an election that would be the final step in the establishment of a democratically elected government. The Transitional Executive Council (TEC) to promote the preparation for and transition to a democratic order was now well established and ready to promote the conditions for unrestricted political activity in the run-up to the elections.* Between 15 April and 15 May 1994, the country saw South Africa's most comprehensive peacetime mobilisation of the security forces to ensure a free election.[1] The main political parties, even the Inkatha Freedom Party, which had only agreed to participate at the eleventh hour, had strong campaign machines. Widespread voter education campaigns among the disenfranchised had started two years earlier, when the ANC had started preparing for an elected constitu-

* Transitional Executive Council (TEC) — see People, Places and Events.

ent assembly. In place, too, since December 1993, was the Independent Electoral Commission (IEC).When the IEC was established, Mandela had phoned its head, Judge Johann Kriegler, a tough and energetic jurist, saying that he and the ANC realised there were difficulties, but Kriegler should know that he had the support and confidence of the party.*[2]

What struck Judge Kriegler was Mandela's ability to connect with people from widely different constituencies. Kriegler observed that when he had an issue to raise, 'Mandela would call personally, unlike the usual CEO whose PA calls you to say the CEO would like to speak to you and then you wait for the CEO.'[3] In mid-April, in a meeting of the TEC at which Mandela was present, Kriegler reported on a meeting with the IFP:

There was at one point talk of a boycott of the elections by the ZCC [Zion Christian Church]. At that time there were several threats of boycott: IFP, North West, Ciskei and the right wing. I went to meet with Bishop Lekganyane to persuade him to support the process, before Easter.[†] He said that he had invited the leaders of all parties

* Johann Kriegler — see People, Places and Events.
† Bishop Barnabas Lekganyane was the leader of the ZCC.

to attend the Easter celebration to set the right tone for the election, which seemed to imply that he would be encouraging participation. At the Easter meeting I sat in the hall next to Mandela for two hours. It was the first time I talked to him as a person. He was like a grandfather. He recognised people as they came in, explaining that this one was married to that one's sister; he was able to identify them from all over the country by family connections — he really knew his natural constituents.'[4]

It was the Kenyan professor John S. Mbiti who observed in his seminal work, *African Religions and Philosophy,* that Africans are notoriously religious; this is borne out to a very large extent in the sizeable adherents of the ZCC with its syncretic mix of Christian and traditional African religious beliefs.[5] It therefore made sense for Mandela, or any political leader for that matter, to woo its bishop, whose influence extended well beyond the borders of South Africa, with hundreds of thousands of the faithful trekking from all points of southern Africa to the pilgrimage in Moria, in what was then the northern Transvaal. They might have come to worship, but for Mandela they constituted a voting public. First and foremost, Mandela wanted to ensure the integrity of the founding election, an essential condition for a peaceful transition to democracy.

Mandela writes that 'the formation of the first democratically elected government of South Africa was preceded by a countrywide election campaign during which ANC leaders in all levels of the organisation systematically combed the entire country, visited rural and urban areas and spoke to all sections of the population.

'It is this team of men and women that made 27 April 1994 unforgettable in the collective memory of the South African nation as a day in which our people came together and united in symbolic action.

'That day concluded months of excitement, expectations and fears following the conclusion of negotiations in November of the previous year.

'The election date was agreed at the negotiations so that for five months the nation waited with bated breath for the arrival of that historic day in the life of South Africa.

'To the black majority, it meant the birth of a dream that had inspired generations, namely, that one day the people will govern.

'For decades, after the conclusion of the colonial wars of dispossession, they had to sit on the sidelines of political life, watching their compatriots voting to rule over them. Now the day was nearing when they would, together with all their compatriots, decide on the politics of their country.

'To many of the white population, the prospect of that day obviously held cause for trepidation, fear and insecurity. To them it would signal the end of minority control and privilege, opening up the frightening prospect of having to share with those whom they subjected for so long and in many respects so cruelly.

'The atmosphere in those months leading up to election day was therefore understandably a mixture of all those different and competing emotions and expectations. As we went around the country campaigning and canvassing our people to come out to vote for the liberation movement, we encountered those various moods.

'It was clear that the hard work done by the liberation movement over so many decades had left an indelible mark on the voting patterns to be expected. All over the country and in all communities, we were greeted with enthusiasm and overwhelming signs of support.

'[In my capacity as] the ANC president, [I] travelled to virtually every corner of the country. In the run-up to the elections in the last six months, [I] personally addressed at least two and a half million people through rallies and meetings across the length and breadth of South Africa. It was moving to observe how the name and reputation of our movement lived in even the remotest rural areas.

'In the long-established tradition of our organisation and of Congress politics, we drew into our campaign the widest possible array of people. As we had done during negotiations, when we managed to win over to our side different parties who originally were thought to be allies of the apartheid regime, we now again adopted that broad approach to unite people even in campaigning. We used modern research techniques and methodologies including polling opinion. Our polling adviser was Stan Greenberg who was adviser to [President] Clinton in his 1992 campaign.

'In the campaign we held People's Forums, focus groups and inserted media adverts seeking inputs from the people. These yielded enormous responses. We engaged with the people face-to-face.'[6]

Mandela and the ANC had long realised that they didn't have the campaign resources to match the National Party's formidable election machinery, which enjoyed the advantage of incumbency. Although credited to Greenberg, the ANC, through an activist such as Ketso Gordhan, had actually reformatted the Nicaraguan strategy of the people's forums to suit local conditions.

In a chapter on the election in the Western Cape, as part of a well-researched study, *Launching Democracy in South Africa*, co-edited by the journalist and political scientist R. W. Johnson and eminent South African sociologist and political scientist Lawrence Schlemmer, contributors Robert Mattes, Hermann Giliomee and Wilmot James write that the media opportunities 'afforded by the forums were important in order to communicate the real symbolic message of the ANC's accountability, representativeness and accessibility and rebuild its image as a "parliament of the people" '.[7] Here, the leaders did not speak; instead they responded to questions from the representatives of the audience in an environment that facilitated democratic exchange.

Writing about the period, Johannes Rantete, in his account of the ANC and the negotiated settlement, observes that the election campaign was personalised 'with much attention being focused on party leaders. De Klerk was eloquent and sharp but could not match Mandela's heroic attributes which saw thousands of people flocking and stampeding to most of the gatherings he attended. Young and old wanted to see with their own eyes a man whose reputation in contemporary world history could be compared to none.'[8]

Knowing that there was a problem regarding voter literacy among the black majority, another legacy of apartheid, Mandela sought strategies to redress this problem, which might otherwise have posed a setback for the ANC.

'We also engaged the masses in an active voter education campaign,' he writes. '[I] organised some skilful personalities to help in this regard. One of them was Leepile Taunyane, then president of the National Professional Teachers' Organisation of South Africa [NAPTOSA]. He replied that [I] was late, he and his colleagues in NAPTOSA had already started the voter-education campaign. We were tremendously inspired because he led a strong and disciplined movement, which had enough resources to wage a powerful campaign. We had made the same appeal to the South African Democratic Teachers Union, who had already taken the initiative also before we appealed to them to join. The ANC sought not to speak to the people, but to speak with the people.

'I conducted the campaign as a member and as president of the ANC, having been elected to the latter position by the first national conference of the organisation after it was unbanned, which was held in Durban in 1991. We conducted mock elections as part of the voter-education campaign. Ten million people took part. This was very important, as in the actual election there were less than one per cent spoilt papers. This spoilt-paper percentage is in line with the performance in elections in democracies with developed economies with a high level of literacy.

'The ANC conducted a positive campaign, focused on rebuilding, reconstruction and a better life for all without forgetting the past. We avoided negative campaigning, avoided attacking opposition parties. To the best of my memory, we never placed a single negative advert in the media.* The opposition, on the other hand, were primarily negative and kept attacking the ANC and its alliance partners.

'As always,' Mandela wrote, 'we were mindful of the minorities in our questions about the future, at such times of great transition. Our movement had always been one concerned for all of the people of our country and we sent that message to the country during our campaign. People responded with enthusiasm.

'We remember, for example, how a young woman from the coloured community, Amy Kleynhans, then the reigning Miss South Africa, joined us on stage during our campaign in Cape Town. She had earlier angered the then state president, F. W. de Klerk, because of her refusal to carry the national flag of apartheid during an international beauty pageant, confirming her allegiance to the new South Africa about to be born.

* There weren't negative advertisements beyond what the election team termed 'contrast adverts'.

'There were other such demonstrations of enthusiastic support. One young teacher from the community left his post to sing songs composed by himself for the campaign. This young man, John Pretorius, later recorded the song "Sekunjalo", which he sang at so many rallies in the Cape during the election campaign.'

Energetic and danceable, this song has an urban beat with gospel traditions woven into the music. The refrain 'free at last' and its attendant lyrics are a joyful celebration of the end of tyranny and the dawn of freedom. Years later, during Mandela's eightieth birthday celebrations, John Pretorius sang a duet of this song with Jermaine Jackson to ecstatic reception at a concert at Ellis Park Stadium.

'As we have mentioned,' Mandela writes, 'everything was not of that positive and joyous scale. In KwaZulu-Natal we had to cope with the continuing political violence that cast a spell of gloom and doubt over the otherwise exciting prospects of democracy. We concentrated a lot of our time on the political situation in that province. On the one hand, we had to campaign for the election victory of our organisation, while at the same time it was our duty to address in a non-partisan way the fate of all of the people in the province. The political violence, no matter by whom it was being committed, was to the great damage of all South Africans. And as always in such circumstances, the innocent carried the brunt of suffering, hence our special attention to the then province of Natal.

'Our election campaign did not always proceed smoothly. As pointed out above, the National Party of De Klerk was extremely negative, and at times plainly immoral in its campaign.

'When I visited Los Angeles in the early nineties, I took a photograph flanked by two internationally famous artists, Elizabeth Taylor and Michael Jackson. In the run-up to the April 1994 election, the National Party published a scurrilous pamphlet entitled *Winds of Change* in which they cut out Michael Jackson; and Elizabeth Taylor and I now appeared all alone. They aggravated that deceitful exercise by making defamatory remarks against both of us. The Independent Electoral Commission forced them to withdraw the pamphlet.

'The National Party campaign was not only immoral, but also racist. They exploited the fears of the racial minorities, especially those of the coloured and Indian communities, by arguing that a victory of the ANC would result in their repression by Africans. They criticised Dr Allan Boesak, a prominent cleric from the coloured community, for campaigning for all sections of the South African population, instead of confining himself exclusively to coloureds.

'Another example of this racism was again directed at me personally. Heidi Dennis, a young coloured teacher from the Beacon Valley Senior Secondary School in the coloured community in Mitchell's Plain, asked me to help them to raise funds to paint their school. I then requested Syd Muller of Woolworths not only to provide funds, as asked by Heidi, but [also] to upgrade the school by building more classrooms and a laboratory.

'When Woolworths completed the project,' Mandela continues, 'we went to launch it. A large group of coloured women staged a protest demonstration against me. One of them screamed and said in Afrikaans, *"Kaffer, gaan huis toe"* ("Kaffir, go home"), a derogatory jibe. All these racist and deceitful manoeuvres were committed by De Klerk's party, a leader I had repeatedly praised inside and outside the country as a man of integrity with whom we could do business.

'The ANC tried to the best of its ability to avoid descending to the level of the National Party. We remained focused and constructive. We strongly urged all South Africans, irrespective of colour or creed, to join the fight for a democratic, united, non-racial and non-sexist South Africa. In that campaign we also experienced difficulties from some of our members who made rash statements contrary

113

to our basic policy. We immediately condemned publicly such behaviour.'[9]

It should have been expected, given the high stakes, that the election campaigns would test the mettle of the major contenders. The National Party, which had so much to lose, could only overstate its record as a vehicle that had brought about change, while the ANC, still untested, had to promise to bring about a new dispensation for all. In the cut and thrust of contention it was inevitable that the election campaign would, according to a Western Cape newspaper report, turn into 'a torrid war of words between the African National Congress and the National Party. Each party accused the other of "dirty tricks" and "underhand electioneering". Each has lodged complaints with the Independent Electoral Commission over the other's campaign conduct, posters and pamphlets.'[10]

In the opening salvo of mud-slinging, the ANC had published a pamphlet depicting the National Party's regional premiership candidate, Hernus Kriel, leading a trio of candidates, two black and one coloured, as dogs on leashes, with fifty-rand notes dropping out from Mr Kriel's pocket. Not to be outdone, the National Party had gone for the jugular. 'Later today,' continues the newspaper report, 'the IEC is due to give a final ruling on a National Party comic book which the ANC alleges is racist and which relies on *"swart gevaar"* ["black danger"] tactics to woo coloured voters. It is entitled "Winds of Change Blow Through South Africa — Will You Make It Through the Storm?" '[11]

The National Party's deployment of *swart gevaar* — the notional devastation that would follow the advent of a black government — went against the grain of Mandela's cherished cause of reconciliation. Despite this, Mandela recognised that whites — especially Afrikaners — had to be made part of the evolving new South Africa. Thabo Mbeki echoed this crucial point in an interview with Joel Netshitenzhe and Tony Trew in Johannesburg in 2014:*

[The] reconciliation business had to do with [Madiba's wish to say] 'Let's protect the democratic gains from this potential threat,' and therefore this became a preoccupation not so much because he was a worshipper of reconciliation in itself but it served a purpose in terms of protecting what we had gained . . . He had to attend to this issue of Afrikaners and showing that he was not a monster, he was not a threat and so on, in order to solve a problem. Because . . . there is no Mandela with regard to this matter about reconciliation who is different from

* Joel Netshitenzhe; Tony Trew — see People, Places and Events.

the rest of the leadership of the ANC — this reconciliation, addressing the issue of white fears, was connected to his concern about this possibility of counter-revolution.[12]

'The white right wing,' Mandela writes, 'was another potentially destabilising factor that affected the general mood during the period leading up to the elections . . . Stories were abounding about whites who were adopting a siege mentality, stocking up their houses with food and other emergency supplies.'[13]

Representatives of local and international media houses and agencies and independent journalists and photographers went all around the country, the majority primed to cover a war zone. They had been promised a war. Media spokespeople from the ANC's numerous foreign missions gave on-the-spot briefings about what visitors should expect in South Africa, downplaying the rumours of mayhem. The citizens, armed only with their green identity documents, waited for the polling stations to open.

Mandela was greatly encouraged by the preparations. 'On the organisational and logistical level, just as much public interest was generated. The Independent Electoral Commission set about preparing for the elections, establishing offices in different parts of the country. Amongst their tasks was to monitor the general atmosphere that could affect the measure to which the elections would be free and fair.

'It filled one with pride,' he continues, 'to observe how many South Africans were warming up to the mechanics of democratic elections. It was said by some commentators that the system of voting for that day would be too complex and complicated for the supposedly unsophisticated voters. We had decided on a system of proportional representation: the electorate had to vote for the national legislature and the provincial one on the same day. All of these were thought to hold complexities that might be confusing to voters.

'In the end, it turned out that South African voters had an almost natural affinity to the process of voting.

'There were scores of foreign observers who also travelled the country, including my future wife, Graça Machel, either assisting in voter education or monitoring the situation during the campaign period, ensuring that the conditions for free and fair elections existed.★ Almost without exception they afterwards commented about the positive spirit that existed in the country.

'There were other mechanisms operating to assist South Africans to operate in the spirit

★ Graça Machel — see People, Places and Events.

of open democracy in the run-up to the elections. Amongst these was the Independent Media Commission to ensure that all parties were fairly treated by the media, both in reporting and coverage.'[14]

There are as many impressions of the days of voting as there are people who were compos mentis during the elections, the days themselves a focal point from which to think about the reality of democracy. For South Africans, this is a long moment etched into their brains the way Americans remember John F. Kennedy's assassination or — for older, diminishing generations throughout the world — the end of either one of the world wars. It was, to use a hackneyed phrase, for most South Africans, an experience to remember for the rest of their lives. Given its import, the election would be spread over two days.

Tuesday, 26 April 1994, a trial run for the election the following day, was reserved for the elderly, people living with disabilities, and South Africans outside the country. For many such people, especially some expatriates in foreign climes, the act of voting clarified their minds about their origins — and allegiances. For the religious, if Mandela's release epitomised liberation from bondage, the first democratic elections marked the reality of the existence of the Promised Land. It was a poignant moment for a frail Archbishop

Trevor Huddleston, the president of the British Anti-Apartheid Movement and a lifelong campaigner for Mandela's release, when he entered South Africa House in London's Trafalgar Square in order to cast his vote in South Africa's first democratic election. Hobbling on crutches, he spoke to the assembled supporters 'in the reading room heavy with colonial history, [thanking] God for being able to participate in "something unspeakably wonderful" '.[15]

People from all walks of life trickled like water from everywhere and formed queues that snaked for miles as they took steps to the centres where they could place their vote. If there was nervousness about right-wing attacks, people didn't show it. It was all about resolve, which was broadcast far and wide.

'At some polling stations in black areas,' according to Paul Taylor of the *Washington Post,* 'lines began forming at 4 a.m. At others, disabled voters were carried to the ballot boxes in wheelbarrows or litters. Countrywide, the prevailing mood seemed less one of exuberance than of quiet resolve. "I'm tired; my back is sore; I haven't eaten all day," a stoical Susan Ndhlovu, sixty-seven, told a South African reporter as she waited in a long line under a hot sun in Bloemfontein. "But I'm staying until I've voted." '[16]

On the morning of Wednesday, 27 April, Mandela 'voted at Ohlange High School in

Inanda, a green and hilly township just north of Durban, for it was there that John [Langalibalele] Dube, the first president of the ANC, was buried.* This African patriot had helped found the organisation in 1912, and casting my vote near his graveside brought history full circle, for the mission he began eighty-two years before was about to be achieved.'[17]

Mandela observes that on the dawn of that day, which symbolised a new beginning, 'the South Africans queued in their millions to cast their first democratic vote, the foundations had been laid during preceding months. That memorable day fittingly capped the positive spirit of hope and expectation that reigned predominant in spite of the tears and trepidations.

'The smooth and orderly manner in which the elections occurred, and the violence-free transformation that followed, completely shattered the depressing predictions of the prophets of doom, who included some of the well-known and respected political analysts. They had predicted that the history of South Africa, especially during the four decades of the apartheid regime, clearly showed that the white minority was determined to cling to power for centuries to come. A wide variety

* John Langalibalele Dube — see People, Places and Events.

of commentators underestimated our determination and capacity successfully to persuade opinion makers on both sides of the colour line to realise that this country is their beloved fatherland, with primary responsibility to turn April 1994 into a memorable landmark in our turbulent history.

'This was the day for which a long line of celebrated legends had fought since 1652 when the foreigner Jan van Riebeeck landed on our shores.* They laboured tirelessly for the liberation of our country: the Khoi leader Autshumao, Abdullah Abdurahman, Cissie Gool and Hettie September, Yusuf Dadoo and Monty Naicker, Bram Fischer and Michael Harmel, Khosi Tshivhase, Alpheus Madiba, Queen Manthatisi, Selope Thema, Moses Kotane, Albert Luthuli, Oliver Tambo, Chris Hani, Robert Sobukwe, Zeph Mothopeng and Steve Biko, and a multitude of others.'[†18]

* Jan van Riebeeck, an employee of the Dutch East India Company, established a refreshment station for Dutch ships in Table Bay, leading to the establishment of the Cape Colony and white settlement in South Africa.

† Autshumao; Yusuf Dadoo; Bram Fischer; Moses Kotane; Zeph Mothopeng; Steve Biko — see People, Places and Events. Abdullah Abdurahman was the first coloured person to be elected to the Cape Town City Council in 1904 and the Cape Provincial

Later, reflecting on the aftermath of the historic national poll to legitimise democracy,

---

Council in 1914 and was president of the African Political Organisation, which fought racial oppression against coloureds. Cissie Gool, daughter of Abdurahman, was the founder and first president of the National Liberation League, president of the Non-European United Front in the 1940s, and the first coloured woman to graduate from law school in South Africa and be called to the Cape Bar. Hettie September was a trade-unionist, a member of the South African Coloured People's Organisations and a founding member of the Cape Town Women's Food Committee in 1946. Monty Naicker was a medical doctor, co-founder and first chairperson of the Anti-Segregation Council and the president of the Natal Indian Congress, 1945–63. Michael Harmel was a leading member of the SACP, editor of *The African Communist,* and a member of MK. He was a co-founder of the Congress of Democrats (COD). Khosi Tshivhase is a Venda king. Alpheus Madiba died in what was ruled a suicide by hanging in 1967 after one day in detention. Queen Manthatisi led the Tlôkwa people during the period of the Difiqane/Mefacane wars, 1815–40, until her son, Sekonyela was old enough to rule. Selope Thema was a leading member of the SANNC and secretary of the deputation on behalf of black South Africans to the Versailles Peace Conference and the British government in 1919.

Mandela couldn't help adopting a sardonic tone towards the naysayers and the timorous who had prepared for a catastrophe.

'After the elections, when all was over and matters turned out so differently to what the prophets of doom had predicted, there was great mirth and levity about those who stockpiled in such fashion. But at the time, it was a matter of great seriousness and it did affect the overall mood.'[19]

The ANC won a landslide victory, taking 62.6 per cent of the popular vote, which Mandela attributed to his party's hard work and its adherence to discipline. Notwithstanding difficulties caused by the late participation of the IFP and the violence that imperilled free political activity in rural areas of Natal, or the hacking of the vote-counting system to boost the National Party, Freedom Front and IFP, which was foiled by the IEC, no one contested the legitimacy of the elections, nor that they had been 'substantially free and fair'.[20]

But, as with all elections — or any contest where there are winners and losers — it was inevitable that some, including elements within the ANC itself, would complain about irregularities. For instance, when a delegation of ANC provincial leaders from Natal came with evidence of irregularities that favoured the IFP, Mandela insisted on accepting the ANC's narrow loss of the province rather than mounting a challenge that might have cost the legitimacy of the election and have serious implications for stability and peace. For his part, De Klerk was also not immune to internal rumblings, with some National Party leaders calling for a legal challenge to the results. He took the view, he says in his memoirs, that 'despite all the irregularities, we had little choice but to accept the outcome of the election in the interest of South Africa and all its people'.[21]

Although elated, Mandela still worried over some of the results. The ANC had failed to win the provinces of the Western Cape and KwaZulu-Natal, and the Northern Cape had been won with under 50 per cent of the vote. The ANC had to address concerns of various constituencies, specifically the white working class, traditionalists in Natal, and the Indian and coloured communities. These issues would be a strong focus for Mandela's leadership of the transition in the coming years.

On the evening of 2 May, after De Klerk conceded defeat in a televised address, the party celebrated at the ballroom of the Carlton Hotel, which abuts the Carlton Centre, Africa's tallest skyscraper, with fifty floors towering above the central business district of Johannesburg. Although advised by his doctor to take it easy as he had a cold, Mandela could not pass up the opportunity to rejoice with his compatriots. Here, to an ecstatic crowd, he briefly spelt out his mission and mandate as president of the country's first democratically elected government.

Mandela said: 'I must apologise, I have contracted a cold and I hope my voice will be able to stand up to the pressures this evening. My doctor, who examined me very early this morning, asked me to rest for today and tomorrow and to do as little talking as possible. And he said if I do that this cold would clear in two days' time. I hope you will not disclose to him that I did not obey his instructions.

'Fellow South Africans, the people of South Africa, this is indeed a joyous night. Although not yet final, we have received the provisional results of the election. My friends, I can tell you that we are delighted by the overwhelming support for the African National Congress.

'Within the last few hours, I have received telephone calls from State President de Klerk, General Constand Viljoen, Dr Zach de Beer and Mr Johnson Mlambo, the first deputy president of the PAC, who pledged their full cooperation and offered their sincere congratulations.* I thanked them all for their support and look forward to work-

* Zach de Beer was the last leader of the Progressive Federal Party and the first leader of the Democratic Party.

ing together for our beloved country.

'I would also like to congratulate President de Klerk for the strong showing the National Party has displayed in this election. I also want to congratulate him for the . . . years that we have worked together, quarrelled . . . and that at the end of our heated exchanges, we were able to shake hands and to drink coffee.

'My congratulations also go to Dr Zach de Beer, as well as to General Constand Viljoen, with whom I have had numerous discussions and whom I regard as worthy South Africans who are going to make a contribution in the Government of National Unity.

'I also look forward to having discussions with the leaders of the liberation movement who have not been able to make the threshold. I will go to my organisation because I have got certain ideas. They have suffered together with us. I was in jail with many of them. We suffered together in the battlefields, and it hurts me a great deal that they should not be able to have made the threshold, which other parties have made.

'To all those in the African National Congress and the democratic movement who worked so hard these last few days and through these many decades, I thank you and honour you.

'To the people of South Africa and the world who are watching: this is indeed a joyous night for the human spirit. This is your victory too. You helped end apartheid; you stood with us through the transition.

'I watched, along with you all, as the tens of thousands of our people stood patiently in long queues for many hours. Some sleeping on the open ground overnight, waiting to cast this momentous vote . . . This is one of the most important moments in the life of our country. I stand before you filled with deep pride and joy; pride in the ordinary humble people of this country. You have shown such a calm, patient determination to reclaim this country as your own, and joy that we can loudly proclaim from the rooftops — free at last!

'I am your servant; I don't come to you as a leader . . . We are a great team. Leaders come and go but the organisation and the collective leadership that has looked after the fortunes and reverses of this organisation will always be there. And the ideas I express are not the ideas invented in my own mind. They stem from . . . the Freedom Charter; from the decisions; resolutions of the National Conference and from the decisions of the National Executive Committee . . .* It is not the individuals that matter; it is the collective

* Freedom Charter — see People, Places and Events.

127

leadership which has led our organisation so skilfully.

'And I stand therefore before you humbled by your courage, with a heart full of love for all of you. I regard it as the highest honour to lead the ANC at this moment in our history, and that we have been chosen to lead our country into the new century.

'I pledge to use all my strength and ability to live up to your expectations of me as well as the ANC.

'I am personally indebted and pay tribute to some of South Africa's greatest leaders including John [Langalibalele] Dube, Josiah Gumede, G. M. Naicker, Dr Abdurahman, Chief Luthuli, Lilian Ngoyi, Bram Fischer, Helen Joseph, Yusuf Dadoo, Moses Kotane, Chris Hani and Oliver Tambo.* They should have been here to celebrate with us, for this is their achievement too.

'Tomorrow, the entire ANC leadership and I will be back at our desks. We are rolling up our sleeves to begin tackling the problems our country faces. We ask you all to join us — go back to your jobs in the morning. Let's get South Africa working.

'For we must, together and without delay, begin to build a better life for all South Africans. This means creating jobs, building

* For biographical notes on these individuals, see People, Places and Events.

houses, providing education and bringing peace and security for all.

'This is going to be the acid test of the Government of National Unity. We have emerged as the majority party on the basis of the programme, which is contained in the Reconstruction and Development Programme.* There we have outlined the steps that we are going to take in order to ensure a better life for all South Africans.

'Almost all the organisations that are going to take part in the Government of National Unity have undertaken . . . to contribute to the better life of our people. That is going to be the cornerstone . . . on which the Government of National Unity is going to be based. And I appeal to all the leaders who are going to serve in this government, to honour that programme. And . . . to contribute towards its immediate implementation.

'If there are attempts on the part of anybody to undermine that programme, there will be serious tensions in the Government of National Unity.

'We are here to honour our promises. If we failed to implement this programme, that will be a betrayal of the trust which the people of South Africa have vested in us. It is a programme, which was developed by the masses

* Reconstruction and Development Programme — see People, Places and Events.

of the people themselves in People's Forums. It has been accepted by state corporations, by government departments, by business, academics, by religious leaders, youth movements, women's organisations. And nobody will be entitled to go to that, to participate in that Government of National Unity to oppose that plan.

'But I must add we are not going to make the Government of National Unity an empty shell. We want every political organisation that participates in that Government to feel that they are part and parcel of a government machine, which is capable of accommodating their views within the context of the Reconstruction and Development Programme. We do not want to reduce them into mere rubber stamps, to rubber stamp the decision of any organisation except to say that that programme has to be carried out without reservation.

'The calm and tolerant atmosphere that prevailed during the elections depicts the type of South Africa we can build. It set the tone for the future. We might have our differences, but we are one people with a common destiny in our rich variety of culture and traditions.

'We also commend the security forces for the sterling work done. This has laid a solid foundation for a truly professional security force, committed to the service of the people and loyalty to the new constitution.

'People have voted for the party of their choice and we respect that. This is democracy.

'I hold out a hand of friendship to the leaders of all parties and their members, and ask all of them to join us in working together to tackle the problems we face as a nation. An ANC government will serve all the people of South Africa, not just ANC members.

'We are looking forward to working together in a Government of National Unity. It is a clear mandate for action. To implement a plan to create jobs, promote peace and reconciliation, and guarantee freedom for all South Africans.

'Now is the time for celebration, for South Africans to join together to celebrate the birth of democracy.

'Let our celebrations be in keeping with the mood set in the elections — peaceful, respectful and disciplined — showing we are a people ready to assume the responsibilities of government.

'I promise that I will do my best to be worthy of the faith and confidence you have placed in me and my organisation, the African National Congress. Let us build the future together, and toast a better life for all South Africans.

'Lastly, I just want to say that in some areas we may not have done as well as we hoped. But that is how democracy functions. There should be no tensions in any region in which we have not emerged as the majority party. Let us stretch out our hands to those who have beaten us, and to say to them: we are all South Africans; we have had a good fight. But now this is the time to heal the old wounds and to build a new South Africa.

'I also want to say that there are sports teams that were supposed to come to South Africa. They have not done so because of the state of emergency. I invite all of them to come to South Africa irrespective of the state of emergency. We the people of South Africa will welcome them with open hands.

'I thank you.'[22]

Sometime later in the evening he was given a gift from James Motlatsi, president of the National Union of Mineworkers. Mandela then returned to the microphone and said: 'Well, I'm sure you'll bear with me. I can't resist saying thank you to Comrade James. You must know that my association with the mineworkers' union can be described only by words intimate, because my first job, my very first job, was in the mine as a mine policeman. So I appreciate this gift because those links between the mineworkers and me have lasted and given me strength and hope throughout these many years. And I thank you.'[23]

Like the boxer he once was, Mandela focused all his energy into one blow that would fell the iniquities and inequalities of the past and fashion a truly democratic South Africa. He was a marvel for the staffers in his office, a human dynamo that aimed to reach all constituencies. Jessie Duarte, then chief operations officer in the ANC presidency, remembers how he phoned every head of state who had assisted the ANC's election campaign.[24]

In the days leading up to his inauguration, he conveyed the message that the election was a new beginning and a summons to a national partnership for change. Following a programme that would have tired a man half his age, on the weekend before he was to be elected president by Parliament, Mandela spoke to congregations in Cape Town at a mosque in the Bo-Kaap, and addressed worshippers in a Sea Point synagogue, as well as Anglicans and Methodists in their churches respectively.[25]

In an event organised by the South African Council of Churches to give thanks for the peaceful elections, Mandela addressed a multifaith service at the FNB Stadium in Soweto, where he thanked Christian, Muslim, Hindu and Jewish leaders for their part in the struggle for liberation.

'Nothing I can say can fully describe the misery of our people as a result of that repression,' Mandela said, 'and the day we have been fighting for and waiting for has come. The time has come for men and women, African, coloured, Indian and White, Afrikaans- and English-speaking, to say we are one country, we are one people.'[26]

Duarte remembers that Mandela

also met all the chiefs of the intelligence and the army. He met General Meiring and a General Brown from the police, and he met Magnus Malan.* This was after the election. He said that they had to hand over decently. He wanted to know the strength of the army, what is in the intelligence apparatus, who were the people there. Clearly he had an idea that things had changed and he said so. He took a great interest in those elements: police, army, the Justice Department. I think that came not only from his background but his experience as a prisoner, things that he had experienced that [had gone] wrong for him, the actual issues about justice. He called Bantustan leaders to say that it was time to move forward together.[27]

Earlier, while still in prison, Mandela had been ambivalent towards the Bantustan system.† Although he 'abhorred it', he 'felt the

* Magnus Malan — see People, Places and Events.
† The apartheid regime selected eleven areas in South Africa which it designated for the occupation

134

ANC should use both the system and those within it as a platform for our policies, particularly as so many of our leaders were now voiceless through imprisonment, banning or exile'.[28]

But in the run-up to the elections, Mandela wanted to avert Walter Sisulu's mordant prophecy from coming true. In 1977, Sisulu had written from prison about the so-called independence of the Bantustans. 'With "independence" for Bantustans, the Nats [National Party] will have gone a long way in dividing our people along ethnic lines. Furthermore, the Nats have sown seeds that may well become a time bomb that will explode in our midst, long after they and white minority rule have been vanquished.'[29]

Therefore, in talking to Bantustan leaders, Mandela wanted to ensure that they were all on side in the creation of a unitary, independent state, and to avert the spectre of tribalism that one of the ANC's founders and presidents, Pixley ka Isaka Seme, warned about in October 1911.* 'The demon of racialism, the aberrations of the Xosa-Fingo feud, the animosity that exists between the

---

of different African groups. They were called 'Bantustans' or 'homelands'.

* Pixley ka Isaka Seme — see People, Places and Events.

Zulus and the Tsongas, between the Basutos and every other Native must be buried and forgotten; it has shed among us sufficient blood! We are one people. These divisions, these jealousies, are the cause of all our woes and of all our backwardness and ignorance today.'[30]

For Mandela, security was key both to a stable transition and to the growth and development needed for socio-economic change.

He writes: 'A few weeks before the general election of 1994, and accompanied by Alfred Nzo and Joe Nhlanhla, who later became Minister of Foreign Affairs and Minister of Intelligence respectively, I had a discussion with General Georg Meiring, Chief of the South African Defence Force, and thereafter with General Johan van der Merwe, National Commissioner of the South African Police, later known as SAPS.*

'I asked each one whether he would serve under an ANC government if we won the election. General Meiring assured us without hesitation that he would serve the new government loyally and provide it with adequate security, an undertaking, which he tried to the best of his ability to honour. General Meiring's failure to resist pressure

* Alfred Nzo; Johan van der Merwe — see People, Places and Events.

from Military Intelligence to discredit his obvious successor, General Siphiwe Nyanda, and other top black army officers tended to tarnish his otherwise clean image.*

'The discussion with General van der Merwe was not that easy. He was accompanied by General Basie Smit, the second in seniority, and by General Johan Swart, former Commissioner of Soweto. General van der Merwe informed us that he would be retiring soon, and intended to hand over command to Basie Smit. I pointed out that I was interested in him only; that if he would not be available, I would then appoint a successor of my own choice.'[31]

Sydney Mufamadi remembers the discussions between the generals and Mandela:

General Meiring had been asked to stay on, and then at one point he took the so-called intelligence report to President Mandela, which was making very serious allegations about senior members of the previously non-statutory forces, MK in particular . . . of plans to engineer a coup against the government. President Mandela took the allegations seriously enough and appointed Chief Justice [Ismail] Mahomed, and those allegations were found to have no basis. Georg Meiring did not last long after that . . .

* Siphiwe Nyanda — see People, Places and Events.

President Mandela saw the strategic necessity of an inclusive arrangement in order to
build the new South Africa. But he needed
to be satisfied his interlocutors were of the
same mind.[32]

Mandela's disinclination to continue with
General van der Merwe was based on a more
fundamental aspect, the violence wracking
the country, and its sponsors. Mandela made
his offer to appoint Van der Merwe as commissioner of the new police service to assure
him and his cohorts that they wouldn't be
prosecuted for past crimes; but they had to
show reciprocity.

'Van der Merwe was not appointed as head
of the new South African Police Service,' says
Mufamadi, 'because, even as we were very
close to the elections in 1994 . . . we continued to have very serious incidents of . . .
politically motivated violence — in parts of
the Reef, the East Rand in particular and
KwaZulu Natal — which suggested that the
structures that were created for purposes of
carrying out that violence . . . had not been
dismantled.' One of the incidents was a 'big
massacre in the Port Shepstone area' in 1995.
'President Mandela was not satisfied that we
could count on the leadership of General Van
der Merwe, who was very hesitant about
participating in the Truth [and Reconcilia-
tion] Commission [TRC].'[33]

Based on the Promotion of National Unity and Reconciliation Act, No. 34 of 1995, the TRC was set up by the GNU to help deal with what had happened under apartheid. The conflict during this period resulted in violence and human rights abuses. In Mufamadi's — and Mandela's — view, the TRC 'was not just going to talk about who did what in the past, but actually close the space for whoever might have been thinking about continuing to carry out incidents of violence, to continue to do so because the truth would have been known about who was in the hit squads . . .'[34]

When General van der Merwe failed to respond to Mandela's overtures, Mandela terminated the offer. Soon thereafter, Mufamadi continues, 'we set up the unit to investigate the infrastructure that was clearly still in place fomenting violence in KwaZulu Natal . . . [which was] led by the then superintendent, Frank Dutton. And what was good about it is that it got the cooperation of quite a significant number of people who were involved previously in the hit squads — they were coming forward with information.'[35]

In speaking and interacting with every part of South African society, Mandela was imprinting his authority as leader on both the ANC and the country. 'What a lot of people didn't realise,' Barbara Masekela observes, 'was that he was not going to be the president of the ANC only. He was going to be the president of all the people of South Africa. I thought it was my duty to expose him to as wide a range of people as possible so that he can have as accurate as possible an insight into society. He appreciated it deeply.'[36]

On 9 May, following his historic and unopposed election as president by Parliament — and mindful of the symbolism of the gesture — Mandela went with Archbishop Tutu, De Klerk and Mbeki to address the people of Cape Town from the same City Hall balcony from which he had greeted South Africans on the day of his release in February 1990.

'The people of South Africa have spoken in these elections,' he said. 'They want change. And change is what they will get.

'Our plan is to create jobs, promote peace and reconciliation, and to guarantee freedom for all South Africans. We will tackle the widespread poverty so pervasive among the majority of our people. By encouraging investors and the democratic state to support job-creating projects in which manufacturing will play a central role, we will try to change our country from a net exporter of raw materials to one that exports finished products . . .

'To raise our country and its people from the morass of racism and apartheid we require determination and effort. As a government, the ANC will create a legal framework that will assist, rather than impede, the awesome task of reconstruction and development of our battered society.

'While we are and remain fully committed to the spirit of a government of national unity, we are determined to initiate and bring about the change that our mandate from the people demands.

'We place our vision of a new constitutional order for South Africa on the table not as conquerors prescribing to the conquered. We speak as fellow citizens to heal the wounds of the past with the intent of constructing a new order based on justice for all.

'This,' he concluded, 'is the challenge that faces all South Africans today, and it is one to which I am certain we will all rise.'[37]

An important element of Mandela's greatness was his inability to take anything — or anyone — for granted. Perhaps more than a quarter of a century in prison had taught him that he was a blank page, a substrate on which the new reality of the country would imprint itself. There was a big gap in terms of detail between the world that had formed him before his incarceration and what that world had changed into on his release. As his personal assistant, Duarte saw Mandela as someone who listened a lot and talked less. She and Masekela had a great deal of interaction with him. He had sought ANC member and politician Frene Ginwala's counsel in appointing his office personnel.*

Mandela had already checked with the National Working Committee (NWC) of the NEC responsible for the day-to-day running of the party about the allocation of posts to the National Party and IFP in the new Government of National Unity. He was also thinking about his inauguration.

Duarte remembers that Mandela had a hand in who would be there, both from other countries and South Africa:

In the first week after the count had come out, we were then preparing for the inauguration. What touched me was Madiba looking with Thabo Mbeki and Aziz Pahad at the list of international guests.[†]

There were people that he insisted had to be invited, must be — 'I'm not going to have this without [Fidel] Castro.' He always went back to those people; those were friends. And he had to have Yasser Arafat at his inauguration. He said, 'I don't care how we do it, my brother Yasser Arafat must be at my inauguration.' That was a big challenge because the poor man couldn't leave Tunisia; he was going to be arrested. He had a view that every African leader who could possibly come should be invited. He said,

* Frene Ginwala — see People, Places and Events.
† Aziz Pahad — see People, Places and Events.

'We need to be part of what Africa is going to look like, and shape it and build it.' He wanted to know 'So who said they're not coming?' and then he'd pick up the phone — 'Oh, my brother, I believe you can't make it but you know I'd really like you to be here' — and people couldn't say no, and they did come.[38]

Mandela's inauguration was rich in symbolism and emotion. Watched by a global television audience of about a billion people, almost 180 heads of government and foreign dignitaries, and over forty thousand local guests of all races congregated in the amphitheatre and gardens of Pretoria's Union Buildings. Resplendent in dress uniforms, military and police forces whose historic mission had been to thwart exactly this moment, were now securing the conditions for a peaceful transition.

Sworn into office by Judge Michael Corbett, Mandela stood to attention with his hand across his breast for the anthems.* The military — some generals wearing medals awarded for wars of aggression — saluted the president and pledged allegiance. In the moment between the singing of 'Die Stem van Suid-Afrika' ('The Call of South Africa' in Afrikaans), the anthem of the old, discredited

* Michael Corbett — see People, Places and Events.

South Africa, and the singing of 'Nkosi Sikelel' iAfrika' ('Lord Bless Africa' in isi-Xhosa), the anthem of liberation, the new South African flag unfurled.

Crafted by a team headed by Mbeki — always a dab hand at drafting speeches — and aimed at South Africa and the world at large, Mandela's speech matched the symbolism provided by the inauguration and its accoutrements. For that brief moment on the podium, if he had been tall before, he was now taller, surer of his ground, addressing all South Africans and leaders representing varying degrees of power, from the wealthiest to the most abject of the world.

He said: 'Today, all of us do, by our presence here, and by our celebrations in other parts of our country and the world, confer glory and hope to newborn liberty. Out of the experience of an extraordinary human disaster that lasted too long, must be born a society of which all humanity will be proud.

'Our daily deeds as ordinary South Africans must produce an actual South African reality that will reinforce humanity's belief in justice, strengthen its confidence in the nobility of the human soul and sustain all our hopes for a glorious life for all.

'All this we owe both to ourselves and to the peoples of the world who are so well represented here today. To my compatriots, I have no hesitation in saying that each one of us is as intimately attached to the soil of this beautiful country, as are the famous jacaranda trees of Pretoria and the mimosa trees of the bushveld.

'Each time one of us touches the soil of this land, we feel a sense of personal renewal. The national mood changes as the seasons change. We are moved by a sense of joy and exhilaration when the grass turns green and the flowers bloom.

'That spiritual and physical oneness we all share with this common homeland explains the depth of the pain we all carried in our hearts as we saw our country tear itself apart in a terrible conflict, and as we saw it spurned, outlawed and isolated by the peoples of the world, precisely because it has become the universal base of the pernicious ideology and practice of racism and racial oppression.

'We, the people of South Africa, feel fulfilled that humanity has taken us back into its bosom, that we, who were outlaws not so long ago, have today been given the rare privilege to be host to the nations of the world on our own soil.

'We thank all our distinguished international guests for having come to take possession with the people of our country of what is, after all, a common victory for justice, for peace, for human dignity.

'We trust that you will continue to stand by us as we tackle the challenges of building peace, prosperity, non-sexism, non-racialism and democracy. We deeply appreciate the role that the masses of our people and their political mass — democratic, religious, women, youth, business, traditional — and other leaders have played to bring about this conclusion. Not least among them is my Second Deputy President, the Honourable F. W. de Klerk.

'We would also like to pay tribute to our security forces, in all their ranks, for the distinguished role they have played in securing our first democratic elections and the transition to democracy, from bloodthirsty forces which still refuse to see the light.

'The time for the healing of the wounds has come. The moment to bridge the chasms that divide us has come. The time to build is upon us.

'We have, at last, achieved our political emancipation. We pledge ourselves to liberate all our people from the continuing bondage of poverty, deprivation, suffering, gender and other discrimination.

'We succeeded to take our last steps to freedom in conditions of relative peace. We commit ourselves to the construction of a complete, just and lasting peace.

'We have triumphed in the effort to implant hope in the breasts of the millions of our people. We enter into a covenant that we shall build the society in which all South Africans,

146

both black and white, will be able to walk tall, without any fear in their hearts, assured of their inalienable right to human dignity — a rainbow nation at peace with itself and the world.

'As a token of its commitment to the renewal of our country, the new Interim Government of National Unity will, as a matter of urgency, address the issue of amnesty for various categories of our people who are currently serving terms of imprisonment.

'We dedicate this day to all the heroes and heroines in this country and the rest of the world who sacrificed in many ways and surrendered their lives so that we could be free. Their dreams have become reality. Freedom is their reward.

'We are both humbled and elevated by the honour and privilege that you, the people of South Africa, have bestowed on us, as the first President of a united, democratic, non-racial and non-sexist South Africa, to lead our country out of the valley of darkness.

'We understand it that there is no easy road to freedom. We know it well that none of us acting alone can achieve success. We must therefore act together as a united people, for national reconciliation, for nation building, for the birth of a new world.

'Let there be justice for all. Let there be peace for all. Let there be work, bread, water and salt for all. Let each know that for each the body, the mind and the soul have been freed to fulfil themselves. Never, never and never again shall it be that this beautiful land will again experience the oppression of one by another and suffer the indignity of being the skunk of the world.

'The sun shall never set on so glorious a human achievement! Let freedom reign! God bless Africa! Thank you.'[39]

For people of Mandela's age, the symbolism of the celebration must have been even more poignant; not only was the inauguration happening in the precincts of an edifice representing ineffable power, but it was in Pretoria, not far from the Central Prison where many had been executed for daring to imagine that such a moment could ever come to pass. The city's main station had been desegregated not too long ago and the pavements still held the memory of black feet that had to jump hastily back onto the road in deference to a white person's approach. Mandela now strode away from the formality of the amphitheatre, across the manicured acreage of greenery, the Botha Lawns of the Union Buildings, down to where tens of thousands of people were gathered.

'Before starting his acceptance speech, Mandela danced briefly to the music of the African Jazz Pioneers, and the crowd danced delightedly with him. Amid the festive carnival atmosphere, a group of youths ran onto the lawn in front of the Union Buildings holding a life-size coffin aloft. "Hamba kahle apartheid" (farewell apartheid) painted on the side of the coffin.'[40]

On the stage, he introduced Mbeki and De Klerk as the deputy presidents, lifting their hands to the air in his, like a referee declaring joint winners in a prize fight.

'I will always remember him holding up my hand, and also the hand of Thabo Mbeki, for all to see,' De Klerk recalled years later. 'It was symbolic of us approaching the future together.'[41] Here, Mandela described Mbeki as a freedom fighter who had sacrificed his youth to work for liberation, and De Klerk as one of the greatest reformers, one of the sons of the soil.

'Let us forget the past,' Mandela said. 'What is past is past.'[42]

Later, at the inaugural luncheon of invited guests, he spoke in a different idiom, from the heart, as he was wont to do when making an impromptu speech.

'Today,' he said, 'is the result of that other force in our country, that of persuasion, that of discussion, that of dialogue, that of love and loyalty to our common fatherland.

'In the days to come this is the force on which we are going to rely. We are still going to have many problems. So,' he concluded, 'the government of national unity has to face all these problems. But I have no doubt that we have the men and women in this country, from all sections of the population, who will rise to the challenge.'[43]

CHAPTER FOUR:
GETTING INTO
THE UNION BUILDINGS

Nelson Mandela spent the night of the inauguration at the State Guest House in Pretoria, which would be his temporary home for the next three months while F. W. de Klerk was moving out of Libertas, the presidential residence — Mandela later renamed it Mahlamba Ndlopfu ('The New Dawn' in Xitsonga, meaning literally 'the washing of the elephants' due to the fact that elephants bathe in the morning).

At about 10 a.m. on 11 May, the day after the inauguration, Mandela arrived at the back entrance of the west wing of the Union Buildings, accompanied by a security detail of the as yet unintegrated units of the South African Police and of MK. Two formidable women — Barbara Masekela and Jessie Duarte — who were at the heart of Mandela's administration as ANC president stepped along as smartly as they could, laden with paraphernalia for setting up office.

Forever in the shade, the temperature in

the corridors was one or two degrees lower than outside, forcing a somewhat conservative dress code upon the staff and officials. Previously, when Mandela had met with De Klerk, the corridors had always smelled of coffee brewing somewhere. This morning there was no such smell and, except for the few people Mandela met at the entrance to the building, the place seemed virtually deserted and forlorn, devoid of any sense of human warmth. Executive Deputy President de Klerk had taken the whole of his private office with him, leaving only the functional and administrative staff.

But conviviality and sartorial elegance were the last things on the minds of Mandela's staff, whose main business on 11 May was the finalisation of the cabinet of the Government of National Unity and the swearing-in of ministers. It was a small team, composed of handpicked professionals, which had to deliver an urgent mandate. As Jessie Duarte observed, Mandela was not passive in the selection of staff. When he sought to enlist Professor Jakes Gerwel as a possible director general and cabinet secretary, she remembers that Mandela 'wanted to know everything there was to know about Jakes.* He asked Trevor [Manuel] . . . before he actually sat down with Jakes and said, "If we win, would

* Jakes Gerwel — see People, Places and Events.

152

you come to my office?" He also spoke to quite a number of activists [about] who this Gerwel chap was; who . . . would go into government with him?"[1] A competent cadre in the president's office was needed to make up for the gap left by the withdrawal of the sixty people on De Klerk's staff. Moreover, nothing had come out of tasking a Transitional Executive Council sub-council on foreign affairs to plan a structure for the new president's office, except for the designation of a small temporary team to tide over the new president until a permanent arrangement could be made. At Thabo Mbeki's prompting, a team headed by Department of Foreign Affairs official Dr Chris Streeter took on the role, with Streeter becoming Mandela's 'chief of staff' until the director general was appointed.

Mandela was quick to dispel the illusion that he would be getting rid of the old personnel. Although strapped for time, Mandela made a point of shaking hands with each and every member of staff. Fanie Pretorius, then chief director in the office of the president, remembers the occasion:

He started from the left side and he shook hands with every staff member, and about a quarter along the line he came to a lady who always had a stern face, though she was a friendly person. When he took her hand, he said in Afrikaans, *'Is jy kwaad vir my?'* ['Are you cross with me?'], and everybody laughed and the ice was broken. He continued and gave the message to all the staff. There was nothing more and everybody was relieved. He was Nelson Mandela at that moment, with the warmth and the acceptance. Everybody would have eaten out of his hands — there was no negative feeling from anybody after that in the staff, at least that we were aware of.[2]

Mandela's personal warmth towards people from all walks of life, from gardeners, cleaners, clerks and typists to those in the most senior roles, did not go unnoticed. Those who came across him in the course of their work describe him as generous, self-effacing and easy-going; a man who knew 'how to be an ordinary person', with a sincerity demonstrated by his 'greeting everybody in the same way whether there is a camera on him or not'; 'there is never the feeling that he is up there and you're down there'.[3]

Mandela was respectful but not in awe of the world in which he found himself. Like all confident people who take their capability for granted, he was unhesitant about the road he needed to take to strengthen South Africa's democracy. Throughout his political life, he had never shirked responsibility, no matter how dangerous, as evidenced by his role as the volunteer-in-chief in the 1952 Defiance Campaign Against Unjust Laws.* Inspired by the sentiment contained in his favourite poem, 'Invictus', 'the menace of the years' had found him 'unafraid'.[4] Imprisoned for more than a quarter of a century, Mandela had become the world's most recognisable symbol against all forms of injustice. He was initially reluctant to become president, perhaps feeling that he had accomplished what he'd set out to do with his stewardship of the heady period from release to the elections.

'My installation as the first democratically elected President of the Republic of South Africa,' he writes, 'was imposed on me much against my advice.

'As the date of the general elections approached, three senior ANC leaders informed me that they had consulted widely within the organisation, and that the unanimous decision was that I should stand as President if we won the election. This, they said, was what they would propose at the first meeting of our parliamentary caucus. I advised against the decision on the grounds that I would turn seventy-six that year, that it would be wise to get a far younger person, male or female, who had been out of prison, met heads of state

* Defiance Campaign Against Unjust Laws — see People, Places and Events.

and government, attended meetings of world and regional organisations, who had kept abreast of national and international developments, who could, as far as was possible, foresee the future course of such developments.

'I pointed out that I had always admired men and women who used their talents to serve the community, and who were highly respected and admired for their efforts and sacrifices, even though they held no office whatsoever in government or society.

'The combination of talent and humility, of being able to be at home with both the poor and the wealthy, the weak and the mighty, ordinary people and royalty, young and old — men and women with a common touch, irrespective of their race or background, are admired by humankind all over the globe.

'The ANC has always been rich with talented men and women, who preferred to remain in the background and to push forward promising young people to positions of eminence and responsibility, to expose them early in their political careers to the basic principles and problems of leadership, and how to manage such problems. The kind of leader has always made a formidable impression on many of us. Comrade Walter Sisulu is such a man; that is why he has always towered above all of us, irrespective of the offices we occupied in the movement or government.

'I urged the three senior leaders that I would prefer to serve without holding any position in the organisation or government. One of them, however, put me flat on the carpet.

'He reminded me that I had always advocated the crucial importance of collective leadership, and that as long as we scrupulously observed that principle, we could never go wrong. He bluntly asked whether I was now rejecting what I had consistently preached down the years. Although that principle was never intended to exclude a strong defence of what one firmly believed in, I decided to accept their proposal.

'I, however, made it clear that I would serve for one term only. Although my statement seemed to have caught them unawares — they replied that I should leave the matter to the organisation — I did not want any uncertainty on this question. Shortly after I had become President, I publicly announced that I would serve one term only and would not seek re-election.

'At meetings of the ANC,' Mandela continues, 'I often stressed that I did not want weak comrades or puppets who would swallow anything I said, simply because I was President of the organisation. I called for a healthy relationship in which we could address issues, not as master and servants, but as equals in which each comrade would express

157

his or her views freely and frankly, and without fear of victimisation or marginalisation.

'One of my proposals, for instance, which generated a lot of sound and fury, was that we should reduce the voting age to fourteen, a step which had been taken by several countries elsewhere in the world.

'This was due to the fact that in those countries, the youth of more or less that age were in the forefront of their revolutionary struggles. It was that contribution which induced their victorious governments to reward them by giving them the right to vote. Opposition to my proposal from members of the National Executive Committee was so vehement and overwhelming that I retreated in order. The newspaper, *The Sowetan,* dramatised the issue in its cartoon column when they showed a baby in napkins voting. It was one of the most graphic manners of ridiculing my idea. I did not have the courage to insist on it again.

'There have, however, been cases where I did not consider myself bound by the principle of collective leadership. One example was when I summarily rejected the decision of a policy conference that the Cabinet should be appointed by conference. I also rejected the ANC's first list of negotiators with the apartheid regime, which was sent to us by the leadership in Lusaka. Out of the eleven names, eight belong to one black ethnic group, and there was not a single woman amongst them.

'To sum up, the principle of collective leadership, of teamwork, is not an inflexible or dogmatic instrument to be mechanically applied irrespective of the circumstances. It must always be examined in the light of the prevailing conditions. But it is an essential guiding principle if we're going to promote unity and mutual confidence among comrades. We deviate from it only in extraordinary circumstances.

'As President of the ANC and of the country, I encouraged members of the organisation, the Cabinet and Parliamentarians to be outspoken at ANC and government meetings. But I invariably warned that to be outspoken did not at all mean one should be destructive or negative.

'One should never forget that the main aim in a debate, inside and outside the organisation, in political rallies, in Parliament and other government structures, is that we should emerge from that debate, however sharp our differences might have been, closer and more united and confident than ever before. The removal of differences and mutual suspicion within one's organisation . . . should always be our guiding principle.

'This is comparatively easy when we try, to the best of our ability, never to question the integrity of another comrade or a member of another political organisation who has a different point of view from ours.

'During my political career, I have discovered that in all communities, African, coloured, Indian and white, and in all political organisations without exception, there are good men and women who fervently wish to go on with their lives, who yearn for peace and stability, who want a decent income, good houses, and to send their children to the best schools, who respect and want to maintain the social fabric of society.

'Good leaders fully appreciate that the removal of tensions in society, of whatever nature, puts creative thinkers on centre stage by creating an ideal environment for men and women of vision to influence society. Extremists, on the other hand, thrive on tension and mutual suspicion. Clear thinking and good planning was never their weapon.'[5]

The ANC — or, more precisely, President Mandela — needed to think clearly and plan well. Without this capability, it would be difficult to synthesise the old, security-oriented, bureaucratised civil service, a carry-over from the insular legacy of apartheid, and the new, somewhat inexperienced personnel, some of whom had recently graduated from overseas academies where they had received crash courses in administration and the rudiments of running a modern economy. While De

Klerk had a functioning administrative office staffed by people who had worked with him for years, Mandela and his deputy, Mbeki, had to start from scratch. The only experience favouring the ANC in the public service was in a small but significant number of people in foreign affairs and the security forces — mainly defence and intelligence — who had been involved in extensive joint planning for integration. For Mandela, therefore, building the office entailed first bringing in senior liberation-movement figures to head sections and act as advisers and, second, refraining from rushing to change the structure or dispense with staff from the old order.

Jakes Gerwel was the first senior appointment, bringing gravitas to the presidential staff. He also brought his extensive political background as a leader of the United Democratic Front and his engagement with the ANC in exile. As vice-chancellor of the University of the Western Cape, a position from which he was about to retire, he had led the transformation of an apartheid university into an intellectual home of the left. Mandela's endorsement of Professor Gerwel shows the high esteem in which he held him. It's even more remarkable that Gerwel came from the black consciousness tradition and wasn't a card-carrying member of the ANC. Many years later, Mandela wrote of him:

'Professor Jakes Gerwel was Secretary of

the Cabinet as well as Director-General during my presidency, positions he held with distinction. He is now Chairperson of the Nelson Mandela Foundation, the Human Sciences Research Council (HSRC), the African Centre for Constructive Resolution of Disputes (ACCORD), the Institute for [Democratic Alternatives] in South Africa (IDASA) and the Institute for Justice and Reconciliation.

'He is also active in the private sector, being Chairperson of Brimstone Investment Corporation, Africon Engineering International, Educor-Naspers, Director of Naspers, Old Mutual, David Philip Publishers, Western Province Cricket Pty Ltd., member of the South African Academy of Science and six other private sector organisations. He was a former Chairperson of the Committee of University Principals. Academically, he acquitted himself exceptionally. He passed the Bachelor of Arts Degree, Bachelor of Arts Honours, Dr Litteratum et Philosophiae, all cum laude. He had no less than six honorary degrees from local and overseas universities.

'He has been honoured with the South African Order of the Southern Cross, Gold, by the President of South Africa (1999), King Abdulaziz Sash, Minister Rank, by Crown Prince Abdullah of Saudi Arabia (1999) and the Order of Good Deeds by Colonel Muammar Gaddafi of Libya (1999).

'His publications include a variety of monographs, articles, essays and papers on literary, educational and socio-political subjects. He is an impressive and fearlessly independent thinker who rose to the position of Rector of the University of the Western Cape and now Chancellor of the University of Rhodes.

'In the field of human relations, he clearly emerges as a true leader who is devoid of paranoid tendencies and who encourages principled discussions. He constantly draws attention to those aspects among comrades, which are designed to strengthen rather than weaken human relations.

'As Chairperson of our Foundation, he is a linchpin in keeping all of us working together harmoniously, and he nips in the bud any incipient developments towards any form of infighting among comrades.

'Few people are aware that he is also a polished negotiator on the international level. It was he and His Royal Highness Prince Bandar, the Saudi Arabian Ambassador to Washington, who were responsible for the Lockerbie breakthrough.*

* Mandela, with his Director General Professor Jakes Gerwel, worked with Prince Bandar in creating a deal that saw two suspects in the Lockerbie bombing handed over for trial to Scottish police in the neutral territory of Camp Zeist, Netherlands. This is discussed in greater detail in chapter thirteen.

163

'As long as there are men and women of this calibre and vision, world peace and stability will continue to be the cornerstone of national and international relations.'[6]

At the time he appointed Gerwel, Mandela had formed a reasonable idea about how he wanted his office to look. Like all obsessively orderly people — at one point he wanted to make his own bed in a hotel — he couldn't function without a solid base. Having Gerwel at the helm served this purpose. He respected Gerwel and would take his advice. Masekela later commented on this aspect of Mandela's character.

'I think it requires a certain amount of humility and self-interest to want the best advice and to take it. He was a little too much admiring of educated people, I would say. He really was seriously impressed by degrees, and so on, and if you expressed some scepticism about someone like that it would be very difficult to convince him.'[7]

Not that anyone would have expressed scepticism about Professor Gerwel, or, for that matter, about Ahmed Kathrada, who was there from the very start as a presidential adviser. Much later, Kathrada was appointed to the post of parliamentary counsellor. A long-time friend and Mandela's fellow prisoner, he had turned down a suggestion that he become a cabinet minister.

'What happened,' Kathrada said, 'is that

the papers had published beforehand their cabinet, and my name was there. I then wrote to Mandela saying that although my name had been mentioned, I'm not interested in being in the cabinet . . . Fortunately there was this bartering with the IFP, which wanted one of the security portfolios, which we couldn't afford to give them, so the easiest thing was to give them mine — correctional services.'[8]

Mandela's whole life had been dedicated to the transformation of the apartheid state into a non-racist, non-sexist constitutional one, where all people enjoyed equality before the law. But these were abstract ideals that could only be made real — or translated into reality — by the effort of talented and committed men and women. His office, then, had to be an engine to galvanise the membership. The choice of Nicholas 'Fink' Haysom as legal adviser came as no surprise; like the other members of Mandela's office, Haysom came with impeccable credentials. A law professor who had been active in combating vigilante and state-sponsored violence a decade earlier, Haysom had played a central role during the negotiations. His expertise was invaluable, given South Africa's evolution into a constitutional state and the need to devise a legal framework to transform the country and re-enter the international community (in this circumstance, Mandela was signing some 800 executive orders each year — on average, two each day[9]).

Joel Netshitenzhe was a member of the ANC's National Executive Committee and National Working Committee with a strong background in communications and strategic analysis. Deceptively casual and with an aversion to formal dress, Netshitenzhe — working with media liaison officer Parks Mankahlana, who'd come from the Youth League — operated a brief that went beyond writing Mandela's speeches: he was also the unofficial link to the various ANC and government constituencies. Trusted by the media, mainly because he exuded confidence and candour — and was known to have the ear of the president — he worked hard to simplify the more complex policy positions in various forums.

'Before Professor Jakes Gerwel became the Director General of the Presidency and began to draft my speeches,' Mandela writes, 'a task which he still performs to the present day, my speeches were drafted by Comrade Joel Netshitenzhe, later assisted by Comrade Tony Trew.

'As is the case in many parts of the world, South Africa has produced a harvest of bright stars, even geniuses, who have helped to transform our country from its painful past, and made it world famous. It is these women and men right across the colour line, who

166

surprised the world in the nineties, a world which hailed South Africa as a miracle country. That response from the international community confirmed once again what we have repeatedly said before, namely, that our wealth does not depend only in our minerals, but also in the calibre of our women and men. Joel Netshitenzhe, Head of the Government's Communication and Information System (GCIS), is an integral part of that wealth.'[10]

In addition, Netshitenzhe's communication unit monitored and analysed government performance across the departments, compensating for the initial absence of capacity, due to a lack of resources, for policy co-ordination, evaluation and implementation in the presidency.

He 'could be polite and controlled in the face of unbearable provocation,' Mandela continues. 'In the numerous meetings I attended with him as President of the ANC and the country, I have never seen him once losing his temper. In this regard he worked cordially with Thabo [Mbeki], who sometimes would volunteer to help write the speech.

'When Rusty Evans retired as Director General of the Department of Foreign Affairs, I requested Joel to succeed Rusty. Joel was polite as usual. But he said that if I insisted, he would consider the offer, but added emphatically that he would prefer to remain in Communications. I tried hard to pressurise him. But, with a broad smile across his face, he persisted in his courteous refusal. I then appealed to the Deputy President, Thabo Mbeki, to persuade him to accept the offer. But the Deputy President advised me to withdraw the offer. Joel had been consistent in exile in his determination to cling to communications. I accepted that advice.'[11]

In an interview with Aziz Pahad in July 2010, Jakes Gerwel said that he had meant to keep the size of the bureaucracy of Mandela's office 'as lean as efficiency allows' and with a focused task.[12] However, when writing to the Department of State Expenditure, Gerwel admitted that, when they entered the office in May 1994, they 'inherited the apartheid-era Presidential office'. They had to accommodate the exigencies of 'the dramatically enlarged democracy, the rapidly burgeoning international relations, the historical position and stature of President Mandela.' All of these had 'profound implications for the functioning of the Office of the President' and could not have been 'taken into consideration at that stage'.[13] An analogy that comes to mind is of parents providing a layette for a single birth, only to be blessed with quintuplets.

Most political leaders make decisions with a

view to minimising threats to their own political survival. Even though he actively participated in meetings and consulted with his advisers, Mandela was confident of his own opinions on issues; once he had adopted a position, this could sometimes pose difficulties. However, he was not inflexible to the point of obduracy when he realised that he wasn't changing people's minds.

Jakes Gerwel remembered his boss's ability 'to simplify and get through a thing. Madiba was very straightforward.' As Gerwel had spent his entire life in universities, 'theorising comes naturally to me,' he said. 'I am suspicious about simple answers, but I had to hear so many times: "Jakes, it must be simpler than that." . . . Madiba could see the essential core and make things simple. He could therefore make a crucial decision — within five minutes, if necessary.'[14]

But Mandela needed more than the cold, crisp analyses of his advisers; he also drew on the counsel of others in the ANC. Having started a practice of marking Mondays as 'ANC day' in his diary, he would spend that day at the ANC head office with the top officials and others, also attending NWC meetings. He had no set timetable, however, when consulting other ANC leaders close to him, like Sisulu.

'Me, in particular,' Sisulu said, uncomplainingly, in a 1994 interview, 'he likes to ring.

169

He wakes me up, one o'clock, two o'clock, doesn't matter, he'll wake me up. I realise after he has woken me up, this thing is not so important — well, we discuss it, but it didn't really require that he wake me up at that time.'[15]

Mandela's involvement in cabinet, however, changed over time. Early in his tenure, Mandela was more hands-on, keeping himself informed on almost all aspects of policy in order to maintain the coherence of the ANC in the GNU, a measure demanded by the intricate process of transformation. Manuel remembers how, on the eve of cabinet meetings, Mandela convened ANC ministers and their deputies in an ANC cabinet caucus at his Genadendal residence in Cape Town.* This he did, Manuel says, 'so that we could caucus positions that we wanted to take and be mutually supportive. It afforded comrades [an environment] to have a discussion that was quite free.'[16]

In his first hundred days in government, Mandela held meetings to guide the ministers or get their support for positions he held. He

---

* The building was formerly known as Westbrook; Mandela changed its name to Genadendal ('Valley of Mercy' in Afrikaans) after the missionary town Genadendal, situated two hours from Cape Town, which provided sanctuary to slaves when slavery was abolished in the Cape Colony in 1838.

maintained a continuous interest in matters concerning peace, violence and stability. As Nkosazana Dlamini-Zuma observes, 'I think for me he was more engaged at the beginning, but maybe it was because I engaged him more at the beginning because I myself was not experienced.'* But despite that lack of experience, Dlamini-Zuma had a burning ambition to make a dent in the tobacco industry by enacting legislation that outlawed smoking in public places and amenities. Measures were also quite advanced to set up a medical school in Durban, the Nkosi Albert Luthuli Hospital. These two initiatives stuck in Deputy President de Klerk's craw.

'De Klerk,' Dlamini-Zuma remembers,

> called me to his office to say, 'You must stop this nonsense of tobacco because it's going to put the farmers out of work and it is not necessary.' Then he told me that I must build the Pretoria hospital. So I said to him, 'Well the first one I have to build is the medical school here [Durban], because King Edward [VIII Hospital] is a mess and its training of medical students is actually a disgrace.' There was a report of an investigation that his own government had done, [which said that] King Edward was not fit to

* Nkosazana Dlamini-Zuma — see People, Places and Events.

171

train medical students, but he had not done anything. So that was the first hospital I must build. He told me, well, Pretoria is Afrikaner heritage and he is going to fight for it in cabinet, and I said, 'It's fine, you can fight for it.' I didn't tell Tata [Mandela] because I didn't think it was necessary.* On the tobacco thing, I told him that I was the minister of health and I had the responsibility for the health of the country — farmers could plant other things; there's no land in South Africa that can only grow tobacco. We will have programmes together with the minister of agriculture to help farmers shift from tobacco to other crops.

I didn't tell Tata — I don't know who told him — I told some colleagues but didn't tell him as I didn't think it was necessary. But one day he called me in and said, 'I hear that De Klerk called you in and said these things?' I said yes. He said, 'Why didn't you tell me?' I said, 'I didn't think it was something I needed to involve you in, I didn't need your decision on anything.' Then he said, 'No, you must tell me if he calls you again, but I have told him that he must never do that; he must never call my ministers and tell them whatever.' So he was quite angry with De Klerk, and intervened.

* *Tata* is an isiXhosa word that means 'father'. It is widely used as a term of endearment for Mandela.

For me he was really a pillar of strength in terms of being able to do the things that were maybe sometimes controversial.[17]

Mandela's tendency to canvass for views outside conventional circles was perhaps controversial. He didn't hesitate to call to a meeting anyone he deemed suitable to throw light onto a subject. These could be ministers, representatives or leaders of sectors of society, or even heads of state. Judge Kriegler observed how Mandela would often call people himself, rather than relying on his assistants to do so, sometimes catching those close to him unawares. This gravitational pull towards people was mutual; people from all corners of society wished to interact with him and vice versa. This in turn gave him an insight into the mood of the public.

Mary Mxadana, Mandela's private secretary, remarked on his relationship with the public, any public, at home or abroad. 'He's not only an ordinary president of a country,' she said, 'but he's a renowned leader, so everyone wants to have his time.' When he was supposed to be resting, unless it was in a place without a phone, and his cell phone was unavailable, 'he would start calling people all over the world'.[18]

Leaders all over the world had borne witness to his greatest moment of triumph, his inauguration, and he felt confident enough to call upon them for support or keep them apprised of developments. He was at the head of a country, which, by all accounts, was on the tip of everyone's tongue. For a whole year, Mandela's ascendance to power and the destinies of the 'new South Africa' — a phrase that gained instant currency — preoccupied the media and eclipsed reports of the Rwandan genocide.

The world watched and asked questions, wondering about the strategies that Mandela would develop in order to govern. What were the bases of the policies that he and the ANC were proposing? For instance, in a television interview in 1994, the American news anchor Charlayne Hunter-Gault asked Mandela, 'What kind of president will you be?'

'Our approach,' Mandela answered, 'has already been demonstrated in the course of this campaign. We do not believe in taking decisions on top [*sic*] and then sending them down to the masses of the people. We have evolved the strategy of the People's Forum where it is the masses of the people who are telling us what they want, what their concerns are, what their demands are. And out of those demands from the masses of the people themselves we have now prepared what we call the Reconstruction and Development Programme [RDP], which is going to create jobs, build houses, provide education facilities, electricity and so on.'

He was asked further how he planned to get those programmes pushed through; whether it would be through legislation, delegation of authority to cabinet ministers — would he 'let them push it' — or would he be 'in there yourself'?

Mandela said: 'I have to be interested in almost every detail, but of course it's difficult to achieve that result where you have to look into the activities of every department in detail. It is sufficient to lay down a framework, and all departments, all cabinet ministers, should work within that framework, and your task is that of supervising and sometimes getting involved in the actual operations of a department depending on the importance of the national issue. I have addressed the leadership of the Dutch Reformed Church and a wide range of agricultural organisations, which are predominantly Afrikaners, and they have given us their overwhelming support — everybody in this country wants peace, wants security for his family and his children, and they want to start the work of building a new South Africa.'[19]

But how did Mandela form the first cabinet of the post-apartheid, democratic and representative government in 1994? What empowered him? What made him know that the time was ripe for the ANC to take its seat as the majority party in government? The answer lay in Mandela's faith in the ANC's policy documents.

'Preparing to govern,' he writes, 'was not only confined to mobilising the international community. It had an internal aspect as well, which was contained, among other things, in the document *Ready to Govern: ANC Policy Guidelines for a Democratic South Africa* adopted at the National Conference, 28 to 31 May 1992.

'The policy document stated that it was necessary to dwell on the problems which would be faced by the first government which would be elected under a new democratic constitution. This would help create an understanding of the magnitude of tasks involved in transforming our country into one where everyone could enjoy a basic standard of living combined with peace and security. Problems would not be solved overnight and there would be no quick or easy solutions. The problems ran deep and the resources were limited.

'Right on top of the agenda were the basic principles of a democratic constitution for South Africa. The will of the people should be expressed by their democratically elected representatives in periodic free and fair elections. It was these elected representatives who would adopt a constitution, which should be the highest law of the land, guaranteeing their basic rights.

'The document declared that South Africa would be a unitary state in which there would be a government at local, regional and national levels. The Bill of Rights and principles of non-racialism, non-sexism and democratic accountability should apply at all these levels of government.

'The structure of government would consist of the National Assembly and which would be elected by universal suffrage on a common voters roll according to proportional representation. It would also have a senate representative of regions and be directly elected, and have the power of review, refer and delay legislation.

'The executive would consist of a head of state who would be a President with both ceremonial and executive powers. The President would be elected by the National Assembly. He or she would have a fixed term of office and be available for re-election only once. The President would appoint and supervise the functioning of the Cabinet, acting through a Prime Minister (subsequently changed to a deputy President) who would be directly accountable to the President and responsible to the National Assembly.

'The Bill of Rights would be binding upon the State and organs of government at all levels, and where appropriate, on social institutions and persons. It would be enforced by the courts, headed by a separate, newly created constitutional court, which would have the task of upholding the fundamental rights and freedoms of all citizens against the state and anybody or person seeking to deny those rights.

'The judges would be independent, and would consist of men and women drawn from all sections of the community on the basis of their integrity, skills, life experience and wisdom. The Bill of Rights would guarantee language and cultural rights; it would acknowledge the importance of religion in our community; it would respect the diversity of faith and give guarantees of freedom of religion. The Bill of Rights would protect the rights of children, disabled persons, women, the right of workers to set up independent trade unions, their right to engage in collective bargaining and their right to strike.

'The ANC declared itself against capital punishment, and would seek it outlawed in the Bill of Rights. The Bill of Rights would protect the right to have a home and family and property rights. It would affirm the rights of all persons to have access to basic educational, health and welfare services.

'There was strong support in the country for the idea of affirmative action, which meant special measures to enable persons discriminated against on grounds of colour, gender and disability to break into fields from which they have been excluded by past discrimination.

'The whole of the civil service would have to be opened up so as to make it a truly South African civil service, and not the administration of a racial minority. It would be accountable to Parliament and the local community it serves.

'There would be a non-racial and non-sexist defence and police force, and a prison service comprising personnel that are well trained, disciplined, humane and loyal to the constitution.

'There would be rule of law in which all South Africans would be free to participate either directly or through their representatives in the law-making bodies, without discrimination based on race, colour, creed or religion.

'As far as personal security and crime, the first priority was to address the crime-producing conditions that prevailed in our society. The ANC declared that there would be no respect for the institutions that enforce law and order unless the people respect the law. They would do so if the laws were just and if they participated both in their making and enforcement. A just criminal system would enhance respect for the courts and obedience of the law.

'This,' Mandela states, 'is the summary of a comprehensive and well-considered statement of fundamental principles of government by erstwhile "terrorists", who had no previous training or experience whatsoever in governance.'[20]

One of those erstwhile terrorists was Tito Mboweni, the country's future minister of labour who, with Saki Macozoma, had been part of the team accompanying Mandela at the World Economic Forum [WEF] in Davos in 1992.* There, they edited down to a few talking points a lengthy speech prepared for Nelson Mandela, making the point that the latter was to appear in a panel with De Klerk and Buthelezi and not in a rally. Even though they tried to prevail on Mandela to tone down the rhetoric on nationalisation, he did speak to other political leaders during dinner about the ANC's economic plans, extolling the virtues of state intervention. While there, Li Peng, the premier of China, asked the chairperson of the WEF to arrange a meeting with Mandela, at which he said that China's experience suggested that nationalisation would be an error.[21] The prime minister of Vietnam, also at the forum, conveyed a similar message.

Hearing this, Madiba advised the ANC team that they should 'forget this nationalisation thing, [and] focus on the basic needs of our people'. According to Mboweni, immediately the team returned to South Africa

* Tito Mboweni — see People, Places and Events.

they presented their report and 'had long conversations' which then led to the Nasrec conference, which came out with *Ready to Govern.*[22]

The framework for a five-year GNU, which guaranteed participation of any party gaining over 10 per cent in the election, was set out in the principles enshrined in the interim constitution of 1993. The April 1994 election results dictated the composition of the first cabinet. It consisted of an ANC president and two deputy presidents — one ANC and one National Party — a permutation that would respectively give the cabinet eighteen ANC, six National Party and three IFP ministers.

But before Mandela had to decide on the composition of the cabinet, he and the ANC had to make another decision about a leadership position. His belief was that structures of governance had to reflect the country's diversity. This was informed by a need to set straight the perception of the ANC as a narrow, nationalistic organisation. In its eighty-second year, the ANC had undergone many transformations. From a Christian-oriented organisation of non-violent petitioners through to the torrid forties when the Youth League had given it formidable force, and all the way to the sixties when it embraced armed struggle, it had drawn strength from its non-racial and non-sexist character. It had largely absorbed vicious body blows administered by the apartheid state in the form of States of Emergency and violence and even cross-border raids in exile — and its survival rested on the sacrifices of certain individuals. Most important of these were Walter Sisulu and Oliver Tambo, whom Mandela could trust with his life. He remembers this.

'Oliver Reginald Tambo,' he writes, 'fondly referred to as OR by his comrades, a humble and brilliant lawyer and devout Christian, who became head of the ANC when Chief Luthuli passed away, was also a skilful and respected leader, who raised the organisation to a position of strength and influence it had never reached before.

'It is a phenomenal leader who can succeed in exile to keep united a vast multi-racial organisation with divergent schools of thought, with a membership deployed in distant continents, and a youth seething with anger at the repression of their people; a youth who believe that anger alone without resources and proper planning can help to overthrow a racist regime.

'OR achieved all this. To political and common law prisoners inside the country, to foreign freedom fighters, diplomats, Heads of States, OR was acknowledged as a shining example of a smart and balanced leader who was sure to help restore the dignity of the oppressed people and put their destiny firmly in their hands.

'He was a hard and diligent worker who never spared himself, and who literally was on duty twenty-four hours a day throughout the year without taking any holiday. His wife, Adelaide, tells the story of how OR worked throughout the night. When he saw her dressed and leaving the house, he asked where she was going to at night.

'It was probably this heavy schedule which contributed to the breakdown of his health. He suffered a stroke, which left him partially paralysed. The officials discussed his position, and were all keen that he should make his enormous wisdom and experience available formally to the organisation. We accordingly appointed him National Chairperson, a position he held until his death in 1993.

'OR's death was like the falling of a giant oak tree, which had stood there for ages dominating the vicinity and beautifying the entire landscape and attracting everything around, people and animals alike. It was the end of an era of a remarkable leader with strong and religious convictions, an accomplished mathematician and musician who was peerless in his commitment to the liberation of his people.

'The officials then agreed that Professor Kader Asmal, a knowledgeable, assertive and lucid thinker, who later became Minister of

Water Affairs and Forestry, and then Minister of Education, should succeed OR. His grasp of almost all problems discussed in the Cabinet earned him the distinction of being referred to as Minister of All Portfolios. We all felt that his appointment would help to reverse the wrong notion that the ANC was an ethnic organisation.*

'I then briefed members of the National Working Committee one by one on the recommendations of the officials. With one exception, all of them accepted that recommendation.

'Shortly thereafter, one of the officials returned and confidentially whispered to me that although the members of the NWC had expressly agreed to the recommendation, they had turned against it, and preferred Thabo instead of Kader.

'The episode worried me because it led to negative speculation among Comrades. When people agree to an important proposal and later change [their minds] without raising the matter with you again, then it becomes difficult to challenge the accusation that they had objections which they did not have the courage to put to you; that they knew that the basis of their somersault was against the policy of the organisation.

'But all of them were well qualified and

* Asmal was a South African of Indian descent.

dependable leaders who had endured a succession of terrible ordeals in their determination to free their country. The episode never affected my confidence in them. The refusal to back Kader was, notwithstanding everything, a democratic one and we accepted it without reservation.'[23]

Mandela consulted widely before the cabinet was finalised. He looked at the contribution of people with track records in structures such as the National Reception Committee and who had ended up in the TEC. He then asked Mbeki, because 'Thabo had spent many years in exile and had also interacted with comrades inside the country; he had a better knowledge than me of people best qualified to serve in the Cabinet'.[24]

And so followed a conversation that Thabo Mbeki remembers vividly:

Madiba said . . . 'Can you prepare a list — names and portfolios — from among ourselves.' It must have meant that we knew already what percentage of the cabinet would be constituted by ourselves [in the ANC], it was a specific number, because remember there was the National Party and the IFP . . . So we sat in [Sydney Mufamadi's] flat across the road [and] prepared a list of names and places. And he said to me, 'Prepare a proposal and . . . leave out the position of deputy president; I will deal

185

with that from our side.' So we prepared the list, names and portfolios, ministers and deputy ministers. I can't recall that it had anything to do with what people had done in the TEC or whatever. It was just saying, like Steve Tshwete became minister of sport and recreation because I knew about his passion for sport — rugby player and all that before he went to jail — while he was in jail, so there was that sort of consideration, that this would be a person who would really pay attention to this particular portfolio because of his particular interest.

Mandela made just two changes to Mbeki's list. He said that Derek Hanekom should be a minister — he believed the fact that he had some knowledge of farming and was Afrikaans would help the government deal with issues relating to Afrikaner farmers — and he said that Joe Slovo should be included. The omission of Slovo's name had been informed by a view developed during the negotiation period that his full-time leadership was needed in the Communist Party. Hanekom became minister of land affairs and Slovo became minister of housing. Mbeki continues:

Later he came back to me on the deputy president thing, to say, 'No, I have been consulting about the deputy president business and I had thought that Cyril [Rama-phosa] should be deputy president and the reason for that is because, you see, there is something that we must be sensitive to . . . you see the problem is what people will say. You had Oliver Tambo as president of the ANC, then I succeeded him as president, and now you . . .' — what was I at the time? National Chair of the ANC — '. . . and then you become deputy president. People are going to say, "Look at the Xhosas; the Xhosas are monopolising power," which is why I wanted Cyril . . . But everybody refused — I spoke to Walter, I even spoke to Kenneth Kaunda and Nyerere, and all of them, all of them said, "No — sure we understand the sensitivity to this tribal thing, but it doesn't carry weight; this is your deputy president." '* So he says, 'Therefore you must become deputy president. It's not about you, it's not because of you; it's because I have to deal with this sort of thing.' And I say, 'That's OK, Madiba.' . . . As I recall . . . that was the only intervention — three interventions — he made with regard to that cabinet, to get Derek Hanekom, JS and myself.[25]

* Kenneth Kaunda was the first president of Zambia from 1964–91; Julius Nyere was the president of Tanzania from 1961–85.

Mandela stresses the issue of judicious cabinet selection, when he writes that, under his instruction, Mbeki 'made sure that all our national groups, as well as the members of the Congress Alliance, were adequately represented.* For good reasons, he left open the position of Deputy President. I approved his recommendation and then briefed, in turn, first the SACP [South African Communist Party], then COSATU [Congress of South African Trade Unions] and last the ANC. I made it clear to all of them that, although I would welcome their comments, the final decision would be mine.

'A brilliant and loyal comrade, Raymond Suttner, who is now our ambassador in Sweden, reminded me that a previous policy conference had decided that the Cabinet should be elected by a national conference. I summarily rejected such a resolution on the simple ground that, in such a case, members of the Cabinet would be chosen not for merit but for popularity, or because they were supported by a powerful faction.

'Each member of the alliance had strong objections against some of the proposed candidates, including the candidacy of the late Alfred Nzo, a gifted, disciplined and experienced expert on foreign affairs. There

* Congress Alliance — see People, Places and Events.

were also objections against Derek Hanekom on the ground that it was unwise to give the land portfolio to a white person. These objections affected others as well. I rejected all these reservations as based not on principle but on purely personal considerations. I presented the list to the officials as recommended by Thabo.*

'The officials approved all the names without exception. Then there followed a discussion on who would be appointed Deputy President. Two names, Thabo Mbeki and Cyril Ramaphosa, were considered. Ramaphosa had led our team of negotiators to the World Trade Centre [in Kempton Park, north of Johannesburg]. He is an impressive, adroit and persuasive individual and influenced both friend and foe at the Centre. He earned for himself a lot of respect and admiration, and emerged as one of the most powerful figures among the constellation of eminent thinkers.[26]

'In his autobiography, *The Last Trek: A New Beginning,* De Klerk describes Cyril as follows:

The ANC delegation was led by Cyril Ra-

* The officials at the time were Mandela, Sisulu, Ramaphosa, Mbeki, Jacob Zuma and Thomas Nkobi. Mbeki and Ramaphosa were not part of the discussion.

maphosa, its chief negotiator. Ramaphosa had previously been Secretary General of the National Union of Mineworkers, where he had gained extensive experience in tough negotiations with the Chamber of Mines, which represented South Africa's large mining companies. Ramaphosa's large, round head was framed by a beard and receding hair of about the same length. His relaxed manner and convivial expression were contradicted by coldly calculating eyes, which seemed to be searching continuously for the softest spot in the defences of his opponents. His silver tongue and honeyed phrases lulled potential victims, while his arguments relentlessly tightened around them.[27]

'Cyril is hailed by men and women inside and outside our organisation as the linchpin in the negotiations, and one of the main architects of the new South Africa. At the 1997 National Conference of the ANC, he was justly rewarded when he received the highest votes for the membership of the National Executive Committee. He was, and still is, a real asset to our organisation.

'Throughout my political career, I have been haunted by the persistent perception that the ANC was and is a Xhosa organisation, notwithstanding overwhelming evidence to the contrary. I pointed out to the officials that Oliver Tambo, Thabo Mbeki and myself come from the same ethnic group. Would we not reinforce that false perception if Thabo became deputy? I asked. Should we not rather consider for this position Cyril, an equally gifted and respected person who came from the Northern part of our country?

'I readily conceded that Thabo was well qualified for this position and that his knowledge of the continent and diplomatic affairs far exceeded that of Cyril. But I insisted that the latter had a lot of clout and pull internationally; in particular with trade unions, and on the vast majority of opinion makers, especially on those who took part in the negotiations.

'Notwithstanding my argument,' Mandela laments, 'the officials were not convinced. They insisted that the general public would accept that, in choosing Thabo, the ANC was guided by merit and not tribal considerations. On the contrary, my concern was not based purely on merit, but on the false perception I felt it was our duty to correct.'[28]

Although Mandela had intended to announce the appointments only after the inauguration, his hand was forced by the media, which had got wind of the debate around the position of the deputy president, with the announcement of the cabinet being made on 6 May 1994. It was an incomplete list and some of the names and their corresponding portfolios would later be changed; by then, too, a decision had been made — after some heated debate — to include a minister without portfolio, with responsibility for the RDP.

Setting up the cabinet was not uncontentious, with De Klerk piqued at inadequate consultation in the allocation of some portfolios. However, Mandela's personal touch in managing the composition of the cabinet was unmistakable. Some of the processes, appearing haphazard at their genesis, ended up bearing fruit. A few of the cogs in the wheel of the machine geared to advance Mandela's dream were blithely unaware of their importance and how their own lives would change. Manuel recalled how, when he was still part of the leadership core in the Western Cape in 1992, he was approached by Cyril Ramaphosa, the secretary general of the ANC.

Ramaphosa told Manuel that Mandela wanted him to head the Department of Economic Planning, an important policy division of the ANC. Manuel, aware of his own lack of training in economics, demurred, pointing out that he had been assigned to work on health issues. Ramaphosa told him bluntly that there were many doctors in the ANC. 'Trevor,' he continued, 'just be clear, this is not a negotiation between you and I; I am conveying a message.'[29]

That was that. Before long, Manuel was accompanying Mandela on foreign missions, such as the 1993 trip to the US when, addressing the United Nations, Mandela said that sufficient progress had been made for sanctions against South Africa to be lifted.

'Part of what he was doing, again,' Manuel says, 'was relationship building, but there was also a very strong posture. He would take delegations along. For instance, a motley crew of us went along to Taiwan, including Pallo [Jordan], [Thomas] Nkobi of course [and] Joe Modise,' to 'secure training, and money . . . but also exposing [us] to different political systems and listening to what we were doing.* He believed in handing over to the young people and preparing them for more intricate responsibilities.'[30]

At some of the investor conferences, which brought together corporate leaders, industry experts and institutional investors in hallowed halls of major world capitals, Mandela would say: 'We've got these young people like Trevor Manuel here. I'd like him to speak to you; I'd like him to answer the questions after I've spoken.'[31]

It was the same thing with Valli Moosa, who, given his involvement in the negotiations, ended up deputising Roelf Meyer, the first minister of constitutional development

* Pallo Jordan; Thomas Nkobi — see People, Places and Events.

and provincial affairs in Mandela's cabinet. Mufamadi, who headed up the peace process, was ultimately destined to become the minister of police, and Joe Modise, who came through MK and the military headquarters of the ANC, became the minister of defence.

Reflecting on all these developments, which pointed to Mandela's strategic thinking, Manuel said, 'I think that by and large those interactions in Madiba's mind were creating early in the process, for want of a better word, a kind of shadow cabinet of people who were assigned certain responsibilities. That process, I think, had a profound impact on the way in which he saw certain things.'[32]

Among the portfolios that featured in discussions, both within the ANC and with De Klerk, was the finance ministry, which ended with an agreement that Derek Keys should continue in his current position as finance minister.* Even though finance was one of the six portfolios to which the National Party was entitled, it was also agreed that this key post should not be identified with any specific party.[33] There were two considerations — experience and worries about how economic decision makers — local African and international — might react. South Africa was still a new entity with untested systems. Any changes — especially the resig-

* Derek Keys — see People, Places and Events.

nation of a trusted finance minister — could have had a negative effect on the markets.

'There are certain positions we will not fight for now, because the country may not be ready for it,' his colleagues remember Mandela saying. He was referring to a number of posts, including the respective heads of the Reserve Bank and the Public Service Commission.[34]

Mandela met twice with De Klerk to discuss the cabinet, first in Pretoria and then in Cape Town, on the evening of the day that the ANC released its first list of ministers, much to De Klerk's unhappiness. According to De Klerk's memoirs, he was shocked at the ANC's announcements 'without making the slightest effort to consult me beforehand' — as was stipulated in section 82 of the interim constitution — and the abrogation of a previous agreement of a National Party security portfolio.[35] Queried about how all three security portfolios were assigned to the ANC, Mandela answered that he had been overruled by the organisation.[36]

What they agreed regarding the assignment of ministers and deputy ministers to the remaining portfolios required some changes in the scope of portfolios allocated to the ANC. That included shifting Asmal from constitutional development to water affairs and forestry, something he learned about only on the day he was sworn in as minister.[37]

Having conducted comprehensive horse trading with the major negotiating parties — especially the National Party and the IFP — Mandela was convinced that the cabinet was both strong and representative of the people of South Africa. He even broached the question of smaller parties participating in government, holding discussions with the PAC (Pan Africanist Congress of Azania), Democratic Party, Conservative Party and Freedom Front. When Mandela came out of prison, De Klerk had proposed that a troika of National Party, ANC and IFP should negotiate South Africa's future, a notion that Mandela and the ANC had rejected in favour of an inclusive approach. Now that the cabinet was in place, Mandela was therefore exasperated at suggestions that it was not fully representative.

'Soon after the formation of the Government of National Unity,' he writes, 'and long before Deputy President De Klerk voluntarily pulled out of the Government of National Unity, the ANC was repeatedly accused of racism, and of promoting the interests of Africans only, and of neglecting those of the minorities. There are still public figures in our country — diehards — who are still peddling this ignoble propaganda.

'I have deliberately set out in full the names of members of the cabinet of the Government of National Unity.* Those who have respect for truth and for themselves, irrespective of their background, will refrain from tarnishing their own image by endorsing what is clearly a senseless propaganda by those who have no credible alternative policy to that of the ANC.

'The subterfuge becomes even more glaring when you discover that, apart from Derek Keys and Abe Williams, the latter a member of the Coloured community, the remaining five Cabinet members of Mr De Klerk's National Party were all White and Afrikaner. There was no African nor Indian. Yet all these national groups formed part of the ANC members of the Cabinet. Out of nineteen, there were seven members of the minorities.

'The domination of Whites in the National Assembly in 1994 was equally striking. Out of two hundred and fifty-six ANC members in the National Assembly, eighty-two represented Coloureds, Indians and Whites.

'Out of eighty members of the National Party, there were eleven Africans, nine Coloureds, four Indians; a total of twenty-four as against fifty-six Whites — more than double the number of other groups.'[38]

* In his original manuscript, Mandela listed the names and positions of his first cabinet in order to show their diverse ethnic backgrounds. One of the pages can be viewed on plate 9.

A younger and more impulsive Mandela might well have carried on itemising the instances of gross insincerity that informed the 'diehards' who were 'still peddling this ignoble propaganda'. He would have extolled the ANC's magnanimity in having accommodated the National Party, whose policies were the root cause of untold misery for the black majority. Satisfying as this might have been to his compatriots, and convinced as he was of the rightness of his cause, Mandela knew that it ageould have sent a wrong signal. He was in control and certainly not one for playing the martyr.

He was seventy-five years old and would need all his stamina and astuteness to convert his personal charisma into durable political currency. While the official opposition had grudgingly agreed to participate in the GNU, there were still pockets of resistance within their ranks who saw this power sharing as capitulation to the ANC. On the other side of the same coin were elements within the ANC, for instance Harry Gwala and his hard-line followers, who felt that the sacrifices made to wrest power from the Pretoria regime were ill served by the architecture of the new order.

For Mandela, however, the urgent task was to ensure that the building blocks towards the construction of the new democracy were in place. He had to acquaint himself with the knowledge that he would be president, a head of state of a complicated country, home to an even more complicated polity. It had all moved with a snarling swiftness, from prison to freedom and thence to the highest position in the country. Like someone catapulted to the head of a huge family following the death of a patriarch, Mandela had to go through some rite of passage, in this instance Parliament, for his installation to be formalised.

CHAPTER FIVE:
NATIONAL UNITY

Nelson Mandela and the men and women who assembled in Parliament on 9 May 1994 to be sworn in as members of Parliament gave full, if diverse, expression to the changes being wrought in the new, democratic South Africa. The ambience of the parliamentary precinct, once staid and forbidding and dominated by dark-suited white men, was one of muted celebration; something huge straining to break out.[1] Then Albertina Sisulu, herself a struggle veteran and leader, rose to nominate Nelson Rolihlahla Mandela as South Africa's first democratically elected president.*

Tears and cheers broke out as the assembly and the public gallery rose as one, cheering a smiling, waving Mandela to his brown leather bench. It had once been the seat of President F. W. de Klerk, who just more than four years earlier had announced, in the same chamber, that he would free the man who had served

* Albertina Sisulu — see People, Places and Events.

more than twenty-seven years in jail. MPs led the rhythmic clapping while an *imbongi* (praise singer) changed Parliament forever, chanting the praises of the new president in his mother tongue of isiXhosa.

Almost everyone who worked with Mandela at the beginning of the first post-apartheid administration, from gardener to cabinet minister, agrees that he had special qualities and, in turn, expected others to match them. Notoriously unable to take no for an answer, he worked hard to obviate any possibility of someone rejecting his offer.

Trevor Manuel, who at the time was minister of trade and industry, provides a somewhat droll note to the otherwise serious, and at times nerve-racking, drama of establishing the first democratic cabinet under President Mandela in 1994.

Mandela hosted a state banquet for François Mitterrand, then president of France, on the evening of 4 July 1994, at the Mount Nelson Hotel in Cape Town. Two days earlier, back in Pretoria, the president had summoned Manuel to a meeting, which also involved Deputy President Thabo Mbeki, Minister of Labour Tito Mboweni and Alec Erwin from the Reconstruction and Development Programme, where he broke the news that Derek Keys was resigning his post as minister of finance.*

Manuel recalls Mandela saying with characteristic candour, 'Look, I've been talking to people, and I don't think the country and the world and white people, in particular, are ready for an ANC finance minister. I hope that you agree with me. I thought I must tell you this and ask if you have any suggestions for a finance minister.' When there were none, Mandela continued: 'I've been thinking about this fellow Chris Liebenberg.† He is retired from . . . [Ned]bank; he's been my banker, he's been the ANC's banker, he's a very good man. White business will really support him. Do you have any difficulty with him?' No one had difficulties. Mandela said, 'Thank you very much, let's have some tea.'[2]

In the afternoon on Monday, 4 July, Liebenberg, who had been abroad, got a surprise call from Mandela, who wanted him to travel from Johannesburg to Genadendal to see him. Mandela left the banquet early to meet Liebenberg at Genadendal.

'When Liebenberg arrives in Cape Town,' Manuel recalls, 'Mandela asks him, "What are you doing now?" Chris Liebenberg tells Mandela that he is retired now. "How old are you?" Mandela asks. Liebenberg says that he

* Alec Erwin — see People, Places and Events.
† Chris Liebenberg — see People, Places and Events.

is sixty. Mandela says, "Yes . . . you're too young to retire, Chris. I've got an assignment for you. I want you to be my finance minister. Derek [Keys] is leaving and I want you to take over." Chris Liebenberg is completely shocked; nothing can prepare him for this. He says, "Having just retired, I will have to consult with my wife about this." '[3]

The seemingly informal and somewhat serendipitous manner in appointing Liebenberg to the position of finance minister is belied by the seriousness with which the ANC leadership formed the cabinet. The appointment of ANC ministers was not informed by caprice. These were people who had acquitted themselves admirably in their various leadership duties in structures at home and in exile. They had all been tested and developed in challenging circumstances. However, there was still a lot of vetting before a name could be given the green light.

A case in point was the aforementioned position of the finance minister. Here, Mandela conducted extensive consultations with some of his ministers, including Manuel, Mboweni and Erwin — and people such as Gill Marcus, an MP who was part of the finance committee, would sit with Liebenberg and deal with the nuts and bolts of fiscal policy.* Mandela concentrated on ensur-

---

* Gill Marcus — see People, Places and Events.

ing that the country was secure, hence his insistence on the ANC holding all the security portfolios. Trusting the two deputy presidents to whom he delegated most tasks — especially Mbeki — meant he could, as has been noted earlier, take a more hands-on approach in entrenching reconciliation. It was Mbeki then, in what others characterised as a prime ministerial role, who ran cabinet meetings on most occasions even when Mandela was present.

'Preparation of bills,' Mboweni remembers, 'and planning memoranda and so on would be submitted to him.' Even though he was hands-off, Mandela would of course keep an interested eye on progress, focusing on the armed forces and the police, and on structural arrangements for the judiciary and Chapter Nine Institutions.* Mbeki also kept him apprised of the work. Mandela would only intervene in situations where he felt that one

* Chapter nine of the Constitution establishes 'state institutions which support constitutional democracy', known as the Chapter Nine Institutions. These are, inter alia, the Public Protector, Auditor General, Independent Electoral Commission, Independent Authority to Regulate Broadcasting, South African Human Rights Commission, Commission for Gender Equality and the Commission for the Promotion and Protection of the Rights of Cultural, Religious and Linguistic Communities.

of his ministers was being wilfully stymied.

A case in point was when Mboweni threatened to resign if certain ministers continued to block the legislation he wished to submit. Even ANC ministers held divergent views on certain issues, so this was not uncommon, although it was undoubtedly frustrating for those sponsoring bills.

On the day of submission, Mboweni recalls how

Mandela asked for an adjournment so that he could have a discussion with those ministers and myself. Well there wasn't a discussion actually, because we just went to his office. It was quite a tiny office, and he said, 'The Minister here has briefed me about his difficulties in getting this bill passed in cabinet, and that if today this bill is not passed by the cabinet he is resigning. I don't want this young man to resign, so when we go back to the cabinet now, you guys must go and support the bill.' Trevor [Manuel] tried to explain [but] Madiba said, 'No, there is no discussion, just go back and support the bill.'

They all went back and Mboweni continued with his presentation, which was supported even by erstwhile detractors. Rather archly, Mboweni ascribes this victory to the 'survival instinct in politics'.[4]

The one political organism that needed to survive, however, was the cabinet itself, the engine of the Government of National Unity. Its strength lay in its ability to make decisions harmonised by a guiding principle. Without this, it would fail. Taking a realistic view of this body blessed with multiple moving parts, MP Roelf Meyer admitted in a 1994 interview that 'it is not going to be possible to have harmony from morning to night. We do not have a coalition in the true sense of the word, but an agreement to cooperate.'[5]

A little more than a year earlier, Mandela had fielded a number of questions from the BBC on exactly the thorny issue of future decision-making. 'We will address these problems,' he said, 'through a government of national unity dominated by the African National Congress. The principle of majority rule will apply. No small party will be allowed to undermine the principle of majority rule . . . [But the ANC] point of view will prevail without undermining the principle of consensus. We will be doing with the Government of National Unity what we are doing now at the multi-party forum . . . we don't impose; we persuade.'[6]

This was at the tail end of the negotiations, where, respectively requested by their teams to find a resolution, Mandela and De Klerk proposed that the cabinet should strive for consensus, and if that failed, the majority view would prevail.[7]

This was accepted and later incorporated in the interim constitution. Under chapter six, which deals with the powers of the National Executive, section 89 (2) stipulates that the 'Cabinet shall function in a manner which gives consideration to the consensus-seeking spirit underlying the concept of a government of national unity as well as the need for effective government'.[8]

Indeed, according to Jakes Gerwel, speaking from the vantage point of secretary of the cabinet, the GNU did make decisions by consensus: 'One would not be aware that it is a multiparty government if you were sitting in on the debates, on the meetings of the cabinet. You would not realise that people come from different parties.'[9]

Kader Asmal, certainly one of the most colourful ministers in Mandela's cabinet, with his characteristic hoarse laugh and the mien of his lookalike, Groucho Marx, must have enjoyed the debates. 'Consensus was allowed to establish itself in a place where everybody was comfortable through a process of argument and counter argument,' he observed in his memoirs. He might have discerned a culture clash between the ANC and National Party in these discussions; for instance, no National Party minister challenged De Klerk in cabinet whereas the ANC was robust in their debates over certain issues, sometimes to the consternation of National Party ministers.[10]

Despite Mandela's talent for nudging people towards their finer instincts, it would be wishful thinking to expect total unanimity among the members of the cabinet; there had to be someone quibbling with the proposal agreed between Mandela and De Klerk, even though it was similar to the principle of sufficient consensus used to break deadlocks during the negotiations. An indignant Chief Buthelezi remembers cabinet decisions being based on 'majoritarianism because . . . I have prepared memoranda in some cases disagreeing with some of the proposed legislation and so on, and all that is said is that, "Well, what the minister of home affairs says must be noted, that's all, but we'll go ahead." '[11]

Mandela sought to breach any chasm that developed out of the divergent and potentially mutually opposing views of the ANC and the National Party. To this end, he established the cabinet committees, which were platforms for finding consensus. Three such committees were set up, each a palimpsest — something reused but altered — from the legacy of the apartheid government. Mbeki chaired the committee on economic affairs and De Klerk those on security and intelligence and social and administrative affairs.

To embed cooperation, Mandela paired ministers and deputy ministers from different parties. 'From the point of view of De Klerk and his party,' he said in an interview, 'three belong to the IFP, six to De Klerk, the ANC has eighteen, twice the combined strength of IFP and National Party. So, if we wanted to, we could just run the government, but we're not doing that. We are committed to making the Government of National Unity something that has got a substantive content, not just a hollow content where we endorse the views of the ANC. It is for that reason that we made sure that in the distribution of portfolios, we should have deputy ministers; if a minister belongs to the ANC, then the deputy minister should belong to the National Party, or IFP. We want it to function properly.'[12]

And function properly it did in the first years, except when Mandela insisted on keeping a firm hand on the tiller in security matters, which rankled De Klerk. 'Madiba's focus with regard to government work was the security issue,' Mbeki remembers:

So he would come to meetings of the cabinet committee . . . that dealt with security matters . . . because he was very concerned about the possibility of counter-revolution, and, like all of us at the time, he thought counter-revolution would come from the right-wing Afrikaner in the army, in the police, in the security sector, who would resort to arms to destabilise and then possibly overthrow the government. That was his particular interest. But with regard to the rest of the work of the cabinet, of government, he would say, 'No, you go and attend to that.'[13]

However, Mandela did intervene directly with ministers on other issues when he felt it was needed, as in the contretemps between Nkosazana Dlamini-Zuma and De Klerk. Ministers from all three parties would come to his office to report back or seek advice, and provide reports when requested.

But as each party had its own structures for maintaining policy coherence — for instance, the ANC had its cabinet caucus and the National Party its strategic policy group — it was inevitable that a structural fault line would develop and generate tensions between the business of cabinet and the reality outside.

There was disagreement on the matter of collective responsibility for cabinet decisions. The National Party and IFP insisted on their right to deviate from collegiality and publicise criticisms of decisions they opposed in cabinet. Even though there were few issues, the differences were sharp and recurrent, complicated further by relations between the party leaders. The truth was that the GNU operated only at cabinet level and not in Parliament or in the provinces.

The advent of local elections towards the

end of 1995 exacerbated tensions as the parties claimed achievements and rejected responsibility for problems. At an early campaign rally, in the contested Pretoria township of Eersterust, Mandela was blunt in addressing the issue.

'Mr De Klerk,' he said, 'has been trying to create the impression that the National Party was playing a leading role in the Government of National Unity and that business confidence and foreign investments were dependent on his participation in the government.' While he appreciated De Klerk's role in the cabinet, he said, 'it is wrong to try and inflate the National Party's role out of proportion. The ANC has eighteen Cabinet members compared with only six from the National Party.' He ended by insisting that the RDP was an ANC initiative.[14]

Even the most uninitiated reader of body language could see that there was a glaring absence of warmth between Mandela and De Klerk. The National Party was undergoing an identity crisis; its parliamentary caucus found itself at odds with the constraining protocols of being in opposition. The ongoing debate about whether it should continue in the GNU tended to seem like an ominous self-fulfilling prophecy. To claw back lost ground, De Klerk became, by his own account, at once critical of decisions and confrontational in pursuit of National Party policy; he did so because his own ministers and deputy ministers did not. 'They did well enough with regard to their own portfolios,' he writes, 'but did not fare so well when it came to making a fighting stand against the ANC in opposing decisions which were irreconcilable with National Party Policy.'[15]

Those decisions deemed irreconcilable with National Party policy added to De Klerk's woes, as did his failure to get retrogressive positions written into the final constitution. It didn't help that he was faced with a challenge from the National Party's Young Turks, represented by Marthinus van Schalkwyk. Much more to the point, however, was De Klerk's admitted unhappiness with the inelegant position he found himself in, which was akin to 'the previous chairman of the board [continuing] to serve on the board of his successor'.[16]

Mandela summed it up in a discussion with Tony Leon, then the leader of the Democratic Party. 'De Klerk,' he said, 'had not reconciled himself with the loss of power.'[17] Mandela had given De Klerk responsibilities, which the latter felt were beneath him as a former minister and president. For someone who had once entertained the idea of a ruling troika of the ANC, National Party and IFP presidency on a rotational basis, this seeming demotion made it difficult for him to convince his party of the correctness of participating in the GNU.

Matters came to a head in a cabinet discussion in January 1995, where De Klerk tabled an agenda item asserting the right of the minor parties to act publicly as opposition. De Klerk's public criticism of the ANC, coupled with his granting of indemnity to 3,500 members of the police force and two cabinet ministers just before the 1994 election, set the stage for a showdown. After ANC ministers had spoken about collective responsibility for cabinet decisions, Mandela attacked De Klerk, citing the indemnity as 'underhand' and labelling the National Party's attitude to the RDP as disloyalty to the government. Leaving the meeting in anger, De Klerk said he and his colleagues would consider their continued participation in the government. The next day, however, the two principals appeared at a media briefing with a joint statement. The misunderstanding had been cleared up and 'we have agreed to make a fresh start, which will help us to avoid a repetition of the situation that arose earlier this week'.[18]

Much like in a doomed marriage, the two men's clashes, symptoms of singularly divergent world views, were cancelled out by public acts of reconciliation. The clashes were born of an impulse to recreate an idyllic past for the minority on the one hand, and, on the other, a single-minded imperative to carve

213

out a liveable future for the majority of South Africa's people.

'Whatever quarrels emerge,' Mandela said, quashing yet another rumour about dissension, 'Mr De Klerk and I understand that we need one another. It's not a question of personal likes; it's a question of absolute necessity that we should be together. I think he understands that as equally as I do.'[19]

KwaZulu-Natal, a province forever beset by problems of violence, created another flashpoint. In September 1995, De Klerk wrote to Mandela suggesting that the best way to address this violence would be a meeting between Mandela, De Klerk, Mbeki and Buthelezi to discuss, inter alia, international mediation and political initiatives to lessen tension and violence.[20] Mandela decided to refrain from mincing his words.

'The problems in KwaZulu-Natal,' he writes in a letter to De Klerk, 'and consequently the solutions to those problems, are deeply embedded in the history of the situation that prevails. You, Mr De Klerk, will certainly acknowledge that the present conflict in the province is as much the creation of the policies and strategies of your party and the government of which you were part and presided over, as of any other factors. We need not here entertain the details of that history; we have discussed that previously. It will be seriously misleading, and not helpful

for finding a genuine solution, to suggest —
as you do in your letter — that the question
of international mediation represents one of
the fundamental underlying causes to the
problems in the province.*

'I have previously briefed you fully on the
discussions I had, as well as the attempts I
made to have discussions with Minister
Buthelezi on this subject. You are aware that
all these initiatives came from me. We would
require, as again I have previously told you,
concrete suggestions as to exactly what it is
you want discussed at the kind of meeting
you propose. A futile exercise in meeting
merely for the sake of meeting, and making
political gestures, aggravates rather than helps
resolve the situation.

'You are as one of the Executive Deputy
Presidents in my government free, and in fact
have the obligation, to discuss with me any
suggestions you may have about any matters
of government policy and direction. It applies in this case as well. What would not be
constructive or helpful would be for you of-
fering as the leader of a third party to medi-

* International mediation on unresolved constitutional issues was part of the 1994 agreement that
saw the IFP participate in the election. For various
reasons, it didn't happen, and Mandela writes that
De Klerk is suggesting in his letter that the lack of
international mediation was a cause of the violence.

ate in what is rather inaccurately being portrayed as simply a conflict between the ANC and the IFP. The historical part played by your party, and the government which it formed, in that conflict totally disqualifies you from performing that role.'[21]

This was a harsh rebuke, and it simply meant that Mandela, the epitome of tact and politesse, even to his adversaries, had reached the end of his patience. The question of violence and the IFP–National Party nexus in its planning and execution, and the bloody toll it took on the people of KwaZulu-Natal and elsewhere had always troubled him. And it would be wrong to forget — or expect that he had forgotten — the humiliating chorus of defiance when, soon after his release in 1990, he called on the people of KwaZulu-Natal to throw away their weapons. If Mandela was civil and polite to both De Klerk and Buthelezi, it was in accordance with his own credo of never being discourteous to another leader.[22] Those leaders, in Mandela's view, were representatives of a constituency. Any rudeness to them thus translated into a massive affront to their followers.

When De Klerk wrote back that he had not been suggesting mediation but a meeting, as a party to the agreement on international mediation, Mandela gave him short shrift. 'Rather than suggesting pointless meetings,' he wrote, 'I would appreciate your input on

216

how to deal with the legacy of the inhumane system of apartheid of which you were one of the architects.'[23]

A break-up in a relationship does not happen suddenly, nor is it triggered by a single cause. The weakest chink in the GNU's armour could have been the wide gulf of an unshared history that separated the sum of its parts; the lack of chemistry between De Klerk and Mandela being the most conspicuous representation of that dissonance. But from the very start, the chances of the National Party staying the full course of the GNU were not that auspicious. De Klerk's cabinet was unhappily divided about decision-making in the GNU, a state of affairs worsened by the party's reduced numbers in the post-election cabinet, which weakened their influence in government. This also strengthened the hand of the faction in the National Party that wanted no truck with the ANC-dominated government.

The clash between De Klerk and Mandela over amnesty in January 1995 seemed to confirm the worst to those opposed to participation. It enfeebled the National Party's Federal Congress in February, dominated as it was by argument over whether to stay in the GNU or pull out, strengthening the perception that the National Party had zero influence in decision-making. In November 1995 its loss of support in municipal elections held almost everywhere (except in KwaZulu-Natal and in some rural areas of the Western Cape and in Cape Town) confirmed the erosion of National Party support.

It was, however, the draft of the final constitution in May 1996 which gave De Klerk the ostensible reason to take the National Party out of the GNU. Even though he knew that the GNU was a transitional arrangement with a five-year duration, De Klerk had always pushed for some formal, permanent multiparty device in the constitution. He cited his failure to wrest this concession out of the ANC as a reason for withdrawing from the GNU three years before the agreed five years was over. The GNU itself didn't provide for National Party influence.

'The GNU worked well to start with,' he writes, 'but it soon became clear that it was a sham as far as any real power-sharing was concerned. The ANC refused to conclude a coalition agreement with us, and preferred to keep us in a gilded cage where National Party ministers had all the trappings of power but none of the substance.'[24]

When the Constitutional Assembly voted on the constitution, the National Party agreed to its adoption. But that evening, De Klerk left early from the dinner celebrating the new constitution. Having got wind of De Klerk's intention to call a meeting to announce the National Party's withdrawal from the GNU, Mbeki left with him in an attempt to dissuade him from withdrawal, to no avail. 'They opted to pull out,' said Mbeki, 'and keep the party support together.'[25]

De Klerk's decision to leave the GNU divided his cabinet colleagues in July 1996. In public comments immediately after the withdrawal and in a parliamentary debate some weeks later, Mandela acknowledged the contribution made by some of the National Party leaders. They had not only played constructive roles in the transition but had also broken with the past to an extent that their party — and consequently its leader — had not done so.

'What concerns me personally,' Mandela said, 'is the departure from public life of outstanding personalities such as Roelof "Pik" Botha, Leon Wessels and Chris Fismer — leaders who worked hard and played a critical role in building national unity and preventing the revival of racism both within parties and in communities where they work.*

* Pik Botha, ebullient long-serving foreign minister in apartheid administrations, oversaw many important transitions, including the end of the Angolan Civil War and Namibian independence. In February 1986, he told a German journalist that he would gladly serve under a black president in the future (J. Brooks Spector, 'Roelof "Pik" Botha, the Ulti-

'We regret their departure from cabinet and Parliament, and hope that they will continue to be of service to the nation.'[26]

As it turned out, except for the brief interlude of the Cape Town Metro election shortly after the National Party withdrawal, the electoral decline of the National Party continued, with its leading figures moving to various other parties and the bulk of its grassroots support migrating to the Democratic Alliance.[27]

When De Klerk tried to get the IFP to join his exit from the GNU, Buthelezi decided to stay put. 'A lot of our people had died,' he said. 'For us as black people it was more important to seek reconciliation than risk escalation of violence.'[28]

In composing the GNU, Mandela had assigned Buthelezi to the position of minister of home affairs, which gave him senior status. Moreover, alert to Buthelezi's sensitivity

---

mate Survivor', *Daily Maverick,* 2 September 2011). One-time apartheid-era Minister of Local Government, National Housing and Manpower Leon Wessels voiced his disaffection with apartheid policies under De Klerk. He later served as a commissioner in the TRC. De Klerk's appointee to CODESA, Chris Fismer served as parliamentary and political adviser to De Klerk and later became minister of general affairs in the GNU.

about seniority, Mandela designated him acting president in times when the two deputy presidents were also out of the country. Despite the historic divergences between the ANC and the IFP, and between Buthelezi and Mandela, the IFP leader managed a more successful alchemy between a public oppositional role with a cooperative stance in cabinet, something De Klerk couldn't achieve. Buthelezi was, in effect, a kind of political Jekyll and Hyde. Jakes Gerwel recalled 'the Wednesday Buthelezi and the Saturday Buthelezi, because he was so mild in the Cabinet on Wednesdays and so aggressive at the IFP's public meetings on Saturdays'.[29] Similarly, the clashes between Buthelezi and Mandela played out in Parliament and in the public arena rather than in cabinet.

A memorable incident involved an irate Buthelezi storming the South African Broadcasting Corporation studio and, on air, confronting an interviewee, Sifiso Zulu, who had accused him of appointing himself the Zulu king's prime minister. Later, Mandela was under pressure to dismiss Buthelezi but was concerned how this would play out in the fraught KwaZulu-Natal situation. After consulting colleagues, Mandela was advised to extract a public apology out of Buthelezi, which he did.

Buthelezi regarded participation in the

GNU as a lever to help achieve the IFP's constitutional goals. Personally, he had not been in favour of participating.

'As a democrat,' he said, 'I do what my people want, even if I don't like it. I did not want to go into this Government of National Unity in the first place, but in the discussion that took many hours, the majority said we should go into that.'[30]

The relationship between Mandela and Buthelezi had a long and winding history, both personal and political, dating back to the time when they were both in the ANC Youth League. It cooled as the IFP shifted away from what Buthelezi described as 'an ANC front' and became characterised by conflict and anger after 1994 as the situation in KwaZulu-Natal impacted on it.[31]

But even during difficult times, they communicated. They corresponded while Mandela was a prisoner, both directly and through Buthelezi's wife, Irene, on both family and political matters.[32] In spite of his differences with the ANC, Buthelezi consistently called for Mandela's release and refused to negotiate with the government until Mandela and other political prisoners were released. In the period running up to the 1994 elections, Mandela frequently spoke with him, recognising him as a significant force. When interviewed about his relationship with Buthelezi, Mandela said that their relations had 'been on a sound basis ever since I knew him as a young man'.[33] By the end, their farewell tributes were, if grudging and ambiguous, nevertheless respectful. Mandela more than once said that he had 'enormous respect' for Buthelezi as a 'formidable survivor, who defeated us [the ANC] in two free and fair general elections'.[34] Buthelezi remained convinced that the difficulties between him and Mandela were a result of the ANC keeping them apart.[35]

For Mandela, the withdrawal of the National Party from the GNU meant taking practical steps, filling the positions left by the departure of National Party ministers. Pallo Jordan was assigned to environmental affairs and tourism, and the ANC deputy ministers took over the portfolios of the departing National Party ministers. But the departure could have made the country jittery; it was incumbent upon Mandela to reassure South Africa — and especially its investors — that the brief hiatus would neither threaten nor deflect the transition.

'Deputy President F. W. de Klerk,' Mandela said, 'informed me earlier today that the National Party had decided to withdraw from the Government of National Unity. As you're aware, the leadership of the National Party has emphasised that their withdrawal is not an expression of lack of confidence in our multiparty democracy, the rules of which are contained in the constitution, which we together adopted yesterday.

'On the contrary, it reflects the fact that the National Party recognises our young democracy has come of age, and would need a vigorous opposition unfettered by the participation in the Executive. We respect their judgement on this matter; as well as the party political considerations, which precipitated their decision.

'As I emphasised yesterday after the adoption of the new constitution, unity and reconciliation within our society depend not so much on enforced coalitions among parties. They are indelibly written in the hearts of the overwhelming majority of South Africa's people. This is [the] course that the government and the ANC have chosen to pursue in the interest of our country. It is a course that we will pursue with even more vigour in the coming months and years.

'The policies that the Government of National Unity has been executing are premised on the needs and aspirations of the country's people. This applies to all areas of endeavour, underpinned by the Reconstruction and Development Programme, to improve the quality of life of the people through sound economic policies of fiscal rectitude and other measures to promote growth and development.

'These policies will not change. Instead they will be promoted with even more focus.

'Though the imperative of Government of National Unity was written into the interim constitution, the onus was on parties which attained more than ten per cent of the vote in April 1994, voluntarily to decide whether or not to take positions in cabinet.

'As the majority party, the ANC welcomed the fact that the National Party and IFP decided to take part in the Executive, especially in the early days of our delicate transition.

'I wish to thank Deputy President F. W. de Klerk and his colleagues for the constructive role that they have played. I am confident that we shall continue to work together in pursuit of the country's interests, and that their withdrawal will have the effect of strengthening, rather than weakening, their commitment to the country's political, security and economic interests.

'Indeed, we are firmly of the view that the National Party has a continuing responsibility to contribute to the process of eradicating the legacy of apartheid which they created. As such, we hope that their decision to play a more active role as an opposition party does not mean obstructing the process of transformation or defending apartheid privilege.

'In this regard, I wish to reassure all South Africans that the course that we have undertaken as a nation is bigger than any party or individual.'[36]

Even though serving to stress the importance of his mission in life and to take a parting shot at De Klerk and his unhappy retirees, Mandela intended that his words would also reassert his authority over the ANC and anyone who might have harboured mutinous notions.

In 1995, a year before De Klerk's withdrawal from the GNU, Mandela had gritted his teeth at flagrant acts of disloyalty and defiance by his estranged wife, Nomzamo Winnie Mandela, whose life since Mandela's release in 1990 already read like a catalogue of disasters. She had been convicted of kidnapping, reviled as a scarlet woman and proved guilty of adultery, which led to Mandela announcing their separation in 1992. Later she faced charges of fraud and presided over a factious ANC Women's League.* Despite all this, and certainly because she presented herself as a champion of the wretched of the earth, she still commanded a lot of vocal support from disadvantaged communities, support given political muscle by people such as Bantu Holomisa and Peter Mokaba of the ANC Youth League.

In February 1995, at the funeral of Warrant

* African National Congress Women's League (ANCWL) — see People, Places and Events.

Officer Jabulani Xaba, who had been shot dead by white police colleagues during a confrontation between striking black officers and their white counterparts, she reportedly accused the government of failing people like Xaba because it had not removed racism from the workplace, and she said that it was time to attend to people's expectations that apartheid imbalances would be addressed.[37] Winnie Mandela's charge could not go unanswered. A week later, after consultations with a range of people, including ministers, deputy ministers and senior ANC officials, Mandela's office issued a statement. It read: 'At the funeral of Warrant Officer Jabulani Xaba, which took place early last week, the Deputy Minister of Arts, Culture, Science and Technology, Mrs Winnie Mandela, levelled serious criticism against the Government of National Unity.

'The criticism was, in the opinion of the President, inconsistent with her position as a member of the government. In keeping with his constitutional responsibilities as head of Government, President Nelson Mandela called on the Deputy Minister to publicly retract her statement and apologise to the Government.

'Accordingly, the President received a letter from the Deputy Minister last night, 13 February 1995, in which the Deputy Minister complied.

'The President has accepted the apology.

'Ministers and Deputy Ministers are custodians of the policy of the government of the day. Their acceptance of positions in Government obliges them not only to help formulate policy in relevant fora, but also to implement to the letter the decisions of government.

'President Mandela views in a serious light any acts of commission or omission, on the part of government officials, which convey an image of disregard or disrespect for the policies and decisions of the Government of National Unity. In accordance with the fundamental principle of cabinet collective responsibility, should this happen, now and in the future, the President shall not hesitate to act firmly against any transgression.'[38]

A month later — following a new round of consultations within the structures of the ANC and an unauthorised trip to West Africa by Winnie Mandela — there was another statement, this time announcing her dismissal. This time the announcement was to the point:

'As President of the Republic, Head of the Government of National Unity and leader of the ANC, I have relieved Nomzamo Winnie Mandela of her position as Deputy Minister of Arts, Culture, Science and Technology.

'This decision has been taken both in the interest of good government and to ensure the highest standards of discipline among leading officials in the Government of National Unity.

'I have taken this decision after much reflection, given that Comrade Winnie Mandela has, in the past, played an important role in the struggle against apartheid, both in her individual capacity and as a leading member of the ANC and the rest of the democratic movement.

'I hope that this action will help the former Deputy Minister to review, and seek to improve on, her own conduct in positions of responsibility, so as to enable her to make the positive contribution to society, which her talents would enable her.

'In order to ensure the smooth functioning of government and uninterrupted service to the nation, I have appointed Brigitte Mabandla as the Deputy Minister of Arts, Culture, Science and Technology. She will assume this position with immediate effect.'[39]

The dismissal became part of a round of political musical chairs, with Winnie Mandela challenging it on procedural grounds. Flanked by family members she held a press conference in a boardroom whose walls were bedecked with photographs and paintings of Nelson Mandela. As the cameras clicked, without preamble she said:

The president's letter, although dated Good Friday, 14 April 1995, was delivered to me in an unsealed envelope at 11:30 p.m. on Thursday night on 13 April 1995 and purports to terminate my appointment as deputy minister only as from Tuesday 18 April 1995. Aside [*sic*] this repeated, clumsy, unprofessional and inept behaviour of the president's office, one thing is clear — and that is that I'm still deputy minister up until 18 April 1995. The president owes it to me as a citizen of this country, in my capacity as a deputy minister. In the circumstances, whilst still deputy minister of arts, culture, science and technology, I publicly resign from that office to pay attention to the more pressing issues I have set out here above.

Getting to her feet and walking out with the entourage, Winnie Mandela turned and waved at the media and said, 'Bye, Ladies and Gentlemen,' and smiled.[40]

The reason for the controversy was that, according to the Constitution, the president should have consulted with the two deputy presidents and leaders of all parties in the cabinet. To avoid leaks, the president delayed the consultation as long as possible. When at the last minute he wanted to consult with Buthelezi, the latter couldn't be found and Mandela reverted to a senior member of the IFP. Although advised that this would pass legal muster, Mandela decided that 'the dismissal of Mrs Mandela should be treated as technically and procedurally invalid'. He did so out of a commitment 'to act within the spirit of the constitution, and further wishes to spare the government and the nation the uncertainties which might follow protracted legal action on this issue'.[41]

When Mandela returned from a foreign visit, Deputy Minister Winnie Mandela was dismissed for the second and final time, in accordance with correct procedures. Dressed in a loose turquoise shirt over khaki chinos, Mandela was a picture of informality as he entered the boardroom. However, his grim face and stern demeanour indicated how seriously he took this unpleasant task. There was a sense of déjà vu among the assembled media contingent, who had been in the room not too long ago. Today, there was no banter, no animated recognition of particular faces that had graced these surrounds, as was his wont; just a dry delivery, rendered more emotional by the very absence of emotion in his tone. Mandela read from a prepared statement:

'After due reflection, I have decided, in accordance with the powers vested in me by the Constitution, to terminate Mrs Winnie Mandela's appointment; and to appoint Mrs Brigitte Mabandla to the post of Deputy Minister of Arts, Culture, Science and Technology. This will take effect on Tuesday 18 April 1995.'[42]

There were mixed reactions from far and wide, some supporting the sacking while others condemned it. The issue was likely to rekindle talk about the estrangement of the president and his wilful wife, especially among the grass roots where Winnie Mandela enjoyed a lot of support. Predictably, a report in the *Los Angeles Times* focused on marital rupture:

At a brief news conference at her Soweto home, Mrs Mandela announced that she was resigning her government post immediately — one day before her second dismissal by President Nelson Mandela, her estranged husband, was to take effect.

Mrs Mandela, a flamboyant politician known for both her chutzpah and her charisma, did not go gently into unemployment. She complained to reporters that her sacking was 'legally invalid and unconstitutional' and that the appointment of her replacement, human rights lawyer Brigitte Mabandla, was similarly 'irregular and unconstitutional'.

She bitterly criticized the president for refusing to detail his reasons for firing her as deputy minister for arts, science, culture and technology, and called his previous statements 'facile'.[43]

At such times, especially the premature

departure of the National Party from the GNU, Mandela must have known that pressure would pile on him — and the ANC — and resuscitate the bile of prophets of doom. To those conditioned to view black leadership with suspicion, the departure of an overwhelmingly — and reassuringly — white National Party cabinet was grist to the mill. Notwithstanding the peaceful elections and a dazzling inauguration, the world was still peopled with worshippers at the altar of racist conservatives like the British journalist Peregrine Worsthorne. 'Black majority rule,' he famously ranted after the ANC's electoral victory in 1994, 'should send a shudder round the world.'[44]

Much later, piqued by another affront, and reacting to the litany of complaints about the record of the ANC in government, Mandela put pen to paper. His words, while chiding, simultaneously act as a reminder of the endorsement his presidency received from the international community. A staggering array of men and women of stature had given the country, President Mandela and the ANC their collective blessing.

'Another perversion shamelessly touted by some opposition parties,' he writes, 'is that the ANC has caused unemployment, homelessness, violence and a multitude of other socio-economic problems. On this particular topic, the *City Press* of 15 May 1994 did not mince words. They said that traditionally an incoming government in most Western democracies is given one hundred days to prove whether it is up to scratch. It would be unfair to use such time frames in our case.

'An ANC Government has very little in common with parties which came to power in the Western world. The ANC has been, until very recently, a liberation movement. It lacks, through no fault of its own, the experience of governing a sophisticated country such as South Africa. But the biggest difference between ourselves and the Western democracies was that, contrary to what some people might wish, South Africa was a Third World country with typically Third World problems.

'The ANC was inheriting a country with immense social and economic problems. The gap between the haves (mostly whites) and the have-nots (mostly blacks) was wide; there was massive unemployment, the economy was in poor shape, the shortage of houses among the poor was growing and informal settlements were proliferating all over our major cities. Violence, be it political or otherwise, was another problem facing the country. And a solution to the education crisis was nowhere in sight.

'This is what the *City Press* wrote only five days after the installation of the new government. The *City Press* has indicted the apartheid regime and those opposition parties who welcomed white supremacy and gobbled up all the fruits of that notorious and rapacious regime.

'Both the National Party and the Progressive Party, predecessor of the Democratic Party of Tony Leon, condemned the armed struggle and sanctions, the principal weapons used by the oppressed to liberate the country. These parties now present themselves as paragons of good government, as people who have never heard of unemployment, homelessness, violence and other socio-economic problems until liberation in 1994.[45]

'The *City Press* of 15 May 1994 wrote that "no amount of words could adequately describe and capture the mood" when the first democratically elected President of South Africa was installed in Pretoria on Tuesday.'[46]

Mandela then recaps the historical nature of the day of his inauguration, not so much for his interlocutors to review the pomp and ceremony of the day, but to see it in the context of how South Africa came of age and, in one fell swoop, aided the world to come of age.

' "Millions of people all over the world," ' he writes, continuing to quote from the *City Press* story, ' "witnessed this historic moment. Those of us fortunate enough to be where the action was, will never forget that momentous day as long as we live.

' "Brushing shoulders and shaking hands with all those famous people, Heads of States, Kings and Queens, church leaders and famous socialists, was an unforgettable experience. It can be easily argued that nowhere else in the world did a single country host so many celebrities in one sitting. Friend and foe sat next to each other. Cuban President Fidel Castro and [the] United States Vice President, Al Gore, smiled at each other. The Israeli President [Chaim Herzog] and the PLO [Palestine Liberation Organisation] leader Yasser Arafat shook hands, and Zambian President Frederick Chiluba and Kenneth Kaunda embraced each other.

' "The generals from the army and the police, who not long ago declared war on the political leaders and on neighbouring states, stood at attention and saluted their former enemies and President, their new boss.

' "Many of us experienced goose flesh when the fighter jets flew over the crowds. There was a lump in our throats as we sang the national anthem and, of course, many of us shed a tear or two when the first black President of South Africa was finally declared," said the newspaper.'[47]

Mandela was heartened to know that his endorsement — and that of the ANC and the new democracy — had come from far and wide. For example, US Republican congressman Amory R. Houghton, Jr described how

he has seen a lot of history — but nothing compares to what he saw Tuesday, when he stood in the throng of 50,000 who watched democracy finally come to South Africa.

'I was in Nicaragua for the inauguration of Violeta Chamorro (de Barrios) and at the Kremlin when the Soviet flag came down and the Russian flag went up, but I've never seen anything like this,' he said in a telephone interview from Pretoria, where he witnessed the inauguration of President Nelson Mandela. 'I just can't believe it . . . There was really the sense of something extraordinary happening,' he said . . . 'There's this sense of forgiveness and reconciliation that dominates this (country) now,' Houghton said. 'And Nelson Mandela is holding this together. He's the George Washington of South Africa.'[48]

Most world leaders have enjoyed an ambivalent relationship with the media, all warily heeding the age-old truism that the media giveth and the media taketh away. Mandela, although deferential to the fourth estate, evinced a less guarded attitude, seeing the media as a necessity for a functioning democracy. Unlike most people who ascend to great heights, he was advantaged by the years of incarceration, where he was out of the public eye and was one of the few people in history whose image or any reproduction thereof could earn one a prison sentence. He grew to epic dimensions in the collective imagination of the world, the slogan 'Free Mandela!', as ubiquitous as he was absent, appearing in reverse in reality on headlines screaming 'Mandela Free!' on the fateful February afternoon in 1990. It was the media that had kept him connected both to world events and what was happening in his country — its disasters, ups and downs, the triumphs and the tears — in all available languages including Afrikaans.

In time, he was able to comment on the role of the South African media:

'In their comments on the inauguration, the South African press reached a high level of patriotism. They regarded the occasion as truly historic, and were intensely objective and full of praise.

'According to *The Argus,* with the inauguration, the final seal was placed on South Africa's acceptance of non-racialism and democracy. And the leaders of the world were there to bear witness to that commitment. South Africa, the paper said, had a government of parliament representative of all citizens.

Beeld hailed the fact that white and black had accepted each other as members of one family.[49] One of the main reasons for the violence was that not every family participated in the political process. When everyone could take part there was a dramatic change, which contributed to the reduction of political violence.[50]

'*Cape Times* referred to the remarkable transformation of the past four years initiated by Mr de Klerk as an historic act of courage and vision.

'This was by no means free of tension and violence. And there had been something miraculous about the dramatic change for the better since the mass of South Africans were given the opportunity to vote in a general election and eighty-seven per cent of those eligible went to the polls, and voted in peace and good order.

'[*The*] *Citizen* hailed the occasion as a great day on which the liberation struggle of Blacks was finally over. That the ANC would win in the end was as inevitable as the rising of the sun. The changes that had come about were traumatic for many people — the old order passing and a new one just beginning, the end of white rule, and the start of Black majority rule, the corridors of power peopled by those who were once banned or exiled or who were in the forefront of the battle for equality.

'*City Press:* "The arrival of the dignitaries at the Presidency for breakfast was reminiscent of a UN Summit in New York. Never before has South Africa been able to bring together such a broad spectrum of world leaders on one occasion. After our day at the Presidency on Tuesday, it really dawned on us that this country would never be the same."[51] South Africa was going through an exciting period, which had captured the focus of the whole world.

'*Daily News:* The unfolding big challenges for all our people proclaimed the swearing-in as more than a moment of high symbolism and emotion for millions of South Africans who had been deprived of their birthright. It marked a moment in which the country shrugged off anachronism and entered the future with purpose and opportunity to play its rightful place in Africa and world affairs. We were being taken into the future at the head of a Government of National Unity. The country was united as never before. And that was what was really new — and gave a chance of success in the year ahead.

'[*The*] *Sowetan* recorded that on May 10, power was transferred from President de Klerk. "People who would never be seen under one roof, like Cuba's Fidel Castro and the United States' Al Gore, plus leaders and representatives from around the globe, all came."[52]

'We might add our own observation and say what rang clearly in the ears of everyone were the words: "We must act together as a united nation for national reconciliation, for nation building, for the birth of a new world."

'In congratulating the two deputy presidents, Thabo Mbeki and De Klerk, [*The*] *Sowetan* added that "De Klerk had the wisdom and vision to choose the right path when he stood at the crossroads."[53]

'[*The*] *Star* picked up the same theme. In a sombre tone but with an optimistic ending, it warned that South African leaders were on trial. Africa was watching to see whether South Africa, with its vast reserves of human talent, its rich natural resources and sound infrastructure, could succeed where most of the continent had failed. This land with its diversity of peoples, religions and cultures, its juxtaposition of First and Third World economies, was in many ways today's world in microcosm. Success in [*sic*] many years of oppression and conflict would be a source of pride to South Africans and an inspiration to Africa and beyond.

'*Rapport:* The number of Heads of State and Government, who attended the inauguration of South Africa's President this week confirmed that South Africa has been accepted back to the international community. Several African leaders indicated that they not only expected South Africa to play a lead-

241

ing role in Africa, but that they would also like assistance from South Africa. In fact the whole world expected South Africa to play a leading role in Africa and not in vain. They are tired of carrying the problems of the dying continent. South Africa was Africa's last hope, said an African expert.

'*Sunday Independent* was only published in 1995 and there is no comment from them.

'*Sunday Times:* "Most people at the inauguration of the President would select the moment when the jets swept across the sky — *our* jets, not *their* jets — as the emotional climax of South Africa's rebirth . . . We had come home at last; we had taken back our air force, and our army, and our police and the country. It had been such a long time, a lifetime, since we could regard our national symbols with possessive pride, free of guilt or shame or anger."[54]

'There are several other national and regional publications that welcomed the new South Africa in glowing terms and boosted our pride.

'We have had robust exchanges with the press. In some, the words used were carefully selected merely to convey no more than what both parties believed to be true. Others were more than robust, leaving the contestants bruised and without balance. Such heated exchanges cannot be avoided or suppressed in a democracy.

'It is good for us, the media and the country as a whole, to know that our journalists can rise to expectations and acquit themselves excellently as on the day of inauguration and on numerous other occasions.'[55]

It cannot be stated often enough that Mandela's lifelong dream was the liberation of the African majority from tyranny and the ushering in of democracy in South Africa. Throughout his life, he was also dedicated to reversing the iniquities of the past and, as president, to preclude, by word or precept, his administration ever sending the proverbial shudder round the world. He was therefore quick to acknowledge those erstwhile members of De Klerk's cabinet who had withdrawn from party politics. Some of them had been, like their ANC counterparts, shocked at De Klerk's precipitate step, leaving some, like Pik Botha, suddenly without the wherewithal to start afresh. A common thread in their later explanations of their decision was a conviction that the National Party lacked the capacity to change in ways that would enable it to play a significant role in the democratic era.

At the National Executive Committee meeting in May 1996, Mandela noted the implications for the National Party. He saw both a challenge, for instance in the vigorous campaign for the imminent Cape Town municipal election, and opportunity in the divisions in the National Party for the ANC to make inroads into the coloured and Indian communities.[56] Later, addressing the NEC in August, Mandela expatiated on the management of the transition and national unity. He was simultaneously shrugging off what might have been read as premonitory signs of the death of the GNU.

'With the withdrawal of the NP from government,' he said, 'the question of the future of the multiparty cabinet has arisen sharply.

'Firstly, we need to examine our relationship with the IFP, both in the context of its participation in the GNU and the political developments in KwaZulu-Natal. What is the best approach required in dealing with this organisation?

'Secondly, I have personally raised the issue of securing the cooperation of the PAC on specific questions and ensuring that they actively participate in the transformation process, including at the executive level.'[57]

From as far back as the late fifties, when the PAC broke away from the ANC, leaders like Mandela had maintained a cautious, almost aloof distance from the splinter party. People like Joe Slovo, vexed by the PAC's critique that the ANC's legitimacy was undermined by the influence of communists, dismissed the PAC as a CIA front. It didn't

244

help that the PAC was formed on 5 and 6 April 1959 at the Johannesburg offices of the United States Information Service (USIS), where its flamboyant leader, Potlako Leballo, who would prove to have a big appetite for intrigue, had been employed. However, Mandela had a high regard for its president, Robert Mangaliso Sobukwe, a committed, respected intellectual who had made his mark as a leader in the Youth League, and who, like Mandela, was a graduate from the University of Fort Hare.

Throughout history, at home and abroad, the attempts to unite the ANC and the PAC had failed. The most notable failure involved the South African United Front (SAUF). Formed abroad after the Sharpeville Massacre of 21 March 1960, it brought together such struggle luminaries as Oliver Tambo from the ANC, Nana Mahomo from the PAC, Fanuel Kozonguizi from the South West African National Union (SWANU) and Dr Yusuf Dadoo from the South African Indian Congress (SAIC). Despite these heavyweights, the differences in approaches to discipline, between the ANC and the PAC especially, put paid to the longevity of the SAUF. Yusuf Dadoo lamented the break:

'The ANC and the SAIC representatives tried hard to maintain the integrity of the United Front . . . They conscientiously held back from expounding their own policies abroad in their desire to maintain faithfully the unity of the Front. They refused, in spite of repeated provocations, to engage in attacks on their principal partner, the PAC. They always confronted their partners with common problems and had even compromised aspects of their policies, all with a view to maintaining the unity and cohesion of the Front.'[58]

The SAUF lasted barely more than a few months, and its dissolution in London on 13 March 1962 led to recriminations that widened rather than bridged the rift between the ANC and the PAC.

In prison, Mandela was witness to the political feuding that sometimes led to physical confrontations, but he had determined to continue playing the role of reconciler, to such an extent that, during a dispute, he refused to testify on the side of the ANC. He writes:

'I regarded my role in prison as not just the leader of the ANC, but as a promoter of unity, an honest broker, a peacemaker, and I was reluctant to take a side in this dispute, even if it was the side of my own organisation. If I testified on behalf of the ANC, I would jeopardise my chances of bringing about reconciliation among different groups. If I preached unity, I must act like a unifier, even at the risk of perhaps alienating some of my own colleagues.'[59]

It was still in this role that, even before the negotiations, Mandela had mulled over the possibility of a united front or patriotic alliance of the ANC, PAC and the Azanian People's Organisation (AZAPO) towards a stronger representation during negotiations.*[60] History, absence of vision, entrenched positions and confusion in the face of untested ideas proved too daunting for this initiative to win the day.

But now, in July 1996, following the collapse of the GNU, whether Mandela still cherished the ideal of cooperation with the PAC or not, Clarence Makwetu, the president of the PAC, turned him down. Mandela admitted as much at his belated seventy-eighth birthday celebration — which he had turned into a festive dinner for veterans, where the invitees included Urbania Mothopeng, widow of the late PAC stalwart Zephania Mothopeng.[61]

This was not the first dinner for veterans that Mandela had hosted. Almost two years earlier, on 23 July 1994, still awed by the ANC's electoral victory, his joy was palpable. It must always be remembered that Mandela

* Formed in 1978 after the crackdown on the Black Consciousness Movement (see People, Places and Events), the Azanian People's Organisation sought to fill the political vacuum left by the banning of the ANC and PAC.

saw the ANC as a representative of the majority of the people of South Africa, black and white; its victory, then, was not abstract or self-indulgent as, say, in the triumph over a soccer rival. It meant another step towards attaining the cherished goal of building a democratic society.

On that occasion, he said: '[This] is a celebration, a homecoming to where all of us belong: the seat of government in our country. At last we are here, where the laws that kept us in bondage were conceived; where the schemes of social engineering that rent our country apart were hatched.

'It is our task today to traditionally grace this whole establishment with the blessings of the veterans. Because, before these settlements and offices are cleansed by your towering presence, they will not be worthy symbols of the new democratic order.

'So I thank you, dear veterans, for taking the trouble of traversing long distances to be here with us. Many an excuse would have been in order if you were not able to come: old age, health, organisational work, business undertakings, and so on. But you dared to defy all these, so we could meet in this unique assembly of the cream of veteran fighters for human rights. I once more thank you.

'I also wish to thank the organisers and fundraisers who left no stone unturned to ensure that this event takes place and becomes the success that it promises to be: Rica Hodgson, Richard Maponya, Legau Mathabathe, Amina Cachalia, Moss Nxumalo, Omar Motani and others.* We however deemed it necessary that from the limited resources allocated to the President's Office, the government should contribute to the catering and other services offered here. Because you deserve this for your role in

---

* Rica Hodgson was a veteran political activist who returned from exile to work with Walter Sisulu. She penned *Foot Soldier for Freedom: A Life in South Africa's Liberation Movement,* an important account of the struggle years. A pioneering black businessman, Richard Maponya inspired entrepreneurship among black South Africans with his successful ventures in Soweto. Legau Mathabathe was the legendary headmaster of the Morris Isaacson High School in Soweto, the epicentre of the June 1976 uprisings. He was credited with contributing towards the growth of the Black Consciousness Movement. A long-time friend and close confidant of Mandela, Amina Cachalia was a campaigner for women's rights and wrote *When Hope and History Rhyme,* an evocative autobiography. Moss Nxumalo is a businessman, former vice president of the National African Federated Chamber of Commerce and Industry (NAFCOC), and a founder of Thebe Investment Corporation. A successful businessman and political activist, Omar Motani worked mostly behind the scenes in his support for the struggle.

bringing about a democratic and non-racial South Africa.

'I welcome you all from the bottom of my heart — including those who join us from abroad.

'Four decades ago — for us veterans, a short space of time! — who would have imagined that we would meet here in a forum of this nature? Yes, we used to dream and sing about the day of freedom and democracy. But we knew it would not be easy to accomplish. We did have great confidence in the final realisation of the democratic ideal. But, prepared as we were to give the anti-apartheid struggle our all, many of us sometimes felt that the new era would dawn only after we had departed.

'In this regard, we should consider ourselves honoured to have been part of the generation that has reaped the fruits of the struggle in our lifetime. There are hundreds — no, thousands — who deserve to be here today but whose lives were cut short by the burden of a wretched apartheid existence. Others fell to the blow of the torturer and the bullet of the defender of apartheid. We salute them all. It is in their honour too that we are here today. When we say thank you for dedicating your lives to the efforts for freedom, justice and democracy, we also extend our profound tribute to them.

'We salute all veterans for daring to stand

up to those who hounded you for your role in the Passive Resistance Campaign, the Great Miners' Strike, the Defiance Campaign, the Congress of the People and other campaigns; for your defiance of those who called you traitors in parliament for telling the truth; for your challenge to those who attached all kinds of insulting appellations to your names for opposing the pass laws and constantly exposing the terrible state of race relations in our country.*

'I refer to you all: veterans from the ANC, the PAC, the SACP, the trade union movement, the Progressive Party, the Liberal Party, Black Sash, the Institute of Race Relations, women's organisations, the Natal and Transvaal Indian Congresses and many, many more. Today, we can together say: when

* Congress of the People — see People, Places and Events. The Passive Resistance Campaign of 1946 was a non-violent campaign against a proposed law by Prime Minister Jan Smuts's government to severely restrict the right of Indian South Africans to own land. At the end of the campaign in 1948, more than 2,000 men and women had been arrested. The African Mine Workers' Strike of 1946 was a general strike of all African miners for a minimum wage of ten shillings a day and better working conditions. The strike, which lasted a week, was attacked by the police, who killed at least nine people and injured 1,248.

we said the truth will triumph, it is because we knew the truth would indeed finally prevail. And we knew too, that South Africa and all her people would benefit by this.'[62]

For Mandela, who was speaking during the heyday of the GNU, it was a time of exuberance where everything seemed possible. Two years later, the new government had a few unpleasant, if necessary, tasks to do. Reality called for certain reconfigurations, mainly the dissolution of the RDP office, one of the main planks of the ANC's manifesto.

Although the RDP occupied an important place in the ANC's election platform, the party questioned whether it should continue as a standalone structure or have its functions spread across various government ministries and departments. After an intense debate and lobbying by the Congress of South African Trade Unions (COSATU), the ANC adopted the second approach.

Veteran trade unionist Jay Naidoo recalls Mandela asking him in 1994 to lead the office for the RDP as a minister without portfolio in the president's office. 'We have a big task ahead,' Naidoo recalls Mandela saying. 'You have been driving the formulation of the RDP from my ANC office and now I want it to be in the centre of all our programmes.'[63]

The position of minister without portfolio is a delicate one in any government, pitting the incumbent against line ministers who feel threatened at possible incursion into their territory. According to some ministers, among them Mufamadi, the office of the RDP had not been included in Mandela's initial list of portfolios.[64] The ambiguity of the institutional position and role of the RDP ministry and its location in the presidency, compounded by its last-minute addition to the executive, both affected its performance and contained the seeds of its dissolution barely two years after its establishment. The complex funding arrangements aimed at helping government departments to reorient their priorities did nothing to lessen interdepartmental tensions.[65] As a completely new structure, the RDP office was also hampered by having insufficient staff.

When he announced its closure, Mandela had to think about all those who had pinned their hopes on its success. These were the multitudes affiliated with the mass organisations of civil society — on the treadmill — 'whose lives', to use Mandela's words, 'were cut short by the burden of a wretched apartheid existence'.[66] As in many cases where he had to persuade people to accept unpalatable measures, he rallied the reservoir of support among the public by being candid about the workings of cabinet.

He said, 'Unity within the Cabinet itself has strengthened as we worked together to identify national priorities, on the basis of the RDP, without being over-constrained by exclusive commitment to the Departments we happen to head.

'As a result of the evolution of policy affecting all the departments of state and the implementation of some institutional changes to give us the necessary capacity to implement those policies, the possibility has increased greatly for the departments each to implement the programme of Reconstruction and Development within the area of its mandate . . .

'The RDP Office will be closed down. I have instructed Deputy President Mbeki to handle the matter of the relocation of the important projects, programmes and institutions, which currently fall under the supervision of the RDP Office.

'The RDP Fund will be relocated within the Ministry of Finance . . . the RDP is not the responsibility of some specialised department but the compass, the lodestar, which guides all government activities.'[67]

Although Mandela was full of praise for Naidoo and 'his colleagues in the RDP Office for the pioneering work they had done',[68] he must have sensed Naidoo's unhappiness about receiving very little notice about the closure and his reassignment to another ministry. He must have been aware of the depth of feeling among elements within the

254

Tripartite Alliance — a political partnership of the ANC, SACP and COSATU, set up in 1990 to promote the goals of the national democratic revolution — which perceived the change as the beginnings of a shift in the country's macroeconomic policy.

These complex transitions were the growing pains of the new democracy. If Mandela was intent on taking those ready for the journey along with him, he first had to deal with those who wanted to get off the bus, including Liebenberg, who resigned in terms of an agreement he had with Mandela when he accepted the position in 1994, that he would only do the job until the next budget.[69] He 'stepped gracefully aside and returned to the private sector, having helped ease the transition to the first ANC finance minister,' writes Alan Hirsch.[70]

In August 1995, about seven months before Liebenberg's departure, Mandela called Manuel to a meeting and told him he wanted him to be minister of finance when Liebenberg stepped down. Mandela told Manuel that as the first black minister of finance he should expect a rough ride. However, Mandela advised him to use the time before Liebenberg left to prepare himself. In addition to his job as minister of trade and industry, he would have to learn the ropes of the finance ministry. He had to understudy Liebenberg without anybody knowing what was going on. The establishment of a committee of ministers working on the budget, which included Manuel, helped. Mandela also told Manuel to skip the annual meeting of the World Bank and International Monetary Fund in 1995 — a meeting Manuel had been attending yearly since 1991 — lest his attendance invite speculation. Manuel recalls:

Madiba would call me quite regularly and say, 'How's it going? Are you following Chris? Are you ready — are you taking an interest in this matter?' And then he said, 'OK, it is all systems go, I'll announce this at the end of Chris's budget, which is the end of March, but there'll be a few changes I need to tell you about. Alec [Erwin is] in finance and I want to move him to trade and industry in your position, but don't talk to him yet. You will need a deputy, and Gill [Marcus] is doing very well in the portfolio committee and I want to move her there — don't talk to her, either.'[71]

In April 1996, after Liebenberg had presented the second budget, Manuel became minister of finance, with Marcus as deputy minister of finance and Erwin as minister of trade and industry.

In all of these dealings, Mandela was confronting situations that required him to maintain a firm hand. He always consulted colleagues and advisers, but on other, more intractable issues — bearing in mind that Tambo, his confidant, was gone — he would check with Walter Sisulu. Sometimes Albertina Sisulu would arrive at Mandela's Houghton home and they would immediately go into a huddle. As a one-time president of the United Democratic Front, who had steered the boat of the mass democratic movement during the country's most combustible period, she was a trusted fount of experience.[72]

Mandela certainly needed to summon all of his reserves of wisdom and tact when it came to the question of the location of Parliament. Seemingly a small, niggling issue at first, the location of Parliament was steeped in the awkward genesis of the Union of South Africa in 1910 as a white minority unitary state. Pretoria in the Transvaal had been designated the administrative capital, the judicial capital was Bloemfontein in the Orange Free State, and the legislative capital was Cape Town in the Cape Province. Natal, whose capital was Pietermaritzburg, received financial compensation for the loss of revenue that would result from the union.

The argument revolved around costs and the economic impact of changing what had been agreed in 1910. Questions arose about what it would cost to have officials regularly travelling between the two capitals; what it would cost to change the arrangement and the economic impact on the capitals. The financial impact of a bigger democratic parliament and its longer sessions became part of the argument, as did the proposition that moving inland would make Parliament more accessible to the public and more exposed to public sentiment.

When this matter was put on the agenda of the first formal meeting of the GNU cabinet, Mandela was aware that it had already triggered competition and the frenzied lobbying by public-relations companies. Speaking at the National Council of Provinces, an assembly of provincial and local governments, Mandela felt the need to calm things down.

'Regarding the question of the seat of Parliament,' he said, 'we have been discussing this, and I hope all members will appreciate that this is a matter that will be handled with great care. It is a very sensitive matter. The only time I saw members of the ANC in the Western Cape agreeing very fully with the members of the NP was on the question of the seat of Parliament. The Transvaalers also speak with one voice on the question, saying that Parliament must be shifted to the Transvaal. Even my name has been involved. When we heard that the Pretoria City Council had said that the President was in favour of Parliament shifting to the Transvaal, I instructed my director general to write to them to say that I had expressed no opinion on this question.'[73]

Cabinet appointed a cross-party subcommittee, headed initially by Mac Maharaj and subsequently by Jeff Radebe, ministers of transport and public works respectively, to look into the matter of costs and the impacts of the proposal, and to make recommendations.* The national executive of the ANC also appointed its own task team.

While the ANC and cabinet task teams were processing the issue, intense city campaigns got under way, with ministers and ANC members getting caught up in the crossfire when protocol required public neutrality. Although Mandela had kept a straight face, he had inadvertently showed his hand during a visit by British Prince Edward in September 1994. The two men were conversing at Mahlamba Ndlopfu, unaware that they were within earshot of the media, when Mandela proudly pointed out to the prince the site behind the ridge where Mahlamba Ndlopfu stood, where he said the new parliament should be located. This media scoop set the president's office scampering about to put out the fires blazing within the ANC and across society.

A year earlier, Mandela had firmly but gently raised the sensitivity of the matter at an ANC caucus meeting. Solemnly, he

* Mac Maharaj — see People, Places and Events.

pointed out that there were strong emotions at play and that the issue should be handled with care. Then he confessed his own personal preference. There should be one capital, 'and it should be Qunu!'[74]

Mandela was, however, far more severe to errant ministers, as evidenced by his notes prepared for an ANC executive meeting on 19 February 1996:

'Nine Cabinet ministers and two deputies have broken protocol to sign a public message to President Mandela, supporting the retention of Cape Town as the seat of parliament. Their message contained in [an] advertisement in *The Argus* today, is viewed as a major political coup for the campaign to keep Parliament in the Cape. The advertisement is also viewed as a sturdy counterpunch to the one contained in the South African Airways magazine, *Flying Springbok,* featuring a multi-personalitied [*sic*] President Mandela promoting Pretoria as a touring attraction . . . ANC cabinet ministers must explain their actions at the earliest possible convenience. A process has been set by the government in this regard.'[75]

If the above reads like a frustrated president's note to self, it would be leavened with humour when recounted two years later in the National Council of Provinces. Mandela said that the names 'of the very Cabinet Ministers who had taken a decision that we must have no option whatsoever until the procedure had been complied with and the reports have come back to us, I now saw on a list that was circulating in the Western Cape, saying, "Let Parliament remain where it is". I called them and said I wanted an explanation. We have taken a decision here that we must not express any opinion on this matter. They said: "No, we saw the names of the members of the cabinet of the NP on a list, and we were thinking, in terms of local government elections, that if we did not join . . . [laughter]." I then called Deputy President de Klerk and said, "You know the decision. Your Ministers have now gone public and signed a petition that Parliament should remain in Cape Town."

'He called his Cabinet Ministers together, and they said: "No, we saw the names of Cabinet Ministers of the ANC on a list and we decided also to join [laughter]." So I warned both parties that the strongest disciplinary action would be taken against them if they again came out in public and expressed an opinion on the matter. That is the government's position on this matter.'[76]

Manuel, one of the six ANC ministers implicated in the campaign, some of whom might have been innocent, remembers a bruising meeting with the president at Tuynhuys and recalls Mandela saying to him:

'So, Trevor, you belong to a faction. Your faction is lobbying through the press to have Parliament in Cape Town. You know our views on the matter. You know that I think that the best option that we had to move Parliament to Pretoria is during the one term that I am president. You know that. You know that I've asked Mac [Maharaj] and Jeff [Radebe] to undertake research. You know all of that, yet you ignore it and become part of this faction to lobby against decisions that are in the national interest of this country.'[77]

Manuel tried to say that he wasn't part of a faction; they'd never met on the issue, but Mandela would hear none of it. 'I'm not interested in your views,' he said. 'You're part of a faction; I want you to hear me, and you're part of a faction along with all of you chaps who live here in Cape Town . . . You know you're a very good minister and you will become better, but if you don't want to be part of the collective then you must leave. How do you want to conduct yourself?'[78]

Although the matter had fallen off the cabinet agenda by the end of Mandela's term, the whole experience gave people, certainly Manuel, a glimpse into Mandela's disposition when he felt thwarted. 'This was Madiba,' Manuel says. 'He had a viewpoint. You could disagree with his viewpoint, but he was head of state, and if you didn't want to be part of the team, you had to decide how you played it.'[79]

For Manuel, it was 'one of the big take-outs of that engagement. It removes the idea of this uninvolved saint who has no views of his own. He was OK with confronting people with issues, even when they weren't comfortable.'[80]

There were numerous instances where Mandela had to crack the whip, increasingly against people from his own corner. He'd internalised Seneca's adage that 'he who dreads hostility too much is unfit to rule'. Even though he understood that the new South Africa was a work in progress, he had to ensure that people took their responsibilities as adults. People had to be dismissed — or be asked to resign — from cabinet or from leadership positions. He found it painful to take action against comrades; he was inevitably disappointed when his trust in others' integrity was not fulfilled. But even when he voiced anger at being taken advantage of, he was ready to rebuild trust.

Those who worked closely with him recall his powerful, and often conflicting, emotions when deciding to act or to refrain from taking action. Ahmed Kathrada spoke of Mandela's loyalty as 'his strength and his weakness. When he is loyal to someone, he's not going to hear something contrary; his loyalty goes beyond. But when you cross him, it goes the other way.'[81]

For Sydney Mufamadi, 'a key facet of his [make-up] was that he did not want to be taken for granted or taken advantage of when he put his trust in the integrity of others'.[82]

Jakes Gerwel described how Mandela's view of human nature informed his actions:

He had this genuine belief — and he often argued with me about the provability of it — that human beings are essentially 'good-doing beings; beings who do good'. We had an incident in government where somebody very senior did something very silly and stupid, and had to step down from that position. But, at the same time, he had played a crucial role in ensuring the stability of the transition period. In the end, we had to part ways with him, and he stepped down. Madiba said to him, 'If there is anything that I can do for you, please don't hesitate to ask me.'

And the man did. A day or two later, he came back asking for an appointment to another international position. Everyone advised Mandela against giving him another chance. Upset, he argued that 'if you are able to follow human beings from the moment that they get up in the morning until they retire at night, you would find that most of them do the proper things most of the

264

time, and that the erring is an aberration'. And he really acted on that. He is not naive, but he has a faith in the goodness of human beings, no matter how they disagreed politically or otherwise, and he always acted in line with that belief. Of course, this attitude also helped to lay the basis for the furthering of social cohesion and national unity in the country.[83]

He sought to achieve this goal by going out to where people were, impelled by a need to see for himself the impact of the new dispensation on them. There was also the allure of the newness of a country from which he'd been separated for decades, which unveiled itself on a daily basis. This was represented by the youth of the land. One of his long-serving bodyguards, Mzwandile Vena, relates how this enthusiasm made Mandela unpredictable and a nightmare for his security detail. He would order his driver to make an unscheduled stop, step out of the vehicle and go across the street to greet a group of children.

'You had to be alert all the time,' Vena says. 'A choir would be singing at an event and without any warning he would just get up from his chair and join the choir. We were forced to improvise all the time.'[84]

An aspect of this spontaneity was part of Mandela's own sense of political timing, when he imparted important messages that subverted orthodoxies. Toine Eggenhuizen, a Dutch ex-priest stationed at the ANC office in London, remembers how Mandela pre-empted the debate about symbols in the run-up to the Rugby World Cup in 1995.

There was some controversy about the Springbok emblem, which many felt was a throwback to the apartheid exclusion of blacks in sport. However, someone had sent a rugby cap with the Springbok emblem to Mandela, which was accepted — and quickly forgotten — by his personal assistant, Beryl Baker. Shortly thereafter, Mandela, as president of the ANC, was addressing a rally in the Eastern Cape. As it was hot, Beryl was worried about Mandela in the sun. Therefore she took out that cap with an apology that she didn't have anything else. Madiba was totally happy with that, with the result that the evening news showed him wearing that cap.[85]

By the time he rehabilitated the Springbok emblem at the memorable Rugby World Cup in Ellis Park — and united South Africans of all races — Mandela had gone a long way towards blunting criticism against the emblem through a gesture that was totally unrehearsed.

CHAPTER SIX:
THE PRESIDENCY
AND THE CONSTITUTION

As president, Nelson Mandela's relationship with the judiciary would be severely tested. And for someone who ended up presiding over the creation of one of the world's most admired constitutions, Mandela's relationship with South Africa's courts had not always been favourable. As a young lawyer he'd had constant skirmishes with magistrates who objected to his seemingly 'uppity' attitude. It didn't help that he was six foot two inches and always immaculately dressed during court appearances, projecting an image that was inimical to the old-school image of an African. He also had a disconcerting knack of ensuring that, whatever the subject of proceedings, he found his way back to what he really wanted to talk about.

The speech he made from the dock on 20 April 1964, during the last months of the Rivonia Trial, is a case in point. Facing a probable death sentence, Mandela told the court — and the world — that he had 'cherished the ideal of a democratic and free society in which all persons live together in harmony and with equal opportunities. It is an ideal which I hope to live for and to achieve. But if needs be, it is an ideal for which I am prepared to die.'[1]

It was only in prison that Mandela completed part-time the law degree he had started in 1949. Through years of study he had been unable to complete the degree at the University of the Witwatersrand. But incarcerated on Robben Island, he studied for his LLB from the University of South Africa (UNISA) by correspondence, finally graduating in absentia in 1989.

After his release, his first encounter with the justice system was an affront to his dignity when he sat — a lonely, if stoical, figure — in the public gallery of the Rand Supreme Court in May 1991, witnessing the mortification of his then wife, Winnie, on trial for assault and kidnapping.

Subsequently, in matters that affected him as president, Mandela's relationship with the judiciary was tested in two instances. Would he, when it came to matters that affected him personally, remember his oath of office and heed the ponderous words that defined his role as president, head of state and head of the national executive? Had he internalised the fact that to hold the highest office in the land made him, as first citizen of his country, indispensable to the effective governance of democratic South Africa? Would he uphold, defend and respect the Constitution as the supreme law of the Republic? Would he affirm that 'in the new South Africa there is nobody, not even the President, who is above the law, that the rule of law generally and, in particular, the independence of the judiciary should be respected'?[2]

The first test came even before the new constitution had been drafted. Running into deadlines for preparations for local government elections, Parliament adopted the Local Government Transition Act before its terms had been completely finalised. To compensate for this, a clause was included giving the president power to amend the Act. Armed with that provision, Mandela transferred control over the membership of local government demarcation committees from provincial to national government. However, that invalidated decisions made by the premier of the Western Cape, Hernus Kriel, who took the matter to the Constitutional Court. The court found for the Western Cape provincial government and gave Parliament a month to rectify the Act.

Within an hour of the court delivering its adverse judgment, Mandela publicly accepted the ruling and welcomed the fact that it showed that everyone was equal before the law.[3] Later, he wrote:

'During my presidency, Parliament authorised me to issue two proclamations dealing with the elections in the Western Cape Province. That provincial government took me to the Constitutional Court, which overruled me in a unanimous judgment. As soon as I was informed of the judgment, I called a press conference and appealed to the general public to respect the decision of the highest court in the land on constitutional matters.'[4]

Mandela discussed the court judgment with his advisers and the speaker of Parliament, Frene Ginwala. She remembers the day: 'He called us to a meeting at his house and told us that he had been informed that it had gone against the government. He said, "How long will it take to change?" I said, "We could reconvene Parliament if necessary . . . ," but even before I could finish, he said, "But the one thing is this: we must respect the decision of the Constitutional Court. There can be no question of denying or in any way rejecting that." '[5]

In a public statement, he went further, announcing that Parliament would be reconvened to deal with the matter and stressing that, apart from Cape Town, things were on track for the elections:

'Preparations for local government elections must continue so that these elections take place as planned. The Court's judgment does not create any crisis whatsoever. I should

270

emphasise that the judgment of the Constitutional Court confirms that our new democracy is taking firm root and that nobody is above the law.'[6]

Mandela was somewhat less sanguine when it came to the other case that had him personally appearing in court. He had worked hard, using the iconic victory in the 1995 Rugby World Cup, to entrench the spirit of nation building and reconciliation among South Africans. But the euphoric surge of unity and embrace of the future had remained within the perimeter of the Ellis Park Stadium, amid the debris of trash and match memorabilia. For some of the spectators, players and rugby administrators, everything was as it had been before the match. Two years on, prompted by reports of maladministration, resistance to change and racism in the sport's governing body, after consultation with Minister of Sport and Recreation Steve Tshwete, Mandela appointed a commission of inquiry, led by Justice Jules Browde, to look into the affairs of the South African Rugby Football Union (SARFU).

The president of SARFU, Louis Luyt, best described as a carpetbagger, had in 1976 founded an English-language newspaper, *The Citizen,* using slush funds from the Department of Information, in what was known as the 'Infogate Scandal', which purveyed propaganda aimed at polishing the apartheid government's image overseas. Singularly un-likeable, Luyt had precipitated a walkout by the New Zealand All Blacks rugby team when, instead of being magnanimous in victory, he made inappropriate remarks at the after-match dinner.*

The president's office issued a statement, saying that 'the cloud hanging over South African Rugby needs to be lifted and the President is confident that the inquiry presents an opportunity to do so, and to dispel any impression that . . . it is retreating into a laager of racial chauvinism. The President believes that rugby will meet the challenge of being one of our most celebrated sports, a sport played and supported by South Africans throughout the country.'[7]

Mandela's intention was to help pull SARFU out of its 'laager of racial chauvinism' but it simply prompted its president, Louis Luyt, to apply to the Pretoria High Court to quash the appointment of a commission of inquiry into the administration of rugby. Judge William de Villiers summoned Mandela to appear before the court as a witness. Not

---

* Defeated All Blacks Captain Sean Fitzpatrick led his team out of the dinner after Louis Luyt said in his speech that the Springboks were the first 'true' world champions. He said the winners of the Rugby World Cup in 1987 and 1991 were not true world champions because South Africa did not participate.

only setting aside legal advice, but also controlling his own feelings — having to testify in court 'made his blood boil' he told journalists — Mandela complied, in the interests of justice.[8] He writes about the episode:

'Judge William de Villiers of the Gauteng High Court subpoenaed me to appear before him to justify my decision to appoint a commission of enquiry into the affairs of the South African Rugby Football Union. Some of my Cabinet colleagues advised me to challenge the subpoena, pointing out that the judge in question was, to say the least, extremely conservative, and that his real aim was to humiliate a black president. My legal adviser as well, Professor Fink Haysom, was equally opposed to my appearance in court. He argued with skill and persuasion that we had sound legal grounds to challenge the subpoena.

'While I did not necessarily challenge any of these views, I felt that at that stage in the transformation of our country, the President had certain obligations to fulfil. I argued that the trial judge was not a final Court of Appeal, and that his decision could be challenged in the Constitutional Court.* In a nutshell, I wanted the whole dispute to be

* The Constitution says that any judgment in the high court on the constitutional validity of the

273

resolved solely by the judiciary. This, in my opinion, was another way of promoting respect for law and order and, once again, of the courts of the country.

'As we expected, the judge had serious reservations about my evidence, and gave judgment for Louis Luyt, the petitioner. But the Constitutional Court set aside the decision of the lower court despite the fact that they maintained that my attitude in testifying was imperious. The Constitutional Court was not wrong. In that situation I have to be bossy and establish that I obeyed the subpoena out of strength and not weakness.'[9]

Mandela's reaction to the ruling in SARFU's favour was his commitment to 'abide by the decisions of our courts'. He said that 'all South Africans should likewise accept their rulings. The independence of the judiciary is one important pillar of our democracy.'[10]

Addressing Parliament later in April, Mandela told the assembled members that they would have to ask themselves 'some very basic questions', as it was 'only too easy to stir up the baser feelings that exist in any society that are enhanced in a society with a history such as ours. Worse still, it is only too

conduct of the president is subject to confirmation by the Constitutional Court.

easy to do this in a way that undermines our achievements in building national unity and enhancing the legitimacy of our democratic institutions. We need to ask such questions because it is much easier to destroy than to build.'[11]

He enjoined the members of Parliament to grapple with constitutional questions, such as the implications of hauling a sitting president to court to 'defend executive decisions', going straight to the principle of the separation of powers and its application in an emergent democracy. He hoped that 'our finest legal brains, both in the courts and in the profession,' would apply their minds to the question.[12]

As a trained lawyer, Mandela probably knew the answers to the questions he was posing, but he was dealing with the Constitution, which he saw as a foundation for the building of democracy — a democracy whose central plank was national unity and reconciliation. He wanted everyone's buy-in, no matter that his own interpretations might have been both correct and justifiable. His appeal to the parliamentarians, then, was for them, in their disparate parties, to help build rather than destroy.

By the time the Constitutional Court set aside the Pretoria High Court ruling that the president had acted unconstitutionally, reaction to Louis Luyt's behaviour — among the public and within rugby — had forced his resignation and led to a decision by the SARFU executive to send a delegation to apologise to Mandela.[13]

Although not codified until the negotiations of the 1990s, the principles of constitutionalism and rule of law had been embedded in the vision of the future shared by Mandela and the ANC at large. The seeds of an empowering constitution can be found in the Freedom Charter, adopted by the Congress of the People and the ANC respectively in 1955, which was drawn up on the basis of popular demands collected from communities across the length and breadth of the country.

Contrary to what happened in struggles for freedom in many other countries, the South African liberation movement made the law a terrain of struggle — defending leaders, members and activists in the courts — and in so doing, affirming the ideal of a just legal system. In 1995, in a lecture, Mandela spoke about using the law to turn tables on the state, as he and the other accused did in the Rivonia Trial:

'The prosecution expected us to try and avoid responsibility for our actions. However, we became the accusers, and, right at the start, when asked to plead, we said that it was the Government that was responsible for the state of affairs in the country and that it was the Government that should be in the dock. We maintained this position throughout the trial in our evidence and in the cross-examination of witnesses.'[14]

In 1985, Oliver Tambo had established a Constitutional Committee, which led to the 1989 publication of the ANC's 'Constitutional Guidelines for a Democratic South Africa'. Embodying the Freedom Charter's political and constitutional vision of a free, democratic and non-racial South Africa, the guidelines were a statement of principle rather than a draft constitution. Even though conditions for a negotiated transition were beginning to take shape, there were still too many uncertainties about the impending transition, and the legitimacy of any constitution would depend on popular participation in its drafting.[15]

The ANC's guidelines were polar opposites of the South African Constitution of 1983, which espoused a system of 'power-sharing' that still ensured white minority control, leaving the excluded African majority to make do with Bantustans and urban councils. The ANC rejected the constitutional protection for 'group rights', which would simply perpetuate the status quo.[16] The ANC guidelines spoke of a unitary state and universal suffrage; a bill of rights guaranteeing fundamental human rights of all citizens; and constitutional obligations on the state and all social institutions to eradicate race discrimination and all of its concomitants.

When drafting a constitution and bill of rights during negotiations, the ANC's Constitutional Committee drew on the organisation's Constitutional Guidelines and also took into account universally accepted democratic principles.[17]

Although not involved in the nitty-gritty of constitutional negotiations, Mandela kept watch over the process to preclude any deviation from the ANC line. Always on hand to break deadlocks, Mandela was informed by two principles, one of process — that the negotiations should be inclusive and ensure public participation; and the other of substance — that the exercise should produce a fully democratic constitution.

The Record of Understanding signed between the ANC and the National Party on 26 November 1992 opened the way for a two-stage process; the first stage, a multiparty negotiating forum, produced thirty-four principles, which were enacted as part of the interim constitution by the National Party government. This provided for the election of a parliament in terms of proportional representation of parties on the basis of universal suffrage. This in turn would sit as a Constitutional Assembly that would draw up a draft final constitution. The Constitutional Court, itself established by the interim constitution, would have to certify that the new draft constitution conformed with the thirty-four principles before it could become law.

While the multiparty forum negotiated the interim constitution, the final constitution was drafted by representatives of the citizenry who were present in the Constitutional Assembly in proportion to the number of votes their parties received in the 1994 election. In contrast to the first stage, there was also direct public participation, including submissions from citizens both in writing and in 'listening' forums in villages, towns and communities.[18]

Valli Moosa remembers that Mandela was very focused on certain issues. 'One of them,' he says, 'was majority rule.'

We would come up with proportional representation, nine provinces, two chambers of Parliament, a Senate and National Assembly . . . [and] a Council of Provinces, and he would always ask the question, 'How does this measure up to the need for majority rule? In what way is this standard majority rule?' He kept an eagle eye on that; he didn't want anything that was going to dilute the will of the majority and result in the elections of organs of power that were not in conformity with the will of the electorate . . . So, the idea of some kind of minority protection, minority rights, special privileges —

anything of that sort he was not going to agree to . . . The other [thing] was that he was clear in his mind that what we were trying to establish was a modern democracy, modern in the sense that it would be non-racial, non-sexist and secular and [would] embody all of the modern concepts and human rights.[19]

His erstwhile deputy, Thabo Mbeki, recalls that Mandela was always present at decisive moments, as much in the drafting of the final constitution as the interim one. 'On the issues which our negotiators raised with me, like property rights, the right to strike, the lockout and those issues, they would come to me and say, "Look, we're having problems about this thing," and then, indeed, Madiba would come into those discussions.'[20]

That Mandela made fewer, though decisive, interventions during the drafting of the final constitution was due in no small measure to matters having been settled in the interim phase and the thorough and intensive process of the Constitutional Assembly. Chaired by the ANC's Cyril Ramaphosa with the National Party's Leon Wessels as his deputy, the Constitutional Assembly involved the whole of Parliament — 400 members of the National Assembly and 90 members of the National Council of Provinces. It was not always straightforward. Ramaphosa remembers some of the difficulties:

> There were moments in negotiating the final constitution, particularly when it was quite clear that De Klerk was getting cold feet about completely agreeing to the final provisions. Madiba would take him on and he was very good at moments like that. We knew that at any moment of deadlock we could rely on Madiba to unlock it. We would push all the difficult issues up to him to hammer them home and to get our position won and confirmed. Madiba was a resourceful leader, and he was knowledgeable and he kept himself abreast with developments, and he wanted to be briefed on a continuous basis.[21]

There was, however, a shadow hanging over the creation of the new constitution. As far back as the mid-1980s, the IFP had either been violently opposed or simply obstructive towards the struggle to bring in a new constitutional dispensation. Recently it had 'flirted with the right wing, hoping to secure special powers and privileges for KwaZulu-Natal'.[22] Rather than participate in the Constitutional Assembly on the same basis as other parties, the IFP demanded international mediation and staged a walkout during Mandela's State of the Nation Address in 1995, deploying a welter of tactics to bolster its stance.

A visibly irritated Mandela characterised the IFP's approach as an attempt 'to assert a status in the constitution-making process, which is far above the support they got in the elections for the Constitutional Assembly'.[23] In a speech at once conciliatory and impassioned, Mandela challenged the IFP to return to Parliament. He said:

'We strongly disapprove of this action. Because it is here in these chambers where the blast furnace of policy formulation is located. It is here, that ideas should be pitted against one another and differences ironed out . . .

'We disapprove of this behaviour from the point of view also of the interests of the country as a whole; it does not reinforce confidence on the part of our people and the international community in the capacity of leaders to use democratic institutions to resolve differences. But our concern goes particularly to those who voted the IFP into these institutions.

'In this context, I wish to address them directly:

'You elected these IFP representatives to articulate your interests and pursue what you hold dear to your hearts. You did so also because you were convinced that they are not cowards who would exit from these hallowed chambers at the slightest hint of a problem. You had confidence that they would stand ground in the National Assembly and the Senate and, within the rules, assert your point of view.

'None of the problems they have raised will be resolved by means of walk-outs. It is your responsibility to call them to order. In the tradition of Shaka, Makhanda, Cetshwayo, Moshoeshoe, Ramabulana, Sekhukhune and Nghunghunyana, send them back to come and slog it out here in parliament and not to run away!*

'Let me once more reiterate the principles which guide the ANC's approach to the issue of international mediation, which has been raised, ostensibly, as the reason for this irrational behaviour.

'Firstly, the ANC has stated over and over again that it is committed to the agreement, which was reached on 19 April 1994. It is precisely for this reason that a sub-committee was formed to look into the matter.

'Secondly, sheer logic tells us that to invite any eminent persons to undertake this task requires that there should be clear terms of reference. This is precisely what the tri-partite sub-committee was discussing.

* Kings and political leaders who shaped the respective isiZulu, isiXhosa, Sesotho, Tshivenda, Sepedi and Xitsonga language groups and were instrumental in their rise to nationhood in the 1800s. Sekhukhune — see People, Places and Events.

'Thirdly, we are examining any steps that might be needed to deal with the issue. On the part of the ANC, we will delegate Deputy President Mbeki to take this matter up as soon as he returns from his trip abroad. In the meantime, I will this afternoon meet Chief Buthelezi at Genadendal in order to explore possible solutions to this problem.

'Fourthly, the ANC — and I believe other rational parties — would not want to be party to an approach that seeks to treat a matter pertaining to the King and Kingdom of KwaZulu-Natal as if the King did not exist. Neither would we accept attempts to arrogate to any political party the right to speak on behalf of any king or kingdom.

'Let me however make one issue very clear. While we do recognise the right of people to undertake any action within the limits of the law; while we are committed to political solutions to this problem; we cannot and must not, as a nation and as a government, allow threats and the actual perpetration of violence to go unchallenged.

'We are confident that South Africans of all political persuasions, including the media, will support the right of government to carry out its obligations to the nation as prescribed in the constitution; that they shall not approach this matter in a manner that encourages irresponsibility, lawlessness and black-mail.'[24]

Mandela's tough speech, aimed more at the rank and file of the IFP than its leaders — and which must have enormously riled Buthelezi and his lieutenants — was also for the ANC itself. The ANC was not blind to Mandela's strivings, and it rankled that, when they were so close to resolving a historic problem, Buthelezi and the IFP would put up these hurdles.

But if others in his camp were frustrated, Mandela was doggedly willing to continue. He met with Buthelezi twice to try to convince the IFP to return to the Constitutional Assembly. But he was unsuccessful on both occasions. In the end there was no international mediation. It was like a football match that ends in a goalless muddle, with the last whistle blown long after the referee has left the pitch. Moreover, the Zulu king, in whose name the Constitutional Assembly had been repudiated, had lost interest, having himself now fallen out with his erstwhile sponsor, Buthelezi.

Unlike the IFP, the National Party pursued its objectives through the agreed process. It held out right to the end on a number of issues, requiring Mandela to use his persuasive skills to end the deadlock and maintain the ANC's positions. In a replay of the scenario in which Mandela and De Klerk had met to iron out sticking points in the final days of the negotiations before the elections, they now met to undo the logjams before the deadline for completing the draft of the new constitution. They worked hard, late into the night, alternating between De Klerk's office in the Union Buildings and Mandela's official residence in Pretoria. Some issues, which could not be completed within the required time, were left for the Constitutional Court's certification process.[25]

Despite his steadfast leadership, Mandela always kept an open mind and would himself yield to persuasive argument. For instance, he would have preferred to keep the four existing provinces rather than split them into nine based on the economic regions defined by the Development Bank of Southern Africa.* Nonetheless, the ANC agreed to the

* The four original divisions from 1910 to 1994 were Natal, Transvaal, Orange Free State and the Cape of Good Hope and ten fragmentary homelands scattered throughout the country. The new provinces are KwaZulu-Natal, Eastern Cape, Western Cape, Limpopo, Mpumalanga, Northern Cape, Free State, Northwest and Gauteng. See the map on page 684. Originally set up to perform a broad economic development function within the homeland constitutional dispensation that prevailed at the time, the Development Bank of Southern Africa was reconstituted in 1994 as a development finance institution. It promotes economic development and growth, human resource development and institutional capac-

division, albeit with slight modifications.

At the end of the two years allocated to drafting the new constitution, the negotiations, deadlocks and interventions were finally over. On 8 May 1996, heaving a collective sigh of relief, the Constitutional Assembly adopted the draft finalised in the wee hours of the morning by Parliament's Constitutional Committee. Mandela welcomed it in an address that touched on both substance and process.

'The brief seconds when the majority of honourable members quietly assented to the new basic law of the land have captured, in a fleeting moment, the centuries of history that the South African people have endured in search of a better future.

'As one, you the representatives of the overwhelming majority of South Africans, have given voice to the yearning of millions.

'And so it has come to pass that South Africa today undergoes her rebirth, cleansed of a horrible past, matured from a tentative beginning, and reaching to the future with

---

ity building by mobilising financial and other resources from the national and international private and public sectors for sustainable development projects and programmes in South Africa and the wider African continent.

confidence.

'The nation teetered on a knife edge over the past few days, with reports of intractable deadlocks and an abyss in waiting. This was to be expected, given the difficult issues we were dealing with, and given the tight negotiating deadlines. But aren't South Africans a wonderful people, to whom the words "deadlock" and "miracle" have come to nestle in comfortable proximity; and alternately, to grip the national imagination like a plague!

'Be that as it may, we dare not, in the midst of the excitement of last-minute solutions, forget the magnitude of the achievement we celebrate today. For, beyond these issues, lies a fundamental sea change in South Africa's body politic that this historic moment symbolises.

'Long before the gruelling sessions of the final moments, it had been agreed that, once and for all, South Africa will have a democratic constitution based on that universal principle of democratic majority rule. Today, we formalise this consensus. As such, our nation takes the historic step beyond the transitory arrangements, which obliged its representatives, by dint of law, to work together across the racial and political divide.

'Now it is universally acknowledged that unity and reconciliation are written in the hearts of millions of South Africans. They are an indelible principle of our founding pledge.

They are the glowing fire of our new patriotism. They shall remain the condition for reconstruction and development, in as much as reconstruction and development will depend on unity and reconciliation.'

As was often the case, Mandela was alive to the reality of the average person on the street, whose strivings and contributions normally went unacknowledged while those in authority basked in rites of self-congratulation. He therefore commended 'the active participation of the people in the drafting of the new constitution [which] . . . broke new ground in ways of engaging society in the process of legislation . . . [and which] reinvigorated civil society in a manner that no other process in recent times has done'.

He pointed out the presence in the public gallery of a cross section 'of civil society, which made their inputs into the process: the legal fraternity, women, local communities, traditional structures, and leaders of sectors dealing with business, labour, land issues, the media, arts and culture, youth, the disabled, children's rights, and many more.

'Beyond those present are the millions who wrote letters and took part in public forums: from the policeman in a charge office in the furthest corner of the Northern Province, to prisoners getting together to discuss clauses, and to residents of Peddie in the Eastern Cape who continued with their meeting in pouring rain to debate the role of traditional leaders.'

Courteous to a fault, Mandela thanked them all — from the chairperson and his deputy, to the management committees in which all the parties were represented, and the staff — 'for their dedication and drive to ensure that we attain this historic moment'. In the same vein, he also thanked the representatives of the international community who had seen the process through, adding that 'your contributions and your force of example provided the fountain from which we drank with relish.'

The one principle that had influenced the ANC's approach in the negotiations, Mandela stated, now departing from his written speech, was that, eventually, 'there should be neither winners nor losers', but that 'South Africa as a whole must be the winner'. This was a commitment from the ANC to avoid any abuse of its majority that might reduce the other parties in the Government of National Unity to 'mere rubber stamps'. Having said that, Mandela warned that 'everybody will understand that we have a commitment and a mandate from the overwhelming majority of our people in this country to transform South Africa from an apartheid state to a non-racial state, to address the question of joblessness and homelessness, to build all the facilities that have been enjoyed for centuries by a tiny minority. We have that commitment and we are determined to ensure that all the people of South Africa live a dignified life in which there is no poverty, no illiteracy, no ignorance and no disease. That is our commitment. We are determined to honour that pledge, and anybody who tries to block us from attaining that objective of carrying out our mandate is like a voice crying out in the wilderness.'

He ended with a note of caution: 'We are dealing with a situation in which, when one talks to Whites, they think that only Whites exist in this country, and they look at problems from the point of view of Whites. They forget about Blacks, namely Coloured, Africans and Indians. That is one side of the problem. However, we have another problem. When one talks to Africans, Coloureds and Indians, they make exactly the same mistake. They think that the Whites in this country do not exist. They think that we have brought about this transformation by defeating the White minority and that we're dealing with a community that is now lying prostrate on the ground, begging for mercy, to whom we can dictate. Both tendencies are wrong. We want men and women who are committed to our mandate, but who can rise above their ethnic groups and think of South Africa as a whole.

'We have now adopted this constitution . . . Every day I go to bed feeling strong and hopeful because I can see new leaders of thought emerging, leaders who are the hope of the future.'[26]

After Parliament had amended the few remaining inconsistencies in the newly created constitution, as directed by the Constitutional Court, President Mandela gave it legal force at a public signing ceremony at Sharpeville on 10 December 1996. The venue was chosen carefully, to symbolise the restoration of rights and dignity at the very scene of the Sharpeville Massacre, where on 21 March 1960, police shot and killed sixty-nine and wounded and maimed one hundred and seventy-six anti-pass demonstrators; the entry wounds in the backs of the victims showed that they had been in flight when shot.

In a country where, traditionally, the laws were crafted for the preservation of white interests, and those of the black majority were a mere afterthought, it was important that a new judiciary emerged out of the embers of the past. And this had to be prominent and vibrant in the execution of its mandate to win back a sceptical constituency. The establishment of a Judicial Service Commission (JSC), as human rights lawyer George Bizos has said, was a strong reaction to apartheid policies.*[27] The pervasive wariness coupled

* George Bizos — see People, Places and Events.

292

with hostility to the law among the black population was evocative of a poem called 'Justice' by Langston Hughes, one of the luminaries of the Harlem Renaissance, which reads:

That Justice is a blind goddess
Is a thing to which we black are wise:
Her bandage hides two festering sores
That once perhaps were eyes.[28]

The judiciary, then, had to unburden itself of the baggage of the past and ensure that Lady Justice was truly impartial. In spite of the pressure to make unjust judgments, some of the officers of the court — white senior counsel practising at the Bar and appointed through ministerial fiat — 'had a strong sense of justice'.[29] These were among the candidates interviewed by the JSC, which subsequently provided President Mandela with a list from which he would select judges of the Constitutional Court. That selection was informed by the Constitution, which stipulated 'the need for the judiciary to reflect broadly the racial and gender composition of South Africa'.[30]

Perhaps inevitably, though, the spectre of race hovered above every interview with prospective judges at the Civic Theatre in Johannesburg. But the creation of the JSC had laid the ground for the establishment of a constitutional state, which would rely on statutory bodies set up to protect democracy and ensure openness of debate and inclusivity. The effects were immediately noticeable. In his memoir, George Bizos recalls a moment of protest during the hearings: 'Students from nearby Wits university gathered at the entrance with placards protesting against two professors of law who were candidates for the court, but who were involved in a dispute on the campus. Chief Justice Corbett met the students and received their memorandum, then invited them into the hearings. Without their posters, but won over by his non-confrontational manner, the students complied, entered the room in a dignified manner and quietly followed proceedings.'[31]

The inauguration of the Constitutional Court in February 1995 fulfilled Mandela's dream of constitutionalism. In his speech, he stressed what that dream meant in reality:

'Constitutionalism means that no office and no institution can be higher than the law. The highest and the most humble in the land, all, without exception, owe allegiance to the same document, the same principles. It does not matter whether you are black or white, male or female, young or old; whether you speak Setswana or Afrikaans; whether you're rich or poor or ride in a smart new car or walk barefoot; whether you wear a uniform or are locked up in a cell. We all have certain basic rights, and those fundamental rights are set out in the Constitution.

'The authority of government comes from the people through the Constitution. Your tasks and responsibilities, as well as your power, come to you from the people through the Constitution. The people speak through the Constitution. The Constitution enables the multiple voices of the people to be heard in an organised, articulate, meaningful and principled manner. We trust that you will find the means through your judgments to speak directly to the people.

'You are a new court in every way. The process whereby you were selected was new. When we look at you, we see for the first time the many dimensions of our rich and varied country. We see a multiplicity of backgrounds and life experiences. Your tasks are new. Your powers are new. We hope that, without abandoning the many sterling virtues of legal tradition, you will find a new way of expressing the great truths of your calling. You will be dealing with the rights of millions of ordinary people. The Constitution, which you will be serving, is the product of their sacrifice and belief. I am sure that I am speaking for all of them when I say that the basic reasons for your decisions should be spelt out in a language that all can understand.'[32]

The leading jurists of Mandela's presidency had earned respect as defenders of justice before the advent of democracy. Michael Corbett, the first Chief Justice of democratic South Africa, was not meeting Mandela for the first time when he administered the oath at the president's inauguration in May 1994. At a state banquet marking Corbett's retirement two years later, Mandela took the opportunity to recount the circumstances of their meeting:

'I first met Michael Corbett in unpromising circumstances some twenty-five years ago,' he said. 'I was a prisoner for life. He was a junior judge on a prison visit to Robben Island.

'There was a particularly unpleasant conflict between warders and prisoners, arising from a brutal beating, and I was the prisoners' spokesman.

'I had no particular expectations of being believed or even listened to. The Commanding Officer tried to intimidate me. But not only did this young judge and his colleagues listen carefully to what I had to say. In my presence, Judge Corbett turned to the Commanding Officer and the Commissioner of Prisons, and protested sharply to the Commissioner over the behaviour of the Commanding Officer. Such courage and independence were rare.'

In his studies for his law degree in prison, Mandela 'came from time to time upon the judgments of Michael Corbett. Their incisiveness reminded me of my earlier encounter with him. So did his dissent in 1979 in the case brought against the Minister of Prisons by my co-accused in the Rivonia Trial, Denis Goldberg.* Alone of the five Judges of Appeal, Michael Corbett held that the prison authorities were not entitled to apply the policy depriving prisoners of all access to news.'

This judgment, Mandela said, was 'scholarly, meticulous and uncompromising in the primacy it gave to important rights . . .

'It is to such actions by good men and women, like Michael Corbett, in every part of our society and of every political persuasion, that we owe our successful transition to democracy. One of the strengths of the new nation, which we are building, is that, by removing the causes of tension and conflict, it creates the space for such people to emerge and play their rightful role. It is in such conditions that the best that is in all of us can flourish. These are the circumstances that are producing a new generation of leaders for a prosperous and just society, at peace with itself.'[33]

In 1994, Mandela appointed Arthur Chaskalson, part of the defence team in the Rivonia Trial and a member of the ANC Constitutional Committee, as the first president of

* Denis Goldberg — see People, Places and Events.

the Constitutional Court. Judge Ismail Mohamed succeeded Michael Corbett as Chief Justice in 1996. Characterised by Mandela as a man for all seasons, the new Chief Justice had been presented with a Byzantine set of measures by the apartheid state to prevent him from practising in various parts of the country.

'In a career of some thirty-five years as an advocate,' Mandela said, 'Ismail Mohamed appeared in numerous trials on behalf of some of the leading figures in the liberation struggle. Like other members of the Johannesburg Bar . . . he helped lead the challenge in the courts to the injustice of apartheid. Because of his reputation for impartiality and firmness, he was accepted as co-chairperson of the multiparty constitutional negotiations . . . He warned us politicians gathered at those negotiations that, as judges, they would fearlessly uphold the Constitution.'

He made good on his threat, Mandela said. When Mandela was cited as first respondent in the case arising out of a constitutional challenge to proclamations Mandela had issued under a section of the Local Government Transition Act, Justice Mohamed and the majority of the Constitutional Court justices struck it down. In Mandela's account, they had stated 'that under our new constitutional dispensation, Parliament does not have supreme authority but is subject to our basic and supreme law, the Constitution. Our parliament, they reminded us, could not, even if it so willed, abdicate its responsibility as the lawmaker.'[34]

Mandela writes, 'All these considerations, as important as they may be, should never be allowed to undermine our democratic Constitution which guarantees unqualified citizenship rights to all South Africans, irrespective of the ethnic group to which they belong. It has a Bill of Rights, to which a citizen can rely if any of his or her rights are threatened or violated. All of us, without exception, are called upon to respect that Constitution.

'There are statutory bodies manned by strong and well qualified public figures who are totally independent of the government. They ensure that the Constitution and its provisions are respected by all citizens, irrespective of their position in government or society.

'They are the Public Protector, National Director of Public Prosecutions, the Auditor General, the Human Rights Commission, the Truth and Reconciliation Commission and the Constitutional Court.'*

'The apartheid regime had put law and

* The statutory bodies also include the Commission for Gender Equality, Independent Electoral Commission and the Independent Broadcasting Authority.

order in disrepute. Human rights were ruthlessly suppressed. There was detention without trial, torture and murder of political activists, open vilification of Appeal Court judges who were independent and gave judgments against the regime, and the packing of the judiciary with conservative and pliant lawyers. The police, especially the security branch, were a law unto themselves. Because of this crude practice, and out of my own convictions, I exploited every opportunity to promote respect for law and order and for the judiciary.'[35]

While Mandela had the highest regard for the Constitution and personally embodied the qualities required for an ethical and courageous leadership style, he was mindful of the legacy of the past, especially when it concerned the judiciary. It was in the courts, when he ran a legal business with his partner, Tambo, in downtown Johannesburg, that he had seen abject human suffering and humiliation.

'The legal profession and the judiciary in South Africa,' he said at a banquet of the General Council of the Bar of South Africa in 2000, 'have no perfect past. There have been failures and lost opportunities, institutional and individual. But it is also true that there have been women and men among South Africa's lawyers, including its judges and advocates, who have been committed to the rule of law and to the achievement of a constitutional democracy. Some have paid a high price for this.

'I believe that people of this kind should be honoured and I am proud to join you tonight to do so. The Bar and the Bench are institutions which are not beyond criticism, but criticism serves no purpose if it is purely destructive and does not acknowledge the dedicated contributions which have been made. These have been made even at the worst times in our history.

'I am glad to hear of the Bar's own attempts to transform its membership and, in particular, to advance legal education; I am especially glad to hear of the creation tonight of the Pius Langa scholarships named after the illustrious Deputy President of our Constitutional Court and Chancellor of the University of Natal.'[36]

The road towards the creation of a legitimate and democratic state had started a long time ago, in the forgotten years of earlier struggles, and had wreaked havoc with the lives of millions. For Mandela, it was an achievement of a task he had set for himself as far back as May 1961. Albie Sachs — a veteran jurist and one of the first twelve judges of the Constitutional Court — reminisces about the period: 'Nelson Mandela had gone underground and called for a general strike. Declaring that the majority of the people had not been consulted about South Africa becoming a Republic outside of the Commonwealth, he had combined a stay-away call with the demand that a national convention be held to draft a new constitution.'[37]

Thirty-five years later, the law, once a cruel instrument for exclusion and oppression, was finally transformed to serve all the people.

CHAPTER SEVEN:
PARLIAMENT

If, in 1994, South Africa's 39 million citizens had been subjected to a comprehensive survey about their impressions of Parliament, it is likely that there would have been as many views as there were respondents. The greatest trick pulled by the apartheid regime was fostering the perception that it revealed all, while in reality it concealed the finer, detailed workings of state machinery from the populace, leaving everyone — black and white — to deal with the effects, which were experienced to differing degrees and seemingly unconnected to the primary source. White people mostly went home satisfied with the government of the day while the black majority gnashed its collective teeth, cursing *uhulumeni* ('government' in isiZulu), the nebulous, featureless entity, much like the golem, which churned out laws that menaced their children. Now and then, the happenings in the imposing and inaccessible white buildings in the parliamentary precinct made headlines.

Generally, though, no one took a great deal of notice.

It was a different matter on 24 May 1994, when Nelson Mandela stood up to give his first State of the Nation Address.

Earlier that day, the assembled crowds had been treated to a veritable splash of colour, from the different uniforms of mounted police and military escorts to the red carpet running from the Slave Lodge to the National Assembly Chamber, artistes that included young drum majorettes from nearby schools and an *imbongi* in traditional battle dress, his stentorian praise poem for Mandela eventually drowned out by the military brass band, which was in turn quietened by the fly-past by the South African Air Force, everything eventually being sealed by the booming twenty-one-gun salute.

But the insignia of different forces, flags and pennants had nothing on the splendid attire of the members of Parliament, which had spectators gawking from the public galleries at the procession of formal dress, conservative and outré, both Western and traditional. Mandela had decreed that with the dawn of democracy, the doors of Parliament were now open to all, thus his first State of the Nation Address became a celebration for all the people of South Africa. And they were here. Inside the chamber, from the galleries, which gave them a panoramic view of the proceedings below, ordinary men and women could see all those who had been at the forefront of the creation of the new South Africa. Some of the guests who had been separated by their various roles in the struggle — an activist awkward in formal dress, compatriots who survived an ambush and lived to tell the tale, or a freshly returned exile with a foreign spouse in tow — hugged one another as their eyes shone with tears.

Mandela first acknowledged Frene Ginwala, the speaker of Parliament, and other illustrious attendees. Then, glasses flashing, he continued:

'The time will come when our nation will honour the memory of all the sons, the daughters, the mothers, the fathers, the youth and the children who, by their thoughts and deeds, gave us the right to assert with pride that we are South Africans, that we are Africans and that we are citizens of the world.

'The certainties that come with age tell me that among these we shall find an Afrikaner woman who transcended a particular experience and became a South African, an African and a citizen of the world. Her name is Ingrid Jonker. She was both a poet and a South African. She was both an Afrikaner and an African. She was both an artist and a human being. In the midst of despair, she celebrated hope. Confronted by death, she asserted the beauty of life. In the dark days when all seemed hopeless in our country, when many refused to hear her resonant voice, she took her own life.

'To her and others like her, we owe a debt to life itself. To her and others like her, we owe a commitment to the poor, the oppressed, the wretched and the despised. In the aftermath of the massacre at the anti-pass demonstration in Sharpeville she wrote that:

The child is not dead
the child lifts his fists against his mother
who shouts Afrika . . .

The child is not dead
not at Langa nor at Nyanga
nor at Orlando nor at Sharpeville
nor at the police post at Philippi
where he lies with a bullet through his
    brain . . .

the child is present at all assemblies and
    law-giving
the child peers through the windows of
    houses and into the hearts of mothers
this child who only wanted to play in the
    sun at Nyanga is everywhere
the child grown to a man treks through all
    Afrika
the child grown to a giant journeys over the
    whole world

Without a pass[1]

'And in this glorious vision she instructs that our endeavours must be about the liberation of the woman, the emancipation of the man and the liberty of the child.'[2]

As powerful and resonant as the words might have been, it was still the case that South Africa's first democratically elected parliament occupied the same buildings as the parliament of apartheid, where laws that had given rise to untold misery were enacted. Some of these considerations had prompted some traditional healers to ask for permission to ritually cleanse the chamber, a spiritual requirement that was instead achieved when Parliament held interfaith prayer services.

By dint of hard work, however, Mandela shaped Parliament into an institution that was oriented by the wishes of the people, the heartbeat of the Constitution. His vision was for a parliament that could enable a profound transformation of society and become a pre-eminent space for public debate. It was to be a place for all the people of South Africa, even those who might have been unwilling to embrace it at the beginning. Ginwala remembers Mandela telling her that the biggest challenge was that 'our people are not used to being in Parliament; the public is not used to Parliament, so we must make sure that everybody, every political party, every South

African, thinks it is their Parliament'.[3]

But if Parliament enacted laws, it did so under the constraints of a sovereign constitution, with the Constitutional Court being the final arbiter — a departure from the apartheid era when Parliament made oppressive laws at will. Even when Parliament sat to draw up the final constitution, its work had to be certified by the Constitutional Court. Cooperation between the parties in the legislature depended, awkwardly, on the 'spirit of national unity' alone rather than constitutional prescription. And although there had been changes to the institution, the ANC still faced hurdles, as it had no technical experience of parliamentary machinery, government or running the economy, which the opposition and the previous administration had in abundance.

However, what the four hundred-odd new MPs did have in common was legitimacy. Each and every one of them had been elected by proportional representation, which replaced the segregated white, coloured and Indian chambers with a single National Assembly that represented all South Africans. Moreover, the system of proportional representation meant that Parliament became a truer microcosm of the country's diversity than any other electoral system. It also spoke to the ANC's concerns about a winner-takes-all or first-past-the-post approach, which

Mandela had favoured until he was persuaded otherwise in discussions with both Essop Pahad and Penuell Maduna. The two men had been members of the ANC team drafting the part of the interim constitution that pertained to issues of representation and they were now drafting the final constitution. Pahad recalls:

We said, 'We want to discuss this matter with you.' He said, 'I know, talk.' So we took him through why we thought that the proportional system is the fairest in the world. He listened and asked many questions about accountability and so on. We said, 'If you go for another system, we can get into a two-party system or, at best, a three-party system and we're going to exclude parties like the PAC, whereas the proportional system is going to allow greater representation of parties in Parliament.' He listened and asked questions and at the end said, 'All right, I agree, but it doesn't mean that this must be forever.' We said, 'Yes, it is left open in the constitution for us to change the system as long as it is broadly proportional.'[4]

Having assembled an electoral college, which chose Mandela to be the country's president, the new National Assembly's next step was to choose its speaker and deputy speaker. Given the importance of these positions, the ANC leadership, especially Mandela himself, and the parliamentary caucus, had to get involved.

Mandela writes, 'An equally contentious question was the election of the Speaker for the National Assembly. Although the ANC had long accepted the principle of gender equality without qualification, actual practice still lagged far behind principle.

'Among my staff as ANC President, there were three women all strong, independent, well informed and outspoken. They brooked no form of chauvinism, either from me or from my comrades. No wonder they came to be known as the three witches.

'They were Barbara Masekela, who later became our Ambassador to France, Jessie Duarte, our Ambassador to Mozambique, and Frene Ginwala. We had numerous discussions on a wide variety of issues. All of them were impressive and hard-working and they helped to purge my system of all contempt for women. I earmarked Frene for the position of Speaker of the National Assembly.

'There was dead silence from my comrades when I first shared the secret with them. I suspected that the fact that I was proposing a female comrade, at that time, irrespective of her qualifications, didn't go down well to those comrades, the overwhelming majority of whom were males.

'There had also been some differences, and even infighting, among exiles abroad, which were still evident in their work inside the country. I, however, made it clear to all concerned that I would tolerate no unprincipled objection to a competent comrade from an organisation, which had been entrusted with the awesome task of governing the wealthiest and most developed country on the African continent. I virtually ordered that every ANC parliamentarian should vote for her as Speaker.

'The other difficulty came from Frene herself. She telephoned me one morning and demanded to know why there were so few women in the Cabinet. In replying to her, I added that I would ensure that she became the Speaker. She vehemently protested that she was not talking about herself; she was raising a general issue, which affected all women.

'As the debate between us was heating, I asked her pointedly to choose between accepting or rejecting my offer. In our discussions, I have always been consoled by the knowledge that she had more respect for my grey hair than for me in person. She paused a bit and then said she would think about the matter. I was relieved when she later agreed to serve.

'Her decision was a landmark as it was the first occasion in our history for a woman to occupy that powerful position in our national legislature. It was a double victory since the deputy speaker was also a confident and able woman, Baleka Mbete-Kgositsile.

'The common view among parliamentarians from all sides of the House is that she [Ginwala] has acquitted herself well without any previous training or experience in this regard. She is non-partisan and often rebukes members for unparliamentary behaviour, irrespective of the political affiliation of the offender.

'Her superb performance and mastery of the functions of her office has not only enhanced respect and support across the political divide. Her remarkable achievement and that of her female colleagues in the House, has clearly demonstrated that the battle for gender equality is being won.

'This rare achievement was rewarded by parliament when she was unanimously re-elected for another five years.'[5]

In line with Mandela's sentiments — that this should be a people's parliament — the arrangement of the MPs' seating was such that each party's representatives, at least, would be visible to the public on television. Committee meetings were opened to the press, and the far-reaching public outreach programmes to acquaint society with the ins and outs of the legislature deepened mutual trust and candour between the people and the institution. This was a counter-intuitive attitude for anyone, party or leadership, assuming power, even in mature democracies, where the temptation is to control information. The whole project of apartheid was to leave black people, from the cradle to the grave, wallowing in ignorance; white people, who might have imagined that they had escaped this fate, were simply deluded, as they, too, had been lied to.

In determining to bring sanity to the country and debunk the lies bandied with alarming fluency from as far back as 1652, Mandela sometimes sounded as if he were trying to convince himself about the rightness of ensuring openness in lawmaking. For example, in his second State of the Nation Address, he said, 'We can therefore claim with justification that such legislation, as has been approved, is representative of the will of the people. It therefore enjoys a degree of legitimacy and enforceability, which all previous laws could never have.'[6]

The original parliament building in Cape Town was built in 1884, in a neoclassical design that incorporated features of Cape Dutch architecture. A heritage site, Parliament housed over four thousand works of art, some of them priceless artworks and some dating back to the seventeenth century. But despite their historical importance and value, the collection did not represent all the people and art of South Africa.

When Parliament decided to remove from its buildings portraits and other works of art from the apartheid era, Mandela supported the action. He said that the decision 'was taken after extensive deliberations within Parliament, and it was agreed to by all political parties. The new democratic Parliament should reflect the image of an inclusive South Africa, in all its diversity. This is an important component of nation-building and reconciliation.'[7]

Mandela paid respect to Parliament in other ways too. Keenly aware of the symbolism of dress, he insisted on wearing a suit to Parliament, in contrast to his usual attire of colourful Madiba shirts. Indeed he was always fastidious about dress — and routine generally. His wife, Graça Machel, relates how he'd wake up every morning to do his exercises, fold his pyjamas and make up his bed until he had to yield to the benign tyranny of Xoliswa Ndoyiya, a senior staff member at their Houghton home. 'He was very clean and tidy,' Machel says. 'You just didn't throw things in his presence. Where he is, everything has got to be orderly . . . impeccably clean. Even the way he would dress, he takes his time to dress; he'd look at himself [in the mirror] and make sure he is perfect.'[8] He combined an unbending practicality with old-world courtesy, which he also expected of others, especially his colleagues.

Ginwala once asked him why he always came to Parliament in a suit when he was already known for his trademark colourful shirts. 'He put on his dignified face,' Frene says, 'and said, "Frene, Parliament represents the people, I have to respect it, and, so, I always wear the suit." '[9]

He was not simply concerned with appearances. He also worried about the inconsistent attendance of some MPs and ministers, both because they were needed in the House as elected representatives and to ensure a quorum was achieved during debates. Sometimes snap debates called by the opposition caught the ANC flat-footed.[10] When this was raised by the Reverend Makhenkesi Stofile, the first ANC chief whip, Mandela agreed to write to ministers about it, but cautioned, 'You must find a way of making sure that you don't put too much of a burden on them because they do have other work.'[11]

Mandela was seventy-five when he became president, and he was not an MP. Parliamentary question time was often boisterous and highly partisan. There was therefore an informal agreement — in deference to his age and status, and the pressures of his programme in the early years of transition — that he should be exempt from answering questions in Parliament.[12]

Instead, Mandela was invited to the ANC

caucus meetings. He attended quite frequently at first, discussing issues with the parliamentary leadership and senior members of the movement, including Ginwala; Govan Mbeki, who was senate deputy president; Stofile, the chief whip; and Mendi Msimang as the caucus chair. He also frequently sounded out his close colleagues and former prison mates, ensuring that their insights were factored into caucus meeting discussions.[13]

Notes Mandela wrote for a caucus meeting in February 1996, almost two years into the new parliament, exemplify his interventions. He continued to be concerned about ANC attendance and conduct in Parliament.[14] He was also unhappy about the tensions between the ANC and other parties arising from the fact that the Government of National Unity's multiparty ethos was not always replicated in Parliament:[15]

1. Have missed several meetings of this caucus due to other engagements I could not avoid.
Caucus is the main engine for our parliamentary work; and if we're going to carry out the mandate of our people effectively, duty of all of us to attend.
Have arranged with my office to arrange my engagements in such a way that I will be able to attend.

2. Must also try to be in close contact with the portfolio committees.
3. Whips to give me report of attendance at the end of every month. Implications of failure to attend. Matter discussed by . . . [illegible]. Utmost discipline crucial. Implications of lack of discipline.
4. Section 43 [concerned with the powers of provinces] under discussion.
5. Did not win through military victory where we dictate terms to a conquered army.
6. Work done — statutory committees result of our hard work.[16]

Mandela's personal notes for meetings show his preoccupation with discipline — especially collective discipline — loyalty and honesty. In one, he observes that the 'organisation has gone through many challenges', referring to some of the upheavals, including the ousting of the so-called Africanists in the fifties and the Group of Eight in the seventies.* These 'were popular in the ANC — but

* These were the dissenting voices in the ANC who broke away to form the PAC. Eight senior ANC leaders, the Group of Eight, were expelled from the ANC for their opposition to white members of the Communist Party, whom they saw as diluting the nationalist agenda of the ANC.

once out it was easy to deal with them'. Then, at the head of a list of affirmations, mnemonics and admonitions to self as well as to an imaginary audience, Mandela remarks that the 'secret is that our struggle is a principled struggle'.[17]

There are a few more such notes, all evocative, speaking to the mindset of a man for whom the democracy was an ideal for which he was prepared to die. To the uninitiated, Mandela's scribbled notes might come across as folksy aphorisms, words a parent might impart to a troubled teenager — 'Never to wash dirty linen in public' or 'Think through brain, not blood' — but they were informed by absolute seriousness. One, reading, 'Let leaders decide who takes part in debate', related to Mandela's determination to pay attention to the work of parliamentary portfolio committees.[18] In comparison to the old apartheid committee system, where, as an observer put it, 'one clerk served five committees that met in secret to rubber stamp the executive's laws and policies', the democratic committees 'had teeth to hold the executive accountable. They had the authority to receive evidence and summon witnesses and facilitate public participation in the parliamentary process.'[19] There was therefore a need for a balancing mechanism for ministers, part of the very executive that had to be held in check, and their participation in

318

portfolio committees where they were part of the legislature. Mandela thus ensured that the poachers took their obligations as gamekeepers seriously.

In January 1996 there was a heated exchange at a hearing of the Portfolio Committee on Defence on legislation relating to integration of the armed forces. The proposed legislation included a suggestion that English be the sole language used within the integrated force. The defence force head, General Georg Meiring, complained to Mandela about the incident. At the next caucus meeting, Mandela reprimanded ANC members of the committee for proposing a policy, which, he said, ran counter to the reconciliation efforts of the ANC and the GNU.[20]

Another issue that threw a harsh spotlight on the relation between the executive and committees concerned a state-sponsored musical, *Sarafina II,* about AIDS prevention, which quickly became a cause célèbre. The story of the musical and the splurging of state monies, together with an incoherent explanation from the Ministry of Health as to the source of funding, itself became a drama that Mandela certainly didn't need. Aware of the intense public interest in the matter, he was keen that it be handled judiciously. Having explained the merits of the project, the health minister, Nkosazana Dlamini-Zuma, offered to resign if it transpired that she had done wrong. Mandela declined her offer. Some, like Ahmed Kathrada — as has been noted earlier — cited Mandela's loyalty as both his weakness and his strength. But despite the exoneration of Minister Dlamini-Zuma from financial liability by the Office of the Public Protector, the incident did damage Mandela's reputation, leading elements of the media at home and abroad to editorialise about the creep of corruption during his watch.

If he knew what was being said, Mandela never let anything deter him from his course, guided by what he had learnt from Sophocles — 'What people believe prevails over the truth'.[21] When considering the character Mandela played in a performance of *Antigone* on Robben Island, the renowned South African author André Brink commented that, 'although, like his fellow actors, he primarily identified with Antigone, he brought to the interpretation of Creon what must have been, in retrospect, a peculiar insight: "Of course you cannot know a man completely, his character, his principles, sense of judgment, not till he's shown his colour, ruling the people, making laws. Experience, there's the test." '[22]

Now the stage was here in the new chamber where, almost fourteen kilometres from the Island, issues of national importance were put before Parliament in the form of special debates or statements. Among these were the dissolution of the Reconstruction and Development Programme office, the Constitutional Assembly's adoption of the Constitution, and the report of the Truth and Reconciliation Commission.

No single issue would arouse as much controversy as the process Mandela instigated of unearthing and confronting the institutionally sanctioned evil of the past through the Truth and Reconciliation Commission. Established by an Act of Parliament in 1995, the TRC's first hearings into South Africa's inglorious past started in April 1996 in East London, in the Eastern Cape, the country's poorest province. It was here that, on the second day, the chairman, Archbishop Desmond Tutu, broke down during the televised public hearing when he listened to the grim accounts by wheelchair-bound Singqokwana Malgas, a former Robben Island prisoner who'd suffered a stroke in 1989 as a result of years of torture in the hands of the security police. Malgas, who spoke with difficulty, said that, in 1963, after being arrested by the East London police and accused of being a terrorist, 'he had been tortured and "assaulted terribly" before being taken to Pretoria, charged and sentenced to twenty-two years in jail. On appeal the sentence was reduced to 14 years.'[23]

There were many such instances, typified by Malgas's horrific account, which laid bare

321

the evil of an unacknowledged past.

Even though Mandela and De Klerk wrangled for months over the commission's terms of reference, for instance, the period of the probe — with a section of the white community fearing that old wounds would be opened — the TRC did lead to the unravelling of the apartheid security apparatus and exposed its covert networks. While the five-volume final report failed to satisfy everybody — white South Africans because it felt like an officially sanctioned hatchet job and black South Africans because it hadn't gone far enough — it became an invaluable record of social history.

In June 1995, Mandela responded to a senator who had raised a question about the progress of police investigations into the killing of IFP supporters outside Shell House, the ANC's HQ in Johannesburg, in March 1994. Intending to close the matter, Mandela said he was responsible for the Shell House shootings. In fact, as later emerged during the TRC's amnesty hearings, Mandela had not ordered security to kill anyone, only to protect the building.[24] But he did what leaders should do: he took direct responsibility. With a curious mix of calmness and asperity, he tackled the issue in a speech to the Senate:

'Regarding the question of the so-called

massacre in Shell House the members of the NP have stood up on the IFP's side. This is in spite of the fact that on the day before the event, I telephoned President De Klerk, as he then was, Gen Van der Merwe and Gen Calitz. I told them that there was going to be that so-called demonstration, and that a lot of people were going to die. I asked them to put up roadblocks around Johannesburg, so as to protect lives.

'They all undertook to do so. Mr De Klerk actually interrupted me and said: "Have you told Van der Merwe about this?" and I said: "Yes, I have." He then said that he would also tell him. No roadblocks were put in place. Those people were allowed to go into the city with their weapons. By 07:00, Radio 702 had announced that Inkatha had killed thirty-two people in Soweto. By the time they came into town, we already had that information.

'They came to Shell House, past the spot where they were supposed to have the meeting. We knew why; therefore I gave instructions to our security that if they attacked the House, they must please protect it, even if they had to kill people. It was absolutely necessary for me to give that instruction.

'What is important now is that the NP and the DP [Democratic Party], which is now to the right of the NP, were not once able to say who killed the forty-five people in Johannesburg. Their sole preoccupation was the nine people who were killed in self-defence. That was the sole purpose of the point of view of the NP and the DP. They showed no concern about the forty-five other people who were killed, thus encouraging the perception that Whites do not care about Blacks.'[25]

A firestorm of public outrage greeted Mandela's statement, and the opposition called for a snap debate. When Thabo Mbeki and Sydney Mufamadi came to see him, even before they raised the matter he said, 'I know why you've come. You're diplomats. I am not a diplomat because I have spent my time fighting with warders. What should I do about my statement?'[26]

After their discussion, a special meeting of top ANC officials was called to devise a strategy and formulate a response for a parliamentary debate. Aware of the significance of the imminent debate, Mandela prepared himself. He knew, however, that the task of explaining himself would be even harder if he didn't take the media along with him. 'Finally,' he wrote, in preparation for the meeting, 'the opinion of the media is important and in some respects crucial. We must always treat it with respect; the whites have powerful weapons and propaganda, which we ignore at our peril. But we must never forget the people out there and our strategy must not ignore their feelings on this

324

subject.'[27]

What Mandela said in the snap debate was in essence a reprise of his earlier speech in the Senate, but it was accompanied by a reminder of the fundamental goals of transition, and stressed that it was imperative that there should be a national effort to achieve those goals. Shell House 'was not a bolt from the blue' he said. The marchers 'were to be directed to attack Shell House, destroy information and kill members of the leadership'. Knowing this, the ANC had alerted the authorities, who failed to take preventative action despite agreeing to do so, resulting in the deaths of more than thirty people, killed in the wake of the Inkatha rampage in Soweto.

'Needless to say,' Mandela continued, 'the surging columns on Shell House, away from the routes to their destination, the shots fired, and the fact that the few policemen deployed there decided to run away, gave credence to the information we had gathered. It is in this context, Madam Speaker, that this incident happened.'

He regretted 'the loss of life, anywhere and under any circumstances. But what parties involved in this vendetta need to pause and reflect on, is what would have happened if the intentions of these plotters had been realised, if, indeed, Shell House had been invaded, documents destroyed and ANC leaders killed!'[28]

He ended on a conciliatory note however: 'Let us therefore dedicate ourselves, in memory of all the lives lost in conflict, to working together to seek solutions to the problems which generate conflict. We must bring an end to violence. The existence of no-go areas, controlled by whatever party, is a shame to our nation. We must see to it that they no longer exist. Above all, we must save human lives.

'As long as we fail to tackle these problems, we will . . . undermine our capacity to improve the quality of life of our people, millions of whom still live in abject poverty. We will be hampered in our drive to ensure that all South Africans enjoy the climate of safety and security, which is their right.

'The nation has set itself the task of reconstruction and development, nation building and reconciliation. It expects [from] its representatives in these hallowed chambers, the seriousness of purpose and the application to duty, which success requires. It is in this spirit that we view the comments that have been made. On my part, I call on all parties to join us in working for a better life for all South Africans.'[29]

At its final sitting in 1999, Mandela reflected on the contribution made by the first democratically elected parliament. He commended the people of South Africa for having chosen 'a profoundly legal path to their revolution', noting that it 'is in the legislatures that the instruments have been fashioned to create a better life for all'. Remembering some of the bruising encounters with the committees, he said that it was in the legislature 'that oversight of government has been exercised'.[30]

Mandela was aware that, while he waxed lyrical about it, Parliament had its detractors. Sometime previously, Joseph Chiole, of the Freedom Front, had let rip against the media, which he felt misinformed the public. 'Members of Parliament,' he said, 'have been, and still are, being discredited, insulted and degraded to such an extent that member-of-Parliament bashing is now a very popular pastime in South Africa . . . Every day, in nearly every newspaper, one reads distorted stories.' Concluding his speech, Chiole said, 'The true situation in South Africa at present is that MPs are terribly frustrated by the fact that they do not have the necessary means at their disposal to render a satisfactory service to the voters and to do absolutely necessary research work as well. On the other hand — I am sorry to say this — if proposals are made by MPs, they are accused of stoking the gravy train.'[31]

Mandela said, 'Questions have been raised, we know, as to whether this House is not a carriage on the gravy train, whose passengers idle away their time at the nation's expense. To those who raise such questions, we say, "Look at the record of our Parliament during these years of freedom." '

He directed Parliament's critics to the 'one hundred laws on average that have been passed by this legislature each year'. These were laws passed so that 'the legacy of our past can be undone and put right . . .

'This,' Mandela concluded, 'is a record in which we can take pride.'[32]

CHAPTER EIGHT:
TRADITIONAL LEADERSHIP
AND DEMOCRACY

The fact that traditional African leadership played a role in the inception of the ANC is usually overlooked or, at best, subsumed by popular folklore. Nelson Mandela always recognised the historical dignitaries, some of whom were southern African royalty, who had been the delegates to the founding conference of the ANC in Bloemfontein (also called Mangaung, its ancestral Sesotho name) on 8 January 1912. In the years of exile, it had also become a traditional practice for the long-serving ANC president O. R. Tambo to use the birthday of the ANC to acknowledge the support of the international community and pledge solidarity with liberation movements worldwide. Mandela's style of leadership was to mark the anniversary by preaching unity, reprising the words of Pixley ka Isaka Seme, one of the ANC's founders and its first president. Mandela would repeat

Seme's memorable call:*

Chiefs of royal blood and gentlemen of our race, we have gathered here to consider and discuss a theme which my colleagues and I have decided to place before you. We have discovered that in the land of their birth, Africans are treated as hewers of wood and drawers of water. The white people of this country have formed what is known as the Union of South Africa — a union in which we have no voice in the making of the laws and no part in their administration. We have called you therefore to this Conference so that we can together devise ways and means of forming our national union for the purpose of creating national unity and defending our rights and privileges.[1]

As time passed, however, due largely to the machinations of, first, the colonial administrations and, later, the apartheid state, the traditional structures of kings and chiefs ended up serving interests unfavourable to the majority of the people. Apartheid's grand design, using the timeless strategy of divide and rule, gave rise to Bantustans, little fragments of so-called 'self-governing' entities,

* Pixley ka Isaka Seme — see People, Places and Events.

with their own political parties and administrations.

For Mandela and the ANC, it was a political imperative to carve out an accommodation for the traditional leadership in democratic South Africa, without compromising democratic principle. When it was founded, the ANC had an upper house of traditional leaders, recognising the earlier role of kingdoms and traditional structures in the resistance against colonial intrusion.

Although the upper house was dropped because it was implicated in entrenching segregation, it was supplanted in 1987 by the Congress of Traditional Leaders (CONTRALESA), which became part of the broad democratic front created by the ANC.* This was in line with the ANC's 1989 'Constitutional Guidelines for a Democratic South Africa', which declared that the 'institution of hereditary rulers and chiefs shall be transformed to serve the interests of the people as a whole in conformity with the democratic principles embodied in the constitution'.

On Robben Island in the 1970s, prisoners debated the developments in the Bantustans, aware of the manipulative arrangements that granted power and privilege to leaders toeing

* Congress of Traditional Leaders (CONTRALESA) — see People, Places and Events.

the apartheid line while at the same time dismissing the rebels. The essence of Mandela's thinking on this was set out in his 1976 essay, 'Clear the Obstacles and Confront the Enemy', in which his words 'Time is of the essence and we cannot afford to hesitate' reflect a great sense of urgency. He then immediately goes to the heart of the problem, saying that 'one of the most burning issues in the country today is the independence of the Transkei and other Bantustans, and the whole question of our tactics towards apartheid institutions'.[2]

Brutally self-critical, Mandela questions the wisdom of totally rejecting the Bantustans and posits arguments about where they could be used — or potentially explored — to further the objectives of liberation. The essay describes the liberation movement as having 'weaknesses' and being 'out of touch', and advocates some accommodation with the Bantustans. This, he suggests, would tip the scales in the favour of the liberation movement and give it a political presence or foothold in the rural areas where it was currently at its weakest. This entente between the liberation movement and the Bantustan would then facilitate the exploitation of the regime's weak spot. The crux of his argument, however, is the fear that the liberation movement could well boycott itself into irrelevance.

'In exploiting our weakness in the rural areas,' he writes, apropos the imminent independence of the Transkei, 'the regime probably realised that the independence of each Bantustan would result in a sharp drop or total disappearance of whatever following we had there.* Once people enjoy the right to manage their own affairs, they have won the only right for which they could join the liberation movement.' He cautions against dilly-dallying, as the lure of the homelands had already snared 'some men who were once politically active'. He warns: 'If we do not iron out our differences and close ranks immediately, we may find it difficult, if not impossible, to resist the divisive pressures once independence becomes a fact.'

By the time Mandela was released, the United Democratic Front had laid the foundation for a broad democratic front that included a goodly number of traditional leaders. Many had decided to stake their fate in resisting the Bantustan system in its totality, or to use it as a platform against its progenitors.

* One of the oldest Bantustans, the Transkei gained nominal independence to become an autonomous republic from the South African state in 26 October 1976, with Paramount Chief Botha J. Sigcau as president and Chief Kaiser Matanzima as prime minister.

In December 1989, just two months before Mandela's release, the Conference for a Democratic Future brought together thousands of representatives from hundreds of organisations, including political parties from several Bantustans. Just two months after his release from prison, Walter Sisulu spoke to the conference on the need for a broad front. 'Our response is to remain steadfast in the search for broader unity,' he said. 'Indeed, we cannot be satisfied with even the broadness of this conference. Our aim is a greater one. It is to unite the whole of our society.'[3]

The sense of urgency never quite left Mandela, even after his release. He pushed for the ANC to bring traditional leaders and Bantustan parties into the camp of the liberation movement and deny them to the National Party. A note written to Walter Sisulu during a meeting underscores his concern: 'Comrade Xhamela, I hope you will soon visit homeland leaders. Delay may lead to our being outwitted by Government.'[4]

When the formal negotiations began on 21 December 1991, Bantustan parties were among the participants. Days before the first meeting of the Convention for a Democratic South Africa (CODESA), Mandela, as president of the ANC, issued a statement:

'In keeping with the spirit of unity, the ANC considers it important that the traditional leaders be involved in the process. It is our view, which we have put to CODESA, that the highest-ranking traditional leaders from all parts of South Africa attend the proceedings on 20 and 21 December as observers. Just as such leaders were present at the formation of the ANC, they should be present at the watershed events that herald the dawn of a new, democratic South Africa.'[5]

After much discussion in the ANC's own councils about the form this should take, a compromise was reached in favour of a special participatory status, with delegations of traditional leaders from all four provinces. Later, as the first election approached, Mandela urged activists to be tactical and not to shun traditional leaders because of their history. When speaking to young people in April 1994, he reminded them that 'it is going to be difficult for our organisation to take root and be strong in the countryside unless we are able to work together with [traditional leaders] in their respective areas. Those who feel that we [should] have nothing to do with the chiefs do not know the policy of the ANC and have no idea how to strengthen the organisation in the countryside.'

The National Party had exploited this weakness. 'That is how,' Mandela said, 'they succeeded in forcing the homeland policy on the masses of our people.

'In our custom and history, the chief is the mouthpiece of his people. He must listen to the complaints of his people. He is the custodian of their hopes and desires. And if any chief decides to be a tyrant, to take decisions for his people, he will come to a tragic end in the sense that we will deal with him.'[6]

This last point was born of a meeting he had with a cross section of traditional leaders soon after his release. Of this he writes:

'Soon after I was released from prison I flew down to East London and met Comrade Silumko Sokupa and the Regional Executive Committee to acquaint myself with the situation in that area. In their briefing they told me that the Head of the House of Rarabe, King Zanesizwe Sandile, would visit me at my hotel that morning. I was shocked because to invite a monarch to visit a mere politician in a hotel was a breach of protocol.

'I instructed the committee to phone immediately and inform the King that I would prefer to pay him a courtesy visit at his palace later during the day. At that moment the King walked in. I apologised and pointed out that many of the young people who occupied leadership positions in the African National Congress grew up in the urban areas. They knew precious little about traditional leaders. It was not so much deliberate disrespect of, as lack of information on, the historic role of traditional leaders and the vital contribution they have made towards the liberation struggle.

'Heroes like the Khoi leader, Autshumayo, Maqoma and Hintsa from the House of Tshiwo, Siqungati and Gecelo from the abaThembu, Cetwayo and Bambatha from amaZulu, Mampuru and Sekhukhune from abaPedi, Makhado and Tshivhase from ama-Venda, and a host of other legends, were in the forefront of the wars of resistance. We speak of them with awe and admiration. Traditional leaders like Dalindyebo Ngange-lizwe of abaThembu and Indlovukazi of amaSwazi, Labotsibeni Gwamile, each paid a large number of cattle to enrol their respective people into the ANC.* Kings hailed from

* Chief Maqoma was commander in the anti-colonial so-called Sixth Xhosa War of 1834–6. Hintsa was the thirteenth king of the amaXhosa and ruled from 1820 until his death in 1835. Siqungati was a Thembu warrior who fought against colonialism. Gecelo was a Xhosa chief who was in the forefront of battles against colonialism in the 1800s. Cetwayo was a nephew of King Shaka Zulu. He succeeded his father, Mpande, as king of the Zulu nation in 1872. Bambatha led a protest known as the Bambatha Rebellion against British rule and taxation in 1906. Mampuru was a king and anti-colonial fighter who was executed by colonial powers in 1883. Sekhukhune was king of the baPedi who fought in two anti-colonial wars. He was assassinated by his rival Mampuru in 1882. Makhado was a warrior king and son of King Ramabulana.

all over the length and breadth of the country to join other African leaders in the formation of the ANC in 1912. An upper House was later created to accommodate the Traditional Leaders.

'Even at the height of the severe repression of the apartheid regime, there were courageous monarchs like Cyprian Bhekuzulu kaSolomon and Sabata Dalindyebo and others who refused to betray their people by accepting the Bantustan policy.*

'When I returned from prison I took along with me Comrade Peter Mokaba, the President of the ANC Youth League, General Bantu Holomisa, then the strongman of the Transkei Bantustan, and Ngangomhlaba Matanzima, a former Minister of Agriculture in

---

Tshivhase was the son of Dibanyika, the first King of the VhaVenda, south of the Limpopo River. Dalindyebo Ngangelizwe was king of the abaThembu from 1879. In 1904, he visited England and attended the coronation of King Edward VII. Indlovukazi was the Swazi queen mother. Labotsibeni Gwamile was the queen mother and queen regent of Swaziland.

* Cyprian Bhekuzulu kaSolomon was king of the Zulu nation, 1948–68. Sabata Jonguhlanga Dalindyebo was paramount chief of the Transkei, 1954–80, and leader of the Democratic Progressive Party.

the same Bantustan.* We visited African Kings and traditional leaders under them in the Eastern Cape.

'To all of them my message was the same: I explained that we fully appreciated the fact that they were forced by the apartheid regime to accept the policy of separate development. Had they not done so, they would have been removed from their positions by that oppressive regime. We the ANC were not there to protect them at that time.

'I went further and stressed that the youth were justified in condemning them as traitors, as traditional leaders, with a few exceptions mentioned above, were vicious in persecuting members of the liberation movement. Now the organisation had been unbanned, political prisoners had been released and exiles would soon be back in the country. The ANC was regaining its strength and legitimacy, and would give protection to traditional leaders. I then urged them to rally behind the organisation and to join the fight for liberation.

'Everywhere we went we were warmly welcomed. Vulindlela Tutor Ndamase was then King of Western Pondoland with headquarters at Nyandeni. Holomisa, who was present at that meeting, had become the

* Ngangomhlaba Matanzima is the chairperson of the Eastern Cape House of Traditional Leaders.

military ruler of the Transkei, where Pondoland was situated. He staged a successful but bloodless coup against Prime Minister Stella Sigcau, Princess of Eastern Pondoland. In welcoming us, Vulindlela boasted that he was not an ordinary traditional leader, but a well-known King. Nobody, he claimed, would ever dare to coup him. It was as if he was challenging the General to try to coup [*sic*] him. It was as if he was challenging the General to try to unseat him. But the General appeared not to be offended by the royal boast.

'We also visited King Xolilizwe Sigcau of the House of Tshiwo. In his welcome speech he strongly attacked the toyi-toyi [dance], which had become a popular form of protest.* He said there was nothing he hated more than the toyi-toyi. He had investigated to find out where this type of demonstration came from, and nobody could help him. He announced that he had banned that form of protest in his kingdom.

'Peter Mokaba then explained its origin. It was a war cry against the apartheid policy. It was not at all aimed against traditional lead-

* Borrowed by the ANC from the Zimbabwe People's Revolutionary Army, this energetic dance, consisting of rhythmic movement and stamping of feet, was integrated into political protest in the beleaguered South African townships in the 1980s.

ers. He regretted the fact that the King thought that it was directed at important community leaders. Mokaba then boldly and gracefully toyi-toyied, gyrating menacingly all the way. The Master of Ceremonies was Mandlenkosi Dumalisile, a senior traditional leader in that House, and Minister of Agriculture in the Transkei Bantustan. When Peter Mokaba concluded his remarks, Dumalisile thrilled the meeting when he, in turn, joined and toyi-toyied. The King, obviously fascinated by Mokaba's eloquence and grace, accepted the explanation.

'Holomisa and Ngangomhlaba Matanzima accompanied me only in the Transkei where my meetings went on without trouble. Despite the diplomatic and courteous language used, I did not fare well in the Bantustans of Bophuthatswana and Lebowakgomo in the Transvaal Province, as the Limpopo Province was then known. The position was equally difficult in KwaZulu-Natal.

'Lucas Mangope was President of Bophuthatswana, and a different customer. I visited his Bantustan in the company of Comrade Joe Modise, who later became our Minister of Defence, Ruth Matseoane, who became our Ambassador to Switzerland, and Popo Molefe, who later became the Premier of North West. Before April 1994, no liberation movement could campaign in Mangope's Bantustan. He first agreed when I requested him to remove all barriers and allow political organisations to campaign freely in his area. Later during the discussion, he suddenly pounced an unexpected question on us and asked, "When you address a meeting in my area are you going to say Bophuthatswana is a Bantustan?"

'I assured him that everybody knows that his is a Bantustan, and that would be the theme of our speeches. He then said that in that case we would be in trouble. His people would feel insulted and he could not guarantee our safety. We told him that we were confident that we would be able not only to protect ourselves, we would win the majority of the people of that area. But we could not convince him. It was a draw. On several occasions thereafter I invited him to Johannesburg and tried to persuade him without success. He is one of the most difficult and unpredictable politicians I have met.

'After overcoming an intricate web of machinations from Mangope and some South African generals, we succeeded with the help of Pik Botha, Mac Maharaj, Fanie van der Merwe and Roelf Meyer in removing Mangope as President and dissolved his government. The Transitional Executive Council replaced him with [the] South African Ambassador in that Bantustan [of Bophuthatswana], Tjaart van der Walt, and Job Mokgoro as a temporary government.

'I also experienced serious problems in the Transvaal Province in the Lebowa Bantustan under Nelson Ramodike, who was the Chief Minister of that Bantustan. There were two powerful claimants to the BaPedi throne, namely Rhyne Thulare and Kenneth Kgagudi Sekhukhune, both of whom were descendants of King Sekwati I.* Rhyne was the son and undisputed successor to Queen Mankopodi Thulare, who became Regent during the minority of her son. She was later deposed by the Royal Council of the tribe as they disapproved of certain aspects of her reign. The Royal Council appointed Rhyne to succeed the mother, but Rhyne declined. The Royal Council then resorted to K. K. Sekhukhune and appointed him Regent. He was ordered to marry what was termed a "candle wife" who would produce a King.† A son was later born of the marriage and named Sekwati III.

'Later Rhyne changed his mind and claimed his rightful position. According to law and custom he was the undisputed heir to the throne. But K. K. Sekhukhune refused to step

* Sekwati (1775–1861) was king of the baPedi people in what is now South Africa's Limpopo Province.
† A 'candle wife' is a woman selected by the nation and married off to the royal household for the sole purpose of producing a male child.

down on the grounds that Rhyne had renounced his claim to the Kingship, an argument which the High Court endorsed. I called several meetings of the tribe without success. I eventually made it clear that this was a dispute which should be settled by the BaPedi themselves and not by the President of the ANC or of the country. But the matter remains unresolved.

'I had a similar problem with the amaVhavenda traditional leaders. I visited King Tshivhase expecting all the traditional leaders in that area to attend. Contrary to my expectations, King Mphephu refused to attend on the ground that he was senior to Tshivhase, and he insisted that, although he was keen to listen to me, I should visit him at his own residence. In spite of the fact that I was again warmly welcomed, it was clear that I had deeply hurt him in thinking that Tshivhase was senior to him. I also discovered that he was working closely with President De Klerk.

'My problems were in no way less with amaZulu traditional leaders . . .

'In due course and in spite of the problems I encountered, the overwhelming majority of traditional leaders throughout the country responded positively and rallied behind the ANC.

'There is no suggestion whatsoever that only one person was responsible for this historic achievement. Leaders like Walter Sisulu, O. R. Tambo, Jacob Zuma, John Nkadimeng, Elias Motsoaledi, Ngoako Ramatlhodi and many others were in the forefront of that campaign.* It was the result of that collective effort that the ANC became all-powerful in both the urban and rural areas.'[7]

The process of aligning traditional leadership with democracy was long and arduous. Whereas traditional leaders were represented in the Multiparty Negotiating Forum, which negotiated the interim constitution prior to the 1994 election, they were absent from the elected Constitutional Assembly which drew up the final constitution, and were not consulted to the same extent. Much like accommodating a troubled relative at a family celebration, the government had to devise strategies, including legislative measures, to reincorporate the Bantustans into the South African state, all the while ensuring that democratic values survived intact. The major headache for all involved was unscrambling

* Nkadimeng was a member of the ANC National Executive Committee, a leading member of the South African Congress of Trade Unions and the SACP and the deputy president of the COSATU. Ramatlhodi was a member of the NEC of the ANC and the premier of Limpopo Province from 1994 to 2004.

elements of the coercive administrative structures inherent in the Bantustans, which were a legacy of the apartheid regime.

Part of Mandela's quest to deepen democracy, using state power, was — like the eating of the proverbial elephant 'one bite at a time' — eliminating hurdles history had put in the way. Some of the legislation towards the creation of a unitary state, such as the Local Government Transition Act of 1993, paved the way for the first local government elections, which were held in most parts of the country in November 1995. This was an exercise that had a bearing on transformation, which, as observed by Allister Sparks, had led to 'redrawing the geopolitical map of South Africa — in itself a transformation of quite remarkable scale. A country that previously consisted of four provinces and ten nominally autonomous tribal "homelands", four of them independent, has been redrawn into one of nine completely new provinces with their own premiers, executives and legislatures, and with the so-called "homelands" eliminated as separate entities and subsumed into the provinces.'[8]

The framework for the elections had been one of the most difficult negotiating issues. They were weighted in favour of white voters and, in some areas, forums for the restructuring of local government were used to resist change. These and other related dynamics led to an uncharacteristic collaboration between CONTRALESA and the IFP, and they marched to the Union Buildings to pressurise President Mandela to give them more power. In some rural areas, traditional leaders called for a boycott of the elections — which proved to be a damp squib as rural residents instead chose to use their newly won democratic right to vote. Although there was a lower voter turnout in some rural areas, this could not be attributed only to the influence of traditional leaders.[9]

If CONTRALESA and the IFP had joined forces in demanding more powers in local government for traditional leaders, their views on remuneration remained divergent. CONTRALESA favoured uniformity of pay across the country while the IFP wanted pay reflecting a special status for KwaZulu-Natal and feared losing their hold on the province if their pay came from national government.

Those who worked with Mandela during the constitutional negotiations were aware of his own background in the Thembu royal family. His attitude, however, was uncompromisingly informed by political imperatives.

Valli Moosa remembers that Mandela acknowledged that

the traditional leaders had a degree of influence in their own areas, so it was

347

important to engage with them. During the negotiations he felt it was important to keep them on side, so that they supported the transition and did not oppose it. Nor did he want the regime to mobilise the traditional leaders against change, and so he engaged with them and kept close to them. He respected traditional leaders from the point of view that they held the respect and following of their communities . . . although he was of the view that many were illegitimate; he said that over and over. But he didn't want them to have any role whatsoever in government; they were not elected.[10]

Given the intricacies of the area, Mandela also believed in taking counsel with his advisers. He writes about how Sydney Mufamadi, the minister of provincial affairs and local government, 'briefed me on the position of traditional leaders, especially after I had stepped down as President of the country in June 1999. He reminded me that when we came into power in 1994, we needed to find a place for traditional leaders in our new system of government. To that end, we created six Provincial Houses of Traditional Leaders, as well as the National House of Traditional Leaders, so that they could play a meaningful role on matters under their jurisdiction.

'The creation of these Houses was in accordance with the policy of the ANC which had at its inception, as we have already said, an upper House for traditional leaders. This measure was taken not only to acknowledge the role which traditional leaders had played in the wars of resistance, but also because it was an important step in our campaign to bury the curse of tribalism. An Inter-Departmental Task Team was set up to recommend to the Government the role which traditional leaders should play in Local, Provincial and National government. But we must strongly resist any concession to them where they will stand outside the democratic process by investing them with authoritative powers. What is very disturbing is their inability to understand the social forces at work inside and outside South Africa.

'South Africans have fully accepted democratic government in which the people's representatives in the central, provincial and local government level are democratically elected and are accountable to their respective constituencies. Besides, the country's youth who now occupy key positions, in society and in all levels of government, in the South African Congress of Trade Unions (COSATU) and in the South African Communist party (SACP), are urbanised and fairly educated. They cannot be expected to compromise the democratic principles by surrendering any aspect of government to those who occupy positions of authority in society not because of merit but purely because of heredity.

'Many of our traditional leaders are also not aware of the lessons of history. They do not seem to know that there were once absolute monarchs in the world who did not share power with their subjects . . . It is Monarchs who . . . themselves or their predecessors, decided to allow elected representatives of the people to govern, and who became constitutional monarchs who survived like Queen Elizabeth II of Britain, King Juan Carlos of Spain, King Albert of Belgium, Queen Beatrix of the Netherlands, Queen Margrethe II of Denmark, King Harald of Norway and King Carl XVI Gustaf. Had these monarchs clung stubbornly to their absolute powers they would long have disappeared from the scene.

'But we must never forget that the institution of traditional leaders is sanctified by African law and custom, by our culture and tradition. No attempt must be made to abolish it. We must find an amicable solution based on democratic principles, and which allows traditional leaders to play a meaningful role in all levels of government.

'I am not clear to what extent a significant initiative of the apartheid government . . . was available in other Bantustans. But in the

Transkei there was a school for the sons of traditional leaders, which gave them basic skills in the administration of areas under their jurisdiction. I would not urge that we should have such schools. But depending on the resources that the government has, it would be advisable to encourage sons of traditional leaders to get the best education.

'Although my own resources are very limited, I have sent a number of sons and daughters of traditional leaders to Universities in South Africa, and to the United Kingdom and the United States of America. A literate corps of educated traditional leaders would in all probability accept the democratic process. The inferiority complex, which makes many of them cling desperately to feudal forms of administration, would, in due course, disappear.

'Some leaders of the ANC have established education trusts to help, particularly previously disadvantaged children, to enter high schools, technicons and universities.* But I would urge that they should consciously try to make scholarships available to children of traditional leaders as well.

'The colonial powers in their efforts to subjugate the people of the African Continent, deliberately refused to acknowledge that

* A technicon is an institution similar to a polytechnic.

351

we had Kings and traditional leaders. They referred to them as chiefs and paramount chiefs. Only the colonial countries themselves had the monopoly of having kings and princes. The era of colonialism and contempt for the people of Africa has gone, never to return. We must recognise our kings and princes.'[11]

The final step during Mandela's presidency towards reconciling traditional leadership with democratic local government was the Municipal Structures Act of 1998. It laid the ground for the first fully democratic local government elections, to be held in 2000, consolidating the countrywide system of elected local authorities. Traditional leaders would be ex officio and non-voting members of councils in areas where communities recognised them. Yet again, some were disappointed and critical, still mounting pressure for more extensive recognition.

The relationship between traditional leadership and violence was a nagging issue for Mandela. This was especially true of the recalcitrance that could be found in Natal, which was unfortunately linked to violence. This concern had motivated him to use one of the first days of his freedom — 25 February 1990 — to visit Durban and address a rally.

After greeting the people of Natal, he said:

'The past is a rich resource on which we can draw in order to make decisions for the future, but it does not dictate our choices. We should look back at the past and select what is good, and leave behind what is bad. The issue of chiefship is one such question. Not only in Natal, but all through the country, there have been chiefs who have been good and honest leaders who have piloted their people through the dark days of oppression with skill. These are the chiefs who have looked after the interests of their people and who enjoy the support of their people. We salute these traditional leaders. But there have been many bad chiefs who have profited from apartheid and who have increased the burden on their people. We denounce this misuse of office in the strongest terms. There are also chiefs who have collaborated with the system, but who have since seen the error of their ways. We commend their change of heart. Chiefly office is not something that history has given to certain individuals to use or abuse as they see fit. Like all forms of leadership, it places specific responsibilities on its holders. As Luthuli, himself a chief, put it: "A chief is primarily a servant of the people. He is the voice of his people."

'The Zulu royal house continues today to enjoy the respect of its subjects. It has a glorious history. We are confident that its members will act in ways that will promote the well-being of all South Africans.

'The ANC offers a home to all who subscribe to the principles of a free, democratic,
non-racial and united South Africa. We are
committed to building a single nation in our
country. Our new nation will include blacks
and whites, Zulus and Afrikaners, and speakers of every other language. ANC President
General Chief Luthuli said: "I personally
believe that here in South Africa, with all of
our diversities of colour and race, we will
show the world a new pattern for democracy.
I think that there is a challenge to us in South
Africa to set a new example for the world."
This is the challenge we face today.'

The biggest hurdle that had to be overcome
was that not much had changed since his
release. 'Yet even now as we stand together
on the threshold of a new South Africa, Natal
is in flames,' he said. 'Brother is fighting
brother in wars of vengeance and retaliation.
Every family has lost dear ones in this
strife.'[12]

It is one of history's enduring paradoxes
that the Natal of the 1990s became the main
obstacle to the transition to democracy. The
province's wars against colonial intrusion are
legendary, not to mention the fact that it was
the birthplace of John Langalibalele Dube
and Pixley ka Isaka Seme, the founders of
the ANC in 1912. Chief Albert Luthuli, the
first African recipient of the Nobel Peace

Prize in 1960 and the president general of the ANC from December 1952 to July 1967, was also from Natal.

In almost all his speeches addressing the tragedy of division that wracked the province, Mandela never forgot to invoke the glorious past of the amaZulu by referencing their involvement in anti-colonial resistance. The re-emergence of militant trade unionism in the 1970s and 1980s owed much to the workers of Natal. But from the mid-eighties, Natal was locked into a violent and deadly conflict that is estimated to have taken twenty thousand lives over the next decade, most of these in the aftermath of the unbanning of liberation movements in 1990.[13]

Apartheid security forces — police and military intelligence — fomented and perpetrated violence and, according to evidence by various operatives, gave material and operational support to Inkatha as the party in control of the KwaZulu Bantustan.[14] However deceitfully the apartheid government tried to limit democratic change in the Kwa-Zulu Bantustan, it found itself outflanked by the ANC, which succeeded in getting virtually all the other Bantustans into its camp.[15]

With active support from within the security forces, Inkatha mounted pressure to secure its constitutional objectives — unconstitutionally, as it were — wreaking havoc across the Reef (now part of Greater Johannesburg), especially the East Rand and parts of present-day Mpumalanga. About a thousand people were killed in the three months before the 1994 elections. Mangosuthu Buthelezi's capitulation at the last hour to participate in the elections was therefore critical in staunching the violence and paving the road to the transition and an unchallenged election.

Despite this, the peace was sporadic with continued outbreaks of violence. Normalising the situation in KwaZulu-Natal was one of the main preoccupations of Mandela's presidency. While not wholly eradicating political violence, he was engaged with the multipronged strategies that, by and large, narrowed its operational space, cutting the umbilical cord that had nurtured covert capacity. Greater security and freer political activity helped normalise the province and integrate it into the emergent South African nation.

Throughout his time in office, Mandela's attitude towards the traditional leaders of KwaZulu-Natal was ambivalent:

'At the outset one must concede that this section of our people are intensely nationalistic, proud and brave. They are immensely inspired by the spectacular achievements of uNodumehlezi, or the black Napoleon as the colonial historians sometimes refer to King Shaka.

'In my long association with amaZulu, I found that the majority are men and women I deeply admire.

'I have enormous respect for Mangosuthu Buthelezi, Minister of Home Affairs, in particular, a formidable survivor, who defeated us in two free and fair general elections, firstly in April 1994 and again in June 1999. We used as ammunition against him, facts which are of common knowledge, that he was a Bantustan leader, that although he refused to take independence as other Bantustans had done, he worked hand in hand with the apartheid regime, that they gave him funds to oppose sanctions and the armed struggle, that he formed the trade union UWUSA [United Workers Union of South Africa] to undermine the progressive and dynamic policies of COSATU and the SACP. We even had more damaging allegations than those set out above. All these failed to tarnish his reputation, and he remains to the present day a powerful public figure that cannot be ignored.

'But few will deny that there is still a hard, arrogant core of influential traditionalists who think that they are superior to other African groups in the country. At a meeting with amaZulu traditional leaders in Durban, Prince Gideon Zulu accused me of having insulted amaZulu in general and their King Zwelithini in particular, when I put him on the same level as King Mayishe II of ama-Ndebele. I sharply criticised such an arrogant approach and bluntly told him that there were many monarchs that were highly respected in our country. AmaNdebele, I pointed out, were a proud and fearless tribe that had made an important contribution in our history. I added that it was a dangerous delusion on the part of amaZulu to think there was only one black King in the country.

'There is a disputed area in the Transkei which is claimed by both Thandizulu Sigcau, King of Eastern Pondoland, and by Zwelithini. The two Kings, Minister Buthelezi and myself attended a meeting in that area. I was shocked and embarrassed when Thandizulu was sidelined and told to sit behind Zwelithini and Buthelezi. In spite of my enormous respect for Zwelithini, I could not keep quiet. I intervened and made sure that Thandizulu sat next to Zwelithini in the front seats.

'There are many members of this famous tribe who are like Deputy President Jacob Zuma and Dr Ben Ngubane of the Inkatha Freedom Party and Minister of Arts, Culture, Science and Technology. These two politicians are a shining example of leaders who consistently put the welfare of the country above personal or party interests. They are broadminded and are committed to the unity of our people.'[16]

Even though Mandela and Buthelezi had a

political and social history — both were former students of the University of Fort Hare and had a shared affiliation to the ANC Youth League — Buthelezi still presented Mandela with a conundrum. Attitudes among the ANC members on the ground, who bore the brunt of the violence in Natal, were hardening with regard to the IFP, with Buthelezi the focal point of their execration. The hostile reaction to Mandela's plea that the warring factions of Natal throw their *pangas* 'into the sea' did not lessen when, a few weeks later, he broached the idea of meeting with Buthelezi in an effort to bring peace.[17]

'The National Executive of the ANC had no objection to me talking to Buthelezi,' he told Richard Stengel, his collaborator on *Long Walk to Freedom*. 'What happened was that in 1990, I went to Pietermaritzburg and I was received enthusiastically. It was difficult — at one time, you know, my shoe came out you see — because there was no proper marshalling and people just crowded around, you know and so on . . . but they were very enthusiastic. I found it difficult even to start my speech, but when I started my speech, in the course of my speech I said, "Mr De Klerk and Mr Buthelezi and I will have to go to the trouble areas and appeal to the people for peace." It was then that people wanted to choke me. The same people who had showed me the love. Once I mentioned the name of Buthelezi, they wouldn't have that. And they said, "You are not going to speak to a man whose organisation has been murdering our people." '[18]

Mandela maintained cordial, some will even say friendly, relations with Buthelezi on the basis that the latter had turned down the blandishments of apartheid self-rule in the Bantustans and kept the prisoner 'informed of what was happening outside'. Many in the ANC didn't, however, including the leadership in exile, like National Executive Committee member John Nkadimeng, who pronounced on a Radio Freedom broadcast that 'the puppet Gatsha [Buthelezi] is being groomed by the West and the racist regime to become a [Jonas] Savimbi, in a future free South Africa.* The onus is on the people of South Africa to neutralise the Gatsha snake, which is poisoning the people of South Africa. It needs to be hit over the head.'[19]

* Jonas Savimbi was the co-founder and leader of the National Union for the Total Independence of Angola (União Nacional para a Independência Total de Angola) (UNITA), the anti-communist nationalist movement opposed to the People's Movement for the Liberation of Angola (Movimento Popular de Libertação de Angola) (MPLA) government in Angola with the covert aid both of apartheid security and the Central Intelligence Agency.

In his book *Gatsha Buthelezi: Chief with a Double Agenda,* Mzala, the nom de plume of the late Jabulani Nobleman Nxumalo, a brilliant ideologue of both the ANC and the SACP, refutes any notion that Buthelezi was ever a positive influence in the long struggle against apartheid. He cites him as missing in action for all the momentous events: opposition to the enactment of the Bantu Authorities Act of 1951, mobilisation during the Defiance Campaign of 1952, and preparatory action towards the Congress of the People and the adoption of the Freedom Charter. 'This campaign involved not only people who were ANC members. People from all walks of life participated in it and sent delegates to Kliptown on 26 June 1955. Buthelezi was neither a delegate nor did he send a delegate.'[20]

Mandela himself explained to Stengel that Buthelezi 'did not honour arrangements which were made between Inkatha and the ANC . . . [and] our people got annoyed with him. You see, Inkatha was started by the ANC to work as a legal arm of the ANC inside the country and there was an agreement to that effect.' But, Mandela states, 'once Inkatha was now established, Buthelezi decided . . . to break away from the ANC and to develop it as his own political organisation, and that soured relations.'[21]

As part of its strategy to stem the violence

in KwaZulu-Natal, the government developed an approach to the conflict where peace was to be the dominant theme of politics; traditional leaders were to be extracted from party political control and security action was to be informed by information gathering and undercover work. Mandela stated that the ANC had been 'unequivocal in its belief that a hidden hand is behind this violence'.[22] He also believed that top leadership should be deployed 'in these dangerous areas', with adequate security measures being taken. 'Nothing,' Mandela felt, 'discourages people on the ground more than the continued absence of the top leadership in these problematic areas.'[23]

Just as Mandela had sought the support of P. W. Botha to counter the threat of violence by the Afrikaner right wing, he now called on King Goodwill Zwelithini. 'My goal,' Mandela said, 'was to forge an independent relationship with the king, separate from my relationship with Chief Buthelezi. The king was the true hereditary leader of the Zulus, who loved and respected him. Fidelity to the king was far more widespread in KwaZulu than allegiance to Inkatha.'[24]

In making this approach, he wasn't surrendering anything; he would bend over backwards to bring about peace. Walter Sisulu had described his comrade and protégé as a very tough person, adding, 'I think there are very few people who've got the qualities of Nelson. Nelson is a fighter; Nelson is a peacemaker.'[25]

King Zwelithini gradually came to accept that, as king of a nation of people who belonged to different political parties, he was the only traditional leader who transcended party political disputes.

The continuing violence and inflammatory talk evoked an angry reaction from Mandela. It all began in 1995 on a May Day rally in Umlazi, a sprawling township some 25 kilometres to the south-east of Durban. The rally was held a week after Buthelezi had called on his supporters, in an address at the same stadium, to 'rise and resist the central government' if the IFP's constitutional demands were not met.[26] As the police used rubber bullets and tear gas to clear the residents that had massed since morning and to prevent IFP supporters from marching to the rally, an undeterred Mandela continued talking. An article in the *Mail & Guardian* described how 'as more shots sent his supporters ducking behind rows of buses outside, Mandela departed from his speech to let loose perhaps the most militant remark of his presidency: "[Inkatha] should know it is [central government] who is giving them money and they are using the money against my government . . . should they continue, I'm going to withdraw the money." '[27]

Caught by surprise, the president's office quickly briefed the media, contextualising Mandela's threat as a 'timely warning' to the province.[28] Had it been left unexplained, it would have been unconstitutional. Later, in Parliament, Mandela elaborated, aware of the political firestorm his remarks had loosed.

The reduction of tensions in the province of KwaZulu-Natal was, he said, 'one of the most urgent priorities faced by politicians'. Referring to the Constitution, he reminded MPs and senators that human life was more important than the Constitution — and he would step in and protect human lives, for that was what was at stake.[29]

'I have briefed the leaders of political parties inside and outside the Government of National Unity, that there is a serious situation in KwaZulu-Natal. Chief Buthelezi has made a public call to Zulus to rise against the central Government. He has said that if they do not get the right to self-determination, it is not worth being alive. Not only has he made this statement, but [also] this threat is now being implemented in that province.'[30]

Citing a long list of violations by the IFP, where lives had been lost, he lashed members of the opposition for their hypocrisy on human rights. He said:

'Members here who have never known about the tradition of human rights and of democracy are now giving gratuitous advice to those people who fought hard to bring about democracy and the culture of human rights in this country. They are talking about the sanctity of the Constitution, and yet, when they were in power, at the slightest excuse, they interfered with the Constitution. They even amended the entrenched process which protected the language rights of people in this country, and took away one of the most important rights of people, the right of the coloured people to vote in this country. Now they are lecturing us on the sanctity of the Constitution.'[31]

In full flight, but weary, Mandela ended his address, explaining what had motivated him to threaten withdrawing funding from KwaZulu-Natal:

'I agree that the Constitution is very important, and it is a matter of serious concern when the President of a country threatens to change the Constitution, but I am determined to protect human life. The perception that whites in this country do not care about black lives is there. I may not share it but it is there. The discussions here, where reference is not even made to the principal reason for my having taken this tough line to protect human lives, unfortunately goes a long way in confirming that perception.'[32]

The issue was again raised when the Senate debated the president's budget a month later, this time along with a question about the pre-election shooting of IFP demonstrators outside ANC headquarters at Shell House in Johannesburg. Here, Mandela reminded the House of the role of the National Party in using the IFP as its cat's paw:

'Whatever the origins of the IFP were, the National Party soon took them over and used them in order to undermine democracy in this country, to undermine the United Democratic Front and now the ANC. Members must remember that when the then President Mr De Klerk was asked in July 1991 whether he had given the IFP R8 million plus R250,000, he said that they had, but that he had stopped it.

'What is happening in KwaZulu-Natal is part of the agenda of the NP. One can see it, even now, from the way in which they themselves are handling the matter [in the debate]. I am sure they are quite honest about the views that they are expressing, but they are so used to managing the IFP, that it can do no wrong . . . It is not accurate to project the problem as a clash between the ANC and the IFP only. The NP is amongst the guilty parties in this whole affair, because they have over decades incited the IFP to do certain things which are not consistent with the law of the country. That is why they find it difficult to break away from the wrongs that the IFP are doing.

'I have been holding discussions with the IFP ever since I came out of prison. For every other meeting we held, the initiative was taken by myself. Not once has the IFP taken that initiative. However, all the other initiatives were taken by the ANC. We have had discussions as organisations. I have called Chief Buthelezi, and had one-on-one discussions with him. All of them failed to resolve anything, but all the NP can say here is that I should hold discussions with Buthelezi.

'Why should I repeat today what I have been doing for the past five years, which has failed to resolve anything? Are they so barren that they have no fresh suggestions to make, except for saying that I should repeat what I have been doing for the past five years? That is what they are saying! If not, they should tell me what I should do. I have used negotiations, persuasion, but there has been no development at all. What should I do now?'[33]

A few days later, as if in answer to Mandela's exasperated question, the cabinet was briefed on the tangible steps being taken to combat the violence in KwaZulu-Natal. A working group consisting of the president, the two deputy presidents and the minister of home affairs was established, marking a shift of emphasis from combative public dispute to concerted security action for stability. Intelligence officers and detectives would accompany additional troops and police deployed in the province. A community safety plan that covered the whole country focused on identified flashpoints, and the Investigation Task Unit continued with its work to identify covert structures of the hit squads.[34]

An intelligence breakthrough had exposed the 'hidden hand' or 'third force' involvement, and led, in 1992, to the conviction of police officers responsible for a 1988 massacre in the Natal village of Trust Feed.* Painstaking detective work revealed the extent to which people at the top of the security establishment of central government and the homelands were implicated.[35]

The exposure of senior political figures created dilemmas, such as the moment in September when the attorney general of the province found himself facing the prospect of prosecuting senior IFP and KwaZulu police officials. In certain instances, placing the peace dividend above the dubious benefit of prosecuting highly placed IFP criminals, the ANC opted for stability. Progress in dealing with violence that had been cultivated over decades was gradual. Violent incidents con-

---

* Trust Feed is a community in KwaZulu-Natal where, in 1988, eleven people were killed. Police Lieutenant Brian Mitchell and four constables were convicted of the eleven murders. They received death sentences that were later commuted to life sentences.

tinued and massacres still happened.

Mandela had to maintain law and order in a flawed, dangerous and irredeemably cruel country, which had spawned monsters like Sifiso Nkabinde, a KwaZulu warlord whose reign of terror only ended in 1999, when he was shot dead in front of his family. Ironically, sometime earlier, while on a killing spree, Nkabinde, a serial defector who had been an ANC leader before going rogue, had unsuccessfully tried to have his own mother murdered. His death was the moment that marked the defanging of the violent progeny of the security structures.

In November 1996, halfway through the government's five-year term, Mandela was able to report to the ANC's NEC on the long journey towards an imperfect peace. His notes reflect his optimism:

'KwaZulu-Natal as a major achievement, among the reasons being firmness, intelligence-driven operations, and the role of political, religious and other leaders. An indication of the success achieved can be gauged from the fact that only 27 cases of violence of a political nature have been recorded in the past 3 months.'[36]

Although violence had not been eradicated by the time of the second national elections in 1999, the situation was much better than it had been five years earlier. The no-go areas, which had sometimes proved fatal for election campaigners, had been reduced. King Zwelithini and a few other traditional leaders in KwaZulu-Natal promoted participation and preached tolerance. But as elsewhere in the country, tensions remained, and the province still had one of the largest concentrations of rural poverty in South Africa. The alignment of traditional leadership with democracy had only just begun — and there was still a lot of work to do. The period of transition had left the Zulu king with exceptional status and powers, both of which would prove problematic in years to come.

Chapter One

The Challenge

An unprecedented challenge faced the first democratically elected government of the Republic of South Africa.

It was a major rubicon to cross for the generation of dynamic and steeled freedom fighters who, for almost half a century, had sacrificed everything for the liberation of their country.

Some of them had given up lucrative careers, spent almost a lifetime under harsh conditions in exile mobilising the international community to condemn apartheid and to isolate white South Africa.

That while South Africa was in due course shunned by almost every country in the world, and apartheid condemned as a crime against humanity was a measure of the success of their historic campaign.

Those in exile crisscrossed the five continents briefing heads of state and government on our situation, attending world and regional gatherings, and flooding the world with material exposing the inhumanity of apartheid.

It was this world wide campaign which made the African National Congress (ANC) and its leaders inside and outside the country, one of the most well-known liberation movement of the world.

The fighters of Umkhonto we Sizwe (M.K) displayed unrivalled courage and infiltrated the country, attacked government installations, and clashed with the apartheid forces and, now

An original manuscript page from the third draft of Mandela's memoir on his presidential years. His private secretary, Zelda la Grange, would type up his handwritten text with her team, then Mandela would annotate her typewritten version or handwrite an entire new draft. Some chapters went through multiple drafts in this manner.

Mandela addresses the people upon his release from prison, City Hall, Cape Town, 11 February 1990. 'I stand here before you not as a prophet but as a humble servant of you, the people,' he said. 'Your tireless and heroic sacrifices have made it possible for me to be here today. I, therefore, place the remaining years of my life in your hands.'

Singing 'Nkosi Sikelel' iAfrika' with his then wife, Winnie Mandela, at his Welcome Home rally at the FNB Stadium, Soweto, on 13 February 1990, two days after his release from prison. More than 100,000 people attended the rally to hear him speak.

Mandela addresses the United Nations Special Committee Against Apartheid, New York, 1990, and urges it to maintain sanctions imposed by the UN and individual governments against South Africa until apartheid is abolished. Economic sanctions against South Africa, which the UN had imposed since 1962, were lifted in October 1993.

In January 1991 the leaders of the warring IFP and ANC, Mangosuthu Buthelezi and Nelson Mandela, met and issued a statement on a joint peace agreement to stop the political violence. This cartoon published in *Die Transvaler* suggests the leaders' underlying feelings towards each other aren't quite so magnanimous.

With IFP leader Mangosuthu Buthelezi and President F. W. de Klerk at a press conference to announce the IFP's late entry into South Africa's first democratic elections, only weeks out from polling, in April 1994.

Mandela and Walter Sisulu salute the coffin of popular political activist Chris Hani, FNB Stadium, Soweto, 19 April 1993. Hani's assassination almost led the country into civil war. In a televised address, Mandela urged the nation to act with dignity and rededicate itself to bringing about democracy (see pages 71–72).

Mandela salutes the crowd during an election rally in Galeshewe Stadium, near Kimberley, 1994. Long-serving bodyguard Mzwandile Vena says that Mandela's unpredictability when he was among the people made him a nightmare for his security detail. 'You had to be alert all the time' (see page 265).

Election campaigning, 1994. Mandela wrote that 'To the black majority' the forthcoming election 'meant the birth of a dream' (see page 105).

Mandela votes for the first time at Ohlange High School, Inanda, 27 April 1994. The venue was near the grave of the first ANC president, John Dube.

In this cartoon, published in *The Sowetan*, Nanda Soobben juxtaposes the hype and excitement surrounding Mandela's inauguration with his voting public's expectations for basic necessities.

Estranged from his wife, Winnie, Mandela's daughter HRH Princess Zenani Dlamini accompanies him at the luncheon following his inauguration, Pretoria, 10 May 1994.

President Mandela flanked by his two deputy presidents – Thabo Mbeki (left) and F. W. de Klerk, the outgoing president, Union Buildings, Pretoria, 10 May 1994.

Outside Tuynhuys, the presidential office in Cape Town, on the day of the opening of the first democratic parliament. Mandela is with (from left to right) MP Cyril Ramaphosa, Zanele Mbeki and her husband Deputy President Thabo Mbeki, Speaker of Parliament Frene Ginwala, Kobie Coetsee, who served as president of the Senate until 2008, and Deputy President F. W. de Klerk.

Mandela with some of his first cabinet and senior presidency officials. He is flanked by IFP leader Mangosuthu Buthelezi to his right and Deputy President Thabo Mbeki to his left.

11. E. P. Jordaan : Minister of Environment & Fisheries Post & Communication

12. S. Sigcau : Minister of Public Enterprises

13. S. W. Tshwete : Minister of Sport & Recreation

14. S. R. Maharaj : Minister of Transport

15. N. C. Dlamini Zuma : Minister of Health

16. A. B. Nzo : Minister of Foreign Affairs

17. D. M. Hanekom : Minister of Lands

18. S. F. Mufamadi : Minister of Safety & Security

19. T. T. Mboweni : Minister of Labour

Professor Jakes Gerwel was Director-General in the Office of the President and Secretary of the Cabinet

Soon after the formation of the Government of National Unity, and long before Deputy-President De Klerk pulled out of that joint Cabinet, the ANC was repeatedly accused of racism and of promoting only the interests of Africans and neglecting those of other the minority groups. There are still people today who still peddle this fable. Irrespective of ethnic group to which they A glance at the above list of members of the GNU below

I have deliberately set out the names of the full Cabinet of the GNU and those who have respect for truth and themselves will refrain from tarnishing their image by endorsing a senseless propaganda and transparent subterfuge by those who have no credible alternative policy to present to the people of to our country to the people of South Africans

How can we be accused of racism

The subterfuge becomes all the more transparent glaring when you consider that apart from Mr Williams, a member of the Coloured community, the remaining 5 cabinet members of Mr De Klerk's National Party were all whites and Africans, no Indian, no African

As far as the ANC is concerned we had no less Yet all these national groups were represented in the ANC cabinet

A page from chapter five of Mandela's manuscript of his memoir of his presidential years. Here he has set out the names of his cabinet in the Government of National Unity to show that his list was fully representative of different ethnic groups. This was in response to accusations that the ANC was primarily occupied with the concerns of Africans. 'There are still public figures in our country – diehards – who are still peddling this ignoble propaganda,' he writes (see page 197).

TOP: With Jessie Duarte, ANC chief of operations in the presidency.

ABOVE: With Joe Slovo, who was appointed minister of housing in the Government of National Unity.

TOP: With Trevor Manuel, who became South Africa's longest-serving finance minister.

ABOVE: Mandela and director general in the presidency Jakes Gerwel, known as 'Prof'.

In Parliament with his long-time friend, former fellow prisoner and political adviser Ahmed Kathrada.

AUGUST (08)	1995	SEPTEMBER (09)	1995	OCTOBER (10)	1995
SUNDAY	6 13 20 27	SUNDAY	3 10 17 24	SUNDAY	1 8 15 22 29
MONDAY	7 14 21 28	MONDAY	4 11 18 25	MONDAY	2 9 16 23 30
TUESDAY	1 8 15 22 29	TUESDAY	5 12 19 26	TUESDAY	3 10 17 24 31
WEDNESDAY	2 9 16 23 30	WEDNESDAY	6 13 20 27	WEDNESDAY	4 11 18 25
THURSDAY	3 10 17 24 31	THURSDAY	7 14 21 28	THURSDAY	5 12 19 26
FRIDAY	4 11 17 25	FRIDAY	1 8 15 22 29	FRIDAY	6 13 20 27
SATURDAY	5 12 19 26	SATURDAY	2 9 16 23 30	SATURDAY	7 14 21 28

THURSDAY

JULY **06**

WEEK No 27
DAY No 187

TIME PLANNER | CONTACT | PHONE NO. | CALL AGENDA:

07:00   30 - 12 - 96

07:30

08:00   Meeting with Officers of the SAPS

08:30

09:00   A report released by the National Information

09:30

10:00   Management Centre of the SAPS showed that

10:30

11:00   1996 saw a reduction in levels of serious

11:30

12:00   crime; crime categories which reflected a

12:30

13:00   reduction include such violent crimes as

13:30

14:00   hijackings, armed robberies, politically motivated

14:30

15:00   violence, murder NOTES; LETTERS; FAX; MEMO; MINUTES; AGENDA & taxi

15:30

16:00   violence.

16:30

17:00   Members of the SAPS need to be congratulated

17:30

18:00   for the reduction in levels of crime is a result

18:30

19:00   of hard work & sacrifices which they made &

19:30

20:00   Continue to make.

20:30

EVE   Notwithstanding the many problems which
DAILY GOALS   PRIORITY
some communities in the E. Cape still have, eg.
taxi violence in Port Elizabeth, violence in
Qumbu, Idolo, Mganduli, as well as gang
related crimes in the Northern areas of P.E.

2650©   &D   Page 173

Mandela was a copious note-taker and would minute meetings in his diary, as he did for this meeting, on 30 December 1996, with officers of the South African Police Service.

President Mandela visits former South African president and staunch supporter of apartheid P. W. Botha, known as 'Die Groot Krokodil' (The Big Crocodile), at his home in Wilderness, 1995.

Actively practising reconciliation, Mandela visited Betsie Verwoerd, the widow of the architect of apartheid, Dr H. F. Verwoerd, at her home in the 'whites only' town of Orania, 1995.

Signing the Constitution of the Republic of South Africa, Sharpeville, 10 December 1996, with (from right) Cyril Ramaphosa and mayor of the Lekoa-Vaal Metropolitan Council, Yunus Chamda.

At Libertas, the presidential residence in Pretoria, which Mandela renamed Mahlamba Ndlopfu, meaning 'The New Dawn' in Xitsonga or, literally, 'the washing of the elephants'.

In his old cell on Robben Island at a reunion of political prisoners, 10 February 1995.

With US president Bill Clinton at the White House, Washington, DC. Mandela took advantage of his personal relationships with international leaders to influence negotiations and conflict resolution.

With Cuban president Fidel Castro. Mandela was insistent that Castro attend his inauguration.

The combination of talent and humility, of being able to be at home

with both the poor and the wealthy, the weak and the mighty,

ordinary people and royalty, young and old, men and women with

a common touch, ~~irrespective of their race or background~~ are admired by humankind all over the globe.

The ANC has ~~also~~ *always* been rich with talented men and women, who

preferred to remain in the background, and to push forward

promising young people to positions of eminence and

responsibility, to expose them early in their political careers to the

basic principles and problems of leadership, and on how to

manage such problems. This kind of leader has always made a

formidable impression on many of us. *Comrade Walter Sisulu is such a man; that is why he has always towered about all of us irrespective of the offices we occupied in the movement and government* I urged the three senior leaders that I would prefer to serve without

holding any position in the organisation or government. One of

them, however, put me flat on the carpet.

He reminded me that I had always advocated the crucial

importance of collective leadership, and that as long as we

scrupulously observed that principle, we could never go wrong. He

bluntly asked whether I was now rejecting what I had consistently

preached down the years.

In this original page of the manuscript, from chapter six, Mandela prefaces his description of his friend and former partner in law Oliver Tambo by commenting that the ANC has always had members who have preferred to remain in the background while mentoring younger members into leadership roles. Later, he has annotated the text with the words: 'Comrade Walter Sisulu is such a man; that is why he has always towered above all of us irrespective of the offices we occupied in the movement or government' (see page 156).

With French president Jacques Chirac at a Bastille Day military parade, Champs-Élysées, Paris, 1996.

TOP: With Palestinian leader Yasser Arafat.

ABOVE: With Graça Machel, Queen Margrethe II and Prince Henrik of Denmark, Copenhagen, 1999.

TOP: With Queen Elizabeth II, travelling along the Mall to Buckingham Palace, London, 1996.

ABOVE: With Prince Bandar bin Sultan of Saudi Arabia and Libyan leader Muammar Gaddafi, 1999 (see page 582).

With Graça Machel, Heathrow Airport, 1997. They began corresponding after Mandela sent her a letter of condolence from prison following the death of her husband, Mozambican president Samora Machel, in 1986. They were married on Mandela's eightieth birthday in 1998.

Mandela insisted on carrying out many mundane personal tasks himself, to the point of making his bed in hotels and polishing his shoes aboard the presidential jet. 'You just didn't throw things in his presence,' says his widow, Graça Machel. 'Where he is, everything has got to be orderly . . . impeccably clean' (see page 314).

X

The apartheid regime had put law and order in
disrepute. Human rights were ruthlessly suppressed,
there was detention without trial, torture and murder of
political activists, open villification of Appeal Court
Judges who were independent and gave judgments
against the regime, and the packing of the judiciary with
conservative ~~lawy~~ and pliant lawyers. The police,
especially the Security branch, were law unto themselves.
Because of this crude practice, and out of my own
convictions, I exploited every opportunity to promote
respect for law and order and for the judiciary.

Two examples will illustrate this point:
During my presidency parliament authorised me to
issue two proclamations dealing with elections in the
Western Cape Province. That provincial government took
me to the Constitutional Court which overruled me in
a unanimous judgment. As soon as I was informed of

In this handwritten page from chapter six of Mandela's memoir, he explains that due to the corrupt and inhumane practices of institutions of law and order under the apartheid regime, he 'exploited every opportunity to promote respect for law and order and for the judiciary' in the new democratic South Africa (see page 300).

At a Tri Nations Series rugby game with Zelda la Grange, who worked for Mandela for nineteen years, first as his private secretary, then as his aide-de-camp, spokesperson and office manager during his retirement years.

Mandela and Graça Machel visit Pollsmoor Prison, 1997, where Mandela himself had been incarcerated ten years earlier, to meet with prisoners following allegations that they had been assaulted.

With Springbok captain Francois Pienaar, Ellis Park Stadium, Johannesburg, after South Africa won the 1995 Rugby World Cup. Mandela's gesture of wearing the Springbok cap and jersey won thousands of Afrikaner hearts.

At the Fiftieth National Conference of the ANC, Mandela steps down as president of the organisation and hands the reins over to Thabo Mbeki, Mafikeng, 20 December 1997. Upon closing the conference, he said, 'I look forward to that period when I will be able to wake up with the sun; to walk the hills and valleys of Qunu in peace and tranquillity' (see page 595).

Receiving the report of the Truth and Reconciliation Commission from the commission's chairman, Archbishop Desmond Tutu, Pretoria, 1998. The commission investigated human rights violations that took place between 1960 and 1994. Aware of doubts about the process, Mandela admitted its imperfections but insisted on a national recognition of the crimes of the past (see page 468).

Greeting children in his hometown, Qunu, Christmas Day, 1995. Describing Qunu to Richard Stengel in 1993, he said, 'the people there, you know, there is a different dimension altogether, and I get . . . so pleased when I listen to them talk; their mannerisms, it reminds me of my younger days'.

Talking to students at the launch of the Nelson Mandela Children's Fund, Pretoria, 1995. Health care and education for children were among his main concerns, and he donated a third of his salary while he was in office towards the fund.

Youth welcome their hero as he demonstrates the famous 'Madiba Shuffle' while dancing to a local band during a visit to Oukasie township in Brits, 1995.

Always recharged by interaction with the public, here Mandela embraces a staff member at Hanover Day Hospital, Hanover Park, 1996.

After his retirement, Mandela became one of Africa's leading campaigners for HIV/AIDS awareness. Here he speaks at a Red Ribbon event in support of HIV/AIDS awareness in 1998.

President Mandela receives a standing ovation after making his final speech to South Africa's first democratically elected parliament before he retires as president, Parliament, Cape Town, 26 March 1999.

In this cartoon by Zapiro, the infant democratic nation lets out a collective wistful sigh as the sun sets on 'The Mandela era' and its first democratic president retires from public office in March 1999.

CHAPTER NINE:
TRANSFORMATION OF THE STATE

On 12 June 1964, one of the darkest moments in the history of South Africa, Nelson Mandela and seven other members of MK started a new life as men condemned to life imprisonment. Even though he made light of that time later, quipping that he had 'gone for a long holiday for twenty-seven years', before he had even left the Palace of Justice in Pretoria the forty-five-year-old Mandela had already decided that he would not be broken by imprisonment. Surviving prison called for immense reserves of mental strength — he had to arm himself with those things that enhanced his inner stability and discard everything that might weaken him. As there were no elders in prison, Mandela had to depend on the books that had sustained him, and internalise what he had read about the lives of others in similar positions.[1]

Nelson Mandela's library, before, during and after incarceration, was full of memoirs and biographies as well as epic novels whose connective tissue is the human struggle and triumph against insurmountable odds. Jan Smuts, Deneys Reitz, V. I. Lenin, Jawaharlal Nehru, Carl von Clausewitz, Kwame Nkrumah and Chief Albert Luthuli sat alongside *Spartacus, War and Peace, Bury My Heart at Wounded Knee* or *Red Star Over China.*[2] Here, too, was the work of Luis Taruc, the Filipino leader of the Hukbalahap guerrillas, whose memoir, *Born of the People,* was a key text for Mandela when he led MK; Taruc's account of peasant resistance and guerrilla warfare is so bleak as to be Sisyphean.[3]

One of the mountains Mandela had to climb was the transformation of the state. As in 1947 when Nehru's joy at becoming India's first prime minister was eclipsed by his distress at the wave of sectarian killings and conflict over Kashmir, Mandela — a midwife to an imperfect birth — had to put on a stoic face at the destruction wrought by apartheid, and work to enthuse a dispirited populace. It was here, also, that Mandela would take a leaf out of Nehru's book when it came to the Indian leader's trust in the involvement of multilateral organisations, like the UN, toward conflict resolution.

It was central to Mandela's leadership that he should continuously give grounds for optimism about the future. He saw this as one of his most important tasks. Knowing that he had inherited a wasteful and flawed state machinery, Mandela had to avoid the failures that plagued newly independent countries when colonial administrations gave way to liberation movements. The settlers, or the previous apartheid administration and its supporters, were South Africans and not an adjunct of a foreign colonising power; the settlers, as it were, were settled — South Africa was their home. The transition inevitably entailed some accommodation of existing state personnel.

Mandela's government had to reorient the state and its priorities. It had to rationalise what had been fragmented. As Allister Sparks put it: 'At the city, town and country level, a hodgepodge of local government institutions with their roots in the incredibly complex apartheid system, where the races were kept physically and politically apart, has been restructured into a compact system.'[4]

While all this was happening, the civil service corps was required to reflect the diversity of the country's population. Mandela took a pragmatic view of such complexities.

'When we win an election we hold office,' he said. 'We don't gain control of political power. To gain political power means that we have to get control of the civil service, of the security forces — that is, the police and the army; we have to have our people in telecommunications and so on. That is going to take some time to organise. For the first months or year we are going to lean very heavily on the present services. But the process of re-organisation will immediately start, to put our qualified people on the policy structures that take decisions. And we must expect that it is going to take some more time as we train more people.'[5]

In addition to this, of course, there was the establishment of the nine new provincial administrations to replace the four existing provinces, ten Bantustans and two quasi-administrations that were meant to service coloured and Indian populations, as well as a new local government system.

The 'sunset clauses' agreed upon during the negotiations guaranteed the jobs of old-order civil servants during the integration period. Similarly, the retention of the heads of the Commission for Public Administration, which would later become the Public Service Commission, secured a smooth transition and reduced the likelihood of counter-revolution.

These successes were sometimes punctuated by difficulties that detracted from progress achieved. The ANC's lack of training and capacity was a source of great concern. Zola Skweyiya, who would become the minister of public service and administration, was blunt: 'When it came to the question of the civil service, the public service, I don't want to tell lies,' he said, 'there never was very much preparation on the side of the ANC.'[6]

With characteristic candour, Mandela also honed in on the problem, saying, 'We had our policies on which we worked for a long time, but we had no experience.'[7]

If the ANC leaders and senior cadre lacked technical expertise in aspects of public service administration, for instance in the security forces, they made up for the deficit by shadowing apartheid functionaries during the negotiations and in the Transitional Executive Council, whose first meeting was on 7 December 1993. The sub-councils of the TEC oversaw regional and local government and traditional authorities, law and order — stability and security, defence, finance, foreign affairs, the status of women and intelligence. Those dealing with security, defence and intelligence developed codes of conduct and mechanisms for oversight and control, which served as a point of departure for the new democratic government after the election. The ANC was determined that these agencies would cease operating in the old ways and conform to the democratic ethos.[8]

As has been said already, for Mandela security was the key to a stable transition; the building blocks towards realising his democratic ideal. The way forward, in his reckoning, was to ensure that officers from the previous regime were embraced and given a stake in the new democracy as active custodians and creators of the future. Furthermore, in these early days for South Africa's fledgling democracy, a great deal of valuable information about human rights violations had yet to be revealed; a precipitate shake-up of the security forces could see evidence destroyed, depriving the government of information that would be crucial to understanding the past and ensuring it was not repeated.[9]

In November 1994, six months into the new dispensation, aware of the involvement of state security elements in seeking to block meaningful transformation, the new minister of safety and security, Sydney Mufamadi, asked Mandela to address the top police command. Mandela spoke to them from behind closed doors, now and then glancing up from the notes he had prepared for the meeting. Knowing that a law respected throughout the world is that a constabulary — any constabulary — must be bonded by a strict code of solidarity, and that cops generally despised weakness, he had to be firm and conciliatory in equal measure, the better to quash cliquish tendencies:

'I welcome the opportunity to exchange views with the command structure of the SAPS [South African Police Service]. You are responsible for law enforcement. You can only achieve this objective if you receive the full support of Government.

'I am here not as a representative of any political party — neither the National Party nor the ANC — but as head of the Government of the country.

'I believe in a police force which is committed to serving the nation as a whole, not a particular political party.

'I believe in a force that maintains the highest professional standards. Such high standards should be maintained even in the course of making a radical restructuring and reorientation of the police services.

'We have to bring about such radical transformation, but we would like to do that with the full cooperation of the Commanding Officer of the Police and the entire Command Staff.'[10]

Very few South Africans do not have a tale of woe involving the police. If the police are often viewed with suspicion throughout the world, it was even more so during the heyday of apartheid and during the transition that Mandela was steering. For as long as there was statutory apartheid, the trope of the cruel cop would feature in South African literature and song — and almost all township theatre would use it as shorthand for state cruelty. Knowing this, Mandela coaxed the police service to reach deep inside itself for solutions towards its legitimacy:

'It would be regrettable if the perception is strengthened that you're opposed to such transformation, that you want to defend the racist nature of the force in which a white minority dominates, and where blacks are relegated to inferior positions.

'You must not appear to be giving in to these changes only under pressure.

'You must never forget that the changes that we are introducing in this country were brought about by the struggle of the oppressed people of our country, some of whom paid the highest price. Many of these died in police custody, and others were so tortured in detention that they are crippled for the rest of their lives. They will never allow, especially now that they are in power, for any Government agency or department to undermine their programmes to better their lives.

'You must also not forget that the eyes of the world are focussed on South Africa.

'Notwithstanding the brutality of the apartheid system generally — and that of the police in particular — during the run-up to the elections, I urged my people to forget the past; to work for reconciliation and for nation building.

'With a few insignificant exceptions, the entire country has responded marvellously to this message. Black and white, Shangaan, Venda and Sotho, Afrikaans- and English-speaking South Africans are now working together to build a new South Africa.

'The police must not appear to be opposed

to this movement and spirit, paying only lip service to the idea, whilst working day and night to undermine what we are doing.'[11]

Mandela continued by telling them he had not only appealed to mainly black South Africans — most of whom had suffered hideously in the hands of the law — to have a change of heart towards the police; he had also taken concrete steps to ensure a peaceful transition. He had met General van der Merwe some months before the elections, addressed the command staff of the SADF and addressed the command structure of the South African Police (SAP) on 16 January 1993.*

'The SAP,' he said, 'have responded very well. They made a formidable impression on the day of the inauguration, as did the SADF. The generals of [the] SAP must not appear to be against this development.

'Ghosts of the past can continue to haunt us if we do not become a visible part of the current changes. Hit squads are still a disturbing feature in the crime situation; and the failure of the SAP to bring them to book is a source of great concern to me.'[12]

He rattled off what troubled him: the lack

---

* The South African Police (SAP) was renamed the South African Police Service (SAPS) when apartheid ended and it was amalgamated with other apartheid police forces.

of disciplinary action when police were shown to have been involved in the military training of IFP members; the failure to search illegal IFP training camps; and turning a blind eye to open defiance by IFP members carrying illegal weapons. He decried the double standards seen in 'the sharp and almost vicious manner in which SAP acts against ANC' whilst folding their arms when Eugene Terre'Blanche led the Afrikaner Weerstandsbeweging in action that killed scores of people in Bophuthatswana before the elections.* Aware of police involvement in crime, he pointed to the impact of high crime levels on discouraging future financial investment in the country, and concluded by voicing his concern about the working conditions of ordinary members of the police.[13]

There would be many such encounters, some occasioned by the urgency of the situa-

* In early 1994 President Lucas Mangope of Bophuthatswana attempted to crush protests demanding the homeland be reincorporated into South Africa. On 7 March 1994, violent protests and a civil service strike reacted to his announcement that the territory would boycott the democratic elections set for 27 April 1994. On 11 March, the AWB sent armed men to support Mangope. They embarked on a random shooting spree in which forty-two people were killed. Three AWB men were shot dead by a Bophuthatswana policeman.

tion, others by Mandela's need to satisfy himself that the police were still on track. Apart from unfailingly attending the meetings of the Cabinet Committee on Security and Intelligence, according to Thabo Mbeki, Mandela also interacted with the police at all levels. The no-holds-barred engagement behind closed doors was matched by Mandela's public appeals to communities to support the police whom he credited with making an effort to embrace the new South Africa.

Mufamadi remembers how, as minister of safety and security, he would suggest when Mandela should meet with the police. Often, though, Mandela 'would also initiate meetings with police just to know what they think about the changing situation'. Mandela would

give advice when he felt it was warranted, and encourage them [the police] to stay focused on their work. There were times when a particular form of crime would show itself as a national priority crime, such as the cash-in-transit robberies that emerged at one point as a disturbing trend of organised crime by people who in some instances had military training. We established a special unit to investigate that. Once Mandela became aware of it, he said, 'Can I meet them and hear what they think about the task? Have we given them enough resources to do their work?' When they [the special unit] made breakthroughs, he would invite them and congratulate them. But at all times, even as he was talking in positive terms, encouraging them to do more of the good work they were doing, he would always draw a line at things he didn't want to see [being] repeated, things that belonged to the past.[14]

In December 1996, when Mandela was supposed to be holidaying in his ancestral home in Qunu, in the Eastern Cape, he initiated a meeting with the police in the province. He had good news for the police officers in the form of a report from the National Crime Information Management Centre of the SAPS, which recorded a marked reduction that year in incidents of serious crime, such as hijackings, armed robberies, politically motivated violence, murder and taxi violence. 'Notwithstanding the many problems which some communities in the Eastern Cape still have,' he said, 'e.g. taxi violence in Port Elizabeth, violence in Qumbu, Tsolo, Mqanduli, as well as gang-related crime in the northern areas of P. E. [Port Elizabeth], the E. Cape as a Province, experienced such a decline in levels of serious crime in 1996.'[15]

The Eastern Cape had been the epicentre of the struggle against apartheid, a province that was the home of a disproportionately large percentage of ANC leadership. As it was his birthplace, Mandela felt conflicted that it was the poorest of the nine provinces and the one most riven with crime. This breakthrough, therefore, was a real achievement, given the fact that, while the police were fighting crime, 'at the same time they were attending to the task of restructuring the police service and amalgamating three agencies within one province, they were amalgamating the Transkei police, the Ciskei police and the then SAP'.

He encouraged those 'who are committed to serving the community', and commented on 'a few elements within the SAPS who do things which bring the police service into disrepute', observing that 'the fact that such elements are often exposed by their own colleagues, will in the long term, convince the communities that the police have irrevocably broken with the past.

'One of the problems which dogged the province is the corruption which pervades the various state departments. The fact that some of the high-profile cases of theft of taxpayers' money remain unsolved, does not contribute to good public image of the police. It is important to bear in mind that the credibility of the SAPS will derive from the feeling that the SAPS is committed to solving problems experienced by our people.'[16]

General van der Merwe had told Mandela

before the 1994 election that he intended to retire early. Much to Mandela's irritation, Van der Merwe had wanted Lieutenant General Sebastiaan 'Basie' Smit as his successor.*[17] Nonetheless, Mandela had wanted him to stay on. He wanted to reassure the general and his subordinates that they were not going to be persecuted for past crimes and misdemeanours and that there was a place for them in the new South Africa — provided, of course, that they participated in building the future and worked towards ensuring that there was no recurrence of past wrongdoings. However, Van der Merwe showed little enthusiasm for the investigations into the continued existence and operations of hit squads or for participating in the Truth and Reconciliation Commission, which was expected to expose structural support for the ongoing violence. The relationship between Van der Merwe and Minister Mufamadi began to deteriorate, and Mandela became convinced that he needed to appoint the first National Commissioner, in line with the new South African Police Service Act. Eventually, George Fivaz, who had been part

* Basie Smit was implicated in the charge of attempted murder when the prominent cleric Frank Chikane was sent poisoned T-shirts in 1989. Smit also awarded a medal to convicted mass murderer and former security policeman Eugene de Kock.

of the police national change-management team, was appointed to replace General van der Merwe.*[18]

In setting out the evolution of the security structures, Mandela was surer of his ground, an architect seeing the various elements of his blueprints becoming more concrete, and in his unfinished memoir he expands on the situation at some length:

'It was under those circumstances that George Fivaz became the new National Commissioner. Mr Sydney Mufamadi became the Minister of Safety and Security. The two were the foremost pioneers in the creation of a new South African police force dedicated to the service of all our people regardless of colour or creed. In the National Crime Prevention Strategy (NCPS), which came out in 1996, and in other policy documents that followed, they candidly analysed the formidable challenges facing the Department of Safety and Security.

'They pointed out that the first democratic elections in 1994 did not bring a system of policing which was well placed to create a legitimate police service out of the eleven police forces constituted under apartheid.

'They reminded us all that policing in South Africa was traditionally highly centralised, paramilitary and authoritarian. While

* George Fivaz — see People, Places and Events.

these characteristics ensured that the police were effective under apartheid in controlling the political opponents of the government, it meant that they were poorly equipped for crime control and prevention in the new democracy.

'Under apartheid rule, they stressed, the police force lacked legitimacy, and functioned as an instrument of control, rather than as a police service dedicated to ensuring the safety of all citizens. Thus historically, the police had had little interest in responding to crimes in the black areas. In 1994, as much as 74% of the country's police stations were situated in white suburbs and business districts.

'Police presence in townships was used to anticipate and respond to collective challenges to apartheid. This mode of policing necessitated the mobilisation of force requiring skills and organisation very different from that needed to police a democratic order in which government seeks to ensure the safety of all citizens. That inheritance had a number of important consequences, which weakened the ability of the Department to combat crime.

'The study pointed out that the authoritarian policing had few (if any) systems of accountability and oversight, and did not require public legitimacy in order to be effective. Thus with the advent of democracy in South Africa, systems of accountability and oversight were not present.

'New mechanisms such as the Independent Complaints Directorate (ICD) — a complaints body tasked with investigating abuses within the SAPS, situated outside of the police, but reporting directly to the Minister — provided the means of limiting the occurrence of human rights abuses.

'The study contends that the South African Police Service had not had a history of criminal detection characteristic of the police in other democratic societies. The collection, collation and presentation of evidence to secure the prosecution of criminals were weakly developed in many areas. This was reflected by, among other indicators, the training levels and experience of the Detective component of the SAPS.

'In 1994, only about 26% of detectives had been on a formal investigation training course, while only 13% of detectives had over six years' experience. In any event, those detective skills present in the police force before 1994 were concentrated in white areas.

'According to the study, the problems of criminal detection were mirrored in the area of criminal intelligence. Intelligence gathering structures were orientated towards the political opponents of the apartheid state. Consequently, crime intelligence, particularly as it pertained to increasingly sophisticated forms of organised crime, required immediate improvement.

'A concentration on policing for purposes of political control meant that prior to 1994 — and in contrast to developments in other societies — the understanding and practice of crime prevention was poorly developed in South Africa.

'The NCPS was the most important initiative aimed at achieving sustainable safety in South Africa. It had two broad and interlocking components, that of law enforcement and that of crime prevention, particularly social crime prevention.

'The study adds that law enforcement initiatives will be weakened if conditions in which they are carried out continue to generate high levels of criminality. International experience had shown that sophisticated crime prevention strategies had only a limited effect when such institutions of policing and criminal justice were poorly developed.

'What was required were social crime-preventing programmes which targeted the causes of particular types of crime at national, provincial and local level. Such an approach also recognised the impact of broader government economic development and social policies for crime prevention. The effective delivery of basic services such as housing, education and health, as well as job creation, had in themselves a critical role to play in ensuring living environments less conducive to crime.

'I have summarised this frank and objective police study to show how Sydney Mufamadi and George Fivaz accurately described the type of police force the new South Africa was inheriting from the apartheid regime. These are the well-considered views of two eminent and courageous leaders with undisputed credentials in their commitment to the country.

'The crisp message from them was that we need a new police force, totally different from the one that served the apartheid state, if we are to succeed in reducing the unacceptably high level of crime ravaging the country. Only a force stripped of its paramilitary and authoritarian characteristics and properly trained in the modern methods of policing in a democratic order could help South Africa to achieve this object.

'Commentators of integrity would compliment the Department of Safety and Security for their analytical ability and vision. No honest analyst, black or white, could expect this goal to be achieved within a period of seven years.[19]

'In his budget speech to the National Assembly on 28 May 1998, Sydney Mufamadi quoted a telling passage from the *South African Institute of Race Relations Survey* [of 1993/94]:

Murder and armed robbery, as well as attacks on the elderly and on policemen, have increased dramatically, while white-collar fraud had also risen sharply in 1992.

The Minister of Law and Order, Hernus Kriel, said in Parliament in May 1993 that more than 20,000 people had been murdered in South Africa in political and criminal violence in 1992. There were 380,000 rape cases in South Africa every year and 95% of the victims were African . . .

In the ten years from 1983 to 1992, the murder rate increased by 135%, robbery by 109%, housebreaking by 71%, car theft by 64%. However, many crimes were unreported.[20]

'Sydney Mufamadi added that that indeed was a picture of an escalation of serious crime which demonstrated grave geometric continuity.

'It is against this background that the achievement of the government in transforming our police force must be seen. It must, however, be conceded that even during the darkest moments of apartheid there were many police, black and white, men and women, of the highest calibre, who were professional in their duties, and who tried to the best of their ability to serve all sections of the population without discrimination.

'But these were few and far between. They

were the exceptions rather than the rule.

'The overwhelming majority fully accepted the inhuman policies of apartheid, and served as the instrument of the most brutal forms of racial oppression this country has ever seen. Some of these men and women are still members of the present force, occupying strategic positions and obstructing in countless ways the creation of a new police force.

'Nevertheless, both Sydney Mufamadi and his successor, Steve Tshwete, George Fivaz and [his successor as] the present National Commissioner Jackie Selebi, have made unprecedented progress in creating a new force capable of policing in a democratic order, and in significantly reducing the high levels of crime.

'On 24 May 1997, and after discussing the matter with me, Deputy President Mbeki announced the appointment of Mr Meyer Kahn, Group Chairman of the South African Breweries Limited, to take on the position of Chief Executive of the SAPS for a two-year period.* The Deputy President explained that that was a new civilian function calculated to direct and accelerate the conversion of the SAPS into an effective law-enforcement and crime-prevention agency. Mr Kahn would report to Safety and Security Minister Sydney Mufamadi.

* Meyer Kahn — see People, Places and Events.

'The Deputy President added that our selection of one of the private sector's toughest and ablest managers — and his willingness to answer the call — underscored the new era of partnership between the public and private sector to end the scourge of crime.

'National Commissioner Fivaz would thus be freed of the administrative burden within the SAPS, and would be able to concentrate his total energy on managing and controlling the pure policing operations of the service.

'The goal, the Deputy President said, was to put the police back on the frontline, and make sure that they were equipped with the right skills and resources to do their job well.

'But the partnership between the government and the private sector actually started a year earlier with the establishment of a non-profit organisation, Business Against Crime (BAC). The prime aim of the organisation was to contribute to the government's crime-combating strategy, policy and priorities, and to transfer much-needed technology skills to government.

'This partnership has been hailed as one of the best practices of its kind in the world. The NCPS was the first initiative of this partnership. After the engagement of Meyer Kahn, other full-time business executives were appointed and funded by the business community.

'These helped to modernise the criminal justice system, combating commercial crimes, organised crime [and facilitating] the installation of electronic surveillance with remarkable success. In one area, electronic surveillance resulted in an 80% reduction in crime, increased conviction rates in cases where crime had been committed, a 90% decrease in the number of police personnel required to patrol the area, and an average response time to incidents of less than 60 seconds.

'This sober assessment comes from Business Against Crime, an important section of the community which has spent considerable resources, time and energy to improve the quality of our police services.

'I asked Meyer Kahn for a report on our agreed strategy to reconstruct the SAPS into an effective law-enforcement agency. He responded on 02 July 1998. Among the structural focus areas he dealt with was the enforcement of the newly launched Code of Conduct with a view to, over time, changing the conduct and behaviour of the police.

'The golden thread that flew from that Code, Meyer Kahn reported, was one of caring. Care for your country, care for your communities, care for your colleagues, care for your assets and, above all, care for your reputation.

'He pointed out that he had by then been in office for eleven months and had no regrets about his appointment. He believed that our new strategies were as good as one would hope to find. He was heartened by the fact that our statistics indicated clearly a stabilisation and mild decrease across the board in terms of all the serious crime in our country. He considered this to be fairly remarkable against the background of a deteriorating external environment of no economic growth and greater joblessness. In addition, the very high and speedy arrest rates by our detectives in respect of high-profile crimes that so damage the morale and reputation of our country certainly indicated that the SAPS still had the skill and dedication to compare with the best in the world.

'However, he placed on record that the increase in the police budget of only 3.7% in monetary terms and on a comparable basis, he found difficult to comprehend. Particularly against the background that fighting crime is recognised by every South African, as well as by international opinion, as the foremost, if not the only priority, in order to create an environment for our democracy and economy to flourish.

'He regretted that a reduction that year in real terms of at least 4% in police spending would inevitably impede even the most basic policing that our people were entitled to expect, and would most certainly place our medium-term strategy of reconstructing the

SAPS in serious jeopardy.

'But the Deputy President, Business Against Crime and Meyer Kahn, acting independently of one another, virtually reinforced the assessment of Sydney Mufamadi and George Fivaz in analysing the formidable challenges facing the Department of Safety and Security in their efforts to transform the SAPS from an illegitimate and discredited service to a credible and efficient force in a democratic South Africa.

'They all spelt out the changes required and in due course assessed the results of such initiatives, the cooperation between the SAPS and the masses of the people, and the gradual decline in the levels of various crimes. Their performance and achievements left all of us proud of our country, of our comrades, our police and of ourselves. We were exuding with confidence and optimism . . .'[21]

'It has been a long haul from the difficult and painful era of the pre-1994 police, who enjoyed no public legitimacy, to the present force which works with the public and which guarantees safety and security to all our people. Without a properly trained and efficient police force which enjoys the trust and support of the public, as the present one does, political and economic stability would have been an elusive daydream.'[22]

The transformation of the military, by contrast, had got off to a promising start, with General Georg Meiring giving his unqualified commitment to serve Mandela's government. This was punctuated by the seamless security around both the 1994 elections and the ceremonial embrace of the inauguration. Before long, however, the transformation of the defence force proved a lot more turbulent than had been anticipated.

The SADF and the defence forces of the nominally independent Bantustans of Transkei, Venda, Bophuthatswana and Ciskei, as well as the KwaZulu Self-Protection Force, had to be merged into an integrated South African National Defence Force (SANDF) together with their traditional enemies, the ANC's MK and the Pan Africanist Congress of Azania's Azanian People's Liberation Army (APLA). Once this was complete, the new entity, the SANDF, had to be rationalised and downsized.

There had been earlier meetings between the SADF and MK, the first in 1990 in Lusaka, and then in 1992.[23] Initiated by Mandela, then ANC president — who told the ANC, 'These people want to talk' — the first practical engagement was in April 1993, when senior ANC military and intelligence leaders met the top five of the SADF.[24]

Chaired by General Meiring during the time of the TEC, a Joint Military Coordinating Committee, with representatives from both the SADF and liberation movement forces, worked towards the creation of a single defence force, to come into effect at midnight on the day the elections began. This entailed 'the integration of a large number of statutory and non-statutory forces into a single, cohesive defence force' and the establishment of 'systems of civilian control over the defence force'.[25]

The ANC prepared for integration by briefing its MK cadres in the camps and by holding conferences throughout the country, some of which Mandela attended, to impart his wisdom. These men and women had joined MK to acquire skills to fight and liberate the country from apartheid oppression and exploitation. Now, while many of their compatriots donned the uniform of the new and integrated national defence force, they would have to divest themselves of the uniforms that had given them a sense of being part of something hugely meaningful.

All soldiers feel naked in the clothes of civilians. Mandela understood this vulnerability, this sense of being robbed of a crutch. He knew, also, that there was a possibility for the strength of the new defence force to be depleted by the introduction of voluntary severance packages, a double-edged sword. It appealed to people with a few years of pensionable service; it was also likely to encourage the exodus of exactly the kind of talent the defence force needed. Knowing that some of the ex-combatants — many of them young and inexperienced — would be excited to receive the large sums of money being offered to those volunteering for demobilisation, he advised them against 'eating the money'. Sadly, in most cases, his advice fell on deaf ears.[26]

Despite the careful preparations, years of enmity, suspicion and conflicting expectations posed huge difficulties for the integration. The rumblings were loudest in the military base of Wallmansthal, some 50-odd kilometres from Pretoria, where, days after the election, the car of two MK generals driving into the base to deal with complaints was pelted with stones by former members. A few months later, some five hundred MK members marched from the base to the Union Buildings, demanding to see the president. Mandela came immediately from his residence and, after listening, acknowledged their grievances as genuine. He discussed the matter with General Meiring, the Acting Chief of Staff Siphiwe Nyanda and Minister of Defence Joe Modise. Interacting further with MK members, Mandela met the SANDF Command Council, the highest decision-making body of the defence force, and urged them to address the fact that the non-statutory forces were being accommodated rather than integrated. The process was very slow; racism was alive and well in the camps, and the living conditions were atrocious.[27]

Seeking to settle the matter, Mandela visited Wallmansthal to address the former MK members there and was immediately faced with the enormity of the situation. After listening for two hours, Mandela had a firm message for both protesters and the top brass. While the soldiers had legitimate grievances, their mistake was to pursue them in a manner that was unseemly for people in uniform. He told them that they had a week to return to barracks, at their own cost, and submit themselves to SANDF discipline; those who weren't back by then, need not return. To the SANDF leadership, he said that the integration process needed accelerating. He added that he was confident that General Meiring and the commanders were committed to making a success of integration.[28]

While some of the soldiers returned to base, a number didn't, sparking rumours of armed protests; this highlighted concerns that demobbed soldiers, from either side, might turn to crime or political destabilisation.

Half the seven thousand soldiers had gone AWOL and were still refusing to return until their issues were resolved. Now he reminded the soldiers of MK history: why it had been formed and its proud record — a record of which they were expected to be custodians, he said.[29]

Two years later, in 1996, Mandela voiced his concern in an interview:

'We have a big army of about 90,000. We don't need even half of that. We need far less because we have no enemies. But, assuming we reduce it by half this year, there would be another 45,000 people unemployed. We already have five million unemployed.

'We then create a great deal of bitterness on the part of people who are trained to use arms. And with arms circulating in this country almost freely, that would be a dangerous thing to do.

'So when we move away from the apartheid budget, we should do so cautiously and gradually and we will be unable to do many things we would like to do.'[30]

Many elected leaders the world over have echoed Mandela's lament about the circumstances that render them 'unable to do [the] many things' they would like to achieve. A few of those have been hobbled by the budget not squaring up to the social needs of the citizens; few, however — except in war-torn countries — have had to roll back the inexorable legacy of problems associated with the past. These were intricate problems facing a society that was still inchoate — soft like clay before it is fired in a kiln. The solution, if applied unwisely, could very well lead to its collapse.

A year earlier, in 1995, South Africa's dishonoured past had risen up, bringing a new set of problems for Mandela and his government. Together with IFP leader M. Z. Khumalo and eighteen others, Magnus Malan, the former apartheid minister of defence, was arrested and charged with being responsible for leading the massacre in KwaMakhutha, Amanzimtoti, near Durban. Thirteen people, mostly women and children, were shot dead at the home of United Democratic Front activist Bheki Ntuli on 21 January 1987. Mandela knew that Malan's arraignment would further divide the country. Magnus Malan — a decorated soldier's soldier and military strategist — was as admired by the apartheid military establishment as he was reviled by the majority that had, directly or indirectly, borne the brunt of his excesses in the enforcement of P. W. Botha's doctrine of Total Strategy.*

In a note for a National Executive Committee meeting, Mandela observed that the 'arrest of General Malan and others provoked

---

* In its commitment to keep South Africa under white control, P. W. Botha's government used the term 'total strategy' to describe its suppression, which was usually disproportionately violent, of the increased black resistance, which it termed 'total onslaught'. This doctrine saw the government conduct cross-border raids on the ANC in neighbouring countries.

wide interest across the length and breadth of the country . . . Before and after the formal arrest we briefed several individuals and organisations, eg. Georg Meiring alone first and later the command structure of the SANDF; business; Archbishop Tutu alone first and thereafter the SACC [South African Council of Churches]; Bishop Lekganyane; DRC [Dutch Reformed Church]; political scientists from all our universities, with the exception of Stellenbosch and PE [Port Elizabeth]; the 26 teachers organisations; the FF [Freedom Front]; and P. W. Botha.'[31]

Briefing the diverse men of the cloth to enlist their appreciation of the nuance of the arrest was one thing, but Mandela was somewhat more offhand with the SANDF. General Nyanda remembers Mandela saying that 'he wanted to come to a regular Monday meeting of the Defence Staff Council. He didn't allow any questions, just came there as commander-in-chief. The essence of what he said was this: "We have gone through a difficult period of change; our people fought for the democracy that we now enjoy. It is at a tenuous stage and if there are people who want to undermine it and reverse things, the South African people will defeat them." '[32]

He made similarly stern remarks when, in January 1996, the parliamentary caucus put forward a motion to scrap Afrikaans as one of the languages of instruction, training and command, requesting instead that English should be the only language used. Mandela felt that tampering with a group's language would 'reduce the country to ashes', and vowed to 'protect' the Afrikaner cultural heritage 'as if it was my own'.[33] Fortunately, the idea was rejected by the minister of defence and cabinet, and by May 1996 the section on language written into the *White Paper on National Defence for the Republic of South Africa* required that the SANDF 'shall respect the constitutional provision on language and shall endeavour to cater for the different languages of its members. Instruction, command and control shall be conducted in a language that is commonly understood by all.'[34]

However, Mandela's spirited defence of the Afrikaners and their culture — and his accommodation of the military's past leadership — was rewarded by a manifest betrayal of trust.

Although the intelligence agencies were supposedly amalgamated under the control of a new national intelligence service, the truth is that military intelligence continued to harbour some who continued to pursue old agendas. Three months after the elections, there was an attempt to pressurise the minister of defence by threatening to publish names of ANC members now in government who had allegedly been informers to the apartheid regime.[35]

Over the next three years, military intelligence fabricated a report purporting to show a plan to disrupt the 1999 elections and bring down the government — a plan that supposedly involved General Nyanda, who was in line to succeed General Meiring. When the report reached him, Meiring took it to the president. A sceptical Mandela found the report implausible; it named people without a motive to upset the applecart, as they were likely to take senior positions when the old-order generals moved on. At the opening of the budget debate in April 1998, Mandela briefed Parliament:

'Several recent developments have underlined the strength of our democracy. Media reports suggesting that a coup plot had been uncovered have turned out to be essentially without foundation and based on the fulmination of an active imagination.

'It may be well to take this opportunity to brief honourable members on the basics concerning the SANDF report, which I received on 5 February, and which had the title "Organised Activities with the Aim to Overthrow the Government". Initial consultations within Government raised questions about the report's reliability and lack of verification. These were still in progress when a leak of some of its contents made it necessary to establish, with urgency, the reliability of the processes of its compilation, verification and subsequent handling.

'The commission of inquiry appointed for this purpose reported to me at the end of March. The intelligence report made the following claims: That an organisation called FAPLA (Force African Peoples Liberation Army) had existed since 1995 and aimed to subvert the 1999 general elections, [and] that it aimed to do so by assassinating the President; murdering Judges; occupying Parliament, broadcasting stations and key financial institutions; as well as orchestrating generalised disorder over a period of some four months before the elections.

'The culmination would be a campaign of attacks in which the present order would collapse, and power handed over to the coup leaders. Some 130 people are named in the report as the alleged organisation's members, leaders or supporters. They include very senior military personnel, political figures and others.

'The commission's main conclusions are as follows: The report was without substance and inherently fantastic. All the witnesses interviewed were sceptical about the existence of FAPLA. Even those compiling it appeared not to have taken it seriously. No serious attempt was made to keep the alleged plotters under surveillance and no attempts were made to authenticate the report.

'Those responsible for compiling the report over three years failed to share it with the appropriate authorities, including the South African Police Service and the National Intelligence Coordinating Committee. The commission was critical of steps taken to keep the record safe and prevent leaks. Those responsible for compiling and handling the report did not communicate it to the Ministers responsible for Intelligence, Safety and Security, who only gained access to it from the President after he received it from the Chief of the SANDF.

'An allegation concerning a particular officer was communicated by the Chief of the SANDF to the Minister of Defence, but not the extent of the allegations, the identity of other senior officers alleged to be involved, nor the details of the conspiracy. The Minister of Defence said he was not prepared to communicate an uncorroborated allegation to the President.

'The commission concluded that such a report should not have been communicated to the President in the way it was. It also commented on the extraordinary procedure of a direct communication to the President and a deliberate avoidance of furnishing the report to any other officials. The commission recommended that the security agencies should investigate why the omissions and failures in the processing of the report took place and what can be done, if necessary legislatively, to avoid repetition in the future.

'I acceded to the request for early retirement by the Chief of the SANDF, as it was an act which put the national interest of the SANDF above his own. The leakage of the report and the critical comments of the Commission of Inquiry over its compilation and transmission clearly put the General in a difficult position in his relationship with the senior officers mentioned in the report and with his Commander-in-Chief, and Minister of Defence. Such a bold, though regrettable, step was therefore clearly warranted.'

Mandela promised that at its next meeting, cabinet would consider the urgent question of the appointment of a new SANDF chief. He added that 'it should be made very clear that our nation has a loyal defence force which has laid the groundwork for its own transformation.' But, he continued, 'neither the original [discredited] Military Intelligence report nor the Commission of Inquiry's report have been made public . . . it would be the height of irresponsibility for any government to peddle untruths and fabrications about people whose reputation could be harmed, despite the lack of truth.

'The public has a right to know that such matters as this are addressed thoroughly and scrupulously through processes in which they can have confidence. The Commission of

Inquiry fulfils these requirements. The briefing of parliamentary committees elaborates the process.'

Mandela did, however, offer to release the report in a redacted form to the Joint Standing Committee on Intelligence, and in order to 'allow broader oversight', the reports were made available to the leaders of the opposition parties.

'It is instructive to note that it is those who opportunistically refused to look at the report [after its presentation to them earlier] who continue to call for its publication. At the same time, they use the fact that they have not seen it to raise doubts about the government's untrustworthiness.

'This is a dangerous game to play with our intelligence services and raises the question of whether the legitimacy of the government is accepted by such people! Or maybe it is simply a reckless pursuit of party advantage, bringing self-appointed champions of democratic conventions close to abdicating their responsibility as political leaders. I myself, in dealing with this matter, have sought to act according to the assumption that all of us in our respective political parties share a common national purpose.'

Mandela continued, throwing down the gauntlet: 'Indeed, there is a more general challenge here. As we approach the election period, parties will have to ask themselves some very basic questions. It is only too easy to stir up the baser feelings that exist in any society, feelings that are enhanced in a society with a history such as ours. Worse still, it is only too easy to do this in a way that undermines our achievements in building national unity and enhancing the legitimacy of our democratic institutions. We need to ask such questions because it is much easier to destroy than to build.'[36]

Again, it is worth remembering Mandela's extraordinary capacity to maintain friendships with people he believed were crucial to the construction of South Africa's democracy. He won over many right-wingers who posed a threat to his project, and enlisted their co-operation; others, like the AWB leader Eugene Terre'Blanche, whom he thought was beyond the pale, he dismissed with undisguised contempt. For example, speaking to Mike Siluma of *The Sowetan,* he said, 'We have marginalised the right wing . . . [Eugene] Terre'Blanche used to draw 2,000 people to his meetings. Today he struggles. He can't even get 100 — even when counting his horse.'[37]

Mandela had embraced and defended Meiring, even in the face of criticism from his own comrades. After Meiring's resignation, Mandela said, 'I accepted his decision to step down with regret because he is an officer I hold in the highest regard because of the invaluable service he had rendered to the South African National Defence Force and to the country and to me personally. Over these four years we formed a very close relationship in which I regarded him as one of my closest friends.'[38] That the general should have played such an active role in the military intelligence plot was therefore a very personal betrayal.

After Meiring's departure Nyanda stepped in as the head of the defence force. The policy framework defining both the function and strategic doctrine for a new military was drawn from the 1996 *White Paper on National Defence* and the 1998 *Defence Review*. It established a Defence Secretariat, which reinforced civilian control, a departure from the apartheid regime's use of military power to impose its interests on the Southern African region. There was recognition of the fact that, as South Africa had been embraced by many international organisations, most notably the United Nations, the Organisation of African Unity (OAU) and the Southern African Development Community (SADC), it was expected to play an active role in these bodies, especially with regard to peace and security in Africa and in the region.* The

* Organisation of African Unity (OAU); Southern African Development Community (SADC) — see People, Places and Events.

policy framework of the *White Paper* and *Defence Review* sought to reverse the military's order of priorities and provided for support for police operations against crime and a requirement to contribute towards reconstruction and development.

The review of the defence force's role and its need for equipment would take nearly three years, and procurement issues arose as soon as Mandela's government took power. A purchase of corvettes from Spain was in progress. According to Trevor Manuel, Joe Modise, the minister of defence, arrived with a stern-faced Mandela at the ANC's first cabinet caucus after the elections. They were obviously still carrying the mood of an earlier exchange. Manuel remembers how 'Madiba said, "Joe?" Joe Modise broke down, crying, "It's not a nice day for me to say this, and it is my birthday, but the president has spoken to me about this contract to buy the corvettes from Spain, and he said that we will cancel the contract. I don't know how I'm going to tell my troops, especially the Navy, that we're cancelling this contract, but the president assures me that we would look at this thing." '[39]

Mandela felt that the government had to look at all the needs of the entire defence force rather than of just one service and that, as a result, the contract should be scrapped.[40]

There was, he said, 'a national consensus

that our Defence Force requires an appropriate capacity and modern equipment. We welcome the fact that debate on these issues is now finding rational reflection in the discussions around the *Defence White Paper* and the *National Defence Review*.'[41]

Given the scope of the expenditure, the cabinet consolidated the complex process of arms procurement into a single component known as the Strategic Defence Procurement Package. The cabinet and a special committee made up of the ministers of finance, defence, public enterprises and trade and industry, chaired by Thabo Mbeki, decided on the allocation of the main contracts. The committee adopted a rule that it would not interact directly with any of the bidders, and there were four independent evaluation groups to add another layer of checks and balances. It was cabinet, however, that would decide on the primary contractors; the latter, in turn, would be responsible for engaging the secondary contractors needed to fulfil their obligations.[42]

This would have wide implications for the South African government and would, in time, earn the inelegant sobriquet of 'Arms Deal'.

Although its integration and transformation had been buffeted by strong winds coming from a questioning media and a wary public, the defence force had changed utterly by the end of the Mandela presidency. It was a complex undertaking, a foray into uncharted territory, and one which could not possibly have succeeded without Mandela's personal stamp, without his characteristic and always timely interventions. The new defence force was initially a hodgepodge of armies with long histories of mutual hostility and disrespect. The liberation contingents looked down on the Bantustan forces, seeing them as a watered-down version of the time-tested enemy, the SADF. In addition, the soldiers of the SADF had to be brought kicking and screaming into the modern era, one in which they would have to view their compatriots as live human beings and not as quarry in their gunsights.

The twin processes of integration and rationalisation had produced a SANDF in which about 40 per cent of its members were from liberation movements and Bantustan forces.[43] Recruitment of black youth into the voluntary part-time force further increased the numbers of new entrants.

Camaraderie began to develop between soldiers from the different forces. The army's support for the police in fighting crime was seen as supportive to communities, a far cry from the apartheid army's unwelcome presence in the townships. A 1999 survey by the Human Sciences Research Council found that trust in the Defence Force among Africans stood at 62 per cent. Interestingly, the study attests that 'trust in the South African National Defence Force (SANDF) exceeded trust in the police and the courts'.[44]

When it came to the transformation of the intelligence services, once both the nerve centre and backbone of the apartheid state, the new democratic government had to dig deep into its intellectual reserves — and explore a sophisticated level of cunning — to negotiate its way through a labyrinth that had taken decades to build. The act of transformation meant examining the entrails of a many-headed monster with an unlimited budget. Its officers had engaged in exchange programmes with their counterparts in the Middle East, especially Israel, and with dictatorships in the Americas, where they learnt the finer arts of torture and the manufactured disappearance of opponents. It was a ubiquitous service that touched every part of life — and death — in South Africa. It was simultaneously quite adept at communicating its nonexistence, bringing to mind Baudelaire's line that 'the finest trick of the devil is to persuade you that he does not exist'.[45]

It was an expression of the state security services' attempts to cover their tracks that, on the eve of the new government coming into power, South Africa saw an unprecedented shredding and burning of secret documents.

The Military Intelligence Department, which had incubated the report that led to Meiring's resignation, was just one of the apartheid intelligence agencies. The new government dealt with restructuring of the agencies early on, but even before that happened, Mandela had requested a comprehensive overview of the security situation. He had a series of meetings with the leadership of the National Intelligence Service, the defence force and the police. He told them what he wanted from the National Intelligence Service, itself slated for restructuring, and that he wanted it at the earliest possible convenience. It was a comprehensive list:

1) Were any documents containing intelligence material destroyed or [possibly 'edited'] and intelligence information wiped off from computers during the period 1 February 1990 and 31 May 1994?
   a) If so, the reason for such destruction what was the material or inform: give full particulars of such material or information
   b) The dates of such destruction or wiping off
   c) The name or names of the persons who authorised such destruction or

415

wiping off.

2) Does the State Security Council and its structures, like the Joint Management Committee, still exist?
   a) If so, who are the members of such State Security Council and Joint Management Committees?
   b) If not, the exact details of when they were dismantled
   c) A list of members before they were dismantled
   d) The purpose of the State Security Council
   e) What happened to its funds and equipment

3) A list of the organisations on which NIS spied and a list of the agents of NIS who penetrated the organisations or institutions spied upon.

4) Does the Civilian Cooperation Bureau still exist? A detailed explanation of its structure and personnel must be furnished.
   a) If not, when was it dismantled? What happened to its funds and other equipment?

5) Does the Directorate of Covert Collection still exist?
   a) If so, who are its members?
   b) If not, when was it dissolved?
   c) What happened to its funds and equipment?

6) The original copy of the Report of General Pierre Steyn must be supplied.*
   a) Precisely for what criminal acts were several senior officers of the army dismissed or asked to resign as a result of that report?
7) Who is responsible for politically motivated violence which has led to the murder of close to 20,000 people?
8) It is alleged that the parties responsible for politically motivated violence were also responsible for the death of freedom fighters like Neil Aggett, Rick Turner, Imam Haroon, Ahmed Timol, David Webster, [Matthew] Goniwe and others, Griffiths and Victoria Mxenge; Pebco Three; Bheki Mlangeni
9) Did the Vlakplaas Unit continue to exist after 1/2?†
   Who were its members and what has happened to them.
   What was or is its purpose before, or if it continued, what did its members do after 1990?

* The report by General Pierre Steyn in 1992 detailed police and military involvement in violence in the run-up to the election.
† The 'Vlakplaas Unit', a division of the counter-insurgency unit of the SAP, was responsible for the torture and deaths of many anti-apartheid activists.

417

If dismantled, what happened to its funds and equipment?

10) Detailed information on the operations of hit squads in the country. According to the Goldstone Report, members of the Vlakplaas Unit were paid between R200,000 and R1 000,000 on ['dissolution'?] is this correct? What were they paid for?[46]

The 1992 report by General Pierre Steyn, to which Mandela refers, had done much to expose the hit squads. While he had been briefed on some of its findings, Mandela hadn't seen the full report. However, it was on his desk shortly after the briefing meeting.

While pointing to the depth of collusion of the intelligence agencies in suppressing resistance, the list explains Mandela's abiding caution — or mistrust — and why resignations from these structures always put him on his guard. In transforming the intelligence agencies, where covert action and corruption were the warp and woof of apartheid functionality, Mandela had to ensure scrupulous enforcement of the constitutional prescript on national security. It holds that national security 'must reflect the resolve of South Africans, as individuals and as a nation, to live as equals, to live in peace and harmony, to be free from fear and want and to seek a better life'.[47]

The first major policy hurdle for the new democratic parliament was the 'fragmentation of the new state's intelligence capabilities. Six intelligence organisations — each of which had been subjected to one or other political authorities or parties that were part of the earlier negotiations — had to be brought under one roof and redirected to address a new security agenda.'[48]

By the end of 1994, policy and legislation were in place to amalgamate the national and Bantustan intelligence agencies with the intelligence departments of the liberation movements. Domestic intelligence functions resided in the National Intelligence Agency (NIA) and foreign intelligence functions resided in the new South African Secret Service (SASS). After some intense negotiations that covered every field from the strategic direction to the technicalities of positions, the ANC showed wisdom in getting its personnel into more strategic positions, unlike what had transpired in the military and crime intelligence agencies.[49] And to ensure tight control and supervision, there would be operational oversight by independent inspectors general for each service, ministerial accountability and, importantly, parliamentary oversight by the Joint Standing Committee on Intelligence.

The new service was formally launched in 1995, with the ANC's Sizakele Sigxashe as its first director general; an ANC deputy headed the NIA while a deputy from the NIS headed the new SASS. The de facto head of the service was Joe Nhlanhla, from the ANC, who was appointed deputy minister of intelligence services under the minister of justice.

Yet again, integration looked good on paper but was, in reality, slow and uneven, dogged as it was by persistent mistrust between old and new personnel. It was also hampered by tensions among the ANC personnel. That was perhaps the reason for the low-quality intelligence that landed on Mandela's desk, leaving him frustrated. According to Jakes Gerwel, the regular intelligence briefings sent to the president's office were 'like reading newspapers three days old'.[50] Mandela was known to have rejected these reports, sometimes with harsh words, in cabinet meetings or in meetings with intelligence officials. In one instance, he had intelligence officials sent away from a cabinet meeting because their report was short on the information he had requested. On certain international issues, the politicians would be actually be more informed than the intelligence reports produced by officers from the previous administration.

In one example, when Alfred Nzo, the foreign minister, was handed a report on participants in the Burundi conflict, he trashed the report.* 'I know these people,' he said. 'I lived with some of them in exile in Tanzania.'[51]

The new intelligence service was hampered by misinformation, originating from former members, or others with links to the new service, about plots from right and left to destabilise or overthrow the government.[52] The Meiring report was one such fabrication and used the work of 'information peddlers' concocted by elements in military intelligence. General Nyanda told Mandela, after the Judicial Commission had declared the report as baseless, that military intelligence was 'one of the most backward and untransformed elements of the Department of Defence'. It displayed 'bias in favour of the old friends of the SADF in analyses and reports on southern Africa and a preponderance of reports on phantom left-wing threats compared to graver right-wing ones'.[53]

At the bottom of all the dirty tricks and chicanery was an intelligence community hidebound by racial prejudice, which could not abide the thought that the new government might succeed — and on its own terms, too.

* Mandela succeeded the late Tanzanian President Julius Nyerere as chairperson of the multiparty Burundi Peace Process.

■ ■ ■ ■

Working most directly with Thabo Mbeki, the SASS operated behind the scenes to support Mandela's international initiatives. Its work in foreign intelligence veered away from the old regime's prioritisation of Europe and the United States to a perspective more in keeping with the new foreign policy directions. This shift was seen in action when South Africa began to play a bigger role in conflict resolution. It was often required to act as a backchannel, facilitating initiatives or mending fences. For example, Mandela had sent his deputy, Thabo Mbeki, to Abuja to intercede on behalf of the Ogoni writer and activist Ken Saro-Wiwa and eight of his compatriots, who were threatened with execution by the Nigerian military ruler General Sani Abacha in 1995. When General Abacha ignored the request for a stay of execution and hanged the nine activists, Mandela reacted with explosive rage.

According to Lansana Gberie, an academic journalist from Sierra Leone, on 27 November 1995, he heard a calm voice issuing a statement on the BBC. It was Mandela saying: 'Abacha is sitting on a volcano. And I'm going to explode it underneath him.' Mandela had great faith in human nature and was driven by a sense of nationalism, which he hoped would permeate the rest of the continent. Abacha might have been corrupt and obdurate, but he was still an African leader and — possibly — not a monster.[54]

When his plea — in the name of quiet diplomacy — for the men to be reprieved fell on deaf ears, Mandela felt thwarted and lashed out, in the same way he had rebuked De Klerk in front of TV cameras. This was not an act aimed at humiliating an adversary, as has been pointed out by Graça Machel. Trust — albeit one that hadn't been consecrated by any formal accord in Abacha's case — had been broken. It took hard work by intelligence officials for any interaction to happen between South Africa and Nigeria.

Another case was the easing of tensions with Egypt after a falling out between Mandela and President Hosni Mubarak after the latter misled him in 1992 with a false commitment to donate funds for the ANC.[55]

At the official opening of the new intelligence agencies' combined headquarters in 1997, Mandela spoke of the 'challenges facing democratic South Africa [that] are without doubt different from the challenges of yesterday. In the past, the single biggest threat to the security of our people came not from outside but from our law-enforcement agencies, including the intelligence services . . .

'In this regard, we have started the difficult but necessary task of changing the state, and the intelligence community in particular, into structures that serve the people rather than terrorise them; structures that protect the integrity of our country rather than destabilise our neighbours; structures that protect democracy rather than undermine it.'

Turning to the work of the services, he described their primary task as becoming 'the eyes and ears of the nation'. He expected both the NIA and SASS to help 'create the environment conducive for reconstruction and development, nation building and reconciliation', warning that 'without a better life for all, any hope for national security would be a pipe dream'. He emphasised the glaring fact that this had not been so in South Africa's recent past, observing that the history of the country 'has confirmed that none can enjoy long-term security while the majority are denied the basic amenities of life'. He asked the intelligence services to 'continue to give valuable support to the police in the combating of crime, particularly organised crime'.

Speaking of which, there had been a spate of thefts from the offices of the intelligence service. 'It is quite clear from the nature of these thefts,' he said, that there are elements within your structures, linked to others outside, who are working with sinister forces, including possibly crime syndicates and foreign intelligence agencies to undermine our democracy . . .

'These are forces that are bent on reversing our democratic gains, forces who have chosen to spurn the hand of friendship that has been extended to them, forces that do not want reconciliation, indeed forces that wish of us to apologise for destroying apartheid and establishing democracy.'

Mandela was, however, confident that there was a solution to the problems. He said: 'The official opening of the joint headquarters of the National Intelligence Agency and the South African Secret Service symbolises another giant step away from an era when intelligence structures were at the centre of division and conflict in our country. It also symbolises the coming together of the different strands of our divided past into a united service working towards a common good.'[56]

With regard to the public service both the ANC and the apartheid government were open to the criticism that they lacked the imperative to transform it. Skweyiya, who was minister of public service and administration from 1994 to 1999, alludes to the 'nightmare', which must have kept Mandela awake for nights on end, of devising formulas for driving the different tiers of government, especially, at the granular level of governance — local government. He says, 'One of the first things that we did was to set up the civil service, create nine provinces of a unitary South Africa, and ensure that there is a bureaucracy that exists there, appoint people to those positions, and ensure that all those provinces and the eleven administrations that existed are rationalised into one, which has been really a nightmare.'[57] The apartheid government, which splurged on planning and preparation for the security forces, economy and international affairs, never gave the civil service much thought.[58] No wonder he had concerns that the new administration was going to cause some problems.[59]

The difficulties that beset transformation in particular areas, such as the public service, had their origins in the architecture of the negotiated transition, most notably the so-called sunset clauses championed by Joe Slovo. Built into the Constitution to deal with the first five years of the transition, the clauses provided, among other things, for the protection of civil service pensions. This served to ensure stability through the retention of staff with institutional memory who would, in turn, ensure capacity for the civil service to fulfil its mandate. But the urgent need to make the civil service more representative resulted in an uncomfortable mix of what Allister Sparks described as 'an ossified old guard and inexperienced newcomers', which rendered the government's mandate more cumbersome and slower than had been planned.[60] Furthermore, when factoring in the cost of voluntary severance pension packages to ease the exit of officials from the previous administrations, it proved too expensive. Advertising the posts of incumbent civil servants from the old order led to the first rift in the Government of National Unity.[61]

One of the problems arose from an ANC oversight in negotiating the interim constitution: the old Commission for Public Administration (CPA) still retained its powers over control of all appointments to the public service. It was only when the final constitution was signed that this anomaly was rectified, with the CPA being replaced in 1996 by the Public Service Commission.

Another hitch, meant to bypass restrictions in making appointments, could be sourced to the placing of senior members of the liberation movement into management positions, with some starting as ministerial advisers, leading to the creation of parallel centres of authority. Added to this were the clashes of cultures between the old and new regimes and an absence of a shared vision, necessitating the granting of more powers to ministers with regard to senior appointments. This unplanned measure became entrenched, with negative implications in later years on the professionalisation of the public service.[62]

Five-year targets were set for the composition of the civil service management. The desired outcomes were that black people, that is, coloured, Indian and African, would comprise 50 per cent; at least 30 per cent of new recruits would be women; and, in ten years, at least 2 per cent would be people with disabilities. Only the level of the latter remained below target.[63]

Less than a month after the start of the new government, Mandela wrote to his ministers, reflecting the urgency with which he regarded the matter of the appointment of women in particular.

'Our country,' he wrote, 'has reached the point where the representation of women is accepted as essential for the success of our policy of building a just and equitable society.

'The Government has to lead in this process by providing visible evidence of the presence of women at all levels of Government.

'I would, therefore, like to request you to prioritise the appointment of women to positions in Government departments, the Civil Service and standing committees.

'I would also like to remind you that the services your Department will provide should bring improvement to the conditions of women as well as men.'[64]

Another hurdle in the public service was the need to rationalise and pare it down to the minimum needed to run efficiently. This couldn't be done through ministerial fiat behind closed doors, but had to involve negotiations with the trade unions, which, until 1993, had been banned from the apartheid public service altogether. There was added pressure from the macroeconomic crisis currently gripping the country, which made matters worse. The minister of finance proposed cutting down the number of civil servants from 1.3 million to a million. This figure was politically unviable, given the level of unemployment and the concomitant impact on the poorest of the poor.[65]

Corruption, too, played a big role in consuming resources and impairing the new government's legitimacy in the eyes of its citizens. It was particularly endemic in, but not isolated to, the former Bantustan areas where patronage and lax oversight greased the wheels of apartheid survival. Starting in the Eastern Cape, and later extended throughout the country, the government mounted action to deal with the problem. It identified 'ghost workers' and investigated abuse of pension funds and state financial resources.

In addition, where there had previously been four provinces and ten Bantustans, there were now nine provincial administrations. The former Bantustan officials, now integrated into the new civil service, brought with them institutional legacies with long-lasting adverse consequences.[66]

While Mandela's engagement with the

transformation of the civil service was less direct than it was with the security forces, he did, however, involve himself in selling the new and more representative civil service to the public. For him, the civil service was to be a resource for society as a whole.[67]

For that to happen, however, there had to be give and take between the public service and the government. In his second State of the Nation Address in February 1995, Mandela commended the dedicated work of the public service and spoke directly to South Africa's civil servants:

'We are committed to the motivation of all public sector workers so that they become a conscious, willing and skilled agent for the transformation of our society according to the objectives spelt out in the Reconstruction and Development Programme.

'As part of this process, Cabinet has given instructions to all Ministers to interact continuously with all members of their ministries and departments to brief them about their tasks, to report on progress achieved, to agree on how to overcome obstacles to the process of transformation and generally to be involved in the struggle for change.

'We have also invited the public sector unions to participate as fully as possible in the budgeting processes so that they make their own contribution to the difficult task of deciding the best possible allocation of the limited resources available to government.'

However, Mandela warned against an adversarial relationship between the executive and the administration, which 'would impact negatively on the common task . . . of serving the people of South Africa.

'Accordingly,' he went on, 'we have been available and willing to address all matters of concern to the public service workers, including questions of salaries, promotions, pensions and other issues relevant to working conditions.'

He called on the public service workers to 'join hands with the government to address other important matters such as the racial and gender imbalances within this service', while observing that the public service 'will never be fully acceptable to the people as a whole and can never be truly responsive to the needs of the people unless it is composed in all its ranks in a manner that reflects the composition of our population.

'To speed up this process, the government will continue to implement measures and programmes aiming at ensuring that those who were disadvantaged by apartheid in the past are given the capacity to catch up with those who were given the opportunity to develop and advance themselves in terms of management and other skills.'

After spelling out the meaning of the affirmative action programme, which aimed to redress the inequalities of the past, Mandela called upon the people 'to refuse to listen to the false prophets who seek to perpetuate the apartheid divisions and imbalances of the past by presenting affirmative action as a programme to advantage some and disadvantage others on the basis of race and colour'.[68]

However, Mandela had to be candid when spelling out both the setbacks and the planned remedial action. He explained to Parliament in February 1996 that although government had meant to stick to its mandate of establishing a 'single, streamlined, efficient and transparent Public Service and to allocate more public resources to capital expenditure', it was time to be 'frank and say that the current service is too large, and it has to be rationalised. There is no other option.

'However, our actions cannot ignore the painful truth that the most affected will be areas that are poor, with low economic activity and little prospect for alternative employment. This means, among other things, searching for creative negotiated solutions that will help stimulate economic activity.

'The rationalisation process will not be vindictive. Neither will it be carried out in a haphazard manner. Rather, it will affect all races and provinces. Discussions are well advanced with the relevant ministry to set up the Presidential Review Commission [PRC], which will redefine the structure, functions and procedures of the Public Service, and relevant announcements can be expected soon.*

'Among the greatest challenges for 1996 is to further build the capacity of government to serve communities. Nowhere is this needed more than at local level, where government interacts on a daily basis with communities. It should therefore be the case that one of the main themes of this year will be the introduction of massive training programmes for the newly elected councillors and their staff.'[69]

During Mandela's presidency, two major reports on the public service were commissioned. The director general of the Department of Public Service and Administration, Dr Paseka Ncholo, led a provincial review task team, which probed provincial administrations. In the report, which went to cabinet in August 1997, Ncholo concluded that 'from an administrative point of view, the system is expensive, chaotic and unaffordable'.[70]

* Chaired by leading academic Dr Vincent Maphai, and featuring an array of experts in various fields, the Presidential Review Commission's terms of reference were published in the *Government Gazette* (no. 17020) on 8 March 1996, with a remit to recommend the transformation of the public service.

The PRC reported in 1998, after two years' work, on how the inherited executive and administration should be restructured to better enable reconstruction and development. Its far-reaching recommendations informed changes made by the next administration. It dwelt sharply on the need for better co-ordinating and integrating structures at the centre of government, in the presidency and cabinet secretariat.

The various commissions and task groups reflected Mandela's desire to acquire as much knowledge as possible in order to fulfil his dream of creating a better society. That society could only come about if the public embraced the ideal of making South Africa the country of their dreams. He said as much on opening the third parliamentary session on 9 February 1996:

'Yes, South Africa is not only on the right road. We are well on our way to making this the country of our dreams. I take the opportunity to congratulate all South Africans, in the public and private sectors — the most prominent in the land as well as the humble member of the community — all of whom are striving to add another brick to the edifice of our democracy. We have set out on this road together, and we should together aim for the stars.'

While praising the achievements of the communities, which 'have laid the foundation to make a real impact on the inequities of the past', he admitted that 'we are only at the beginning of a long journey'. It was 'a journey we should undertake with expedition, if our consciences are not impervious to the cries of [the] desperation of millions. But this is a journey, too, that requires thorough planning and tenacious industry, if we are to remain on course and capable of sustaining our march . . . All of us, all South Africans, are called upon to become builders and healers. But, for all the joy and excitement of creation, to build and to heal are difficult undertakings.

'We can neither heal nor build if such healing and building are perceived as a one-way process, with the victims of past injustices forgiving and the beneficiaries merely content in gratitude. Together we must set out to correct the defects of the past.'[71]

CHAPTER TEN:
RECONCILIATION

In a fleeting news clip that was broadcast to the world on 12 June 1964, the day he was to start serving his sentence, Nelson Mandela is partly obscured by the wire mesh over the window of the van transporting the condemned men.[1] Although unseen, the prisoners leave an indelible stamp of rebellion as clenched fists appear through the ventilation holes on the side panels of the sealed vehicle, a physical complement to the language of defiance from the spectators, many of whom had packed the gallery during the trial.

Even though the police officials had used a back exit to avoid the crowds, many people were still able to cheer their heroes to prison. Above the harsh throb of traffic and the stuttering growl of the outriders' motorcycle engines, Mandela could hear the shouting outside, the call-and-response chants and songs that had throughout time rallied the faithful to battle. A powerful voice shouted in isiXhosa, *'Amandla!'* and the people responded, *'Awethu!'* The chant was then repeated in English, with the voice calling out 'All power!' and the crowd responding, 'To the people!' Never in the history of struggle in South Africa had there been anything as eloquent as these five simple words to express the agony of millions and their resolve to reverse centuries of oppression.

For a black person to enter prison in June 1964, some sixteen years after the National Party came into power, meant being at the mercy of functionaries trapped at the lowest rung of the state's administrative hierarchy. Simply, white prison staff were usually of Afrikaner stock, ill-educated and powerful. These were mainly young men and women, the likes of whom had prompted American writer James Baldwin's observation that 'ignorance, allied with power, is the most ferocious enemy justice can have'.[2]

The black warders, also victims of the violence driving the apartheid policy, which had turned them into instruments of oppression, were mostly a more benighted version of their paler brethren. However, it was the white officials who had the responsibility for Mandela and the political prison population.

This was Mandela's new world, a world in which African prisoners were first subjected to the indignity of being stripped naked and then forced to wear shorts, as opposed to the long trousers worn by Indian and coloured prisoners. He had taken pride in how he dressed in the outside world — dress symbolising his own sense of self. When he was to be sentenced at an earlier court appearance, in 1962, he had eschewed a Western suit for a jackal-skin cloak with beadwork, which he wore with defiant grace, to symbolise his Africanness.

In 1965, when he was serving a life sentence on Robben Island, there was no suggestion of future generosity in a series of grainy pictures that were smuggled out and published by the International Defence and Aid Fund in London, in which a shaven Mandela and his compatriot Walter Sisulu are deep in discussion.* All around them is the unremitted bleakness of the rock quarry and walls of stone. It was, as the late Indres Naidoo called it, truly an 'island in chains'.[3] It was not a place to nurture the spirit of reconciliation.

Yet, thirty-one years later, the image of a beaming Mandela kitted out in the Springbok rugby strip at the victorious end of the Rugby World Cup in 1995 has in itself become graphic shorthand for reconciliation and sanity. It adds to the mystery that has always surrounded the man the media once called

* The photographs were taken by Cloete Breytenbach who worked for the *Daily Express* in London.

the Black Pimpernel.

In the early 1960s, the National Party's penal system was one of the most dreaded coercive arms of the apartheid state. Mandela had already had earlier brushes with the law, most notably as the ANC's volunteer-in-chief during the Defiance Campaign Against Unjust Laws, which had kicked off on 26 June 1952, and he was one of the accused in the marathon Treason Trial from 1956 to 1961. Prior to being sentenced to life imprisonment, he had been serving a five-year sentence, since 7 November 1962, for leaving the country without a passport and inciting workers to strike.*

In all these encounters, Mandela had evinced great dignity. A sense of dignity derives from an unwillingness to be demeaned, and Mandela had recognised quite early into his incarceration that he would have to thwart the designs of the regime and its minions. As with all people forced to fight for their lives, he would discover his own strength in the height of battle. Outside, before his arrest, he had enjoyed the support of the ANC and its infrastructure; prison was different and needed different tactics. Here, he had himself, his close comrades and a prison population that consisted of people of

* Treason Trial — see People, Places and Events.

varying political affiliations. However, they all had one thing in common: they were political prisoners seeking the downfall of the apartheid regime. Together they learnt to use the rules to their advantage. They defied those they found unacceptable and, eventually, after repeated flouting, the rules became unenforceable.

In recalling the period, Michael Dingake, who was released from the Island in 1981 after a fifteen-year sentence, wrote that among all the inmates, Mandela 'was the most tireless participant in discussions — in formal discussions restricted to ANC members and in informal, bilateral or group discussions with members of other organisations. Some of us, whenever we could, preferred to engage in *mlevo* (palaver or idle talk). Not Comrade Nelson. Every day, but every day, in addition to his organisation's programmes, he had numerous appointments with individuals, always on his own initiative, to discuss inter-organisational relations, prisoners' complaints, joint strategies against prison authorities and general topics. Nelson Mandela is an indefatigable activist for human rights.'[4]

An energetic and forceful political organiser — and a maverick among ministers in Mandela's first cabinet — Mac Maharaj had proven a handful for his jailers on Robben Island. He devised ingenious plans for smuggling Mandela's writings out of prison. Functioning as a troubleshooter who unravelled difficult situations during the transition, he wasn't anybody's cheerleader, which others could find disconcerting. He ascribes his former inmate's success in surviving incarceration to the older leader's 'extraordinary self-control'.

'Mandela's greatest achievements stem from engaging with others by proceeding from *their* assumptions and carefully marshalling arguments to move them to his conclusions. His line of advance is developed on the other party's line of attack. In private, he never stops trying to understand the other side, be it the enemy, an adversary, an opponent or his own colleague.'[5]

But what was to heighten Mandela's stature among supporter and foe alike was his unerring sense of timing. He seized every opportunity to make an impact, never, in the process, allowing an affront, however insignificant, to pass unchallenged. He confronted the authorities at every turn, invoking the rights of prisoners and resisting any form of humiliation against him and his fellow inmates. Over time, he fought the prison officials, for small things, little freedoms, for the long trousers. Slowly, inevitably — mainly through the testimonies of freed prisoners and friendly jurists who could visit the men inside — the struggles and privation inside

441

prison became known to the outside world. So, too, did the invincibility of the spirit of one man.

It is possibly only in popular culture, sports and the arts — especially music, film and dance — that the world has been able to get a richer picture, as it were, of Mandela's infectious humanity. The liberation songs inspiring a generation of political activists, from the 1960s to the 1990s, invoked Mandela's name. Internationally, artists like Miriam Makeba and Hugh Masekela, once caged birds at home who were freed to soar in exile, collaborated with global household names like Harry Belafonte, Quincy Jones and many others to popularise the struggle of the people of South Africa — a struggle that had become synonymous with Mandela's name.* Tony Hollingsworth, who produced the star-studded 'Mandela concerts' at Wembley Stadium in 1988 and 1990, credits Mandela's global appeal for the success of the extravaganzas.

The struggle in South Africa, which forced the world to examine its own conscience — hence the various resolutions at the United

---

* Miriam Makeba and Hugh Masekela were two of South Africa's most prominent musicians. They fled the country during apartheid and built successful careers abroad.

Nations condemning apartheid as a crime against humanity — found its anchor in Mandela. As the struggle took shape, its message of courage spreading to all corners of the world, it bore on its face the image of one man. It was common for representatives of the ANC to open their address to world bodies with the words: 'We greet you in the name of Nelson Mandela and the struggling masses of South Africa.'

The longer he was incarcerated, the more the world opened its arms to Mandela's political kith and kin, especially those residing in exactly those areas from which South Africa was barred. Exiles like Barry Feinberg, Ronnie Kasrils, Pallo Jordan, John Matshikiza, Billy Nannan — and many others who later occupied important positions in the new South Africa — went on to form Mayibuye, the cultural unit of the ANC, which read to audiences, sang and did short sketches about life in South Africa, their repertoire including Mandela's speech at the dock.*

* Barry Feinberg was an anti-apartheid activist, exile, poet and film maker. He now lives in South Africa. Ronnie Kasrils was a freedom fighter for MK. He served in Mandela's cabinet as deputy minister of defence and later, under President Mbeki, as minister of intelligence. John Matshikiza was an actor, poet, theatre director and journalist.

Their tours of various countries in Western Europe in the 1970s were continued in the 1980s by the Amandla Cultural Ensemble, which, having originated in the ANC camps in Angola, would once in a while have President O. R. Tambo making a guest appearance and conducting the ensemble.[6] Elsewhere, cultural activists like James Phillips established and trained choirs in West Germany, Holland, Belgium, Sweden, Wales and the United States to sing the liberation songs in the indigenous languages of the people of South Africa. For the packed audiences at the Kulturhuset in Stockholm, seeing a troupe of young flaxen-haired, rosy-cheeked people singing and shimmying to 'Shosholoza Mandela' was infinitely more eloquent than any political speech.

By the time he was released, Mandela had become the world's most famous political prisoner. He became, according to some, the most recognisable brand after Coca-Cola — and not only in Western circles.[7] The Rwan-

---

He went into exile with his parents, Todd and Esme Matshikiza, as a child and returned in 1991. He died in South Africa in 2008. Billy Nannan was an anti-apartheid activist who went into exile in the 1960s after being detained and tortured. He worked for the ANC in London until his death there in 1993.

dan president of the World Youth Alliance, Obadias Ndaba, writes:

From the late 1980s and early 1990s, a lot of people in my remote world named their newborns after him. Today, I have a number of childhood friends called Mandela even though the name itself has nothing to do with our culture. As such, I grew up with a mindset associating the name Mandela with something good to emulate: love, freedom and peace, which weren't present under the madness of [the late Zairean dictator] Mobutu [Sese Seko]. As a people of cattle herders, we even rejoiced in the fact that Mandela herded cattle as a child.[8]

Nelson Mandela defied expectation in his single-minded quest to humanise his adversaries and — in word and deed — even his own people who were scarred and traumatised by the excesses of the apartheid regime. He embraced his erstwhile jailers, like Christo Brand and James Gregory and Jack Swart, giving them a place of honour during his inauguration on 10 May 1994. He had lunch with Percy Yutar, the prosecutor who — according to George Bizos — had 'showed his lack of respect for ethical legal practice'.[9] During the Rivonia Trial of 1963–4, even though Mandela and his co-accused had been charged with sabotage, Yutar had voiced his preference for them to be charged with high treason, an offence that was more likely to lead to their death by hanging.[10]

Mandela believed that reconciliation and national unity were one side of the same coin, of which reconstruction and development were the other side — something that could be arrived at 'through a process of reciprocity' in which everyone should 'be part — and be seen to be part — of the task of reconstruction and transformation of our country'.[11]

Mandela's nation-building project required that there should be harmony between the diverse elements of South African society. That harmony could only be achieved if those who had benefited from the exploitations of the apartheid era understood that it was now time to share their resources for the benefit of all. Only then would South Africa have a chance of shaping an equitable future. The alternative was conflagration.

Politically, even though the ANC had gained the lion's share of representation in the Government of National Unity, Mandela wanted to explore the notion of smaller parties participating in government. He held discussions with the Pan Africanist Congress of Azania, Azanian People's Organisation, Democratic Party, Conservative Party and Freedom Front. Although the Constitution made no provision for the inclusion of those parties in cabinet, Mandela said that he was prepared to work for a change in the Constitution to accommodate them.

This was not an act of misplaced altruism but an understanding of, among other policy precepts, the Freedom Charter, which declares that 'South Africa belongs to all who live in it' and 'All national groups shall have equal rights'.[12] But Mandela knew that he would be remiss if he ignored that the very route towards the vaunted ideal of equality started off from a series of historical inequities. And he knew that current injustices had their root in historical inequities. Mandela was determined to face the challenge of getting the group that had monopolised power to accept its loss of power and commit to the creation of a just and reconciled society.

That society couldn't be created without hard work. Mandela had to enter the minds of the peoples forced by time and history to stare at each other from across a wide gulf. He had immersed himself in studying Afrikaans history and culture, roping in his erstwhile jailers as part of his research. He was as familiar with how the Afrikaners would seek to control their fears by holding on to power, as he was of the potential harm if the black masses suspected that their hard-won victories would fall short of securing them lasting political power. Women's rights advocate and former First Lady of South Africa Zanele Mbeki, in an aside to a friend,

447

encapsulated the tragedy of perceptions between blacks and whites. Blacks, she said, see whites as people who've gone to heaven without first dying.[13]

Mandela had singled out Afrikaners for his initiative of reconciliation for the simple reason that they were a population group that was largely behind the ascendance to power of the National Party. Much more than that, however, was the knowledge that the Afrikaners were also indigenous to South Africa without a home elsewhere.* They were reputed to be straight shooters without the guile or insincerity of their English-speaking counterparts, whom black people credited with having started it all. The Colour Bar was a British colonial invention; the Afrikaner, in devising apartheid, merely worked from a reliable template.† Mandela knew, also, that if the Afrikaners — who share a history of

---

* Afrikaners, which means 'Africans' in Dutch, are descended from seventeenth-century Dutch, German and French settlers to South Africa. They rose to political and economic prominence after the 1948 elections won by the Afrikaner party, called the National Party, and established apartheid, which officially ended forty-six years later after the advent of democracy.

† Apartheid South Africa had a legally enforceable 'Colour Bar' which designated certain jobs to people based on their racial classification.

448

poverty with Africans — accepted the change represented by the new democracy, they would form the backbone of its defence.

Despite all that, Mandela was aware of nuances within communities and that he would be making a mistake if he merely painted Afrikaners with a broad brush and overlooked the fact that, as a group, they were socially differentiated and politically divided over the transition.

Although civil war and violent disruption of the first democratic elections by proponents of Afrikaner self-determination had been averted, undercurrents of dissent still raged on, undiminished, when the new government took office. Even these lost their sting with the establishment of the Volkstaat Council, which helped to persuade the Afrikaner community that they had a home in the broader South Africa. Afrikaner self-preservation in the face of an inexorable tide of change was a much more compelling motivation for the hardliners' decision to participate in the process. Seizing the moment, Mandela, who always pursued an accommodation with those who might be disaffected, ensured that agreements were inviolate, thus minimising the risk of anyone taking destructive action, which would bring ruin to the country.

He spared no effort in his determination to avoid anything that would destabilise the country. Most of the wreckers were motivated by emotion. Much later, he would articulate the need for a leader to subject emotions to rational thought. He told Oprah Winfrey: 'Our emotions said, "The white minority is an enemy. We must never talk to them." But our brain said: "If you don't talk to this man, your country will go up in flames, and for many years to come, this country will be engulfed in rivers of blood." So we had to reconcile that conflict, and our talking to the enemy was the result of the domination of the brain over emotion.'[14]

If De Klerk had earlier faced opposition from the hawks of the apartheid security services when he broached an accord with the newly freed Mandela, there was a certain irony, which Mandela must have appreciated, in his having to face headwinds from various quarters opposed to the *volkstaat*. As always, Mandela had to be mindful of the uncompromising attitudes held by some within ANC ranks, who could not abide any territory being hived off for the benefit of a special interest group; the ANC policies commit to a unitary South African state. Mandela was also aware that, even at the time when he was still in exploratory talks with apartheid officials in prison, there had been attempts to delink him — and thus alienate him — from his political base, the ANC. There was always the feeling in the higher councils of the ANC, that the regime — in its time-tested wish to divide and rule and sow confusion among the ranks of the liberation movement — had strived to give an impression that Mandela had been 'compromised'.

There were hotheads within the ANC who still bristled at the transition, which was limping peacefully along. Those imbued with the spirit of Harry Gwala or even Chris Hani, would have preferred an armed takeover by MK, free from the constraints of negotiation politics. But, for Mandela, these were the crucial rounds in a boxing bout where the opponent, who'd delivered telling blows at the beginning of the fight, was beginning to wobble at the knees. Therefore, for the sake of seeing the project of reconciliation through, Mandela would press on and not be stampeded into reneging on previous commitments towards the *volkstaat* as a sop to certain elements within the ANC. In June 1995, following the Volkstaat Council submitting its first report — in which it abandoned the idea of an Afrikaner homeland and opted for a Cultural Citizens' Council, an economic development subregion and a share in the Pretoria area — Mandela responded in the Senate to the arguments regarding the *volkstaat*. He said:

'On the more general question on the report of the Volkstaatraad [Volkstaat Council], I wish to reiterate that my organisation, and I personally, will study the report with sensitivity. We will do so, taking into account the cooperation by these leaders in the peaceful transition. At the same time, we remain firmly committed to the principles of democracy, non-racialism and equality.'[15]

He felt it necessary to remind the assembly of the fires that had been put out. 'Many do not know what dangers faced this country just before the elections,' he said. 'However those of us who negotiated as far back as 1986, and especially shortly before the election, know that we were on the brink of a catastrophe, which could have plunged this country into bloodshed . . . It is easy for you to say that there will be no *volkstaat* in this country. That is easy for you because you did not do the work. You do not know what dangers we have averted.

'I am not going to play cheap politics with the future of this country. If people have been turned round and are now cooperating, we as responsible leaders must sit down and see how we can meet them. I have said before, and I wish to repeat it, that the decision on the question of the *volkstaat* is going to lie with the people of South Africa. They have to tell us whether or not they want a *volkstaat*. It is not a question that is just going to be dealt with in an opportunistic manner.'[16]

While thinking he had given short shrift to the naysayers, Mandela was presented with

452

another conundrum when, in March 1996, a sports commission recommended that the Springbok symbol be dropped. Invoking the threat of the right wing, Mandela criticised people both inside and outside the ANC who 'are not aware that there are still powerful elements among whites who are not reconciled with the present transformation and who want to use every excuse in order to drown the country in bloodshed. That is the reality of the situation. But many people do not appreciate this.'[17]

Another touchy issue was the national anthem. Before the 1994 election, the use of both 'Nkosi Sikelel' iAfrika' (Lord Bless Africa) and 'Die Stem van Suid-Afrika' ('The Call of South Africa'), to be sung in sequence, was agreed upon by the ANC and National Party in the Transitional Executive Council as an interim arrangement. On becoming president, Nelson Mandela assigned a team to produce a much shorter and less awkward version, which combined elements from the two diverse anthems.[18]

However, during the drafting of the final constitution, in September 1996, the National Executive Committee of the ANC made two decisions about the anthem before Mandela arrived at the meeting. The first one was that the new constitution should not specify the anthem but provide that it be determined by the incumbent president. The second was that the national anthem should be 'Nkosi Sikelel' iAfrika' translated into four languages. Mandela only learnt of this after the meeting. He told his colleagues in the National Working Committee that such a decision should not be taken in his absence and demanded that the NEC review it.[19] The question of the anthem was left as it had been in the interim constitution, and in October 1997, when the team had completed its work, Mandela proclaimed the hybrid composition to be the national anthem.

In all these circumstances of reconciliation, Mandela was willing to take risks, knowing that his actions could be subject to misinterpretation. This wasn't new. In the heady times of post-election South Africa, it was possible to forget the risks that had been taken, the gambles, to bring the country to where it was. Mandela had started out as volunteer-in-chief of the 1952 Defiance Campaign, eventually becoming commander-in-chief of MK in 1961, during a period where — as with the contemporaneous Freedom Riders of the American civil rights movement in the Deep South — a black person risked death for proclaiming his or her right to be treated like a human being. To be a volunteer then was to be, in the eyes of a police force that itched for action, a troublemaker.

Mandela took risks when he became the commander-in-chief of MK; when he went underground; and, certainly, when he stood at the dock and made a speech of defiance, knowing full well that the judge passing sentence on him had the power of life and death over him. If the overhaul of an unjust system had called for courage, Mandela was fated to know that bending the selfsame system to the service of democracy would require even greater determination — and shrewdness.

He found that he had to call upon his inner reserves of strength and skill — and his powers of persuasion — to deal with the concerns arising from the black community. These were the people who had routinely been deceived by racist power. Although, when he came out of prison and told the expectant multitudes that he was coming 'not as a prophet but as a humble servant of you, the people', it's unlikely — given the highly combustible period in South African history — that the people took his disclaimer seriously.[20] His release, symbolising liberation from the burden of oppression, violence, poverty and pain, was for them a fulfilment of a prophecy. He personified the pledges made in countless political campaigns that there would be peace, freedom and prosperity. Even though the ANC and its Tripartite Alliance partners were largely non-racial, no one had prepared the masses for the fact that their march onward would be rerouted towards reconciliation.

Mandela had embarked on the path of reconciliation, which meant addressing himself to white fears and coaxing the timorous into acceptance of the road to peace. If Mandela had won admiration for listening to people with opposing views, as psychologist and anti-apartheid activist Saths Cooper said when recalling his time with him on Robben Island, he now had to cater to a constituency, which, while agreeing with him on almost everything, was unhappy with Mandela's preoccupation with reconciliation.[21] In this instance, Mandela found himself increasingly having to defend the charge that his brand of reconciliation meant addressing white fears at the expense of black needs. This accusation persisted, even though he explained the dialectical connection between reconstruction and development on the one hand and nation building and reconciliation on the other — and that the beneficiaries of consequential stability would be all South Africans, most importantly the black majority. It had been a feature of his presidency from its earliest days. Replying to a question from an ANC member in the Senate budget debate in 1994, he went to great lengths to clarify the issue, saying:

'The socio-economic programme which we have set ourselves, requires immense resources. We cannot face these problems if

456

there is instability in our country.' He said that the government 'was faced with a problem, which some of us have raised from time to time. I refer to the difficulty of the White minority in this country, with its background of privileges, which excluded the Blacks, not only from the centres of power, but also from enjoying the resources of this country.'

The white minority, he said, 'now faces the possibility of a partnership with a majority, which has been excluded — and that has led to the feelings of insecurity that the democratic changes . . . might lead to the domination of Whites by the Black majority. That attitude is lacking in their approach to problems by our White counterparts in the country.'

The obverse of this related to black people from the liberation movement who had internalised resistance to a point where it had become a tradition 'at a time when they are required to build, and who feel they should oppose anything which will result in eventual reconciliation and nation building'.

To illustrate the point, Mandela told a characteristically self-deprecating story about a conversation he'd had 'with a leading Afrikaans-speaking personality . . . [who] said I had no idea what I had done for their people, the Afrikaners. He felt that this was his country too. According to him, it was not only I who was liberated, but that he was liberated too. He was prepared to serve South

Africa and this was due to my strength.

'I was beginning to swell with pride when he turned around and said this was also a sign of a grave weakness on my part. He said that I was concerned with assuring whites and neglecting my own people who put me in power. I was quick to tell him about the President's Project, which I had dealt with in Parliament.* He knew all about those projects and he stated that the perception that had been created — and which was more dangerous than facts — was the one he had put to me.

'He went further and informed me that the press and mass media were not interested in the things which I was telling him. He knew that I had not abandoned my people but the perception fostered by the mass media was that I was not attending to the affairs of the country. What strikes them is that a man who has spent a long time in jail should now adopt this conciliatory approach. They have created this perception that this is all that I am concerned with. It would appear that even

* These were projects under the direct supervision of the president, which included providing free medical care for children under six and pregnant women, a nutritional feeding scheme for needy primary schools, electrification of 350,000 homes and the restoration of services and job creation in rural areas.

my own comrades, who know my activities amongst our own people, have been caught up in this propaganda fostered by the mass media.'

Mandela then turned to the question put to him by his ANC interlocutor: 'My comrade has now warned me that there is an element of truth in the saying that I have neglected our people and that I am now concentrating on whites. However, I appreciate the spirit in which this has been said, because people are angry, impatient and they have suffered for centuries and they are still suffering today . . . the Reconstruction and Development Programme is there to address the basic needs of the masses of the people in this country. These needs are those of Blacks — that is, Africans, Coloureds and Indians. This is the purpose of the RDP.

'The Government of National Unity in this country will stand or fall on the basis of delivery in regard to all the schemes that are involved in the RDP. Our Ministers are working 24 hours a day to ensure that we better the lives of our people, that there are sufficient jobs, sufficient schools, educational facilities and houses, electricity, transport and the introduction of clean, healthy running water. All these are intended to serve the interests and the basic needs of the masses of the people in this country.'[22]

The changes wrought by the new democracy reduced the National Party, once a bastion of Afrikaner political expression, to a minority partner in a transitional government. The heads of the security forces, public service and Reserve Bank had been retained temporarily in the name of stability, and the arch-conservative Freedom Front had agreed to pursue its objectives by legal and constitutional means.

But reduced representation did not translate into a diminution of power in white society. White people had had a head start in controlling economic resources, to the detriment of the black majority, who bore the brunt of centuries of structural inequality, the effects of which could not be summarily erased. Black people might have had the numbers but South Africa's cultural, educational and religious institutions, even its agriculture, provided the basis of white power. And Mandela had said as much at a reception hosted by the mayor of Pretoria on 26 August 1994.[23]

Reconciliation, therefore, had to transcend formal institutions and engage directly with the different sectors of society. Typically, it was Mandela who set about confounding expectations, especially in the appropriation of quintessentially Afrikaner symbols. His dramatic — and unexpected — show of support for the national rugby team in the 1995 Rugby World Cup was one of the earliest examples of this. Soon after, he gave a tea party for widows of leaders from both sides of the struggle at his official residence in Pretoria. In addition, he visited those who were too infirm to attend, including Betsie Verwoerd, the widow of the hated architect of apartheid, Dr H. F. Verwoerd, in her home in Orania in the Northern Cape.* After P. W. Botha had a stroke, Mandela visited him at his retirement home in George in the Western Cape. The fact that the media covered these poignant moments — a grey-haired Mandela patiently listening to P. W. Botha lecturing on the consequences of government policies, or helping Betsie Verwoerd read a demand for a *volkstaat* in Afrikaans — ensured that inclusiveness was given a national profile. But so, too, was the fact that Mandela was in command.

A few days after the Rugby World Cup victory, Mandela met representatives of twenty mainly right-wing or conservative organisations, an interaction organised by the leader of the Freedom Front, Constand Viljoen. When a journalist asked on one such occasion what the reasons behind these meetings were, Mandela explained that it was all about nation building and reconciliation. It was important, he said, 'to keep lines of communication between such organisations and

* H. F. Verwoerd — see People, Places and Events.

the government open, to remove any misunderstandings that could lead to tension'.[24]

Speaking to the Afrikaanse Taal-en Kultuur-vereniging, known as ATKV (Afrikaans Language and Cultural Association), Mandela said he understood their fears of a language policy that would prejudice Afrikaans. He assured them that the protection and promotion of all the country's languages, Afrikaans included, was an unshakeable policy of both the government and the ANC.[25]

In 1996, the Ruiterwag, the youth wing of the Broederbond — a powerful and secretive organisation, whose main aim was to advance Afrikaner culture, economy and political power — invited Mandela to a conference of young Afrikaner leaders. Mandela urged them to lead their communities in becoming active agents of reconstruction and development.[26]

Still fired up from his meeting with the young Afrikaner leaders, and wishing to spread the message to society as a whole, Mandela dashed to the packed First National Bank Stadium in Johannesburg, where the Africa Cup of Nations football tournament was starting. There he was drowned out by the overflight of planes as he ran over the allotted time, explaining to the soccer fans that he had just come from the meeting with the Afrikaner Ruiterwag.

Mandela also ventured into universities such as Stellenbosch, Pretoria, Potchefstroom — historically Afrikaans in language and culture — and spoke at churches, usually by invitation, but on occasion uninvited, to the delight of worshippers. Wherever there was a pulse of Afrikanerdom, he spoke. His message remained constant throughout.

'For me,' he wrote, 'it is of the utmost importance that we all engage in serious discussion about our common future in this country . . . When I last spoke of the testament of reconciliation and national unity, which I want to leave behind me, the markets almost crashed. I hope it won't happen again. But I do want to repeat today that I see it as one of my most important tasks to work for national reconciliation, and to leave behind me a country in which there is lasting peace because all the people and groups in the country live together in mutual acceptance, respect and national consensus.'[27]

Knowing that Afrikaners had concerns about Afrikaans education and Afrikaans schools, he distributed copies of the Freedom Charter to his audiences. He told them that the Freedom Charter, drawn up and accepted in 1955 at the Congress of the People, 'is the basic policy document of the ANC. Today it is still the basic guideline for the organisation. So, when I speak reconciliation and respect for all the languages and cultures of our land, it is not, as is often claimed, simply an individual position. It is a position contained in the basic policy of the ANC, the majority party in the Government of National Unity. I am saying this so that you will know that respect for the variety of our society has deep roots in the political organisation that is in office in our country today . . .

'The liberation struggle, which has been fought for eight decades in our country, was underpinned by deep thought and searching for answers to questions about the nature of our society. The so-called "national question" is one which has constantly occupied the liberation movement. How are the interests of the different national groups to be accommodated within non-racial unity? And it is important, before we start this discussion on Afrikaner interests, to bear in mind that the national question concerns not only Afrikaners. If one asks about the place of a language group or culture in our shared land, then one must at the same time also consider the interests of others.'

Mandela stressed that the future of Afrikaans 'cannot be equated with racism. At the same time there is a minority of people who do indeed exploit the question for racist purposes. There is a minority that uses the pretext of concern for Afrikaans to try to protect existing privileges by standing in the way of changes, which are in the interest of the nation as a whole.

'Those who are genuinely concerned about Afrikaans should speak out against such an approach and those who adopt it. In so doing you will also help to ensure that the majority of your compatriots do not suspect a hidden agenda whenever the question of Afrikaans is raised.' Conciliatory to the end, Mandela exhorted the Afrikaners to 'conduct this discussion in a positive spirit! We are here to listen to each other and to seek solutions to any problems that may exist.'[28]

When Mandela signed the Accord on Afrikaner Self-Determination between the Freedom Front, the ANC and the National Party in April 1994, the Accord had established the idea of a *volkstaat* and the clouds of civil war had cleared.

On the day of Mandela's election as president he broke from the ceremonial procession as he entered the National Assembly, to shake hands with Viljoen, now a member of Parliament. Viljoen recounts how, after the inauguration, Mandela told him: 'I have a great desire to be a president not only of the ANC but to be a president of everybody, and I wish to give you free access to my office. If you have anything for the Afrikaner you would like to come and discuss, you can just ask.'

'And believe me,' Viljoen says, 'it never took more than two days to see the president if there was something I wanted to discuss.'[29]

The continued existence of a Volkstaat Council made its way into the new constitution as a transitional institution.[30] There was also agreement on the constitutional recognition of rights of voluntary communities as opposed to the group rights of apartheid. This in turn created a basis for voluntary cultural councils in each sphere of government and the establishment of the Commission for the Promotion and Protection of the Rights of Cultural, Religious and Linguistic Communities (also known as the CRL Commission), with powers to investigate complaints and resolve conflicts.[31]

In reality, however, the Volkstaat Council achieved little of substance. Its funding dried up in 1999, its founding legislation was repealed in 2001 and its reports went to the CRL Commission. The idea that Afrikaner concerns needed either a separate territory or a dedicated political party had lost the hold it once had.[32]

The Volkstaat Council had provided a forum, an ark in which a beleaguered people could find shelter, albeit from a storm that existed more in their imagination than in reality. The truth was that the turbulent waters had been calmed. The shift of political power played a part, as did reconciliation, in particular Mandela's decision to devote a lot of his energies to an engagement with Afrikaner society. He did this knowing the history of antipathy towards the Afrikaners. 'Feelings become particularly strong when our people think of the Afrikaner, the group that dominates the political institutions of the country, and sober discussion becomes difficult.'[33]

He took as his starting point the view that it was a mistake to 'treat him [the Afrikaner] as a homogenous group with a uniform and unalterable attitude on race matters, holding that no useful purpose will be served by trying to reason with him'.[34]

He went steadfastly on, speaking to those Afrikaners whom he felt could be part of his project to build a stable democracy. At first this was puzzling, especially to some of the Afrikaners themselves. Beset by guilt, they naturally expected a hostile and vengeful reaction from Mandela and the black people he led. When the reverse happened, there was surprise and bafflement and — according to well-known poet and academic Antjie Krog — much more.[35] In Krog's interaction with members of the Afrikaner community during her stint as a radio reporter covering the Truth and Reconciliation Commission, she found that Afrikaners interpreted African people's readiness to forgive as weakness and inferiority. If half of what African people had endured had been visited on Afrikaners, they reasoned, the country would be steeped in blood.

In July 1995, the London-based journal *South African Times* asked various people what their birthday wishes would be for Mandela, basing their answers on what they imagined Mandela would want. In response, satirist Pieter-Dirk Uys asked, 'What would Mandela want? A long life? Yes, yes, yes. A happy life? With all our hearts. A normal life? How? He doesn't have to prove anything. Now, dangerously, he can tease and challenge, jeopardising his position as a rare and endangered species, in order to get across his point of view. It is so obvious what that is. The man is committed to forgive and reconciliate. The man embodies the best in all religions. Love your neighbour, even though he locked you up for twenty-seven years!'[36]

'It was Mandela,' Viljoen later recalled, like someone finally putting together the last piece of a jigsaw puzzle. 'Mandela mesmerised the Afrikaners. He was so acceptable. He created such a big expectation towards a real solution in South Africa that even the Afrikaner people accepted the idea.'[37]

The Truth and Reconciliation Commission (TRC), headed by Archbishop Desmond Tutu, has become as symbolic of the new South Africa as apartheid had been of the old regime, coming second only to the new constitution. To the outside world, it has been a vivid demonstration of South Africa's courageous mission to deepen democracy.

From its inception, the commission probed human rights violations and evolved mechanisms for those who owned up to their crimes. The naked truth about the apartheid regime's hit squads and third-force violence had been brought into the public domain by the work of courageous journalists, most notably of the *Vrye Weekblad* and the *Weekly Mail*. As the hearings were conducted under the unwavering gaze of cameras, the full horror that had been perpetrated in support of apartheid was brought into the living rooms of a public that no longer had the luxury of pleading ignorance. The process also dealt with the gross human rights violations perpetrated in the pursuit of the liberation struggle. The TRC, then, became an equal-opportunity offender in the eyes of those brought before it, who usually regarded their actions through the prism of justifiable trespass. Throughout the country, there were debates about whether the violations committed by freedom fighters could ever be deemed coterminous with state violence under apartheid.

Without a leader of Mandela's stature and moral standing, the TRC could not have done its work. He had to deal with arguments about the TRC at each stage: during the negotiations over the founding legislation, in the appointment of the commission, during the hearings and when the report was eventually published.

For instance, taking advantage of Mandela's offer of the 'open door', Constand Viljoen had initially tried, albeit to no avail, to persuade Mandela against the TRC, saying it would have negative rather than positive consequences.[38] Although later convinced of the merits of participating in the TRC, Viljoen had to consider the vulnerability of his supporters if the cut-off date for political offenders qualifying for amnesty remained at midnight on 6 December 1993, the date on which the TEC was established. He enlisted the help of the TRC's Vice Chairman Alex Boraine to urge Mandela to move the deadline to 10 May 1994 so that he and his supporters could apply for amnesty for involvement in the plans to disrupt the election by force. Supported by De Klerk, Mandela resisted Viljoen. However, the retired general's persistence paid off as he was finally able to convince Mandela to support an extension of the date for the submission of amnesty applications from December 1993 to the date of Mandela's inauguration in 1994.

It was not a decision Mandela was comfortable with: 'We have been negotiating . . . since 1990, and people who committed offences after the start of negotiations are to me not at all entitled to consideration.' Nevertheless, he acknowledged Viljoen's role, saying, 'We have been able to avoid a Bosnia situation because of the cooperation of leaders from a wide range of political affiliations . . . I could not continue to ignore his persistent appeals to me.'[39]

Viljoen later appeared before the TRC and applied for amnesty for his plans to disrupt the elections by force.

Niël Barnard, the former head of the National Intelligence Service who had started secret talks with Mandela in prison at P. W. Botha's behest, also tried to prevail on Mandela. He arranged a meeting with Mandela and Johan van der Merwe, the head of the police, at a safe house. The two security officials tried to argue that the whole process would be divisive and would not yield any permanent benefit. Hearing them out, Mandela said he understood their arguments but disagreed with them. The past had to be opened up to inform people what had happened. It was the only way to start healing the country's wounds.[40]

It was not going to be easy.

When P. W. Botha was summoned to appear before the TRC, in October 1997, he refused, creating a dilemma for Mandela.

In an interview with the South African Broadcasting Corporation, Mandela pointed out that it was a 'mistake to think that this transformation just took place without any hassle. We were faced with a situation of civil war here where the right wing decided to stop the election by violence. We had to negotiate, to use people who were influential, who could stop that. I am not going to say any particular individual assisted us in that regard. But we had to use people who were our mortal enemies in order to defuse that. And we have to think about that when problems arise.

'I have spoken to P. W. Botha twice on this question about the TRC. I've spoken to all his children. I have briefed the South African Defence Force, the South African Police Services, the Dutch Reformed Church and others, because I know a little more than you do as to what is happening below the surface.

'And it's a serious mistake to look at matters from the point of view of what you see and which everybody notices. There are issues, which one has to consider, which many people are unaware of. It is necessary to try and defuse this situation. But our determination to do so cannot go so far as to allow people to defy the law. I have done my bit and I can assure you that P. W. Botha is not above the law and I will never allow him to defy the TRC. And I have urged his family to help to prevent his humiliation. And if he continues along this line, then the law must take its course. There is no question about that at all.'[41]

To haul a person such as P. W. Botha, the last of the Afrikaner warrior generals, before a tribunal was quite an undertaking. But even though Mandela had sought Botha's help to quieten the right-wingers, who were spoiling for a fight, he still held the rule of law to be paramount. The law was the law. He didn't want to see the old man pilloried, but if it came to that, so be it. He therefore asked Barnard to help him persuade Botha. Barnard declined. Botha would refuse. Forcing him would only make a martyr of him.[42] It's possible that Barnard was correct or — perhaps more likely — simply didn't want to tangle with Botha, who had become even more irascible with age. Mandela might have been a man of firm convictions, but he wasn't rash. The last thing he wanted was a resuscitation of the ghost of Afrikaner insurgence. In the end, Botha never did appear before the TRC.

The seven-volume report of the Truth and Reconciliation Commission, published in 1999, with some of the volumes running to hundreds of pages, was a painstaking — and often painful — record. Part of it sought 'to provide an overview of the context in which conflict developed and gross violations of human rights occurred'. Volume two focused 'on the perpetrators of gross violations of human rights, and attempts to understand patterns of abuse, forms of gross violations of human rights, and authorisation of and accountability for them'.[43]

It had been as difficult to run the process as it had been to garner usable information. Despite these difficulties,

a vast corpus of documentation was collected . . . However, the sources of information, while rich, were not evenly distributed, presenting difficulties in the identification of organisations and individuals who became perpetrators of torture, killing and other gross violations. The amnesty applications received from former members of the South African Police (SAP) represent an invaluable source of new material. The Commission received many applications from serving or retired police officers, specifying their role in gross violations of human rights. Some of these cases, such as the death in detention of Mr Steve Biko, were well known both at home and abroad; others were unknown outside a very small circle of the perpetrators themselves. The information contained in amnesty applications revealed a deeper level of truth about the fate of a number of individual victims.[44]

Unsurprisingly, there were reservations and criticisms from all sides. Noting them, Mandela accepted the report, saying: 'I had no hesitation in accepting the report of the TRC presented to me in October, with all its imperfections.

'It was inevitable that a task of such magnitude, done in so short a time, and so early in a process that will still take many years to accomplish, would suffer various limitations. And indeed the report itself highlights many of these.

'It was also inevitable, given the nature of the divisions that do still run through our society, and the freshness of the wounds still to be healed, that the judgements of such a body will jar with how some or others of us see matters.

'As we anticipated, when the report was handed over in October, questions arose about an artificial even-handedness that seemed to place those fighting a just war alongside those who they opposed and who defended an inhuman system.

'Further still, the practical consequences of the compromise that gave birth to the amnesty process as an instrument of peaceful transition are painful to many of the victims of human rights violations and their families.

'Many who lost loved ones or who lived through terror that seemed incomprehensible in its cynical inhumanity will wonder at what seems to be the dismissal of the existence of a "third force": the fact of the existence of a deliberate strategy and programme by the powers that be, as they then were, to foment violence among the oppressed, to arm and lead groups that sowed death and destruction before and especially after 1990 . . .

'Questions have also been raised regarding the impartiality or otherwise of the Commission. And some have sought to find in the work of this body, a witch-hunt against a specific language group.

'It is not my task to pronounce upon all these issues, and some of them may no doubt appear in a different light when the TRC gives a more complete account after the amnesty process is completed.

'It will be for the national debate we are starting here today, to come to a resolution where that is possible.'[45]

Having acknowledged the problems, Mandela insisted on the need for a national recognition of what had happened in the past, and the concerted effort that would be needed to make the TRC's recommendations a reality.

'The success of reconciliation and nation building,' he said, 'will depend on all sectors of society recognising with the world, as did the TRC, that apartheid was a crime against humanity, whose vile deeds transcended our borders, and sowed the seeds of destruction whose harvest we continue to reap today.

'About this, there can be no equivocation: for it is this recognition that lies at the very heart of the national pact that is our new constitution, of our new democracy and the culture of human rights that we are building together.

'For all its limitations, the TRC has performed a monumental task in helping our nation towards this understanding.'[46]

Whatever its limitations and successes, the TRC provided an opportunity — in the full glare of domestic and world attention — to shine a spotlight on the unacknowledged crimes and suffering of the past.

But responses to the TRC remained widely divergent. A survey by the Human Sciences Research Council in December 1998 showed the polarisation. Among African people, 72 per cent thought the TRC was 'a good thing for the country', while the same percentage of white people thought it a bad thing.[47]

Some of the respondents to the survey — among them those who regarded the reluctant and forced cooperation of perpetrators, such as De Klerk and others in the National Party, as a gross betrayal — wanted to let bygones be bygones. For them, acknowledgement of complicity with — or benefit from — a system that was being exposed as anachronistic was hard to take. Not a few of them retreated into the argument that their having agreed to relinquish political power was adequate penance.

For some of the victims, however, reliving the horrific experiences reintroduced them to forgotten traumas. There was an expectation from the majority that — beyond reparations

— the TRC process would exact from the beneficiaries of apartheid meaningful contributions towards redressing the historical wrongs through faster transformation.

Mandela was aware of these tensions, as he was alive to the fact that a sizeable section of the white community had gradually come to embrace the TRC process and its implications for the new constitutional dispensation. In his 1997 State of the Nation Address, Mandela acknowledged that the government was 'conscious of the concerns that some Afrikaner people have regarding, in particular, the work of the Truth and Reconciliation Commission.

'It is, of course,' he continued, 'no longer as easy as it once was to speak in any monolithic way about "Afrikaners", just as it is not that simple for anyone to claim to speak on behalf of the Afrikaner people.

'Afrikaners are spread throughout our society in different spheres, holding different positions and different viewpoints, speaking in different voices.

'Afrikaners are an inextricable part of our rainbow nation, reflecting amongst themselves the rich diversity, which is its strength.

'Yet we do take notice of the voices raised in Afrikaans concerning the TRC; voices suggesting that it represent a witch-hunt.'

Pointing out that the objectives of the TRC were clearly set out in the interim constitution and in legislation, Mandela advised parliamentarians — and the country at large — that all must 'emerge from this process with a clearer picture of that part of our history. We must do justice as far as we can to those who suffered and we must end up on the road to lasting reconciliation, determined never to repeat such injustices one against another.

'There is no place for any sense that a racial, ethnic, linguistic, religious or other group is collectively in the dock. The diversity of Afrikaner people means that Afrikaners will know that when a specific perpetrator of gross human rights violations, who is an Afrikaner, appears before the Commission, it is not the Afrikaner in general who is being called to account. Because, as with other language and cultural communities, it is not in the nature of the Afrikaner as such to be brutal to others.

'All of us, as a nation that has newly found itself, share in the shame at the capacity of human beings of any race or language group to be inhumane to other human beings. We should all share in the commitment to a South Africa in which that will never recur.'[48]

Mandela engaged in the drive for reconciliation in the full hope that a future South Africa would roll back the past horrors visited on the majority of the population. As in most legends of courage, the man or woman must

479

first go away and experience great privation to be able to return to serve the people. On sultry evenings in the ANC camps in Angola, the soldiers would chant and dance in what was called the 'Jazz Hour', a time of reaffirmation. While the revelry continued in the square, a section of a platoon would give literacy classes to the uneducated, the word having filtered through the walls of Robben Island, across thousands of kilometres, that Mandela and the other political prisoners were studying, arming themselves for a return to their native land.

CHAPTER ELEVEN:
SOCIAL AND ECONOMIC
TRANSFORMATION

Any student of history — and Nelson Mandela was certainly that — would accept that the white people who had benefited from the plunder of the past, and who still had a firm grip on socio-economic institutions, would fight tooth and nail to maintain the status quo. When it transpired that there wouldn't be any traumatic upheaval and that the oft-heard call to 'chase the white man into the sea' was as empty as the cry of seagulls, they changed tack, seeking to impute all societal ills to the ineptitude of the current administration.

Whether behind prison walls, at the head of transition negotiations or, finally, as the face of the ANC and democracy at the elections, Mandela had been kept abreast of South Africa's problems — the right-wing threat and high levels of crime and poverty — but until he took power he did not have the total picture. Once in office, he soon realised that the biggest hurdle was the socio-economic one.

At the inception of the Government of National Unity, Mandela could not ignore the analysis of the economy by the Reconstruction and Development Programme itself. The section on building the economy states that 'the South African economy is in a deep-seated structural crisis, and as such requires fundamental restructuring'.[1] This was due to the white minority's decades-long use of its exclusive access to political and economic power for the promotion of its own sectional interests, to the detriment of the black majority. South Africa 'has now one of the world's most unequal patterns of distribution in income and wealth'.[2] Speaking in Addis Ababa on 15 December 1994, Algerian secretary of the Economic Commission for Africa (ECA) Layashi Yaker made an assessment of the African economy in 1994 and of prospects for 1995. He saw South Africa's economic growth accelerating if 'labour and employers . . . build a new pragmatic relationship, based on a sympathetic understanding of each side's basic concerns as they set out to correct the labour market distortions entrenched by forty years of apartheid'.[3]

Mandela saw the mandate given to his government as the first step towards addressing the economic legacy of apartheid characterised by imbalances currently weighted against the black majority.

For the new government, the first steps towards addressing the socio-economic deficit were taken when the new cabinet assembled the day after the inauguration. They had no agenda apart from a general mandate to change the country in accordance with precepts from policy workshops, conferences and people's forums. An item recorded on the day reads: 'The President stressed the importance of the immediate and enthusiastic implementation of the Reconstruction and Development Programme and called on all members for their support.'[4]

This mission had its origin in *Ready to Govern,* the policy framework adopted at the ANC national conference held towards the end of May 1992. The vexed question of state ownership of economic assets versus privatisation had also been under discussion. When he came out of prison, Mandela had been an ardent advocate of the nationalisation of key sectors of the economy, a view he had been forced to revise, as we have seen in chapter four. In the wake of the global loosening of ties on the mobility of capital, the ANC formulated guidelines that spoke of a mixed economy.

The 1992 Ready to Govern conference had formally registered the change, recognising the need for flexibility after a debate that went on for hours. ANC policy thereafter avoided the words 'privatisation' and 'nationalisation'. Public ownership was to be flexibly expanded according to 'the balance of the evidence in restructuring the public sector to carry out national goals'.[5]

Definitions notwithstanding, when the government mooted the privatisation of state assets, there was considerable dissent within the ANC. But it was Mandela's view that this 'should be settled in negotiations on a case-by-case basis'.[6]

The country was in the grip of an economic crisis whose severity became even more apparent after the election. The need to turn it around had informed the ANC's decision to work towards a Government of National Unity rather than a protracted process of mass mobilisation and negotiations, which, even if ultimately successful, would have come at a huge cost.

The state was in no condition to implement programmes for improving people's lives, especially the poor. Fragmented along apartheid lines, the state had been effective only in serving white minority interests and suppressing the majority. It was artificially expanded to accommodate patronage, both in national government and in the subordinate administrations. Its narrow focus rendered it ineffectual in policy development. For instance, ANC representatives involved in negotiations over the establishment of a Transitional

Executive Council found to their surprise that the apartheid state had only weak mechanisms for financial oversight and control.[7] National coordination and strategic direction had been carried out, mainly with security considerations in mind, by the National Security Management System, which De Klerk had dismantled in 1989, leaving an even bigger vacuum at the centre.

Given the systematic legacy of neglect and impoverishment, tackling poverty and inequality would need both comprehensive transformation of the state and sustained growth and redistribution.

Constructing the policy and legislative architecture for change got off to a quick start. The first full cabinet meeting tabled about twenty memoranda. This could be credited to the foresight of the cabinet secretariat, which had indicated from the get-go that ministerial and departmental memoranda were the staple raw materials of cabinet meetings.[8] These were the beginnings of prolonged procedures; some memoranda took up to two years to emerge as White Papers — and then more time to find operational authority in legislation. Therefore, the changes deferred by oppression would not be immediately realised with the advent of democracy. The first years were devoted to preparing the legislative framework to empower the state to effect the much-needed, and long-awaited, transformation.

Research, sometimes unrealistically, pointed to a widespread acceptance among the poor that meaningful change would take time. The reality was that the spectre of volatile impatience was never far from the national conversation. Ever optimistic, Mandela, who was alive to the impatience, would say that it would take 'at least five years' for the changes enshrined in the policy manifesto to take root.[9]

It was therefore with a great sense of urgency that the programmes focusing on 'major areas of desperate need' had to be implemented within the first hundred days, as announced by Mandela in his address to Parliament in May 1994.[10] These were to piggyback on pre-existing activities; their success would make a visible impact, the numbers indicating that progress would become a staple in the president's communications. Other projects, however, needed more preparation. Putting in place housing and land reform was analogous to building a castle, which would need deep foundations and sturdy walls to withstand the buffeting winds of time. The programmes had to grapple with obstacles deeply entrenched in the South African state and society at large.

Housing and land are central to any liberation struggle, and Mandela knew this only too well. In his unpublished memoirs, he writes:

'The plundering of indigenous land, exploitation of its mineral wealth and other raw materials, confinement of its people to specific areas, and the restriction of their movement have, with notable exceptions, been the cornerstone of Colonialism throughout the land.

'This was the form British Colonialism took in South Africa, so much so, that after the passing of the Land Act of 1913 by the South African government a white minority of barely 15 per cent of the country's population owned about 87 per cent of the land, while the black majority — Africans, Coloureds and Indians — occupied less than 13 per cent. They were forced to live in squalor and poverty or to seek employment on white farms, in the mines and urban areas.

'When their Nationalist [*sic*] Party came to power in 1948, Afrikaners acted with unbelievable cruelty and sought to rob blacks even of these meagre rights to land they still possessed.

'Communities large and small, who had occupied areas from time immemorial, where their ancestors and beloved ones were buried, were mercilessly uprooted and thrown into the open veld, there to fend for themselves. And this was done by a white community led by an educated but infamous clergy and its

487

successors who used their skills and religion to commit various atrocities against the black majority, which God forbade. Yet they hypocritically claimed that their evil schemes were inspired by God.'[11]

Here in the manuscript, Mandela has included a note in parentheses to 'quote Sol Plaatje on The Land Act of 1913'.*[12] Plaatje's words on the issue of dispossession read: 'Awaking on Friday morning, June 20, 1913, the South African Native found himself, not actually a slave, but a pariah in the land of his birth.'[13]

Mandela continues, 'It was against this background that the African National Congress Reconstruction and Development Programme highlighted the importance of land reform by calling for the abolition of the Land Act, and by guaranteeing residential and productive land to the rural and urban poor, labour tenants, farm workers and previously disadvantaged farmers.'[14]

Six months after taking office, Mandela's preamble to the *White Paper on Reconstruction and Development* promised that the transformation will permeate every level of government, every department, and every public institution. The government's RDP activities therefore should not be seen as a new set of projects, but rather as a compre-

* Sol Plaatje — see People, Places and Events.

hensive redesign and reconstruction of existing activities. Growth and development are more than interdependent. They are mutually reinforcing. Addressing inequalities will expand markets at home, open markets abroad and create opportunities to promote representative ownership of the economy. The expansion of the South African economy will raise state revenues by expanding the tax base, rather than by permanently raising tax rates.'[15]

Success in both endeavours required the government to get into 'active partnership with civil society, and with business and labour in particular . . . [to] jointly pursue the broader challenges of extending opportunity to the millions of adult South Africans who can currently find no place in the formal economy . . .

'Our people have elected us because they want change,' Mandela said, in conclusion. 'Change is what they will get. Our people have high expectations which are legitimate. While the Government cannot meet all these needs overnight, we must put firmly into place the concrete goals, time frame and strategies to achieve this change.'[16]

In his first address to Parliament in May 1994, Mandela announced that R2.5 billion had been redirected from within the budget to fund the RDP in the coming year and that, to demonstrate its seriousness, government would in the next one hundred days implement a set of Presidential Lead Projects. These focused on free medical care for children under six and pregnant women; a nutritional feeding scheme in every needy primary school; to continue with the programme to electrify 350,000 homes in the current financial year; and a public works programme to rebuild townships and restore services in rural and urban areas. In addition, there would be a one-off 5 per cent reconstruction levy on individuals and companies with taxable incomes of more than R50,000.[17]

Given the inherited economic crisis of the early years, the government was often forced to strike a complex balance between engaging in poverty eradication or stimulating growth. The point of departure for implementing the democratic mandate was that, short of dependence on international loans, resulting in loss of sovereignty, the economy had to be on a sustainable path that promoted growth and attracted domestic and foreign investment. The government also had to reorient the state by reallocating existing resources.[18] This included reducing the volatility of the exchange rate. In a television interview after his presidency, Mandela said: 'The president of the IMF came here and said, "The reason why your currency is unstable is because your foreign reserves are very low. I am prepared to help you, to give you funds." And I say, "No, the difficulty with you is that you impose conditions which violate the sovereignty of a country." He says, "No, I will not do so." I was happy. I then called the deputy president, Thabo Mbeki, and said, "Man, this is what the IMF says." He said, "Nothing doing." I won't go into the reasons, which they advance, but I regarded them as better than me in questions of this nature and I accepted their suggestion that we don't want to be indebted to anybody. We want to rely on our own resources and taxation and so on.'[19]

In October 1994, cabinet adopted restructuring as 'a contribution to the transformation of the public sector to promote implementation of the RDP, growth and prosperity'.[20] Leading by example, the president and his two deputies all took a 20 per cent cut in their salaries while ministers took a 10 per cent cut; there was to be a freeze on salaries of senior officials and an increase in the minimum wage of public servants of R15,000.[21] This might have been a drop in the ocean insofar as the budget was concerned but it was an effective message on combining cost-cutting and narrowing the wage gap. Mandela saw the salary cuts as an example to be emulated as South Africans dealt with the apartheid legacy of social ills.

While promoting the RDP, the government

had to reduce the fiscal deficit, by not spending more than what was in the coffers, to avoid a debt trap over time. Government spending was therefore shifted towards more capital expenditure with the RDP financed mainly via restructuring of budgets towards RDP priorities. The civil service would be re-organised and trained to provide effective and efficient services to all citizens (as we saw in chapter nine). Development of human resources, labour market reform and collective bargaining rights for all were 'essential if we are to succeed in attaining the objectives contained in the RDP'.[22]

The austere economic environment, a legacy of past misspending, inevitably had a negative impact on the financing of RDP objectives. Each day led to more worrying discoveries about the depth of the crisis. During the negotiations, Derek Keys, the National Party government's finance minister, had briefed Trevor Manuel, then head of the ANC's Department of Economic Policy. Manuel conveyed to Mandela what he had learnt. Mandela concluded that extended negotiations would end with a democratic government inheriting an economy that was beyond recovery.[23]

Mandela never forgot this. Years later, while campaigning in the 1999 elections, he responded to a question about unemployment with an explanation of the state of the economy he and his government had inherited:

'I would like to place the question of unemployment in context because it would be a mistake to think that the question of joblessness has just dropped from the skies, that there is no history. We all know that in the decade leading up to April 1994, R5.1 billion left the country as a result of political uncertainty.

'Secondly, the economic growth of the country was negative. And there was high inflation, which was in two digits; also the budget deficit was in two digits.

'But what was even more shattering was the discovery when we took over, that this country had a public debt of no less than R254 billion, which we are now paying at the rate of R50 billion a year. That is R50 billion which we do not have in order to create jobs and to reduce the rate of unemployment. That is the background to this issue.

'Now, it is not very easy to deal with because one of the major decisions we took when we took over as the government was to reduce the rate of inflation, to reduce the budget deficit, and we have succeeded enormously in that regard.

'But to reduce the rate of inflation and the budget deficit meant that there should be a drastic cut in government expenditure and we took that decision. And we are ruthless in making sure that we cut down government expenditure, bring down the rate of inflation as well as the budget deficit. From an inflation which was in two digits when we took over, about 13 per cent, we were able to reduce it to between 4 and 5 per cent . . . And we therefore inherited a situation whereby there was huge unemployment in this country. We did not have and do not have the resources to address that unemployment . . .

'We are able to go to the United Nations at a time when we owed more than US$100 million in the form of arrears for membership, which the apartheid government did not pay when it was suspended . . . I had to go to the United Nations and to speak to [Bill] Clinton, Boris Yeltsin, Jacques Chirac and others, Jiang Zemin, and to ask them to write off this debt, which they did.

'I then came back to my country confident that now that I have got this arrears debt written off, I'm going to get this R254 billion written off and I asked the Minister of Finance to give me a breakdown of this debt. I nearly fell on my back when I was given these particulars. More than 90 per cent of this debt we owed to our workers there. What the apartheid regime did here was to take pension funds and to support, to enrich themselves out of those pension funds. We could not write off that debt because, if we wrote off that debt, a government which writes off a debt, which it owes to its workers, we would lose all credibility. So we have no alternative but to pay that debt.'[24]

Going back to 1994, apart from what was owed to South African pension funds, there were loans from foreign banks and the IMF.*

Initially, to deal with the limited resources, government agreed to keep recurrent state expenditure to a sustainable level and thereby reinforce the RDP ministry and fund as a lever for reorienting the civil service towards reconstruction and development, greater efficiency and more representative personnel.[25]

These measures, including limited privatisation of state assets, proved inadequate to attract much-needed investments. There was a disappointing response from the private sector, despite the government's investor-friendly approach. Many businesspeople

* The IMF loan agreed by the TEC was US$889 million (R2.8 billion) under the IMF's Compensatory and Contingency Financing Facility (CCFF) to 'help countries cope with temporary exogenous shocks affecting export earnings without resorting to undue and unnecessary adjustments'. The objective was to avoid a balance-of-payments crisis in the run-up to the 1994 election, caused mainly by a drought in 1992, which cut cereal exports. The CCFF loan represented 1.5 per cent of total government debt.

suspected the government of hiding a big stick with which to beat them up.

In August 1995 — following a recommendation by the NEC of the ANC — the cabinet established a special ad hoc Committee on Growth, chaired by President Mandela and including the ministers of finance, trade and industry, home affairs and the minister responsible for the RDP, as well as the two deputy presidents.[26] Among the committee's remits was overseeing the National Growth and Development Strategy. This was an extensive process due for completion during 1996.[27] Before the deadline came up, however, the government responded to volatile currency and insufficient investor confidence with an announcement in June 1996 of a macroeconomic plan, the Growth, Employment and Redistribution (GEAR) strategy.

In introducing GEAR, Mandela had to urge belt-tightening, to court investors, to reopen doors into the world economy. He also had to engage with the ANC's alliance partners and deflect demands from ministers vying for a bigger slice of the available cake.

Heated discussion occurred around the full implications of the GEAR policy. There were vociferous critiques of what some saw as a 'movement from a development policy with a socialist resonance — the (RDP) — to one decidedly neo-liberal in form and substance — the Growth Employment and Redistribution (GEAR) policy'.[28] Notwithstanding such brickbats, however, there was a general, if grudging, acceptance by society that GEAR should be given a chance. It received a further shot in the arm at the ANC's fiftieth national conference in December 1997 where it was resolved that the 'emphasis in the RDP on macroeconomic balance has been a consistent part of ANC policy and has been mentioned in every policy document since 1990. The strategy for Growth, Employment and Redistribution (GEAR) aims at creating the environment of macroeconomic balances required for the realisation of the RDP. In this, therefore, the GEAR does not seek to displace the RDP.'[29]

Whenever he was asked about the social system that the ANC was pursuing, Mandela's response exemplified his pragmatic approach. 'We are not concerned with labels,' he said, after a lecture he gave in Singapore in 1997, 'whether our system is capitalism or socialism. We are concerned with delivering services to the masses of our people who were denied all the basic rights of citizenship, who could not go to school, who could not acquire knowledge, skills and expertise. We have declared in our election manifesto that our aim is to better the lives of our people.'[30]

There were criticisms from the business sector, too. Mandela commended corporate responses to his personal appeals to fund the building of schools and clinics or for participation in projects such as Business Against Crime, and Rural Safety. In reality, however, business was proving reluctant to invest in the country's future. Business couldn't be depended on as a partner in reconstruction and development.

The application of the GEAR policy was not always coherent. But it was generally intended to achieve balance. However, the difficulties of this were often exacerbated by external events, such as the Asian financial crisis from 1997 to 1998. The Reserve Bank's retrograde policy attempts to defend the exchange rate by using its minuscule foreign currency and gold reserves had the reverse effect of shooting the interest rates up to the levels last seen in the 1980s.

One of the proposals of the Labour Market Commission, which Mandela had supported, was for a social contract of government, business and labour. Although the National Economic Development and Labour Council was launched in 1995 with great hopes that it would help forge that contract, by the end of Mandela's presidency the goal was only achieved in word rather than in deed.

Dealing with the inherited economic crisis was just one prerequisite for addressing the twin scourges of poverty and exclusion.

Reflecting back on this period, Mandela later writes: '[Previously,] we refer to the view of Mr Meyer Kahn in which he expressed his disappointment that the increase in the police budget was only 3.7 per cent in monetary terms. There were many others, Cabinet Ministers included, who also complained about the cutting down of government expenditure.

'I discussed the matter with Ms Gill Marcus, [who in 1999 became] Deputy Governor of the South African Reserve Bank, and she said that looking back over South Africa's development since 1994, there is no doubt that our country has achieved a number of remarkable successes. Economic policies had to address the consequences of decades of apartheid discrimination, while at the same time meet the stringent requirements of a rapidly changing world where globalisation was the dominant trend.

'While South Africa was emerging from its long period of isolation, it emerged into a world that itself was undergoing rapid changes. The information age and new technologies, deregulation and liberalisation have all contributed to a world we hardly recognised. The challenge for us was not just to catch up with the rest of the world, but in fact to become part of a dynamic world in which international principles and standards, codes of conduct, best-practice rules, corporate governance and so on, set the parameters in which countries are judged as fit investment destinations or trading partners.

'Integration into the international financial network was reinforced by South Africa's participation in various international forums, including bodies such as the World Trade Organisation, the International Monetary and Fiscal Committee, the Group of 20, the International Organisation of Securities Commissions (which promotes the development of efficient securities and future[s] markets) and the Basel Committee Core Principles Liaison Group, concerned with sound banking supervision.

'Government initiatives to integrate South Africa into the international financial markets focused on foreign investment and the liberalisation of capital flows.

'The challenges facing a new democratic government in 1994 were daunting, and often underestimated. The phenomenal achievements are often not recognised because the magnitude of the problem is not fully realised. Unravelling the apartheid state infrastructure, including the Bantustans, which were extensively underpinned by an intricate legal spider's web, was a feat in itself. But above all, the new government found economic chaos and coffers that were virtually empty.

'While we recognise that many challenges still face us, not least among them tackling the high level of unemployment and attaining higher rates of growth, even our sharpest critics will acknowledge that an ANC government has put in place sound monetary and fiscal policies, and that the economy is better managed than ever before.

'Prior to 1994, South Africa's economic growth rates were in decline. In the 1985–1990 period, the South African economy's annual average growth rate was 1.0 per cent, falling to 0.2 per cent in the 1990–1994 period. In contrast, during the period 1994–2000, South Africa recorded an annual average economic growth rate of 3.0 per cent. Although not yet sufficient to absorb new entrants into the job market, significant structural reforms have been introduced, creating solid foundations that should help ensure future sustainable growth.

'The government had to grapple with a large budget deficit. It had to come up with a new economic policy mix aimed at stabilising the macroeconomic fundamentals and build foreign investor confidence.

'The opening up of the South African economy from 1994 (as measured by SA merchandise imports plus exports relative to GDP) has had many positive effects, not least among them the development of a significant export market. The importance of external demand for South Africa's products is reflected in the five consecutive quarterly current account surpluses on the Balance of Payments that we have recorded as at June 2001.

'The government deficit has been reduced to two per cent of GDP in 2000, markedly lower than the 7.2 per cent in [the] fiscal year 1992/3. This is far below the deficit level of most developed economies.

'On the monetary policy front, the South African Reserve Bank has helped to improve the interest rate environment, another growth-positive factor from the very high levels of 25 per cent in the eighties to 13.75 per cent in June 2001. The low or normalised interest rate levels are conducive to stronger fixed capital investment.

'The rate of inflation has come down significantly. From a level of 15.5 per cent in the period 1985–1990 to 12.5 per cent in the period 1990–1994, inflation has maintained an average of 7.3 per cent in the period 1994–2000. Recognising the importance of price stability, the government and the South African Reserve Bank introduced an inflation-targeting framework, with an initial target of between 3–6 per cent average in 2002. Thus the prevailing inflation trend is downwards.

'A critical issue that faces many countries in transition is collection of taxes, one of the key hallmarks of governance. South Africa's young democracy faced an even greater challenge given that the African majority had resisted taxation (e.g. Bambatha poll tax rebellion*), as they were not willing to fund their own enslavement. Therefore the task was not only to bring millions of new taxpayers into the net, but also to ensure everyone paid their fair share. Tax reform was an integral part of the overall fiscal strategy.

'The success with regard to reorganising the entire tax system, including customs and cross-border management, has played a significant part in government being able to reduce its borrowing requirement, and hence also the budget deficit. It has enabled significant tax reform to take place . . . Corporate income tax has been significantly reduced.

'Despite cutting taxes, both personal and corporate, and virtually eliminating fiscal drag, the South African Revenue Service has consistently exceeded the stringent targets set for total revenue collection. This has been achieved by improved infrastructure, smarter methods of work, better systems and enforcement, as well as recognition by the taxpaying population that everyone has a responsibility to pay their fair share.

'Foreign investor confidence has improved markedly as a result of the government's

* The rebellion, which originated in Greytown, KwaZulu-Natal, in 1906 and was led by Chief Bambatha, was a protest against a one-pound poll tax aimed at forcing black people from rural areas to work in the mines.

commitment to macroeconomic discipline. In the year 2000 alone, the turnover in the bond market rose to a record R10.5 trillion and a record turnover in shares of R537 billion.

'Debt service costs rose during the 1990s from 15 per cent to over 20 per cent of the budget in 1998/9. This steadily eroded the resources available for delivery of services; for instance, the amount spent on servicing debt was roughly equal to the amount spent on education, the greatest expenditure items on the budget. This trend has been reversed and it is expected that by 2002/3 debt service costs will fall to 4.4 per cent of GDP, releasing an additional R10bn to spend on services. By 2005, it is estimated that interest on debt will be reduced to 16.4 per cent of consolidated spending.

'The macroeconomic strategy followed since 1996 focused firmly on building foundations for sustainable long-term growth. This requires higher levels of savings (currently hovering around the 15.5 per cent of GDP ratio) and investment. Government dissaving has significantly reduced, and it will not be long before the local government sector will make a positive contribution to the national saving effort.

'The budget deficit has been lowered from 7.2 per cent of GDP in 1992/3 to 4.6 per cent of GDP in 1996/7 and to 2.0 per cent of GDP in 2000/01.

'Had the government not followed this course, our economy would not have performed so well.'[31]

Towards the end of Mandela's presidential term in 1999, the first parliament had passed over five hundred new laws, eighty-seven of them of a socio-economic character, creating a framework for the transformation of South African society.[32]

Mandela comments: 'By the end of September 1999, 436 land-redistribution projects involving 55,507 households had received ministerial approval. These projects involved 13780,4463 hectares of land, which totals 1.6 per cent of the total rural land in the country.*

'Legislation also seeks to restore land and

---

* The strange-looking figure of '13780,4463' hectares of 'land approved' for land-redistribution projects is an error in Mandela's original handwritten manuscript. It is unknown what the actual figure approved was. However, a 2014 report by the Department of Planning, Monitoring and Evaluation lists land-redistribution hectares 'delivered', which would have been less than hectares 'approved'. By 1999 a total of 521,276 hectares of land had been delivered for land-redistribution projects. By 2014 this had increased to 4,313,168 hectares (*Development Indicators 2014*, p. 35).

provides other remedies to people dispossessed by racially discriminatory laws and practice. By 31 December 1998 a total of 13,931 households had land restored to them involving 264,615 hectares of land. R13 million has been paid to a further 782 households as compensation.

'Legislation to protect labour tenants from eviction was passed. It also provided a mechanism to labour tenants to buy land on which they were staying. At the end of September 1999, 349 labour tenant projects involving 434 households and 7,181 hectares have been approved by the Department of Land Affairs.

'Another piece of legislation increases the security of tenure of farm workers and protects them from unfair eviction.

'Much progress has been made since 1994, notwithstanding certain challenges, some of which are matters of common knowledge.'[33]

Housing, like land, mirrored — most dramatically — the consequences of South Africa's history of legislated inequality. As with land reform, both the housing programme and its enabling legislation had to undo multiple restrictions and barriers put in place by apartheid.

'Segregation was the bedrock of the apartheid government with overcrowded and poorly policed black townships situated far away from white areas.

'The primary object of the democratic government was to introduce a uniform and non-discriminatory national housing policy, and to replace the more than 17 administrations managed by Bantustan, Coloured and Indian officials.

'We were faced with the formidable challenge of providing accommodation for the multitude of people who never enjoyed the most elementary privilege of having a shelter, and with a backlog of between two and three million. It was the top priority of the new government to reduce that backlog.

'Apart from the new government building houses, we also provided finance to enable emerging building contractors, some of whom are women, to participate in the industry. We also devised a scheme to enable poor people to have loans to extend their houses. Low-income earners are provided with alternative finance packages. People had to have houses irrespective of their circumstances.

'For some time the pace of delivery was hampered by lack of capacity to implement it across the three levels of government. Notwithstanding formidable problems, such as the existence of slums throughout the country, we were able to make progress.

'From 1994 up to March 1999 a total of R10.7 billion was spent on housing delivery and we approved subsidies to over 800,000 units providing shelter to three million people.

'Through Operation Mayibuye in the Gauteng Province, we restored ownership of property to those who left their properties because of unrest.*

'We launched a pilot project on hostels redevelopment and converted 32 single-sex hostels into family homes, while 25 are currently being upgraded.

'Our programme has supported the involvement of women in an industry that was hitherto the monopoly of males.

'We also have housing subsidies for the disabled and for people in the rural areas.

'A pilot project on energy-saving houses, concentrating on the low-income market, is gaining popularity, and has reduced the incidence of carbon-monoxide poisoning

* It is likely that Mandela is in fact referring to Operation Masakhane (Let's Build One Another) here, rather than Operation Mayibuye. In a speech he gave on the project in 2 September 1997, Jay Naidoo, who was the cabinet minister responsible for the ANC's Reconstruction and Development Programme, said that the main aim of Masakhane was to facilitate 'the restructuring of governance institutions so as to put the country on a path of sustainable development'. The programme actively urged residents to pay for services such as water, electricity, sewerage and refuse collection.

among these groups.

'The low-cost housing delivery has contributed directly and indirectly to economic growth as well as to a marked increase in the Gross Domestic Product.

'It is estimated that for every house built, one permanent and three temporary jobs are created. Since the beginning of our programme we have created 681,203 permanent jobs and two million temporary ones.

'Furthermore, the housing sector has an influence on the balance of payment through imports used directly in housing construction.

'By concentrating on the disabled, pensioners and a wide range of homeless people we have put the poor at the centre of our housing policy delivery agenda.

'We are steadily improving the capacity to deliver more houses at the average of 200,000 houses per year. We have also passed legislation bringing security of tenure to labour. Tenants on farms [are] one of the most oppressed and exploited section of our people.

'To sum up, through the various schemes sketched above, we have managed to house three million people in the last five years, approved over a million subsidies, restored a people's human dignity by turning single-sex hostels into family units.★

★ During the apartheid era, migrant workers came

509

'We have for the first time in the history of our country introduced a non-discriminatory policy which saw the most vulnerable members of our society getting access to affordable homes — widows, pensioners, the unemployed and the disabled.'[34]

Although the ANC's target of one million houses in the first five years was not met, Mandela took comfort that his government had made the kind of progress that was unequalled anywhere on the globe. Millions of people were given the dignity and security of decent shelter. Yet the backlog hardly showed signs of diminishing. The government of South Africa became the unintended victim of its own success in dislodging apartheid; the removal of restrictions on the movement of Africans led to massive internal migration and stimulated social change, which saw families unbundle into smaller units. By 1999 the proportion of informal households (or households in informal areas) had grown from 7.5 per cent to 12.3 per cent.[35]

Mandela was also concerned by the size of the houses, which couldn't be helped given the government's limited resources. On see-

---

to the cities to work and were provided bleak accommodation in blocks of hostels and were forbidden from bringing their families.

ing the first houses, he joked that the occupiers' feet would stick out of the front door. Possibly influenced by memories of a succession of poky cells that he had lived in from the time of his arrest in 1962 to his release in 1990, he asked Joe Slovo, the minister of housing, if there wasn't an alternative approach, such as serviced sites on which people could be subsidised to build their own houses.[36]

Stephen Laufer, then Joe Slovo's adviser, remembers that the Ministry of Housing explored various ideas to deal with the housing deficit facing the government. The issue of subsidised housing was rejected as a throwback to apartheid practices; there was, however, a thought of creating housing depots, suitably staffed and equipped with expertise and materials to help people to build their own dwellings. This wasn't, however, followed up after Joe Slovo's death in 1995.[37]

Mandela took a special and personal interest in the areas where the poorest of the poor are usually the most vulnerable — education and health. He worried in particular about the efficacy of the school-nutrition scheme, access to primary health care for pregnant women and children under six, and the building and upgrading of clinics and schools both by government and through partnerships he personally forged with private sector corporations.

Sensitive to the inequalities ravaging South African society, Mandela pursued his own personal mission. From the time he walked out of the gates of Victor Verster Prison in Paarl, on the afternoon of 11 February 1990, Mandela had sought to get the business community to have more empathy with the majority — and to encourage it to undertake targeted social-investment initiatives. While making these overtures, he was also aware of a counter-narrative operating in the media, which portrayed the new political players, especially MPs, as money-grubbing, and he did as much as he could to dispel that image. Occasionally, however, such comments came from those he respected, and these were much harder to bear. For example, John Carlin, who had interviewed Mandela on numerous occasions, wrote a piece for UK newspaper the *Independent* headlined 'ANC Boards the Gravy Train: John Carlin in Johannesburg on the Underdogs Who Have Become Fat Cats in a Few Months'. In it he said that 'Mandela promised in his election victory speech that the era of the fat cats was over, that the "government of the people" would tolerate no more gravy trains. What he failed to anticipate was that the gap between government and people would widen after the dawn of democracy.' In the same report,

Archbishop Desmond Tutu was quoted saying that the new government had ' "stopped the gravy train only long enough to get on" '.[38]

Yet even before the ANC received such stinging criticisms from trusted friends and allies, Mandela had decided to donate one-third of his salary to promoting the cause of children's rights. In a speech given in June 1994 to mark the anniversary of the Soweto Uprising, he said:

'I am consulting with relevant individuals and bodies, for me to set up a Presidential Trust Fund representative of people beyond the ANC and the mass democratic movement, to specifically deal with the problems of street children and detainees. I intend to make a contribution of R150,000 a year to this fund, irrespective of the decision that Parliament will make about the salaries of elected representatives. Further details will be announced in due course.

'The Fund I have referred to will assist in alleviating these problems. But I do recognise, as all of you do, that a lasting solution lies in comprehensive socio-economic uplifting programmes. At the same time, the youth, especially from disadvantaged communities, need to realise that we cannot rely only on governmental programmes and charity. We also have to take initiatives in our communities to pool our meagre resources for projects such as bursaries and skills upgrading.'[39]

The Presidential Trust Fund was to form the basis of the Nelson Mandela Children's Fund, which became a vehicle not only for helping build partnerships with business leaders but also ensured that these partnerships were not dependent on state machinery and could thus produce swift results in areas of great need. Although the results were visible and impressive, Mandela acknowledged that they were no substitute for the mass provision of services by the state.

But he knew that South Africa's destiny was irreversibly intertwined with its capacity to educate its people. Progress was reliant on it, and education had always been close to his heart. 'The emancipation of people from poverty and deprivation is most centrally linked to the provision of education of quality,' he said.

'While the poor and suffering masses of our people bore the weight of the liberation struggle, we acknowledge that we would not have advanced in the manner we did if it was not for the education that many of our leaders and cadres obtained. We recognised that emancipation from illiteracy and ignorance was an important part of our liberation struggle, and that education was key to that.

'It was for that same reason, for example, that one of the first things we set out to do when we were incarcerated on Robben Island prison, was to prepare for the education and further education of ourselves as inmates. Many political prisoners learnt to read and write for the first time on Robben Island. Many obtained degrees and further degrees on the Island. And the informal education through reading and discussion was probably the most significant part of our stay in that prison.

'One of the cruellest ways in which the apartheid system hit at our people was through the deliberate undermining of the quality of public education and the destruction of non-state education through, for example, the churches that sought to provide quality education. Today [as] we seek to reconstruct and develop our country, we have to battle that legacy of inferior education deliberately provided to the masses of our people.

'Had it not [been] for the missionaries, I probably would not have been here today. They are the people who introduced education to blacks in South Africa . . . They bought the land, built the schools, equipped them, employed teachers who taught us. Right from primary school to the University of Fort Hare, I was at missionary schools. The Presbyterian Church, the Methodist Church, the Anglican Church and the Catholics. And that is why religion is in our blood because we are the product of missionary education.

'We place education and training at the centre of the developmental policies of our democratic government. We realise that without a broad corps of educated, highly skilled and well-trained people, we cannot become the winning nation we wish to be in order to provide better lives for all our people.'[40]

Future historians will doubtless ask probing questions about Mandela's work with the poor, his predilection for delving into avenues — or competencies — that should have been the province of ministries or government departments. How was it possible, for instance — or even desirable — that his efforts would supplant the work of the ministries of education and health? In picking up the slack and attempting to mitigate the brutal effects wrought by more than three centuries of organised plunder, did he never wonder if his contribution, important as it might have been, was a mere palliative for a chronic disease? When he walked through the townships and informal settlements and saw the devastation and ruin, the children with bloated stomachs and spindly legs and faces on which flies danced with glee, wasn't there a moment when he felt an inexpressible urge to grab De Klerk by the scruff of the neck and force him to look — *look at the ruin you're now pretending to have never been party to?*

Such questions, of course, would have been distractions from Mandela's single-minded programme to construct the democracy he had set out to build from the moment he started negotiations with his captors. Their handiwork — the destruction that the nation now had to repair — was much more present in its lack, an absence born of neglect. There were barely any clinics; those that existed stood forlorn in village slums, in need of upgrading. Such neglect has a lot to do with the attitude of those who were supposed — and even paid — to provide these services; it speaks of an unspeakable brand of callousness.

Here, again, as in the priority programmes to be addressed in the first one hundred days, Mandela tacked on ongoing government programmes of building and upgrading facilities such as clinics and health-care centres, persuading the private sector to augment or even start up projects in partnership with government. He also used his standing to change attitudes that hindered the provision of services such as health care.

Speaking much later at a conference, Mandela reminisced on some of his efforts. 'When I was president of South Africa,' he said, 'I went round the country with the then Minister of Social Welfare Geraldine [Fraser-] Moleketi. Every city or rural area we went to, we told parents to bring the children who are suffering from terminal diseases, like HIV/AIDS, cancer, tuberculosis, malaria. "We also want you to bring children who are disabled, either physically or mentally." And the fact that the president of a country is seen sitting at table with children with HIV/AIDS and suffering from terminal diseases, children who are disabled, makes the parents less ashamed of their children. And the parents will say: "If the president of a country and the minister of welfare can sit at table and enjoy a meal with our children who suffer from terminal diseases, why must we be ashamed of them? We want them to come out and be seen and to enjoy life like ordinary individuals." '[41]

Mandela appreciated people being treated like ordinary individuals, mainly because his life — and the lives of his compatriots — in incarceration had been an endurance test, an obstacle course where to want to be treated as an ordinary person, a human being, was to court trouble. He was all too familiar with disease and death. Those close to him had died and he had been unable to bury them. Now, too, he was keenly aware of the attitudes towards those suffering from AIDS, a scourge loosed on the land, leaving a trail of death and destruction.

'Now,' he explained to journalists at his last media briefing as president, on 10 May 1999, 'the question of AIDS of course is a very difficult problem, because we are faced with a conservative community. You will have seen that a lady in KwaZulu-Natal who confessed that she [was] HIV-positive was murdered, was stoned to death. And this is not an isolated case. As far back as 1991, I went to Mpumalanga, and I called a meeting of parents and I then addressed them on the question of AIDS, and I said to them, "In our community, you don't talk about sex, no matter what you want to say about it. Sex is taboo." And I said, "But we are facing this threat, which might develop into an epidemic. No single government has got resources to deal with it. It is something that must be dealt with by the government and the community." And I say, "The time has come for you to teach your children about safe sex; that a person should have one partner, must have contraceptives and so on." I could see as I was addressing them that I was saying something, you know, which was revolting to them. After the meeting, they came to me and said, "How can you talk like this? You want to encourage prostitution amongst our children? You think that there is a parent you see who can actually tell his or her child that you must have safe sex, you must have contraceptives and so on?" And my explanation was just meaningless.

'And I went to Bloemfontein. This time I

was warned; now, I had to be careful, and I asked the principal of the school. "Look, I want to talk about AIDS." And she said to me — now, this is a principal with a degree, a university degree — she says to me, "Please don't. If you continue like this, you will lose an election." And, of course, I was keen not to lose an election. I had to abandon it.

'So, a massive campaign of education is absolutely necessary to convince the public that they must now abandon old traditions and taboos because this is a disease that attacks the economically active section of the population. It can destroy the economy of the country . . . But it's not very easy because we're faced with this problem of the conservatism of the community as well as the churches. There are still some churches that feel that we are not handling the matter correctly by talking to parents and children and urging them to have safe sex; who say that nobody should have sex until that person is married. You still have churches with that point of view today.

'But, nevertheless, this is something that is being dealt with. It has to be. There must be a number of initiatives educating the public and, of course, making sure that this drug [AZT] is available, but not at the expensive rate as it still is. It must be affordable, and we haven't got resources to be able to give it free of charge . . . We just don't have the resources. And we will acquire and distribute in accordance with our resources.'[42]

There may have been a lack of resources, but the new democratic government had Mandela at its helm — a man with unshakeable faith in his own power to get things done. It was power with its source in the people themselves. Everywhere he went, he was still greeted with the same enthusiasm as when he accepted the oath to lead the country as its first democratic president; he reciprocated this warmth with animated dignity, much like an athlete buoyed by supporters to achieve an amazing performance. He was seventy-five years old when he was sworn in as president of the Republic of South Africa, an age when most people choose to be retired, but he wasn't most people and, like many of his compatriots who had languished in prison, he regarded retirement — a sedentary existence — as a rehearsal for, if not an invitation to, permanent rest in what Thabo Mbeki called a 'small house of wood'.[43] Retirement, temporary or permanent, had to wait. Mandela still had work to do — and the list of what needed to be done was long.

The ANC's 1994 election manifesto had made specific commitments to what would be done over the next five years. It was an ambitious programme and throughout his presidency Mandela kept an eagle-eyed watch to see whether or not the mandate had been met. He wanted the public to be aware of the successes; he also wanted government's eyes on the goals still to be achieved. Opening Parliament for the last time, Mandela summarised how South African lives had changed during the five years he had been president.

He told Parliament that the census of 1996, 'whose result was made public last year, has for the first time, given South Africa a detailed comprehensive portrait of itself. And it is against its dimensions that we must measure our progress.'

Mandela then went on to read the statistics, citing successes in supplying millions with water near their homes; similarly with electricity, access to telephony, school nutrition programmes and services to the community living with disabilities.

'This,' he said, 'means more than the dry rhyme of statistics. The words of Ms Gladys Nzilane of Evaton, who received keys to her new house last year, ring true to the heart: "I hear people on radio and television saying the Government has failed, but I do not believe that . . . [The Government] has given us life."

'In this, she was echoing the feelings of millions, including Mama Lenah Ntsweni of Mpumalanga who was the three millionth person to receive safe and accessible water a few weeks ago.'

Mandela continued to list the developments, the jobs and the construction of facilities that would benefit society for generations to come. He set the government's achievements against the burden of what was not yet done, and alluded, albeit without going into detail, to problems in a process that had neither been smooth nor continuous. He also acknowledged that some targets had been missed. But, with all that, he was still optimistic:

'From the jobs summit, new initiatives have emerged,' he said, 'in a splendid partnership between business and Government, to start major projects that will put more roofs over the head of those in want. As this project starts unlocking the problem of limited public resources, so will its beneficiaries multiply — from the supplier of building materials to the small building contractor; from the new employees to those who will occupy these dwellings.'[44]

The five years of Mandela's presidency had seen enormous social change, though less than had been hoped. Change was still greatest where action depended least on the national partnership that Mandela continually sought — greater where it concerned public service to families and households rather than economic advancement and opportunity; greater in alleviation of poverty than reduction of inequality.

There were other deficits, signs of the

infirmities of the social order, which impacted on the lives of the majority of the people in the most immediate and visceral fashion. South Africans, especially black people, had always lived with violence — the structural violence evolved by the apartheid state apparatus, which was camouflaged and intangible; and the violence of crime, which spoke of the breakdown of the social fabric. The latter was more conspicuous and dramatic. Some would even go as far as to say that having a dark skin in a racist society was an invitation to violence.

The opposition tended to blow the crime situation out of all proportion, spreading stories and surveys that aimed to show that the democratic government was incapable. There was also the insistent refrain that violent crime had started on the day the new government came to power. Research in hand suggests otherwise. An article in *The Conversation* goes a long way in enlightening readers about the true state of affairs. It says that 'from 1994 onwards, the murder rate [in South Africa] fell by an average of 4 per cent a year' and that 'the murder rate didn't begin rising in 1994 — exactly the opposite. There was steady increase to the 1950s, a slightly more rapid rise to the 1960s, some years of relative stability, and then a massive spike to peak in 1993. Then things turned around.'[45]

The majority of newspapers, catering to a

panicked readership, made an issue of high levels of crime but ignored those police statistics showing that the crime rate was beginning to decline.[46] Mandela would have none of it. He writes:

'Opposition parties, some of whom created or inherited that authoritarian and repressive force, and others who condemned white supremacy, but opposed every legitimate action used by the oppressed to liberate the country, now accuse the government of being soft on crime. Hardly do they ever praise the government and business for their excellent performance and for the efficient and devoted SAPS [South African Police Service] now bequeathed to our country.

'The reason for this peculiar attitude on the part of some South African politicians is not far to find. As pointed out in a previous chapter, the white minority has ruled South Africa for more than three centuries.

'Some of them, drunk with power and without vision, never imagined that they would in their lifetime, suffer the trauma of losing that political power to a majority they were taught from birth to despise.

'Even in the face of the far-reaching peaceful transformation that has taken place, plus the zeal with which the ruling party has promoted and implemented the policy of reconciliation, the background, education and political training of some sections of the opposition make them deaf and dumb to what is currently happening in our country.

'We have shown in a previous chapter that since April 1994 our voter support has increased considerably in both the general and local government, as well as in the mega cities. All this information has made no impression whatsoever to some members of the opposition. They still harp monotonously on false propaganda which nobody else, except themselves, believe[s] in. They criticise the government for lack of delivery, predict a split in the Congress Alliance and accuse the government for being soft on crime. If there were a grain of truth in all these accusations, why then would our support continue to grow as it has done over the last seven years?

'The so-called New National Party is on the way out, never to return.* They have no leader of the calibre of former President De Klerk who had the courage and vision to take the right turn when he reached the crossroad.

'But, South Africa has produced great liberals who courageously condemned apartheid. Although they disagreed with our methods of political action, and insisted that we should

* The New National Party was formed in 1997 after the National Party left the Government of National Unity the previous year. The party's first leader, F. W. de Klerk, was succeeded by Marthinus van Schalkwyk, but it eventually disbanded in 2005.

confine ourselves to purely constitutional forms of struggle, they were far less arrogant and destructive than some of their heirs.'[47]

However, the crime problem fed into larger issues. Addressing religious leaders at the Morals Summit called by the National Religious Leaders Forum in 1998, Mandela made the point that 'the inhuman system under which we lived so long undermined and eroded respect for one another and for life itself. That apartheid was a sin and encouraged sinful behaviour is no longer a matter of debate.

'The symptoms of our spiritual malaise are only too familiar. They include the extent of corruption in both [the] public and private sector, where office and positions of responsibility are treated as opportunities for self-enrichment; the corruption that occurs within our justice system; violence in interpersonal relations and families, in particular the shameful record of abuse of women and children; and the extent of evasion of tax and refusal to pay for services used.'[48]

Coming from a past where authority was resisted, where state structures were fair game and the mantra of the day was 'We shall support everything the regime opposes and oppose everything it supports', there was a need for a mental switch. Mandela said, 'It was to be expected, given our past, that we would encounter problems of this kind, but not, I believe, how great they would be. Nor that it would be as difficult to mobilise our society in a united effort to eradicate the problems.'[49]

Even at the time when he committed to leading his country, in May 1994, Mandela must have been hearing the echoes of words from some of his most trusted colleagues. One of them, Gill Marcus, then deputy governor of the Reserve Bank, had summarised the complexity of an emergent South Africa. Talking to Allister Sparks, she said: 'There was a feeling that if you dealt with apartheid, a lot of other things would ultimately fall into place, but that has not been the case. It is much harder than we expected; a lot of problems are much more deep-seated.' She continued: 'So much is expected of us simultaneously that there is no room for sequencing. There is too much to do and we are trying to do it all.'[50]

For Mandela, 'to do it all' meant aligning the skewed past with the realities of the day. For that to happen, though, the requisite change had to be driven by people of integrity. He was concerned about the potential of power to corrupt former freedom fighters and the reluctance of those who had benefited from the past to use their ill-gotten privilege towards the effort to build the future. He called for a change in attitude and values, a paradigm shift in thinking to engender a new patriotism. He urged people to work for the common good rather than narrow personal interest.

He renewed this call at the Congress of South African Trade Unions conference in September 1994, following a strike by public sector workers. He said:

'There are at least five million people who are unemployed; who don't know where to get a meal during the day; who don't know where to sleep; who don't know how to clothe their children; how to pay for their school fees. That is your problem to solve. In striking, don't look at your own personal interests, or just the interests of your union; you must take a broad approach. You must create conditions where business can actually expand and absorb these five million people who are unemployed. It is your task to do so. You must also know that, although we are entitled to fight for better living conditions, we must pace ourselves; the higher the cost of production, the more business want to retrench people and increase the army of the unemployed — bear that in mind.'[51]

He would make a similar call for high standards five years later, in Parliament. Society, he said, had also to bear in mind the need to maintain the 'balance between freedom and responsibility. Quite clearly, there is something wrong with a society in which freedom is interpreted to mean that teachers or students go to school drunk; warders chase away management and appoint their own friends to lead institutions; striking workers resort to violence and destruction of property; businesspeople lavish money in court cases simply to delay implementation of legislation they do not like; and tax evasion turns individuals into heroes of dinner-table talk. Something drastic needs to be done about this. South African society — in its schools and universities, in the workplace, in sports, in professional work and all areas of social interaction — needs to infuse itself with a measure of discipline, a work ethic and responsibility for the actions we undertake.'[52]

Delivering the State of the Nation Address in the last year of his presidency, Mandela's impatience shone through the speech, as did his frustration. But he sounded composed when he touched on issues that were close to his heart. This was when he spoke of the 'reconstruction of the soul of the nation, the "RDP of the Soul" '. He explained, 'By this, we mean first and foremost respect for life; pride and self-respect as South Africans rather than the notion that we can thrive in senseless self-flagellation. It means asserting our collective and individual identity as Africans committed to the rebirth of the continent, being respectful of other citizens and honouring women and children of our country who are exposed to all kinds of domestic violence and abuse. When I say Africans, I mean everybody [who regards the] continent of Africa [as] their home. It means building our schools into communities of learning and improvement of character. It means mobilising one another and not merely waiting for Government to clean our streets or for funding allocations to plant trees and tend schoolyards.

'These are things we need to embrace as a nation that is nurturing its new patriotism. They constitute an important environment for bringing up future generations. They are about the involvement of South Africans in building a better life. Thus we shall take not just small steps, but giant leaps to a bright future in a new millennium.'[53]

On the day he bade farewell to Parliament in March 1999, Mandela was in a more forgiving frame of mind. He took a long backward look at the overall goals the government had set itself and itemised the challenges:

'Those challenges were: to avoid the nightmare of debilitating racial war and bloodshed and to reconcile our people on the basis that our overriding objective must be together to overcome the legacy of poverty, division and inequity.

'To the extent that we still have to reconcile and heal our nation; to the extent that the consequences of apartheid still permeate our society and define the lives of millions of South Africans as lives of deprivation, these challenges are unchanged.'[54]

In contemporary South Africa, progress has been made but society still has to grapple with the periodic reappearance of the old fault lines. It happens when organisations and their leaders sense advantage in stirring up or playing to fears and vestigial prejudices, or where communities and social groups feel vulnerable to attack. The challenges remain in direct proportion to the extent to which the reciprocity essential to reconciliation was withheld. Nonetheless, South Africans can now never hear the word 'reconciliation' without associating it with Nelson Mandela.

CHAPTER TWELVE:
NEGOTIATING THE MEDIA

There is an old Afrikaans proverb normally used for someone whose story or testimony beggars belief: *'Hy lieg soos 'n koerant'* ('He tells lies like a newspaper'). With his conscious rehabilitation of the Afrikaans language from its dishonoured status as the oppressor's tool, Nelson Mandela had likely heard of the saying. However, his attitude to newspapers — and the media at large — was born of practicality. From the early 1990s when he sat in his office at ANC headquarters at Shell House being briefed by Jessie Duarte about his schedule, the Afrikaans newspaper *Beeld* would be well within his reach on the desk.

From the moment he took the oath of office, Mandela accepted that, as president, he embodied the Constitution and all its provisions, including section sixteen with its guarantees of the right to freedom of expression, which also embraced the press and other media. He was a lawyer, first and foremost, and read with interest some of the judgments involving the media, especially the ruling by Justice Cameron that 'a defamatory statement which relates to "free and fair political activity" is constitutionally protected in the Interim Constitution, even if false, unless the plaintiff can show that the publisher acted unreasonably'.[1]

The media in South Africa had never been busier than in the build-up to the 1994 elections, a situation that lasted all the way to the end of Mandela's presidency. The locus of all their coverage of events in South Africa was Nelson Mandela. Emboldened by its new-found freedom, the media covered cases of wrongdoing or virtuousness among public officials with equal enthusiasm. A rash of columnists passed their verdict on the emergent democracy, mainly holding Mandela up as a model of integrity while casting aspersions on the government's handling of issues such as crime.

As a result, there was a paradox at play, a tension between how Mandela saw himself and how the public — the world — saw him. Knowing the delicate nature of the new South Africa and his place in it, he approached the media institutions gingerly, much like a boxer sending out light jabs at an opponent, sizing him up and, at the same time, not being entirely surprised at the opponent's hefty uppercut. 'We have had good fights with the media,' he said. 'Such differences cannot be suppressed or avoided in a democracy.'[2]

Like all leaders, he had mixed feelings about the media, seeing it as a necessary evil. As Thami Mazwai, a doyen of black journalism in South Africa, recalls, 'He respected the independence of the media as an institution. That was Mandela the statesman. But then Mandela the politician tended to react very forcefully where he thought there was an unfair interpretation of the ANC or the government, or himself.'[3]

There had long been a close relationship between the media and the liberation struggle, dating from the nineteenth-century colonial days when leading African thinkers had aired their views in the press. This helped to articulate black unity and resistance that gave birth to the ANC in 1912.[4]

Mandela himself admitted that in the 1950s, when he was banned and restricted to Johannesburg, he had depended on the press for information. However, he also said, 'Although I read a variety of newspapers from around the country, newspapers are only a poor shadow of reality, their information is important to a freedom fighter not because it reveals the truth, but because it discloses the biases and perceptions of both those who produce the paper and those who read it.'[5]

On 29 March 1961, when the Treason Trial ended, with all the accused acquitted, Mandela went underground soon after. Clandestinely, he met with the editors of the more liberal of the newspapers, briefing them on the ANC's campaign towards a national convention. He created news to 'feed the mythology of the Black Pimpernel by taking a pocketful of "tickeys" (threepenny bits) and phoning individual newspaper reporters from telephone boxes and relaying stories of what we were planning or of the ineptitude of the police'.[6]

If he played a cat-and-mouse game with the police, he was, however, straight in his dealings with the media, imploring, to no avail, English-language newspaper editors to support a publicised stay away in opposition to South Africa's departure from the Commonwealth and the impending arrival of the republic.* The newspapers discouraged the strike and downplayed its impact, adopting a role which Mandela deemed 'thoroughly shameful'.[7]

Later, in prison, he found that, his ambivalence notwithstanding, the newspapers were 'more valuable to political prisoners than gold or diamonds, more hungered for than food or tobacco; they were the most precious contraband on Robben Island'. They were more important for disseminating news to

---

* South Africa withdrew from the Commonwealth in 1961 when it became a republic.

the outside world about the struggle of the prisoners. 'In order for a hunger strike to succeed,' Mandela said, 'the outside world must learn of it. Otherwise, prisoners will simply starve themselves to death, and no one will know. Smuggled-out information that we were on a hunger strike would elicit newspaper stories, which in turn generate pressure from support groups.'[8]

The ambivalence was reflected in his farewell briefing to a select group of editors and opinion makers on the fifth anniversary of his inauguration in May 1999. He said, 'We have made repeated statements, especially in the run-up to the 1994 general elections that we regard a free press as a pillar of democracy and that we have no intention whatsoever of restricting that freedom of the press.'

He acknowledged that the government and the press had not always seen eye to eye. 'We have had our differences,' he said, 'because when the press criticises us and we reply then the press says, "Well, the freedom of speech is threatened," which suggests that they are the only ones who can exercise the freedom of speech — when we are criticised we must keep quiet. We don't accept that and we'll never accept it. If you criticise us, you must also give us the right to criticise you . . . We do not want lapdogs; we want watchdogs. And you have played that role and I think that it is proper that you should continue to be fiercely independent. All that we want is that even when you criticise and we don't agree with your criticism, there should be integrity in what you say.

'And many of you have that quality in dealing with issues, especially when you are dealing with a government such as ours where each individual has never had the experience of governance before he or she became a cabinet minister. There are many mistakes that we have committed, and so this debate in the country, this national debate must go on. And there will be differences. The important point is that the press is there to be used by us as a mirror in which we can see our own performance and we have changed our attitude on a number of things because we realised from the way in which the press reacted that we were either wrong or we did not make sufficient preparations for the nation to accept the point of view that we have taken . . .

'Nevertheless,' he concluded, 'at the same time, we must not be too much in a hurry, because you cannot change some of the issues that we face overnight. It's a process to change them. And I am satisfied that within that context, the press is playing an important role.'[9]

An expression of this conviction about the media's inalienable right to perform its role free of the fetters of state control was made when Mandela addressed the Congress of the International Press Institute in 1994. He said: 'It is only such a free press that can temper the appetite of any government to amass power at the expense of the citizen. It is only such a free press that can be the vigilant watchdog of the public interest against the temptation on the part of those who wield it to abuse that power. It is only such a free press that can have the capacity to relentlessly expose excesses and corruption on the part of government, state officials and other institutions that hold power in society.

'The African National Congress has nothing to fear from criticism. I can promise you we will not wilt under close scrutiny. It is our considered view that such criticism can only help us to grow, by calling attention to those of our actions and omissions which do not measure up to our people's expectations and the democratic values to which we subscribe.'[10]

He was hands-on in the projection of his public persona, and became, in time — given the avalanche of invitations to speaking engagements — the victim of his own popularity. Finding himself deluged by a full schedule, he would complain to his nattily dressed, quick-witted and energetic spokesperson, Parks Mankahlana, that his schedule left too little time to read state documents and the newspapers, and to reflect on issues.

He joked that he missed his days on Robben Island where he had time to think, and suggested free time in the afternoon whenever possible.[11]

Mandela managed communications in performance by making statements through the way he dressed. When he donned the Springbok rugby jersey at Ellis Park, he was saying something of grave importance to all South Africans, and to the world. He was also making a statement when he eschewed the top hat and tails at the inauguration in favour of a simple suit, and he always wore formal attire for appearances in Parliament. In time, he started wearing the loose, colourful 'Madiba shirts' that came to be associated with him in engagements with the public.

Mainly planned by his advisers, the engagements with the media were also at his own initiative. He met with Afrikaans editors in 1995 to thrash out the burning issue of the future of the Afrikaans language; and when the tension in KwaZulu-Natal was at fever pitch over the drafting of the Constitution, he invited the newspaper editors of the province to a meeting to brief them on the direction contemplated by the government on the issue.[12]

Through Mankahlana, Mandela maintained direct relations with individual journalists and editors. Press conferences were an arena where Mandela showed his prodigious memory for names, calling the journalists by their first names, even those he had met many years ago. He showed old-world courtliness; he would be simultaneously friendly and firm with all those he encountered. Serving Mandela, Mankahlana would go as far as venturing into newsrooms to offer stories, spending — it seemed — very little time at his desk in the office.[13]

If Mandela had an issue to raise with editors or senior journalists, he would pick up the phone and, as often as not, invite them over for a meal — and put his point across. Recalling this, Mazwai says that Mandela 'tried to walk the tightrope and react in such a way that there was no invasion in the right of the media to write and tell it like it is. What he tended to do would be to invite specific journalists to breakfast. Then he would say, "Look, this is what you said, but this is in reality what the situation is." That was how he tried to manage the situation.'[14]

For instance, Mandela had an off-the-record meeting with the editor of *Die Burger* when he felt that the paper had given an insufficient explanation of the context of the shooting at the ANC's headquarters at Shell House in March 1994.[15] In the same vein, he invited the editor of *City Press* to a meeting when he felt he had overlooked an important idea in an editorial arguing that the cricket and rugby bosses were using Mandela to make reconciliation a one-sided process at the expense of black people. Both agreed, with neither side conceding anything, that it was a useful discussion.[16]

Sometimes Mandela's contact with the media was attended by farce, which he shrugged off. Jakes Gerwel remembered an incident that made him appreciate a different side of his principal. The men's porn magazine *Hustler* had named Mandela its 'Arsehole of the Month', leading to indignant voices calling for a distribution ban on the issue. In contrast, a highly amused Mandela quipped, 'We should not be banning things.'[17]

Although he received a daily analysis of the news media soon after the working day began, Mandela would by then have read several newspapers, mostly while having his breakfast at home. By the time he reached his office, he would have, as often as not, telephoned ministers and members of his communications team to get their responses to issues featuring in the media.

He was happy to delegate the drafting of his speeches when confident, as was the usual case, that his views and priorities would be reflected. There were times that he would indicate what needed stressing, but, since he was astute enough to know that the journalists unfailingly latched on to comments not covered in a prepared speech, he would ask that important points should not be included in a prepared speech. Often journalists covering his events would only prick up their ears and start using their pens when he started speaking extempore. He would often preface his remarks by saying that what he had just read was what his bosses had told him to say — and now he would speak from the heart.

Contrary to popular belief that Mandela was prone to speak off the cuff or shoot from the hip, the truth is that most of those comments were deliberate on his part; he had thought them through but knew he'd face opposition if he consulted with his colleagues. Moreover, the frequent repetitions that characterised his speeches were not from forgetfulness. In self-deprecatory prefaces to his speeches he made the point that his staff told him he was wont to repeat himself. But this was a strategy to not only put an issue on record but also to ensure that it became a focus of public discourse. For example, the scorecard of expanding access to basic services became a mantra of communication in every kind of setting, formal or informal, prepared or unscripted, in speeches or notes.

Famously known as a nightmare for VIP protection units — at home and abroad — Mandela preferred unmediated social interaction with the public. He got a charge out of the constant affirmation by ordinary people from all walks of life. The end of a day of interaction with the public would be more satisfying than sitting in his office or through cabinet meetings. 'You have made me feel like a young man again, with my batteries recharged,' he would remark.[18]

While he recognised that he had become a world icon, likely to attract interest in just about every aspect of his life, Mandela was also quite firm in drawing a line when the interest became overly intrusive. He was as reticent about sharing what had caused him pain — for instance, his divorce from Winnie Madikizela-Mandela — as he was of putting his relationship with Graça Machel, which was unquestionably a source of joy for him, in the media spotlight. When he and Graça Machel married, even his spokesperson was not let in on the secret, leading him in all good faith to assure the media that there was no wedding at exactly the moment it was taking place.

Even though transparency was the watchword for the democratic government, it had to operate within boundaries that couldn't just be confined to personal matters. There was also the line between transparency and the need for the government to be able to work quietly in areas where public knowledge would either undermine that work or make it even more difficult. Knowing that any measure that approximated abrogation of freedom of speech or access to information would ignite outrage with proponents of an open society, Mandela would call upon journalists to understand the processes under way. Journalists grew used to hearing him saying: 'We are dealing with very sensitive matters and so I hope you will not press me for details.' This was done in such a firm yet gracious manner that it was accepted.

There was often less rapport, however, between government and the media when it came to how the two institutions saw transformation. The government, which perceived itself as receiving a raw deal when a target of inaccurate reporting, construed these inaccuracies as ideological. The journalists, piqued at the undermining of their professionalism, simply regarded these charges as impossibility. Mandela was convinced that that negativity about the ANC-led government was no different from rearguard action, witting or unwitting, in defence of past privilege.

'South African media,' he had said in February 1994, 'are still largely dominated by persons drawn almost exclusively from one racial group. With the exception of *The Sowetan,* the senior editorial staffs of all South Africa's daily newspapers are cast from the same racial mould. They are white; they are male; they are from a middle-class background; they tend to share a very similar life experience. The same holds true for the upper echelons of the electronic media, again, with a very few recent exceptions.

'While no one can object in principle to editors with such a profile, what is disturbing is the threat of one-dimensionality this poses for the media of our country. It is clearly inequitable that in a country whose population is overwhelmingly black (85 per cent), the principal players in the media have no knowledge of the life experience of that majority.'[19]

The implicit expectation that black editors and journalists would necessarily be more empathetic in their reportage soon proved false. Mandela then increasingly shifted towards media ownership. This reflected an ANC stance, which, much earlier, had resulted in tensions between the ANC and black journalists. The journalists felt that the ANC was impugning their integrity and professionalism in portraying them as powerless to report on terms other than those approved by the white owners and editors; this disregarded the role they had played under very difficult circumstances. The nascent Black Editors Forum initiated meetings with the ANC in August and September 1994 to try to resolve the issues. At one of the meetings, Mandela supported the call for affirmative action in the media and the appointment of more black editors. The journalists regarded the meeting as very positive. Mazwai said, 'We were eating out of his hand.'[20]

But the relationship with the media continued to be fraught. Media criticism against the government — and, by extension, the ANC and Mandela — centred on the expulsion of Bantu Holomisa from the ANC and his dismissal from government, as well as allegations of corruption against Minister of Health Nkosazana Dlamini-Zuma with regard to the musical *Sarafina II* as previously discussed in chapter seven. Mandela interpreted this as a media crusade against the transformation of the country and against the ANC. He made two charges against black journalists, souring relations with the media for a year or more.

Some, he said in a television interview, failed to understand the country's problems. Black journalists who accused him of putting white fears before black needs, he said, failed to understand the strategy of neutralising those who wanted to stop the 1994 election by violence.[21] Professor Guy Berger, then head of the School of Journalism and Media Studies at Rhodes University, commented on the ambivalence of black journalists towards the pace of change: '[They] often seem to feel the need to remind whites in general and their white colleagues in particular, of past and present prejudices and white power. Having been victims much more than white journalists, many are reluctant to accept reconciliation without redress. The result has been a critical stance of official reconciliation policy, which has incurred the wrath of Nelson Mandela himself who feels they fail to appreciate why he made the compromises that left redress only a small part of the picture.'[22]

Mandela put his thoughts down on paper and stressed that he was singling out 'some senior black journalists'. 'What you have today is a type of senior journalist — and there are a few — who regret that we have destroyed white supremacy in this country, and who are taking out their venom on the one organisation that has brought about radical changes in this country. They have no conception of the problems facing the country. As I said before, they think — they assume — that we defeated whites on the battlefield and that the whites are now lying on the floor helpless and begging us for mercy.

'We had to adopt a strategy to sideline, to marginalise, those elements which wanted to stop the elections by force. Some senior journalists are not even aware of that. And it's only a few senior black journalists who have got a secret agenda.'[23]

The other charge was that some black journalists had been co-opted by backward-looking interests. Mandela wrote what he had been saying repeatedly on public platforms: 'Both black and white journalists are waging a biased and venomous campaign against the ANC.'

He went on to rail against the media for raising issues of both Holomisa and Dlamini-Zuma, decrying the role of 'some senior black journalists' who had 'been co-opted into this sordid affair . . . Traditionally white parties and their surrogates are bitter against the democratic movement for having destroyed white supremacy and the privileges monopolised by the former ruling minority.'

Of the co-opted journalists, one of them 'was disarmingly honest and frank' when asked by a senior ANC leader. He said the ANC neither paid nor promoted him as a journalist — his newspaper did. The unprecedented bias in commenting on public affairs has never been more clearly illustrated than in the case of maverick Bantu Holomisa whose situation, Mandela believed, was being taken advantage of by these journalists by using him 'as an instrument to destroy the ANC; and totally ignored the basic facts which ought to inform objective comment'.[24]

The political report Mandela presented to the ANC's 1997 national conference contained elements of his concern with media ownership and governance. He said: 'Even a cursory study of the positions adopted by the mainly white parties in the national legislature during the last three years, the National Party, the Democratic Party and the Freedom

Front will show that they and the media which represents the same social base have been most vigorous in their opposition whenever legislative and executive measures have been introduced, seeking to end the racial disparities which continue to characterise our society.'[25]

Along with warnings that some of apartheid's networks continued to pose a security threat — together with concerns about the oppositional role of some NGOs — this comment elicited a storm of criticism from much of the media and opposition parties. Thinking about how he would respond to this when he closed the conference, Mandela came back to the question of media ownership, and instead of retreating, he decided to sally forth. In the notes he prepared before giving his closing address, he writes: 'The panic among opposition parties and in some editorials in response to my political report was not unexpected.

'The striking feature of the NP and DP towards criticism has always been that of a bunch of individuals who have delicate skins and frail nerves; they cannot take criticism. Enlightened members of both these parties deserted them and left behind an arrogant group of unscrupulous racists whose sole aim is to demonise the democratic movement and unashamedly to conduct a virulent campaign of disinformation.'[26]

He continues to write about how the departure of luminaries from the Democratic Party, people who were 'now serving our country with distinction', has 'put the DP firmly on the right of the NP'.[27]

Similarly, people of distinction, who 'could no longer feel at home with a membership that was determined to defend apartheid and its privileges for the white minority', deserted the National Party.[28]

The same media that 'tried to cover up the fact that a Third Force existed in this country . . . now argue that there are no counter-revolutionary elements in this country.

'The hostility of the white media in this country has induced principled commentators to say that South African journalists write as if they are foreigners in their own country.

'Thami Mazwai, a senior black journalist, who was jailed for his principled stand and who later was elevated to the position of chairman of the National Editors Forum, tried to encourage a spirit of patriotism among his colleagues, in vain. He was forced to resign.'[29]

However, upon closing the conference, Mandela decided to refrain from reading out what he had penned, and instead summarised his opinions on the matter in one sentence: 'The response of some political parties and sectors of society, including the media to my

Political Report, was not unexpected; and if anything, it confirms everything that we said.'[30]

One of the first resolutions of the South African National Editors' Forum (SANEF), an industry association born in October 1996, was critical of Mandela's remarks about black journalists. Twenty-two black journalists later asked to meet him, angered by Mandela's remarks, which the journalists felt were denigrating them. A robust exchange was followed by a joint press conference at which Mandela said that he favoured a free press that acted as a watchdog on government, but that as long as conservative whites controlled the media, black journalists would not be free. Having hotly contested that proposition, the journalists agreed to disagree.[31]

In the end, disappointed as he was at the pace of transformation of the media — and critical of the quality of much of the content — Mandela combined acceptance of differences between media and government as a feature of democracy, delivering somewhat qualified praise that held the near uniformly euphoric coverage of his inauguration as ideal:

'We have had robust exchanges with the press,' he writes, 'in some, the words used were carefully selected merely to convey no more than what both parties believed to be true. Others were more than robust, leaving the contestants bruised and without balance. Such heated exchanges cannot be avoided or suppressed in a democracy.

'It is good for us, the media and the country as a whole, to know that our journalists can rise to expectations and acquit themselves excellently as on the day of inauguration and on numerous other occasions.'[32]

Ultimately, Mandela showed consummate skill in managing public relations. He had emerged from prison at a time when media communication had changed into a system in a perpetual state of flux, a voracious beast that had a depthless appetite for the sound bite. Somehow — and it could be said, with a little help from his unsleeping communications staff — he seemed to have studied and embraced this new reality; using his stature, he exploited the media's own needs to communicate important messages that were in line with his mission in a difficult transition.

He accepted with grace the media's intrusiveness, understanding that it was also driven by its own fascination with Mandela the man. Using his status of celebrity, which grew in correspondence to his age, he mastered the discipline of self-control to impart important messages about the collective interests of humanity and the place and role of South Africa in a globalising world.

CHAPTER THIRTEEN:
ON THE AFRICAN
AND WORLD STAGES

Africa for Nelson Mandela was as complex a place as South Africa had been when he came out of prison. He had gone to jail exactly at the time when more and more African states were gaining independence or, in given instances, wresting it from the grip of colonial administrations. Even his language, or choice of words, reflected this connection with a frozen period in the past; for instance, he still used the ancient word 'emancipation' for liberation, conjuring up the parlance favoured by scholars and political activists of yore, whether W. E. B. du Bois or Marcus Garvey, or that could be found in books such as Harriet Beecher Stowe's *Uncle Tom's Cabin* or Booker T. Washington's *Up From Slavery.*[1]

If his language was quaintly anachronistic or limned with whimsy, he was determined to ensure that democratic South Africa's relationship with the rest of Africa would be based on hard realities. The Africa he had visited while underground, which had also given him a glimpse into what it was like to be treated like a full human being — and which had nurtured the liberation movement at great cost to itself — would get his full attention.

During his first six months of liberty, Mandela spent half his time outside South Africa. Even though he visited three continents — Africa, Europe and North America — Africa was his main focus and the first to be visited, apart from an urgent dash to Stockholm, Sweden, to see his ailing friend and mentor, O. R. Tambo, in hospital.

The Africa to which Mandela returned after his imprisonment was very different from the one he had known. Many of the leaders had passed on, with natural causes, coups, exile or executions having taken their toll. So, too, had the geopolitical situation altered, with the current leaders now grappling with the implications of momentous global changes. In July 1990, therefore, while the OAU summit of African heads of state and government crafted resolutions aimed at accelerating the final stages of South Africa's liberation, it had to take on board the changing East–West relations, the end of the Cold War and the formation of new regional economic blocs.

The diminution of direct involvement of external powers in African affairs was an opportunity for its peoples and governments to take full responsibility for their destinies through regional cooperation, further democratisation and popular participation. Given that the 'daunting dual challenge of economic development and democratic transformation' required peace and stability, conflict resolution was crucial.[2] The logical expression of the new paradigm was the establishment in 1993 of the OAU Mechanism on Conflict Prevention, Management and Resolution, which would partner with the United Nations. The Southern African Development Community, although embryonic, was also expected to play its part in the future.[3] It had succeeded the Southern African Development Coordination Conference, which had been formed in 1980 by heads of independent states to coordinate investment and trade and to reduce economic dependence on apartheid South Africa. In 1992, with Namibia now independent and South Africa in transition to democracy, the coordinating conference was upgraded into the SADC, the focus of which had shifted to economic integration.

Mandela and the ANC participation in the OAU meetings and summits laid the basis for the contribution that democratic South Africa would make in the quest for peace and development in Africa and the world. It also saw the beginnings of some of Mandela's efforts towards conflict resolution. By the time South Africa joined the OAU in 1994, the union had charted a new course. It expected to meet challenges. There would be tensions — Africa being so vast with many member states with varying priorities — between collective commitments to the promotion of peace and democratisation on the one hand, and respect for the sovereignty of member states on the other. If the OAU didn't get help from the UN and other countries, it would have a hard time marshalling resources and experience to develop peacekeeping and conflict-resolution capabilities. There was, however, an optimism: the new directions were clear.

Therefore, when President Nelson Mandela addressed the OAU summit a month after his inauguration, in June 1994, it was a moment of great excitement. For many, it was an emotive fulfilment of a promise. Mandela's speech, carefully crafted to articulate his country's nascent 'Africa policy', set out his country's perspective, commitments and responsibilities towards the continent. He said:

'The total liberation of Africa from foreign and white minority rule has now been achieved. Our colleagues who have served with distinction on the OAU Liberation Committee have already carried out the historical task of winding up this institution, which we shall always remember as a frontline partner for the emancipation of the peoples of our continent.'

Then, in what must have sounded dramatic even to his own ears, Mandela said, 'Finally, at this summit meeting in Tunis, we shall remove from our agenda the consideration of the question of Apartheid South Africa.'

This agenda item had been tabled at conventions, summits and seminars of just about any meeting of progressive forces for as long as Mandela had been in prison. Its removal from the agenda signalled a victory of immense proportions — a victory that belonged to a significant section of the world community.

Mandela punctuated this by saying that one epoch 'with its historic tasks has come to an end. Surely, another must commence with its own challenges. Africa cries out for a new birth, Carthage awaits the restoration of its glory.

'If freedom was the crown which the fighters of liberation sought to place on the head of mother Africa, let the upliftment, the happiness, prosperity and comfort of her children be the jewel of the crown.'

On the imperative for Africa to 'bend every effort to rebuild the African economies', Mandela reminded the leaders that the fundamentals 'of what needs to be done are known to all of us. Not least among these is the need to address the reality that Africa continues to be a net exporter of capital and suffers from deteriorating terms of trade. Our capacity to be self-reliant, to find the internal resources to generate sustained development, remains very limited.'

He pointed to the pitfalls of self-pity where leaders blame external agencies for problems when they should be doing a little soul-searching. He paid homage to the 'great thinkers of our continent' and upbraided Africa for failure to deal with the human tragedy of Rwanda, which 'stands out as a stern and severe rebuke to all of us for having failed to address these interrelated matters. As a result of that, a terrible slaughter of the innocent has taken and is taking place in front of our very eyes.'

Mandela pledged: 'We know it as a matter of fact that we have it in ourselves as Africans to change all this. We must, in action, assert our will to do so. We must, in action, say that there is no obstacle big enough to stop us from bringing about a new African renaissance . . .

'The vision you shared with us was one in which we would use the resources of our country to create a society in which all our people would be emancipated from the scourges of poverty, disease, ignorance and backwardness.

'The objective we all pursued was the creation of a South Africa that would be a good neighbour and an equal partner with all the countries of our continent, one which would use its abilities and potentialities to help advance the common struggle to secure Africa's rightful place within the world economic and political system.'[4]

During Mandela's presidential years, South Africa played an active role in the reshaping of the OAU. In 2002, this culminated in the launch of the African Union (AU) in Durban, complete with new systems and structures to match the post-liberation demands of the continent. Mandela's presence in the OAU, says Nkosazana Dlamini-Zuma, 'had a profound influence' because 'here was a man that the OAU and the member states had worked with over the years right from the beginning when MK was established. He had been to many African countries before his arrest. And when he was in prison, the OAU played an important role in supporting the struggle for his release and that of other political prisoners, as well as the struggle in South Africa. So, for this man who was also a world icon to be part of the OAU had a tremendous impact.'[5]

In 1996, he also had an equally huge impact as chairman of the SADC. Anxious to lead an organisation that wouldn't be another bureaucratic talk shop, addressing the SADC summit in Malawi in September 1997, Mandela broached the challenges that the SADC would face in harmonising development with security and — as had been the experience in the OAU — reconciling respect for the sovereignty of member states with commitment to democratic principles, features not uniformly realised in all the states. For him it was imperative that the representatives of member states 'ask frank questions and give honest answers about the state we are in and where we intend to go'.[6]

After a long delivery that contained some of the points he had raised sharply at the 1994 OAU summit, which reflected his preoccupation with democratic processes, Mandela listed the tasks for the intergovernmental organisation. He stressed that there'd be no real progress without gender equality, respect for human rights and the 'basic tenets of good governance'.[7]

One of the issues he did not touch on was the status of the Organ on Politics, Defence and Security Cooperation (Organ), a formal institution of the SADC that had been launched in June 1996. Chaired by President Robert Mugabe, and having met on the eve of the summit, in Gaborone, Botswana, over the past months the Organ had been the subject of intense debates centring on its structure and remit, which could supplant the summit itself in that it could 'operate at the Summit level and . . . function independently of other SADC structures'.[8] Irked by lack of transparency in the Organ — and wanting his structures straight and simple — Mandela was not entirely convinced that the Organ had to operate on a summit level, as is evidenced by his notes:

1. Attended SADC summit in Gaborone in June 1996 and agreed with the decision to form the Organ.
2. Was, however, not aware that it would operate on a summit level [rather than a] ministerial level.
3. Discovered when we met in Luanda on 1 October 1996 that Organ was itself a summit. It came to me as shock — Unaware of existence of any organisation.
   They may be
   Had I known, I would not have accepted chairmanship [of the SADC].
4. Then travelled all the way to see President Mugabe to discuss issue. Thereafter saw Pres. Masire as my predecessor and Pres. Chissano as Vice Chairman. Later four of us met in CT.*
5. On all these occasions they explained in great detail why the Organ had to operate on a summit level. Agreed that

* Robert Mugabe, president of Zimbabwe since 1987; Quett Masire, president of Botswana, 1980–88; Joaquim Chissano, president of Mozambique, 1986–2005.

matter be brought to this [Blantyre, Malawi] Summit.

6. Met the 2 Presidents in Gaborone and suggested solution.[9]

The next day the summit heard the members' views, with no clear consensus emerging other than that there was a need for the Organ, given the region's challenges. The decision postponed, Mandela was urged not to resign. Another discussion six months later at a meeting of heads of state in Maputo again ended without resolution.[10] There was, however, greater consensus that the Organ should be a subcommittee of the SADC rather than a separate entity.

Much has been said about Mandela's relationship with Mugabe, including the fact that it was clear from the very start that there was no love lost between the two leaders. Mugabe, who had been the elder statesman all along, fawned over by his younger counterparts in awe of his combative anti-imperialist stance, felt somewhat eclipsed by Mandela, who arrived on the scene with laudable moral and ethical credentials. Furthermore, as someone widely credited with saying that the only white man to be trusted was a dead white man, it was hardly surprising that Mugabe was not enamoured of Mandela's reconciliation project. Given the exigency of the survival of the SADC, however, the two men worked together on various issues, even though the status of the Organ continued to be a source of tension between them. Quett Masire recalls in his memoirs how the uneasy rapport continued over the years.[11]

The instability in the Congo and the African Great Lakes region impacted negatively on most of the SADC countries. South Africa's involvement with the conflict began with its agreement to participate in a multinational force being established in eastern Zaire to cope with a humanitarian crisis arising from an estimated one million refugees escaping genocide in neighbouring Rwanda. Zaire's President Mobutu Sese Seko asked South Africa to facilitate talks between the Zairean government and Laurent Kabila's Alliance of Democratic Forces for the Liberation of Congo-Zaire (ADFL). Having established itself in the east, the ADFL was advancing towards the capital, Kinshasa. Persuaded by the United States, Kabila's ADFL took part in a series of proximity talks in South Africa in February 1996. These opened the way to face-to-face talks between Mobutu and Kabila aboard the SAS *Outeniqua* in Pointe-Noire at the mouth of the Congo River. Also present at the talks was the special representative of the OAU and UN.[12]

Informed by the success of talks to bring about a new and democratic dispensation in

South Africa — and to cast out the revanchist spirit among belligerents — Mandela believed that the end to the Zairean debacle could be similarly achieved. He thought that it would only take persuading the ageing — and universally discredited — Mobutu to leave office with dignity and Kabila to accept an inclusive approach to forming a new government.

The advance of rebel forces diminished Kabila's appetite for an inclusive solution. Citing fear as a deterrent to his joining the follow-up talks on the ship ten days after the initial talks, Kabila vacillated publicly, angering Mandela whom the media overheard giving the rebel leader a dressing down. It was arranged for Kabila to come the next day to Cape Town so that Mandela could brief him on the proposals drawn up after the first meeting; these had been widely consulted with governments in Africa, France and the United States. While on board the SAS *Outeniqua,* Mandela also phoned several heads of state in the region to discourage them from military intervention in the Democratic Republic of the Congo.[13]

Mandela heard that Kabila had not halted his advance on Kinshasa, despite giving his word to the contrary. Mandela's notes for his meeting with Kabila convey his frustration:

1. Advance to Kinshasa

Bizima Karaha statement*
Surround but don't attack

2. Something grossly wrong with one who makes a firm & clear statement & later denies making statement. Tends to destroy mutual confidence & respect that should exist among comrades.
Understands your concern over security
But many people find your claim ridiculous, to say the least.

3. Promised twice to go on board at Pointe-Noire
Lack of normal courtesies = Deputy President [Mbeki], UNO [United Nations] & OAU representative, President Mobutu.
Kept us waiting for whole day without any information of your whereabouts
Unfortunate attitude towards a dying man, insensitive, no human feelings, no respect.†
Martti Ahtisaari — famous int. diplomat

4. Lack of appreciation for the enormous

* Bizima Karaha, who was the ADFL's foreign minister before and after Kabila became president of the Democratic Republic of Congo in 1997, was also involved in the peace talks.

† Mobutu had prostate cancer and died in Morocco on 7 December 1997.

expenses at taxpayers' cost that my country has spent,
ship itself
30 soldiers.
5. [You have been] rushing to the press.
6. Your image being tarnished; no longer have the moral high ground.
7. Unfortunate things being said about you. [I] have defended you & I am sure others as well have done so.
8. Sadako Ogata*
9. Kofi Annan†
[Have] given me tough job. But you are busy destroying mutual trust.
How can I serve [a] person who treats me without respect?'[14]

The military intervention in Lesotho on 22 September 1998 by the SANDF and, to a negligible degree, the Botswana Defence Force (BDF), put the SADC and its leadership — including Mandela — in the crosshairs of the international human rights community. And, as is common with all such

* Sadako Ogata was the UN's high commissioner for refugees from 1991 to 2000 and had met with Mandela in March 1997 to discuss the refugee crisis in Zaire.
† Kofi Annan, secretary-general of the UN, had endorsed the peace talks in the hope that it would lead to a ceasefire.

undertakings, the intervention was well intentioned. It followed a disputed election that was simultaneously hailed as peaceful by both domestic and international observers and, according to detractors, who said it had been rigged, characterised by deep tensions and animosity.

The mutiny by the army and two written requests from the prime minister of Lesotho for intervention prompted the SADC's conclusion that the political process couldn't proceed without military stabilisation of the security situation, which was to be undertaken by South Africa and Botswana on behalf of SADC.[15]

On 22 September, six hundred South African troops entered Lesotho, and they were joined later by two hundred troops from the BDF. Resistance by members of the Lesotho Defence Force (LDF) was much stiffer than had been anticipated, and eight members of the SANDF and twenty-nine of the LDF lost their lives.

Acting South African President Mangosuthu Buthelezi (Mandela was out of the country) briefed the National Assembly as the intervention was taking place and, with the minister of defence, spoke further to the cabinet the next day. The cabinet supported the SADC's assessment that the aim of the intervention, called Operation Boleas, was to stabilise the situation and create an environment in which negotiations could continue to bring about a lasting settlement.[16]

On his return to South Africa from North America, Mandela said, 'We went there not to fight but in order to ensure that these violent activities — which were illegal — were stopped so that the parties could sit down and explore a peaceful settlement. We are there for that purpose. We did not fire first.'[17]

The objectives of the SADC were achieved. Lesotho adopted a number of political and constitutional changes, including a proportional representation electoral system to give small parties a greater say than the previous first-past-the-post system.

'There's no doubt,' Mandela said, 'that SADC's collective initiative succeeded in creating space for that country's political leaders to find a peaceful resolution of their differences; and we ought to take this opportunity to congratulate the Botswana and South African Defence Forces on their decisive contribution; and to pay tribute to those who lost their lives.'[18]

Conflict, especially where there's a loss of life, gives rise to recriminations. The SADC invasion, as it was called in many reports, invited hard questions and accusations that South Africa — Botswana was let pretty much off the hook — had acted ultra vires; that the SADC's intervention was inconsistent with the UN Charter and that there should have been authorisation for the intervention from the UN Security Council. Despite difficulties in achieving its objective — some operational, negative public reactions in Lesotho, etc. — the first military intervention by South Africa and the SADC was successful; however, the SADC was still not fully equipped to conduct such interventions. The intervention provided all involved with an object lesson towards the evolution of a more appropriate approach to peacekeeping and regional conflict resolution.

There were a few other situations that Mandela sought to address, committed as he was to the principle of extending the culture of human rights across the continent. There was a corresponding pull from the peoples of those countries from the south to the north who felt that South Africa had a moral obligation to come to their aid in recompense for their support of the liberation struggle.

For the continent to survive, however, there was a need for the creation of a climate conducive to investment. The turmoil and strife often had their origins in unstable economic circumstances. Addressing this issue, Mandela said, 'We need support from the old industrial countries. They owe us that support, not as a question of charity but because we are entitled to it. Our region and many others were subjected to the most brutal form of exploitation in the colonial era.'[19]

As usual, while Mandela had effectively written the playbook on the merits of reconciliation, which was aimed at securing the future, he was equally reluctant to let the iniquities of the past, such as the impact of colonialism, go unaddressed. Africa's rebirth would not be possible in isolation; it had to happen in collaboration with the rest of the world.

In his almost two thousand days as president of the Republic of South Africa, Mandela brought an intense spotlight on his country, and simultaneously engaged South Africa — a country that had been engrossed in its own drama — in world events. The adulation showered on a black person by admired luminaries, especially from the Western world, edified a sizeable section of whites. Of greater importance was the acceptance of South Africa in prestigious world bodies and the abolishment of the country's status — felt more acutely by white people during the boycotts and embargoes — as a skunk among nations.

The emergent South African foreign policy, evolved in part from the multifaceted relations developed by the ANC over the years, which had more foreign missions than the apartheid government, reflected the dynamic changes the world was going through with the end of the Cold War.

Alongside South Africa's focus on African renewal, relations with countries of the south occupied a vital place. Mandela outlined his vision in his address to a summit of Mercosur (Mercado Común del Sur — the Southern Common Market), which comprises several Latin and South American economies, in 1998. He spoke of the 'unity of experience of the developing world and the great potential for strengthening the South through co-operation and building relations amongst ourselves and at the same time how this could be the basis for advancing a mutually beneficial partnership with the countries of the North . . .

'Common contexts led us both — in the Southern part of Africa and in the Southern cone of Latin America — to establish and build regional associations informed by a commitment to democracy; by the imperatives of development in a rapidly globalising world economy; and by the recognition that peace and security are dependent on development, social equity and proper environmental management in the context of the goal of sustainable development . . .

'Amongst the greatest opportunities for fruitful cooperation lies in coordinated interventions in multilateral organisations in order to promote policy and action that is in the interest of developing countries . . .

'One thinks, as a striking example of the potential for such cooperation, of the initiative on nuclear matters of the Zone of Peace and Cooperation in the South Atlantic, which includes both Mercosur and SADC members.

'In advancing the idea of linkages and co-operation between the world's four existing or prospective nuclear-weapon free zones, the organisation has pointed a way towards consolidating the status of a Southern Hemisphere and adjacent areas free from the threat of nuclear weapons.*

'Such a development, built on the fact that the four zones and demilitarised Antarctica comprise more than half the earth's land mass, could promote non-proliferation and reinforce progress towards nuclear disarmament. The success in achieving consensus on such a complex matter indicates the potential of South–South cooperation for helping shape the emerging world order. The fora for such concerted action are numerous. Democracy has brought South Africa the opportunity to play its part in this process, and it is strongly committed to doing so to the full; whether as a new member of the African–

* In the 1960s the ANC joined the Non-Aligned Movement in its call for four nuclear-free zones in Africa, Asia, Latin America and Europe.

Caribbean–Pacific group of countries; as a member of the Organisation of African Unity and SADC; as chair of UNCTAD [United Nations Conference on Trade and Development]; or a member of the newly established Indian Ocean Rim Association.'[20]

Four years earlier, when delivering his first speech as president of the United Nations Assembly, Mandela had stressed the urgency of reshaping the priorities of the international community and the interdependence of nations and regions.

'The very response of the international community to the challenge of apartheid confirmed this very point that we all understood, that as long as apartheid existed in South Africa, so long would the whole of humanity feel demeaned and degraded.'[21]

The United Nations, he said, 'understood this very well that racism in our country could not but feed racism in other parts of the world as well. The universal struggle against apartheid was therefore not an act of charity arising out of pity for our people, but an affirmation of our common humanity.

'We believe that an act of affirmation requires that this Organisation should once more turn its focused and sustained attention to the basics of everything that makes for a better world for all humanity.'[22]

Mandela was a firm believer in the capacity of the multilateral bodies to effect change, no matter how long it took. For him it was satisfying to watch a trend take shape; while this was born of common sense — the understanding that the more consensus there was to deliver a decision, the more legitimate it would be — it was also based on the strategic culture of the ANC. The journey towards the establishment of a democratic South Africa — the various steps from negotiations to the signing off on the new constitution — had been characterised by a painstaking adherence to the principle of consensus. Mandela had faith in the sensibility of a collective coming to a decision that would change society.

At the Non-Aligned Movement (NAM) summit that met in Durban in 1998, Mandela stressed the imperative of reshaping the global order. Formed at the height of the Cold War in Bandung, Indonesia, in 1955, during the collapse of the colonial system and the rise of the independence struggles in Africa, Asia and Latin America, the NAM was crucial to the decolonisation process and played a key role in the preservation of world peace and security.

Mandela said: 'We have to remake our common world anew. The violence we see all around us, against people who are as human as we who sit in privileged positions, must surely be addressed in a decisive and sustained manner.'[23]

He was speaking of the 'violence of hunger

which kills, of the violence of homelessness which kills, of the violence of joblessness which kills, of the violence of malaria and HIV/AIDS which kill and of the trade in narcotics, which kill. I speak of the destruction of human lives, which attends underdevelopment . . . the violence of war . . .

'What I am speaking of are the twin issues of development and peace, which have been the central objectives of our [Non-Aligned] Movement from its foundation and remain its principal challenges.'[24]

Taking the message to the northern hemisphere, Mandela addressed a joint session of the United States House of Congress. As on previous occasions, he first had to wait until the cheering from an otherwise sedate chamber of grandees had died down before launching into his speech. In the hushed silence, his voice carried to the furthest corners of the hall, the distinguished men and women nodding now and then when the speaker struck a note that resonated with their convictions. He spoke of Martin Luther King, Jr, and quoted T. S. Eliot and Walt Whitman.

'It will perhaps come to pass, to be that this interconnectedness will produce among you, the distinguished members of these Houses of Congress, as among other actors on the world stage, policies which will spring from a common recognition of the fact that success or failure in the conduct of human affairs, can no longer be measured within the limited sphere defined by national boundaries that are the legacy of an ancient reality, away from which life itself has moved society a thousand leagues. If what we say is true, that, manifestly, the world is one stage and the actions of all its inhabitants part of the same drama, does it not then follow that each one of us as nations, including yourselves, should begin to define the national interest to include the genuine happiness of others, however distant in time and space their domicile might be.

'You, honourable members of the US Congress, are part of and represent the most powerful nation in our universe. I am, on the other hand, an African.

'I come out of a continent with whose travails and suffering you are very familiar. You will therefore understand it easily why I stand up to say that for such a powerful country as yours, democracy, peace and prosperity in Africa are as much in your national interest as ours.

'Because I am an African, you will, I am certain, understand why I should stand here and say that it is our deeply held belief that the new world order that is in the making must focus on the creation of a world of democracy, peace and prosperity for all humanity.'[25]

He made more overseas visits, building

trade and economic ties with countries of the Asia–Pacific region, well on its way to becoming one of the world's main economic areas. He went first to India and then it was Japan and South Korea and later the Philippines, Malaysia, Singapore, Bangladesh, Thailand and Pakistan and, at the end of his presidency, China.

Mandela extended his tours to Scandinavia and Finland too, which had given unstinting support to the ANC during the hardest periods of the struggle. The help had been both material and political and assisted the efforts of almost all of the southern African liberation movements. Late in his presidency, he thanked the Scandinavian people for past support and voiced his confidence in future cooperation:

'The achievement of our goals depends also on others achieving the same goals. In this modern world, whatever happens in one country has an impact elsewhere, even across the globe. The integrated development of Southern Africa; peace and stability throughout our continent; and the forging of an international order which ensures that world economic growth translates into development are all essential parts of our approach as we establish our place in the international community of nations.'[26]

Some of Mandela's initiatives to extend human rights to jurisdictions far and wide — as witnessed by his disastrous interaction with Nigerian general Sani Abacha, as discussed in chapter nine — met resistance and ended in failure. The only sanction against Nigeria for the execution of Ken Saro-Wiwa and the other Ogoni activists was a three-and-a-half-year suspension from the prestigious Commonwealth of Nations. The impact of this experience constituted a broader shift in South Africa's foreign policy towards a greater involvement of multilateral bodies without closing the space for interventions by President Mandela.

He did, however, manage a breakthrough in the matter of Lockerbie. He had ruffled official feathers in the US when, on a goodwill tour of African states in May 1990, he had thanked Muammar Gaddafi for Libya's support. He further reacted to the ruins of Gaddafi's residence, which had been targeted in a 1986 US bombing of Libya, ostensibly in retaliation for an act of terrorism for which Libya was allegedly responsible. 'Whatever differences there may be between countries, and people,' Mandela said, 'it is unacceptable that any one attempts to murder an opponent and his family.'[27]

By the time Mandela went to Libya again, in 1992, arrest warrants had been issued in Scotland for two Libyans suspected of the bombing of the Pan American passenger plane as it flew over Lockerbie in Scotland in

1988. There had been 270 fatalities, including passengers and crew as well as local residents on the ground.

Libya didn't want to hand the suspects over, and the country mobilised the Arab League and the OAU; these bodies were as much concerned about Lockerbie as about the United States' unilateral imposition of sanctions on Libya and their impact on the rest of Africa.[28]

Mandela's approach was that if there was clear evidence of the suspects' culpability, they should be tried by the International Court of Justice in The Hague, to obviate the humiliation of a head of state. He urged 'the countries concerned to show statesmanship and leadership. This will ensure that the decade of the 90s will be free from confrontation and conflict.'[29]

Mandela had spoken to a series of international representatives about his statement. Hank Cohen, US assistant secretary of state for African affairs, confirmed that the statement tallied with a resolution on Lockerbie due to be adopted by the UN Security Council later that day. Others on Mandela's list were UN Secretary-General Kofi Annan, UK Minister for Overseas Development and Africa Lynda Chalker and the Spanish and French embassies.

Notwithstanding this flurry of activity, the UN Security Council had imposed air-travel sanctions on Libya because the suspects had not been handed over. On his way to a Commonwealth Heads of Government meeting in Scotland, Mandela called on Gaddafi, hoping to convince him to reach an understanding with the West.[30] Before arriving in Libya, Mandela called for the lifting of sanctions against Libya, a position adopted by the OAU summit earlier in the year.[31]

This time, Mandela entered Libya by car from neighbouring Tunis to avoid violating the UN embargo on air travel to Libya. Addressing the media in Libya, he reiterated his position:

'The Organisation of African Unity has called for the . . . suspects . . . [to] be tried by a neutral country. That is a position, which I discussed in 1992 with the Americans, with President [Jacques] Mitterrand, with King [Juan] Carlos of Spain, as well as Prime Minister [John] Major. Our position is that the suspect must be tried by a neutral country. We cannot accept that one country should be complainant, the prosecutor and the judge at one and the same time. Justice must not only be done but must also be seen to be done.'[32]

Asked if the angry reaction, especially from the US Government, affected him, Mandela responded: 'Well, a politician must not have a delicate skin. If you're a politician, you must be prepared to suffer for your principles. That is why we chose to remain in prison for twenty-seven years because we did not want to change our principles.' Gesturing to Gaddafi, he said, 'This is my friend. He helped us at a time when we were all alone, when those who are now saying we should not come here were helping the enemy. Those who say I should not come here have no morals and I'm not going to join them in their lack of morality.'[33]

The negotiations became protracted and combined the efforts of Mandela, his envoy, Jakes Gerwel, the Saudi diplomat Prince Bandar bin Sultan and the UN. These worked on a solution that involved three countries and their leaders, that is, Gaddafi, Bill Clinton and Tony Blair. The initiative was bolstered by growing multilateral support within the OAU, NAM and the Arab League, and by a ruling from the International Court of Justice that it had jurisdiction over the Lockerbie matter; this implied that it was a legal matter rather than a matter of international security for the UN to deal with.[34]

Within this context, Mandela and his envoys created a space publicly for negotiation towards compromise while persuading, and even applying pressure, in private. For instance, he would praise Gaddafi in public, bestowing on him the highest honour that could be bestowed on citizens of other countries. In private, however, when he felt it was necessary, he would admonish Gaddafi about the need to speak civilly of others, such as the United Nations, even if he did not agree with them.[35] Mandela used his personal relationships with Gaddafi, Clinton and Blair during these crucial moments, exemplifying the role of direct personal relations among leaders in his approach to negotiations and conflict resolution.

The upshot of this diplomacy was that, on 19 March 1999, Mandela was able to stand tall and tell the Libyan people that the Lockerbie matter had been concluded. 'It is with great admiration for the Libyan people that I can today announce to the world that Libya has decided to write to the secretary-general of the United Nations to give a firm date for the handing over for trial in the Netherlands of the two Libyan nationals named as suspects in the Lockerbie case . . . You the Libyan people have proved Africa's potential to be the leaders of peace, equality and prosperity for all as we enter the new millennium. We salute you and wish you well and Godspeed.'[36]

Some of the choices that Mandela made were uncomfortable but they were taken in the broader interests of the country. One such case was the policy switch that South Africa had to make when it chose to derecognise the Republic of China in order to recognise the People's Republic of China.* Jakes Gerwel remembered the moment when it was no longer possible for Mandela to postpone the decision:

> He always said: 'Look, we cannot indecently end the relations with Taiwan because of what they had done prior to the elections.' Suddenly, one morning, he told me: 'The time has come.' I always said to others, in the beginning one got the sense of being a political adviser to Madiba — but Madiba is in some sense inadvisable; he's got what the Germans call that 'finger-tip feeling'. The old man sometimes makes a political call because he has an intuitive sense for timing. That's what happened. He woke up one morning; he first called the ambassador to tell him that we were going to go this route, and then made the announcement.[37]

At a special briefing to the media at his

---

* This is in line with the 'One China' policy enforced by the Beijing government, which maintains that the People's Republic of China is the only government representing all Chinese people. It has its roots at the end of the civil war in 1949 when Chiang Kai-Shek's defeated Kuomintang retreated to Taiwan and made its seat of government while the victorious Communists, led by Mao Zedong, centred their rule in mainland China.

home in November 1996, Mandela explained that he had met the respective representatives of the two Chinese governments and 'expressed the hope that within the next twelve months it would be possible to achieve a smooth transition, acceptable to both the People's Republic of China and the Government of the Republic of China in Taiwan, in terms of which South Africa accords diplomatic recognition to the People's Republic of China, but continues to conduct constructive relations with Taiwan'.[38]

His quest to persuade the world to take multilateralism seriously continued and he became a frequent mediator in international affairs. In all these circumstances he showed his usual respect for fellow human beings. For instance, shortly after articulating his government's acceptance of the People's Republic of China over Taiwan, he invited the Taiwanese Foreign Minister John Chang to South Africa for talks, after which he and Mandela held a joint press conference at the Union Buildings.[39] This was not so much a matter of Mandela's sugaring the pill as of showing South Africa's dilemma that the choice made was due to the exigencies of diplomacy.

Mandela's very last overseas visit as president, which saw him take his leave of the international community, was a trip to China. In his final speech, at Beijing University, he reiterated the imperative of a multilateral approach to development, peace and security. He decried what was happening in Kosovo: 'On the one hand, human rights set out in the Universal Declaration of Rights are being violated in ethnic cleansing. On the other hand, the United Nations Security Council is being ignored by the unilateral and destructive action of some of the permanent members. Both actions must be condemned in the strongest terms.'*[40]

Returning to South Africa, Mandela was asked why he had not raised the issue of human rights in China during his visit. His grave concern for the authority of international organisations was underlined by his response.

'Experience in history has shown that it's not the individuals who change the policies of countries; it is organisations. South Africa shifted from its apartheid policy because of

* Mandela was referring to the Kosovo War, on the one hand to actions by Yugoslav forces against Kosovo Albanians, for which Yugoslav officials were subsequently convicted of war crimes and crimes against humanity, and on the other hand to NATO's intervention, without UN Security Council authority, bombing Yugoslavia to force withdrawal of Yugoslav forces from Kosovo. Mandela made the comments five weeks before the UN Security Council acted to end the war.

the intense pressure exerted by the liberation movement and other democrats inside and outside the country, especially the liberation movement supported by the international community. That is what changed the policy of South Africa. You can't expect an individual to be poking his nose into the domestic affairs of countries. You must respect that, but if you want to do something in regard to the domestic policy of a country, then you use international bodies or regional bodies. And it's a misconception to think that an individual can be a factor in influencing, chang[ing] the policy of a country.'[41]

EPILOGUE

Nelson Mandela walked out of the prison gates on 11 February 1990 into a country desperately in need of a solution to its age-old problems — problems that had caused incalculable harm. He had an idea of the world into which he was being released, but it was an incomplete picture gleaned from censored news reports and smuggled confidences towards the end of his incarceration.

Once outside, the abstract became concrete and tangible; the dust and the noise and the blood became real. Every day, during the process of the negotiations, he rubbed shoulders with men and women, some of whom were sponsors of the carnage. They smiled at him, deferring to age and something unquantifiable in a man who had emerged from incarceration unbowed and in whose eyes they saw reflected the enormity of their deeds. In the eyes of his own people, he saw the pain of trying to make sense of it all.

One of the first acts of the representatives

of the past involved the generals and leaders of the security services; one of them handed Mandela a file, which, he said, contained the names of highly placed people in the ANC who had been agents of the apartheid regime. Mandela scanned the file but handed it back to the source. His vision of a new society would not be hobbled by the past. He had told himself that this project would involve all people, friend and foe alike. There was neither time nor resources to waste on witch-hunts.

Mandela was seventy-five years old when he became the first president of a democratic South Africa. His mentor, Walter Sisulu, whom he affectionately honoured by his clan name of Xhamela, was eighty-one; his other old friend and confidant, Oliver Tambo, who had returned from exile after three decades, had died a year earlier. Many of the time-tested comrades, some of whom had been on Robben Island with him, had also aged and it was clear that, even though they had survived prison, the clock was ticking.

He might have been bereft of the counsel of some of his oldest comrades, but he was bolstered by the knowledge that the millions of South Africans who had voted for the first time on 26 and 27 April 1994 were behind him. The resounding mandate given to the ANC emboldened him to steer the ship of state with confidence.

He wanted to resolve as many of South Africa's problems as possible in the little time he had. It was part of the reason he kept up such a punishing schedule over the course of his presidency. But he also recognised that prison had made him resilient and had taught him that since he could not control time, he needed to embrace it and let it work for him.

Prison, a place of punishment, instead became a place where he was able to find himself. A place where he could think, indulging in the one thing that gave him a sense of self. And it was, of course, in prison that his vision for rebuilding South Africa into a new democratic nation was born.

Given the millions of moving parts that constitute a nation, making that vision a coherent reality was always going to be a daunting task. The first thing Mandela did was to declare that his presidency would be one term only. Very few leaders have the selflessness to do this. History is replete with examples of those who have sought to extend their stay in office. Mandela, however, made this covenant because he knew he had the support of people he trusted implicitly and who would guide him.

There's a beautiful isiZulu proverb: *'Inyathi ibuzwa kwabaphambili'* ('Those who have walked ahead of you, who know the lie of the land, will tell you if the road is safe or if there is a wounded buffalo in the forest'). Mandela always had a fair idea of the direction he wanted to take. But he had two guides, both a few years older than him, to whom he would turn for advice on dangerous and risky ventures: Sisulu and Tambo.

Graça Machel remembers that when there was a breakthrough in the initial talks with P. W. Botha's lieutenant, Kobie Coetsee, which resulted in the subsequent release of political prisoners, Walter Sisulu chided Mandela.

'Why,' Sisulu asked, 'did you not engage in this sooner?'

Mandela replied: 'I was waiting for instructions from you!'[1]

Before Mandela's release, it was Tambo who was kept apprised of each move that Mandela made in the pre-release engagement with his captors. Even though the distance and conditions of confinement made the exchange of sensitive information difficult — and opened up possibilities of mischief and disinformation — the ANC in Lusaka was kept informed. At some stage there were even rumours that Mandela was selling out, and it was Tambo who kept those rumours in check.

This relationship, and Mandela's trustworthiness, convinced the ANC to use Mandela's image and iconic status — even though he was 'legally' a non-person — as the face of its international campaigns. His name, therefore, and the different graphics of his face, became synonymous with the struggle against apartheid. In the camps, very few leaders have had liberation songs composed in their honour. When Mandela was released from prison, many a beneficiary of apartheid, who had expected a caricature of a bloodthirsty avenger, was instead confronted with an exemplar of reconciliation. Revenge they expected, as they knew what *they* had done to him. But Mandela did not conform to their image of him. On the other side of the fence, the antics of their heroes, Botha and his extreme shadow, Eugene Terre'Blanche, suddenly seemed unacceptable.

World leaders from countries that *they* admired were beating a steady path to this ex-prisoner's door. It was the same with the rich and famous. At home and abroad, wherever Mandela went, he attracted vast crowds and adulation.

But all the renown, the celebrity status, was in the service of the people of South Africa. Despite the glitter, many things were achieved. Mandela's grace delivered where bellicosity would likely have reduced South Africa to ashes. The right wing — including those who believed that civil war would have led to some mutual respect among the belligerents — was armed and champing at the bit. Mandela quickly and calmly neutralised that faction. It was a classic manoeuvre, one that should be emulated in other areas of conflict.

Could he have carried out the work of reconciliation differently?

Perhaps. Perceptions matter. When people see you with Betsie Verwoerd or P. W. Botha — and the context is unclear, or the symbolism is lost in the clamour — then they might well jump to conclusions. Black South Africans have a long history of being betrayed and needed constant reminders that their brightest son did not desert them.

In addition — and this has to be said — there might have been elements within the ANC who, for whatever purpose, found a reason to sponsor the view that Mandela had lost touch with the ordinary person. This, of course, was shrugged off by those who understood that the ANC was, as has been repeatedly said, a broad church. And it was an expression of doubt that Mandela himself would have appreciated. He sought, throughout, to tell the world that he was not a saint, 'even on the basis of an earthly definition of a saint as a sinner who keeps on trying'.[2]

There was a poignant symmetry to Mandela's life. On the first day in the Union Buildings as president in 1994, the area had seemed lifeless and forlorn as he walked along the corridor to what was to be his office for the next five years. On the last day, in 1999, when he was no longer the president of South Africa, the building was deserted when he went to collect his personal effects.[3] It was a public holiday, the afternoon of the day Thabo Mbeki was inaugurated as president.

There had been many farewells before this day. Taking leave as president from the people of South Africa and from countries and multilateral organisations across the world, Mandela conjured up a life of quiet reflection spent in his home village in the countryside. From that idyllic vantage point, he would watch developments, concerned at the problems facing South Africa and the world but nevertheless hopeful that leaders would rise to the challenges of peace, equity and development. It was going to be time for him to enjoy life in a way that the pressures of governing, and his life as an activist before that, had simply rendered impossible.

The long goodbye had begun at the time of the ANC's 1997 national conference. In a television interview the evening before the conference, Mandela bared his feelings as he prepared to step down from the leadership of the ANC. He said:

'One of the things I have missed very much is the opportunity to sit down and think. The tight programme that I have, as president of the organisation, does not allow me that opportunity. I also miss the opportunity to read, which I had in prison, as ironical as that might appear to be. But the opportunity to sit down and think is part and parcel of your political work and I have missed that tremendously. And finally, the opportunity for me to sit down with my children and grandchildren and to listen to their dreams and to try and help them as much as possible.'[4]

When he closed the ANC conference in Mafikeng, it was as if he were envisioning his home village. 'I look forward to that period,' he said, 'when I will be able to wake up with the sun; to walk the hills and valleys of Qunu in peace and tranquillity.'[5]

During the last year of his presidency, he took that image along to diverse countries and communities, from the UN General Assembly to a crowd of people gathered in the street during an election walkabout.

'Every one of you knows that I'm stepping down as president of this country, and I'm walking around just to say goodbye to all of you and to thank you for the support and even love that you have given me. I am going to my country village. That is where I'm going to be because I am essentially a country boy. I want to see a blade of grass, I want to see the birds as they are flying around, and I want to listen to the noise of the streams.'[6]

There was a mix of lightness and pathos among the MPs and guests at the final session of Parliament as Mandela recounted for the last time what had been achieved and what was still to be done. As always, he emphasised that South Africa's progress was the result of collective effort, which would continue.

'Each historical period,' he said, 'defines the specific challenges of national progress and leadership; and no man is an island.

'And for me, personally, I belong to the generation of leaders for whom the achievement of democracy was the defining challenge.

'I count myself fortunate in not having had to experience the rigours of exile and decades of underground and mass struggles that consumed the lives of such giants as Oliver Tambo, Anton Lembede, Duma Nokwe, Moses Kotane, and J. B. Marks, Robert Sobukwe and Zephania Mothopeng, Oscar Mpetha, Lilian Ngoyi, Bishop Alpheus Zulu, Bram Fischer, Helen Joseph, Alex La Guma, Yusuf Dadoo and Monty Naicker.* Unfortu-

---

* Anton Lembede was a co-founder of the ANCYL, established in 1944, and its first president. He died in 1947 at the age of thirty-three. Duma Nokwe was the first black lawyer to be admitted to the Transvaal Supreme Court. However, he was prevented from practising because he was accused in the 1956–61 Treason Trial. He was secretary general of the ANC, 1958–69. John Beaver Marks was president of the ANC in the Transvaal, the Transvaal Council of Non-European Trade Unions and

nately, Steve Biko passed away in his youth, but he was a rising star. If he had been given the chance, I would have counted him among these.

'I count myself fortunate that, amongst that generation, history permitted me to take part in South Africa's transition from that period into the new era whose foundation we have been laying together.

'I hope that decades from now, when history is written, the role of that generation will be appreciated and that I will not be found wanting against the measure of their fortitude and vision. Indeed, Madam Speaker, I have noted with deep gratitude, the generous praise that has often been given to me as an individual. But let me state this:

---

the African Mine Workers Union. He was deployed by the ANC to join the headquarters of the External Mission in Tanzania, 1963. Bishop Alpheus Zulu was a member of the ANC, president of the World Council of Churches during the 1960s, and Bishop of Zululand and Swaziland. After he retired, he joined the IFP. Alex La Guma, one of South Africa's foremost writers of the twentieth century, was the leader of South African Coloured People's Organisation. His work on the Freedom Charter led to his arrest and charge of high treason. Upon his death in Havana, Cuba, he was the Caribbean representative for the ANC.

'To the extent that I have been able to achieve anything, I know that this is because I am the product of the people of South Africa.

'I am the product of the rural masses who inspired in me the pride in our past and the spirit of resistance.

'I am the product of the workers of South Africa who, in the mines, factories, fields and offices of our country, have pursued the principle that the interests of each are founded in the common interest of all.

'I am the product of South Africa's intelligentsia of every colour, who have laboured to give our society knowledge of itself and to fashion our people's aspirations into a reasonable dream. I am the product of South Africa's business people in industry and agriculture, commerce and finance — whose spirit of enterprise has helped turn our country's immense natural resources into the wealth of our nation.

'To the extent that I have been able to take our country forward to this new era, it's because I am the product of the people of the world who have cherished the vision of a better life for all people everywhere. They insisted, in a spirit of self-sacrifice, that that vision should be realised in South Africa too. They gave us hope because we knew by their solidarity that our ideas could not be silenced since they were the ideas of humanity.

'I am the product of Africa and her long-cherished dream of a rebirth that can now be realised so that all her children may play in the sun.

'If I have been able to help take our country a few steps towards democracy, non-racialism and non-sexism, it is because I am a product of the African National Congress, of the movement for justice, dignity and freedom that produced countless giants in whose shadow we find our glory.

'When, as will be the case in a few months, I once again become an ordinary citizen of our land, it shall be as one whose concerns and capacities are shaped by the people of our land.

'I will count myself as amongst the aged of our society; as one of the rural population; as one concerned for the children and youth of our country; and as a citizen of the world committed, as long as I have the strength, to work for a better life for all the people everywhere. And as I have always done, I will do what I can within the discipline of the broad movement for peace and democracy to which I belong.

'I will then count myself amongst the ordinary men and women whose well-being must, in any country, be the standard by which democratic government must be judged.

'Primary amongst these criteria is the

Reconstruction and Development Programme aimed at building a better life for all.

'Primary amongst these criteria are national unity and reconciliation amongst communities and citizens whose destiny is inseparable.

'Honourable Members; It is a measure of our success as a nation that an international community that inspired hope in us, in turn itself finds hope in how we overcame the divisions of centuries by reaching out to one another. To the extent that we have been able to reciprocate in renewing hope amongst the people of the world, we are grateful indeed and feel doubly blessed. And it goes without saying that we should all live up to those expectations, which the world has of us.

'As I was reminded yet again, on the visit which I have just made to the Netherlands and four Nordic countries, the world admires us for our success as a nation in rising to the challenges of our era.

'Those challenges were: to avoid the nightmare of debilitating racial war and bloodshed and to reconcile our people on the basis that our overriding objective must be together to overcome the legacy of poverty, division and inequity.

'To the extent that we still have to reconcile and heal our nation; to the extent that the consequences of apartheid still permeate our society and define the lives of millions of

South Africans as lives of deprivation, those challenges are unchanged . . .

'The long walk continues!'[7]

SUPPLEMENTARY
INFORMATION

APPENDIX A:
ABBREVIATIONS FOR
ORGANISATIONS

ADFL	Alliance of Democratic Forces for the Liberation of Congo-Zaire
ANC	African National Congress
ANCWL	African National Congress Women's League
ANCYL	African National Congress Youth League
AVF	Afrikaner Volksfront
AWB	Afrikaner Weerstandsbeweging
CODESA	Convention for a Democratic South Africa
CONTRALESA	Congress of Traditional Leaders
COSATU	Congress of South African Trade Unions

GNU	Government of National Unity
IEC	Independent Electoral Commission
IFP	Inkatha Freedom Party
JSC	Judicial Service Commission
MK	Umkhonto weSizwe
MPLA	Movimento Popular de Libertação de Angola (The People's Movement for the Liberation of Angola)
NAM	Non-Aligned Movement
NCPS	National Crime Prevention Strategy
NEC	National Executive Committee
NIA	National Intelligence Agency
NP	National Party
OAU	Organisation of African Unity
PAC	Pan Africanist Congress of Azania

SACP	South African Communist Party
SADC	Southern African Development Community
SADF	South African Defence Force
SAIC	South African Indian Congress
SANDF	South African National Defence Force
SAPS	South African Police Service
SASS	South African Secret Service
SAUF	South African United Front
SWAPO	South West Africa People's Organisation
TEC	Transitional Executive Council
TRC	Truth and Reconciliation Commission
UDF	United Democratic Front

UNITA   União Nacional para a
         Independência Total de
         Angola
         (National Union for the
         Total Independence of
         Angola)

APPENDIX B:
PEOPLE, PLACES AND EVENTS

African National Congress (ANC)
Established as the South African Native National Congress (SANNC) in 1912. Renamed African National Congress (ANC) in 1923. Following the Sharpeville Massacre in March 1960, the ANC was banned by the South African government and went underground until the ban was lifted in 1990. Its military wing, Umkhonto weSizwe (MK), was established in 1961, with Mandela as commander-in-chief. The ANC became South Africa's governing party after the nation's first democratic elections on 27 April 1994.

African National Congress Women's League (ANCWL)
Established in 1948. Actively involved in the 1952 Defiance Campaign and the anti-pass campaigns.

African National Congress Youth League (ANCYL)

Founded in 1944 by Nelson Mandela, Anton Lembede, Walter Sisulu, A. P. Mda and Oliver Tambo as a reaction to the ANC's more conservative outlook. Its activities included civil disobedience and strikes in protest against the apartheid system. Many members left and formed the Pan Africanist Congress of Azania (PAC) in 1959. Banned between 1960 and 1990.

Afrikaner Volksfront (AVF — Afrikaner People's Front)

Founded on 19 May 1993 as an organisation to unite white Afrikaans speakers, it included organisations such as the extreme right Afrikaner Weerstandsbeweging (AWB) and former generals of the apartheid-era army and police. It demanded independence for Afrikaans-speaking white South Africans and campaigned for an Afrikaner volkstaat or homeland.

Autshumao (spelt by Mandela as Autshumayo)

(d. 1663). Khoikhoi leader. Learnt English and Dutch and worked as an interpreter during the Dutch settlement of the Cape of Good Hope from 1652. He and two of his followers were banished by Jan van Riebeeck to Robben Island in 1658 after waging war with the Dutch settlers. He was one of the first people to be imprisoned on Robben Island and the only person to ever successfully escape.

Barnard, Dr Lukas (Niël)
(1949–). Academic. Professor of political studies at the University of the Orange Free State, 1978. Head of South Africa's Intelligence Service, 1980–92. Held clandestine meetings with Mandela in prison in preparation for his subsequent release and rise to political power. This included facilitating meetings between Mandela and Presidents P. W. Botha and, later, F. W. de Klerk. Director-general Western Cape Provincial Administration, 1996–2001.

Biko, Stephen Bantu
(1946–77). Anti-apartheid activist and African nationalist. Leader of the Black Consciousness Movement. Founder of the South African Students Organisation (SASO), 1968, and its president in 1969. Co-founder of the Black People's Convention in 1972. Banned and forbidden from participating in political activities in 1973. Arrested and murdered by the police, August 1977.

Bizos, George
(1928–). Greek-born human rights lawyer. Member and co-founder of the National

Council of Lawyers for Human Rights. Committee member of the ANC's Legal and Constitutional Committee. Legal adviser for Convention for a Democratic South Africa (CODESA). Defence lawyer in the Rivonia Trial. Also acted for high-profile anti-apartheid activists, including the families of Steve Biko, Chris Hani and the Cradock Four in the Truth and Reconciliation Commission. Appointed by Mandela to South Africa's Judicial Services Commission.

Black Consciousness Movement

Anti-apartheid movement targeting black youth and workers. Promoted pride in black identity. It emerged in the mid-1960s in the political vacuum created by the continued banning and imprisonment of members of the ANC and the PAC. Had its origins in the South African Students Organisation led by Steve Biko, who founded the movement.

Botha, Pieter Willem (P. W.)

(1916–2006). Prime minister of South Africa, 1978–84. First executive state president, 1984–89. Leader of South Africa's National Party. In 1985, Mandela rejected Botha's offer to release him on the condition that he rejected violence. Botha refused to testify at the Truth and Reconciliation Commission in 1998 about apartheid crimes.

Buthelezi, Mangosuthu

(1928–). South African politician and Zulu prince. Member of the ANC until the relationship deteriorated in 1979. Founder and president of the Inkatha Freedom Party (IFP) in 1975. Chief minister of KwaZulu. Appointed South African minister of home affairs, 1994–2004, and acted as president several times during Mandela's presidency.

CODESA (Convention for a Democratic South Africa)

The platform on which nineteen political groups met from December 1991 to negotiate a new dispensation in South Africa. At CODESA 1, a Declaration of Intent was signed and five working groups were appointed to develop a new constitution for a democratic South Africa, make arrangements for an interim government and decide upon the future of homelands, among other issues. However, during CODESA 2, which commenced in May 1992, talks broke down over discussions around majority rule and power sharing. More than a month later, in June, Mandela suspended talks following allegations of police involvement in the massacre at Boipatong. Eventually, behind-the-scenes meetings between cabinet minister Roelf Meyer and ANC member Cyril Ramaphosa were followed by the resumption of the negotiations through the Multiparty Negotiating Forum, which met for the first time on 1 April 1993.

Coetsee, Hendrik (Kobie)
(1931–2000). National Party politician, lawyer, administrator and negotiator. Deputy minister for defence and national intelligence, 1978. Minister of justice, 1980. Held meetings with Mandela from 1985 about creating conditions for talks between the National Party and the ANC. Elected President of the Senate following South Africa's first democratic elections in 1994.

Communist Party South Africa (CPSA)
(See South African Communist Party.)

Congress Alliance
Established in the 1950s and made up of the ANC, South African Indian Congress (SAIC), Congress of Democrats (COD) and the South African Coloured People's Organisation (later the CPC). When the South Africa Congress of Trade Unions (SACTU) was established in 1955, it became the fifth member of the Alliance. It was instrumental in organising the Congress of the People and mobilising clauses for inclusion in the Freedom Charter.

Congress of the People

The Congress of the People was the culmination of a year-long campaign where members of the Congress Alliance visited homes across the length and breadth of South Africa recording people's demands for a free South Africa, which were included in the Freedom Charter. Held 25–26 June 1955 in Kliptown, Johannesburg, it was attended by 3,000 delegates. The Freedom Charter was adopted on the second day of the Congress.

Congress of Traditional Leaders in South Africa (CONTRALESA)

Formed in 1987 in KwaNdebele, one of South Africa's homelands or 'Bantustans'. With the support of the then banned ANC and the United Democratic Front (UDF) it grew into an anti-apartheid pressure group in the homelands of South Africa. CONTRALESA remains a force for greater rights for traditional leaders.

Constitution of the Republic of South Africa

Negotiated in the Constitutional Assembly from May 1994 to October 1996 during the Government of National Unity (GNU). During the CODESA talks — started in 1991 — the National Party and ANC had agreed to create an interim constitution, which would be the basis for a final constitution. The final constitution was to be drawn up by members of the two houses of Parliament sitting as a Constitutional Assembly. On 8 May 1996 the final constitution was adopted by the National Assembly, and one day later, second deputy president F. W. de Klerk announced the withdrawal of his National Party from the GNU, with effect from 30 June. After amendments required by the Constitutional Court, the final text was adopted by the Constitutional Assembly in October 1996.

Corbett, Michael
(1923–2007). Chief justice, 1989–96. First met Mandela while visiting Robben Island. He later administered the oath of office when Parliament elected Mandela as president of South Africa on 9 May 1994, and the next day at his inauguration.

Dadoo, Dr Yusuf
(1909–83). Medical doctor, anti-apartheid activist and orator. President of SAIC. Deputy to Oliver Tambo on the Revolutionary Council of MK. Chairman of the South African Communist Party (SACP), 1972–83. Leading member of the ANC. First jailed in 1940 for anti-war activities, and then for six months during the 1946 Passive Resistance Campaign. Was among the twenty accused in the 1952 Defiance Campaign Trial. He went underground during the 1960 State of Emergency, and into exile to escape arrest.

Awarded the ANC's highest honour, Isitwa-landwe Seaparankoe, in 1955 at the Congress of the People.

de Klerk, Frederik Willem (F. W.)

(1936–). Lawyer. President of South Africa, 1989–94. Leader of the National Party, 1989–97. In February 1990 he unbanned the ANC and other organisations and released Mandela from prison. Deputy president with Thabo Mbeki under Mandela from 1994 to 1996. Leader of New National Party, 1997. Awarded the Nobel Peace Prize in 1993 with Nelson Mandela, for his role in the negotiated end to apartheid.

Defiance Campaign Against Unjust Laws

Initiated by the ANC in December 1951, and launched with the SAIC on 26 June 1952, against six apartheid laws. The Campaign involved individuals breaking racist laws such as entering premises reserved for 'whites only', breaking curfews and courting arrest. Mandela was appointed national volunteer-in-chief and Maulvi Cachalia as his deputy. Over 8,500 volunteers were imprisoned for their participation in the Defiance Campaign.

Dlamini-Zuma, Nkosazana

(1949–). Medical doctor, anti-apartheid activist, politician. Completed a medical degree at the University of Bristol, 1978, then worked for the ANC's Regional Health Committee and later Health and Refugee Trust, a British non-government organisation. Returned to South Africa after the ANC was legalised and took part in the negotiations at CODESA. Appointed health minister, 1994. Minister of foreign affairs (1999–2009) under President Mbeki and under President Motlanthe. Served as minister of home affairs under her ex-husband, President Jacob Zuma, from 10 May 2009 to 2 October 2012. President of the African Union from late 2012 until early 2017.

Duarte, Jessie Yasmin
(1953–). Anti-apartheid activist and politician. Special assistant to Mandela after his release from prison and before he was elected president of South Africa. Member of the provincial cabinet of Gauteng. Appointed deputy secretary general of the ANC, 2012. South Africa's ambassador to Mozambique.

Dube, John Langalibalele
(1871–1946). Educator, publisher, editor, writer and political activist. First president general of the SANNC (renamed as the ANC in 1923) established in 1912. Established the Zulu Christian Industrial School at Ohlange. Established the first Zulu/English newspaper *Ilanga lase Natal* (Sun of Natal) in 1904. Opponent of the 1913 Land Act. Mandela voted

at the Ohlange school in 1994 for the first time in his life, and then visited Dube's grave to report that South Africa was now free.

Erwin, Alexander (Alec)
(1948–). Politician, trade unionist and academic. Participated, on the side of the ANC, in the negotiations to bring an end to white minority rule and was a member of the Development and Reconstruction Committee. Elected to the National Executive Committee (NEC) of the ANC in 1990. Deputy minister of finance in Mandela's first cabinet, then minister of trade and industry. Minister of public enterprises under President Mbeki from 29 April 2004 to 25 September 2008.

Fischer, Abram (Bram)
(1908–75). Lawyer and political and anti-apartheid activist. Leader of the CPSA. Member of the Congress of Democrats (COD). Charged with incitement for his involvement in the African Mine Workers' Strike for better wages in 1946. Successfully defended Mandela and other leading ANC members in the Treason Trial. Led the defence in the Rivonia Trial, 1963–64. Continually subjected to banning orders and in 1966 he was sentenced to life imprisonment for violating the Suppression of Communism Act and conspiring to commit sabotage. Awarded the Lenin Peace Prize in 1967.

Fivaz, George

(1945–). Appointed by President Nelson Mandela as the first national commissioner of the new South African Police Service. His primary responsibility was to unite eleven policing agencies into a single united South African Police Service and secondly to align the new police service to new legislation and the process of transformation in South Africa. When his term of office expired in January 2000, he was succeeded by National Commissioner Jackie Selebi.

Freedom Charter

A statement of the principles of the Congress Alliance, adopted at the Congress of the People in Kliptown, Soweto, on 26 June 1955. The Congress Alliance rallied thousands of volunteers across South Africa to record the demands of the people. The Freedom Charter espoused equal rights for all South Africans regardless of race, land reform, improved working and living conditions, the fair distribution of wealth, compulsory education and fairer laws. The Freedom Charter was a powerful tool used in the fight against apartheid.

Gerwel, G. J. (Jakes)

(1946–2012). Academic. Director-general in the office of President Mandela, 1994–99. Secretary of the cabinet in the Government of National Unity, 1994–99. Chancellor of Rhodes University. Distinguished Professor in the humanities, University of the Western Cape. Chairman of the Nelson Mandela Foundation.

Ginwala, Frene Noshir

(1932–). Anti-apartheid activist, journalist, politician, member of the ANC. Left South Africa in 1960 after helping to establish safe escape routes for anti-apartheid activists. She helped Oliver Tambo and Yusuf Dadoo to set up the first office in exile for the ANC. A journalist, she became the managing editor of two Tanzanian English-language newspapers, *The Standard* and *Sunday News.* She returned to South Africa in 1991. The first woman to serve as the speaker of Parliament in South Africa, she held this position from 1994 to 2004.

Goldberg, Denis

(1933–). Anti-apartheid and political activist. Member of the SACP. Co-founder and leader of the Congress of Democrats (COD). Technical officer in MK. Arrested at Rivonia in 1963 and subsequently served a life sentence in Pretoria Local Prison. On his release in 1985 he went into exile in the UK and represented the ANC at the Anti-Apartheid Committee of the United Nations. Founded Community HEART in 1995 to help poor black South Africans. Returned to South Africa in 2002 and was appointed special adviser to Minister of Water Affairs and Forestry Ronnie Kasrils.

Government of National Unity (GNU)
The government of South Africa between 27 April 1994 and 3 February 1997 under the leadership of the ANC and according to the terms of clause 88 (2) of the interim constitution of South Africa, which required that any party holding twenty or more seats in the National Assembly could claim one or more cabinet portfolios and enter the government. The National Party and the IFP obtained cabinet positions for their leaders and MPs. F. W. de Klerk took his National Party out of the GNU on 3 June 1996, citing the exclusion of joint decision-making from the final constitution, and the National Party's lack of influence on government policy.

Gumede, Josiah Tshangana
(1870s–c. 1947). Political activist and newspaper editor. Co-founded the ANC, 8 January 1912 (as the South African Native National Congress). In 1906 he travelled to England to discuss land claims of the Sotho people. President of the ANC, 1927–30. His son, Archie Gumede, was an ANC activist and served time in prison. Nelson Mandela corresponded with him from prison.

Gwala, Themba Harry

(1920–95). School teacher and political activist. Worked in the underground of the ANC until his arrest in 1964. Charged for sabotage and sentenced to eight years in prison which he served on Robben Island. Continued his activism on his release in 1972 and in 1977 he was sentenced to life imprisonment and returned to Robben Island. He was released early, in November 1988, as he was suffering from motor neuron disease, which had robbed him of the use of his arms. Elected to the National Executive Committee of the ANC, 1991. After the election in 1994 he served on the KwaZulu-Natal legislature.

Hani, Thembisile (Chris)

(1942–93). Anti-apartheid and political activist. Member of the African National Congress Youth League (ANCYL) from the age of fifteen. He also joined the SACP. Member and eventually head of MK. He was active in the ANC underground in the Eastern and Western Capes, and eventually went into exile, where he rose through the ranks of MK. Returned to South Africa in 1990. General secretary of the SACP from 1991. Assassinated outside his home in Johannesburg in 1993 by Janusz Waluś. Posthumously awarded the ANC's highest honour, Isitwalandwe Seaparankoe, in 2008.

Hartzenberg, Ferdinand (Ferdi)

(1936–). Politician and maize farmer. Served as minister of education in the cabinet of P. W. Botha, 1979–82. One of the more conservative members of the National Party, he left the ruling party in 1982 to establish the Conservative Party (CP). Served under Andries Treurnicht as the deputy leader of the party, then led the party after Treurnicht's death in 1993. The CP boycotted the 1994 elections in South Africa. Was the second and last leader of the CP when it merged with the Freedom Front and the Afrikaner Unity Party in 2004 to form the Freedom Front Plus. Retired from politics after the merger.

Holomisa, Bantubonke (Bantu) Harrington

(1955–). Politician, military commander. Began his military career in the Transkei Defence Force in 1976 and rose to the rank of brigadier by 1985. Forced the prime minister of the so-called independent state of Transkei to resign in October 1987, and two months later overthrew his successor, Stella Sigcau. Commander of the Transkei Defence Force and head of its government from 1987 until 1994 when it was reintegrated into South Africa. Elected onto the National Executive Committee of the ANC in 1994 and served as deputy minister of environment and tourism under President Mandela. Expelled from the ANC on 30 September 1996 after accusing the party of corruption. In 1997 he co-founded the United Democratic Movement (UDM), a party which he has led in Parliament since 1999.

Inkatha Freedom Party (IFP)
Originally the Inkatha National Cultural Liberation Movement, known as Inkatha, it was established by Chief Mangosuthu Buthelezi in 1975. Established itself as a political party on 14 July 1990 and Buthelezi was elected leader. It promoted a federalist national government which would provide regional autonomy. The IFP joined the Freedom Alliance, a coalition with white right-wing groups to oppose the ANC. It threatened to boycott the 1994 elections but joined at the eleventh hour. It obtained 10.5 per cent of the national vote and three cabinet positions in President Nelson Mandela's government. The IFP threatened to leave the GNU but did not.

Jordan, Zweledinga Pallo
(1942–). Anti-apartheid activist and politician. Worked for the ANC in London from 1975. Head of the ANC research division, 1979–88, based at the Centre for African Studies at Eduardo Mondlane University in Maputo, Mozambique, where, in 1982, he was badly injured when a parcel bomb sent by the apartheid regime exploded in the of-

fice, leaving him deaf in one ear and killing his colleague, anti-apartheid activist Ruth First. Minister of posts, telecommunications and broadcasting in Mandela's government, 1994–96. Minister of environmental affairs and tourism, 1996–99. Minister of arts and culture under President Mbeki, 2004–09.

Joseph (née Fennell), Helen

(1905–92). Teacher, social worker and anti-apartheid and women's rights activist. Founding member of the COD. National secretary of Federation of South African Women (FEDSAW). Leading organiser of the Women's March of 20,000 women to Pretoria's Union Buildings. An accused in the 1956 Treason Trial. Placed under house arrest in 1962. Helped care for Zindziswa and Zenani Mandela when their parents were both imprisoned. Awarded the ANC's highest honour, Isitwalandwe Seaparankoe, in 1992.

kaBhekuzulu, King Goodwill Zwelithini

(1948–). King of the Zulu nation. Installed after the death of his father, King Cyprian Bhekhuzulu kaSolomon, in 1968. A regent was appointed until he became of age. After his twenty-first birthday and his first marriage, Zwelithini was installed as the eighth monarch of the Zulu people on 3 December 1971.

Kahn, Jacob Meyer (Meyer)
Businessman. Chief executive officer, South African Police Service, 1997–99. Group MD for brewer SABMiller (formerly South African Breweries), 1981–2012 and also as its executive chairman, 1990–2012.

Kathrada, Ahmed Mohamed (Kathy)
(1929–2017). Anti-apartheid activist, politician, political prisoner and MP. Leading member of the ANC and of the SACP. Founding member of the Transvaal Indian Volunteer Corps and its successor, the Transvaal Indian Youth Congress. Imprisoned for one month in 1946 for his participation in the SAIC's Passive Resistance Campaign against the Asiatic Land Tenure and Indian Representation Act. Convicted for his participation in the 1952 Defiance Campaign. Banned in 1954. Co-organiser of the Congress of the People and a member of the Congress Alliance General Purpose Committee. Detained during the 1960 State of Emergency. One of the last twenty-eight accused in the Treason Trial acquitted in 1961. Placed under house arrest in 1962. Arrested at Liliesleaf Farm in July 1963 and charged with sabotage in the Rivonia Trial. Imprisoned on Robben Island, 1964–82, then Pollsmoor Prison until his release on 15 October 1989. MP from 1994, after South Africa's first democratic elections, and served

as political adviser to President Mandela. Chairperson of the Robben Island Council, 1994–2006. Awarded Isitwalandwe Seaparankoe, the ANC's highest honour, in 1992; the Pravasi Bharatiya Samman Award from the President of India; and several honorary doctorates.

Keys, Derek

(1931–). Politician and businessman. Finance minister in South Africa under both President de Klerk and President Mandela after a career in business. In December 1991, De Klerk appointed him minister of economic coordination and of trade and industry. The finance ministry was added to his portfolio in 1992. After being appointed to Mandela's cabinet he resigned on 6 July 1994. He was replaced by Chris Liebenberg on 19 September.

Kotane, Moses

(1905–78). Anti-apartheid and political activist. Secretary general of the SACP, 1939–78. Treasurer general of the ANC, 1963–73. Defendant in the 1956 Treason Trial. One of the twenty accused in the Defiance Campaign trial. In 1955 he attended the Bandung Conference in Indonesia. Detained in the 1960 State of Emergency, then placed under house arrest. He went into exile in 1963. Awarded the ANC's highest honour, Isitwalandwe Seaparankoe, in 1975.

Kriegler, Johann
(1932–). Judge. Appointed chairperson of the Independent Electoral Commission (IEC), December 1993. The IEC's mandate was to deliver South Africa's first elections based on universal adult suffrage. One of the first to be appointed to the Constitutional Court, 1994. His term ended in 2002. Since retirement, has carried out work on five continents for the United Nations, the African Union, the Commonwealth of Nations and a host of non-governmental organisations. Currently deputy chairperson of the Board of Section27, a public interest law centre seeking to achieve equality and social justice in South Africa.

Liebenberg, Chris
(1934–). Banker, politician. Worked his way up from the position of messenger in a bank to become one of the top bankers in South Africa, serving as the CEO of Nedbank. Minister of finance under President Mandela 1994–96. Mandela asked him to take over from Derek Keys who resigned as finance minister months into his presidency.

Luthuli, Chief Albert John Mvumbi
(1898–1967). Teacher, anti-apartheid activist and minister of religion. Chief of Groutville

Reserve. President general of the ANC, 1952–67. From 1953 he was confined to his home by government bans. Defendant in the 1956 Treason Trial. Sentenced to six months (suspended) in 1960 after publicly burning his passbook and calling for a national day of mourning following the Sharpeville Massacre. Awarded the Nobel Peace Prize in 1960 for his non-violent role in the struggle against apartheid. Awarded the ANC's highest honour, Isitwalandwe Seaparankoe, in 1955 at the Congress of the People.

Machel, Graça (née Simbine)

(1945–) Mozambican teacher, human rights activist, international advocate for women's and children's rights, and politician. Married Nelson Mandela, July 1998. Widow of Mozambican president Samora Machel (d. 1986). Member of the Mozambican Liberation Front (FRELIMO) which fought for and won independence from Portugal in 1975. Mozambican minister for education and culture after independence. Among numerous awards she has received the United Nations' Nansen Medal in recognition of her long-standing humanitarian work, particularly on behalf of refugee children.

Madikizela-Mandela, Nomzamo Winifred (Winnie)

(1936–). Social worker and anti-apartheid and women's rights activist. Member of the ANC. Married to Nelson Mandela, 1958–96 (separated 1992). Mother of Zenani and Zindziswa Mandela. First qualified black medical social worker at the Baragwanath Hospital in Johannesburg. Held in solitary confinement for seventeen months in 1969. Placed under house arrest from 1970 and subjected to a series of banning orders from 1962 to 1987. Established the Black Women's Federation, 1975, and the Black Parents' Association, 1976, in response to the Soweto Uprising. President of the ANCWL, 1993–2003. ANC MP.

Maharaj, Satyandranath (Mac)

(1935–). Academic, politician, political and anti-apartheid activist, political prisoner and MP. Leading member of the ANC, SACP and MK. Convicted of sabotage in 1964 and sentenced to twelve years' imprisonment which he served on Robben Island. Helped to secretly transcribe Mandela's autobiography, *Long Walk to Freedom,* and smuggled it out of prison when he was released in 1976. Commanded Operation Vulindlela (Vula), an ANC underground operation to establish an internal underground leadership. Maharaj served on the secretariat of CODESA. Minister of transport, 1994–99. Envoy to President Jacob Zuma.

Malan, Magnus

(1930–2011). Military commander and politician. Cadet in South Africa's permanent force in 1949, serving in the navy and, at one time, as a marine on Robben Island before joining the army as a lieutenant. Chief of the army, 1973. Chief of the South African Defence Force, 1976. Minister of defence, 1980–91. President de Klerk removed him from his post in July 1991 after a scandal involving secret government funding to the Inkatha Freedom Party and other opponents of the ANC. Charged with other officers for the 1987 murder of thirteen people, including seven children, in November 1995. All were acquitted after a seven-month trial. President Mandela urged the public to respect the court's decision.

Mandela, Winnie

(See Madikizela-Mandela, Nomzamo Winifred.)

Manuel, Trevor

(1956–). Anti-apartheid activist and politician. Appointed regional secretary and national executive member of the UDF, 1983. Between 1985 and 1990, he was repeatedly detained without trial or placed under house arrest for his political activities. Elected to Parliament in 1994 and appointed minister of trade and industry by Mandela. South Africa's longest-serving finance minister, he served under Mandela in 1996 and also served under Thabo Mbeki and then Kgalema Motlanthe until 2009. Between 2009 and 2014 he served as minister in the presidency for the National Planning Commission under Jacob Zuma. Chaired the International Monetary Fund's Development Committee. Special envoy for development finance for UN Secretaries-General Kofi Annan and Ban Ki-Moon. Co-chaired the Transitional Committee of the Green Climate Fund, 2011, a UN fund to help poorer nations combat and adapt to climate change.

Marcus, Gill

(1949–). Political activist, politician, banker. Born to political activist parents who left South Africa for exile in 1969, Marcus began working full-time for the ANC in London in 1970. Elected to Parliament in 1994 and served as the first chairperson on the Joint Standing Committee on Finance. Deputy minister of finance in Mandela's government from 1996 until 1999 when she left government to take up the position of deputy governor of the South African Reserve Bank. She held the post for five years and then became professor of policy, leadership and gender studies at the Gordon Institute for Business Science before going into business. Governor of the South African Reserve Bank from July 2009 to November 2014.

Masekela, Barbara Mosima Joyce
(1941–). Political activist, academic and ambassador. Left South Africa in the 1960s and studied in Botswana, Swaziland and Ghana. Graduated with a BA from Ohio State University and was assistant professor of English literature at Staten Island Community College, New York, and then at Rutgers University, New Jersey, until 1982. Served as the chair of the US regional political committee of the African National Congress. Headed the ANC's Department of Arts and Culture, 1983. Returned to South Africa in 1990 and was elected to the ANC National Executive Committee in 1991. Became Mandela's personal assistant in 1990. Has served as South Africa's Ambassador to the United States, France and UNESCO.

Masemola, Jafta Kgalabi (Jeff)
(1929–90). Teacher and member of the ANC Youth League, then the PAC. Known as the 'Tiger of Azania', he was a founder of the armed wing of the PAC. After being arrested in 1962 and charged with sabotage for blowing up power lines and smuggling freedom fighters out of South Africa he was sentenced

to life imprisonment in July 1963. On 13 October 1989, while still in prison, he met with Nelson Mandela at Victor Verster Prison. It was rumoured that they discussed unity between the ANC and the PAC. Released from prison on 15 October 1989, and on 17 April 1990 he was killed in a mysterious car accident.

Mbeki, Archibald Mvuyelwa Govan (clan name, Zizi)

(1910–2001). Historian and anti-apartheid activist. Leading member of the ANC and the SACP. Served on the High Command of MK. Father of Thabo Mbeki (president of South Africa, 1999–2008). Convicted in the Rivonia Trial and sentenced to life imprisonment. Released from Robben Island Prison, 1987. Served in South Africa's post-apartheid Senate, 1994–97, as deputy president of the Senate, and as a member of its successor, the National Council of Provinces, 1997–99. Awarded the ANC's highest honour, Isitwalandwe Seaparankoe, in 1980.

Mbeki, Mvuyelwa Thabo

(1942–). Politician and anti-apartheid activist. President of South Africa, 1999–2008. Deputy president, 1994–99. Son of Govan Mbeki. Joined the ANCYL in 1956 at the age of fourteen. Left South Africa with other students in 1962. He quickly rose through the ranks of the ANC in exile, and underwent military training in the Soviet Union. He worked closely with OR Tambo and led the ANC delegation that held secret talks with the South African government, participating in all subsequent interactions with the South African government. He served as president of the ANC, 1997–2007.

Mboweni, Tito Titus
(1959–). Anti-apartheid activist, politician and banker. Left South Africa in 1980 and joined the ANC in exile in Lesotho. Returned to South Africa in 1990 after the unbanning of the ANC. Minister of labour in Mandela's cabinet from 1994 to July 1998. Appointed head of the ANC's Policy Department, 1998, which was responsible for managing ANC policy processes. Upon joining the South African Reserve Bank in July 1998 as adviser to the governor, he resigned all of his elected and appointed positions in the ANC. Appointed governor in 1999. Appointed international adviser of Goldman Sachs International, June 2010.

Meiring, Georg
(1939–). Military commander. Joined the South African army in 1963 after obtaining an MSc in physics from the University of the Orange Free State. Chief of the South African Defence Force, 1990–93 with the rank of

lieutenant general. Appointed first chief of the South African National Defence Force, 1993–98.

Mhlaba, Raymond (clan name, Ndobe)
(1920–2005). Anti-apartheid activist, politician, diplomat and political prisoner. Leading member of ANC and SACP. Commander-in-chief of MK. Arrested in 1963 at Rivonia and sentenced to life imprisonment at the Rivonia Trial. Imprisoned on Robben Island until he was transferred to Pollsmoor Prison in 1982. Released in 1989. He was involved in the negotiations with the National Party government leading to the democratisation of South Africa. Member of the ANC National Executive Committee, 1991. Premier of the Eastern Cape, 1994. South African high commissioner to Uganda, 1997. Awarded the ANC's highest honour, Isitwalandwe Seaparankoe, in 1992.

MK
(See Umkhonto weSizwe.)

Mkwayi, Wilton Zimasile (clan name, Mbona; nickname, Bri Bri)
(1923–2004). Trade unionist, political activist and political prisoner. Member of the ANC and the South Africa Congress of Trade Unions (SACTU). Union organiser for African Textile Workers in Port Elizabeth. Volun-

teer in the 1952 Defiance Campaign, and later active in the campaign for the Congress of the People. Escaped during the 1956 Treason Trial and went to Lesotho. Joined Umkhonto weSizwe and had military training in the People's Republic of China. Became MK's commander-in-chief after the arrests at Liliesleaf Farm. Convicted and sentenced to life in what became known as the 'Little Rivonia Trial'. He served his sentence on Robben Island. Released October 1989. Elected to the Senate in the National Parliament in 1994, then deployed to the Eastern Cape Provincial Legislature, where he served until his retirement from public life in 1999. Awarded the ANC's highest honour, Isitwalandwe Seaparankoe, in 1992.

Mlangeni, Andrew Mokete (clan name, Motlokwa; nickname, Mpandla)

(1926–). Anti-apartheid activist, political prisoner and MP. Member of the ANCYL, ANC and MK. Convicted at the Rivonia Trial in 1963 and sentenced to life imprisonment. Served eighteen years on Robben Island and was transferred to Pollsmoor Prison in 1982. Awarded the ANC's highest honour, Isitwalandwe Seaparankoe, in 1992.

Modise, Johannes (Joe)

(1929–2001). Bus driver, anti-apartheid activist and politician. Charged with Mandela and 155 others in the Treason Trial of 1956. All were acquitted. Became a freedom fighter in the 1960s and rose to the position of commander-in-chief of MK, the armed wing of the ANC, holding this position for twenty-five years from 1965 to 1990. After Mandela's release from prison, Modise returned to South Africa and joined the ANC's negotiating team in discussions with the ruling National Party. The initial discussion resulted in the Groote Schuur Minute, which paved the way for the return of all exiles and a negotiated end to the apartheid system. Minister of defence in Mandela's cabinet, 1994–99.

Mokaba, Peter

(1959–2002). Political activist and politician. After working for a short time as a teacher, Peter Mokaba was arrested in 1982 and convicted of possessing weapons and undergoing military training as a member of MK in Mozambique and Angola. He was sentenced to six years' imprisonment but was released after a year, following a successful appeal. Founding member of the South African Youth Congress, and later the organisation's first president in 1987, Mokaba was hero-worshipped by a large section of South Africa's youth. President of the ANCYL, 1991–94. Deputy minister of environmental affairs and tourism in Mandela's cabinet.

Moosa, Mohammed Valli (Valli)

(1957–). Anti-apartheid activist, politician and businessman. Member of the UDF. Participated in the multiparty negotiations to end white minority rule. Deputy minister for provincial and constitutional affairs in Mandela's cabinet. After the National Party left the GNU in 1996, he became minister in this department. From 1999 he became environment and tourism minister. He went into business after leaving government.

Moroka, Dr James Sebe

(1892–1985). Medical doctor, politician and anti-apartheid activist. President of the ANC, 1949–52. Convicted in the Defiance Campaign Trial in 1952. During the trial he appointed his own lawyer, disassociated himself from the ANC and pleaded for mitigation. As a consequence he was not re-elected president of the ANC, and was replaced by Chief Luthuli.

Mothopeng, Zephania Lekoame (Zeph)

(1913–90).Teacher and anti-apartheid activist. Joined the ANCYL, 1940. Joined the PAC and was elected its president in 1989 while in prison. Jailed for two years in 1960, and again in 1964, and spent time on Robben Island in the same section as Mandela. Arrested again in 1976 and sentenced to fifteen years in jail. He was released early, in 1988, after he was diagnosed with cancer. Under his leadership, the PAC refused to join the multiparty negotiations for a democratic South Africa.

Motsoaledi, Elias (clan name, Mokoni)
(1924–94). Trade unionist, anti-apartheid activist and political prisoner. Member of the ANC, SACP and Council of Non-European Trade Unions (CNETU). Banned after the 1952 Defiance Campaign. Helped to establish the South Africa Congress of Trade Unions (SACTU) in 1955. Imprisoned for four months during the 1960 State of Emergency and detained again under the ninety-day detention laws of 1963. Sentenced to life imprisonment at the Rivonia Trial and imprisoned on Robben Island from 1964 to 1989. Elected to the ANC's National Executive Committee following his release. Awarded the ANC's highest honour, Isitwalandwe Seaparankoe, in 1992.

Mpetha, Oscar Mafakafaka
(1909–94).Trade unionist, political activist and a member of the ANC. Detained for four years following the Sharpeville Massacre on 21 March 1960. Sentenced to five years' imprisonment in 1983 after being convicted of terrorism and for inciting a riot. In the same year, he was elected co-president of the newly formed UDF. He spent the last period

of his detention under guard at Groote Schuur Hospital. He was a diabetic and had his leg amputated and was confined to a wheelchair. Released on 15 October 1989, along with a group of political prisoners, following Mandela's official request that they be released.

Mufamadi, Fohlisani Sydney

(1959–). Anti-apartheid activist, politician, trade unionist and teacher. Joined the ANC, 1977. Founding member of Azanian People's Organisation (AZAPO), 1978. Joined the SACP, 1981. Elected Transvaal publicity secretary for the UDF, 1983, a position he held until 1990. Elected assistant general secretary of COSATU, 1985. Minister of safety and security in Mandela's cabinet until 1999. Minister of provincial and local government, 1999–2008.

Naidoo, Jayaseelan (Jay)

(1954–). Politician and trade unionist. As a student he became active in the South African Students Organisation that was banned in 1977 just after its leader Steve Biko was murdered in police detention. Became a community-based organiser and joined the trade union movement. Elected the first general secretary of the Congress of South African Trade Unions at its launch in 1975. Served as minister without portfolio in

President Nelson Mandela's cabinet with responsibility for co-ordinating the Reconstruction and Development Programme. Later served as minister of posts, telecommunications and broadcasting. Chair of the board of directors and of the partnership council of the Global Alliance for Improved Nutrition.

National Party
Conservative South African political party established in Bloemfontein in 1914 by Afrikaner nationalists. Governing party of South Africa, June 1948 to May 1994. Enforced apartheid, a system of legal racial segregation that favoured minority rule by the white population. Disbanded in 2004.

Netshitenzhe, Joel Khathutshelo
(1956–). Anti-apartheid activist and politician. Spent many years in exile from South Africa, working for the ANC. Head of communications in President Mandela's office. Head of South Africa's Government Communication and Information System (GCIS), 1998–2006, before heading the Policy Unit in the presidency. Served on South Africa's first National Planning Commission, 2010–15. Executive director and board vice-chairperson of the Mapungubwe Institute for Strategic Reflection (MISTRA).

Ngoyi, Lilian Masediba

(1911–80). Politician, anti-apartheid and women's rights activist, and orator. Leading member of the ANC. First woman elected to the ANC Executive Committee, 1956. President of the ANC Women's League. President of Federation of South African Women (FEDSAW), 1956. Led the Women's March against pass laws, 1956. Charged and acquitted in the Treason Trial. Detained in the 1960 State of Emergency. Detained and held in solitary confinement for seventy-one days in 1963 under the ninety-day detention law. Continuously subjected to banning orders. Awarded the ANC's highest honour, Isitwalandwe Seaparankoe, in 1982.

Nkobi, Thomas Titus

(1922–94). Anti-apartheid activist, treasurer, member of Parliament. Joined ANC, 1950, and participated in the Defiance Campaign Against Unjust Laws and the 1955 Congress of the People. National organiser of the ANC, 1958. Arrested during the 1960 State of Emergency for his role as one of the initiators of the Mandela M-Plan to establish underground networks of the ANC. Went into exile, 1963, mainly living in Lusaka. ANC treasurer general, 1968–73. Returned to South Africa, 1990, and was re-elected as treasurer general of the ANC and as a member of Parliament.

Nyanda, Siphiwe

(1950–). Politician, political activist and military commander. Joined MK, the armed wing of the ANC, in 1974. Appointed MK chief of staff in 1992. Served on the Transitional Executive Council which oversaw the end of white minority rule. When MK was incorporated into the South African National Defence Force (SANDF) in 1994, Nyanda rose through the ranks to Chief of the SANDF in 1998. He remained in this position until 2005. Minister of communications under President Jacob Zuma, 2009–10.

Nzo, Alfred Baphetuxolo

(1925–2000). Leading member of the ANCYL and ANC. Participant in the 1952 Defiance Campaign, and the Congress of the People. In 1962, Nzo was placed under twenty-four-hour house arrest, and in 1963 he was detained for 238 days. After his release the ANC ordered him to leave the country. He represented the ANC in various countries including Egypt, India, Zambia and Tanzania. He succeeded Duma Nokwe as secretary general in 1969, and held this post until the first legal ANC conference in South Africa in 1991. He was part of the ANC delegation that participated in talks with the De Klerk government after 1990. Appointed minister of foreign affairs in the newly democratic South Africa, 1994. Received a number of awards including the Order of Luthuli in Gold, 2003.

OR

(See Tambo, Oliver.)

Organisation of African Unity (OAU)

Formed on 25 May 1963 in Addis Ababa, Ethiopia, with thirty-two signatory governments and eventually including all of Africa's fifty-three states excluding Morocco, which withdrew in 1984. It aimed to eradicate all forms of colonialism and white minority rule on the African continent. It also aimed to co-ordinate and intensify the cooperation of African states to achieve a better life for the people of Africa and to defend the sovereignty, territorial integrity and independence of African states. It was disbanded on 9 July 2002 by its last chairperson, South African President Thabo Mbeki, and replaced by the African Union.

Pahad, Aziz Goolam

(1940–). Politician and anti-apartheid activist. Went into exile in 1964 and became a full-time campaigner for the banned ANC from 1966. Instrumental in developing the Anti-Apartheid Movement in the United Kingdom and in Europe. Elected onto the National Executive Committee of the ANC in 1985. Returned to South Africa after the ANC was legalised in 1990 and participated in the negotiations to end white minority rule. Served as deputy minister of foreign affairs under President Mandela and his successor, Thabo Mbeki. Resigned from cabinet in September 2008.

Pan Africanist Congress of Azania (PAC)
Breakaway organisation of the ANC founded in 1959 by Robert Sobukwe, who championed the philosophy of 'Africa for Africans'. The PAC's campaigns included a nationwide protest against pass laws, ten days before the ANC was to start its own campaign. It culminated in the Sharpeville Massacre on 21 March 1960, in which police shot dead sixty-nine unarmed protesters. Banned, along with the ANC, in April 1960. Unbanned on 2 February 1990.

Plaatje, Solomon Tshekisho (Sol)
(1876–1932). Author, journalist, linguist, newspaper editor and political publicist, and human rights activist. Member of the African People's Organisation. First secretary general of the SANNC (renamed as the ANC in 1923), 1912. First black South African to write a novel in English (*Mhudi,* published 1913). Established the first Setswana/English weekly, *Koranta ea Becoana* (Newspaper of the Tswana), 1901, and *Tsala ea Becoana* (The Friend of the People), 1910. Member

of the SANNC deputation that appealed to the British government against the Land Act of 1913, which severely restricted the rights of Africans to own or occupy land.

Pollsmoor Maximum Security Prison

Prison in the suburb of Tokai, Cape Town. Mandela was moved there from Robben Island along with Walter Sisulu, Raymond Mhlaba, Andrew Mlangeni and, later, Ahmed Kathrada in 1982.

Qunu

Rural village in South Africa's Eastern Cape Province where Mandela lived after his family moved from his birthplace of Mvezo.

Ramaphosa, Matamela Cyril

(1952–). Politician, businessman and trade unionist. First secretary of the powerful National Union of Mineworkers, 1982. Instrumental in the establishment of Congress of South African Trade Unions (COSATU). Chairman of the National Reception Committee which coordinated Mandela's release from prison. Elected ANC general secretary, 1991. Played a pivotal role in the negotiations to end white minority rule for which he earned the praise of Mandela. Left government for the business world when in 1994 he lost out as deputy president under President Mandela to Thabo Mbeki. Elected deputy president of the ANC in December 2012 and has served as deputy president of South Africa under President Zuma from 2014.

Reconstruction and Development Programme (RDP)

Implemented by Mandela's ANC government, the RDP was designed to address the huge socio-economic disparities created by apartheid. It focused on alleviating poverty and addressing massive shortfalls in social services. It was subordinated to the Growth, Employment and Redistribution (GEAR) macroeconomic strategy from 1996.

Rivonia Trial

Trial between 1963 and 1964 in which ten leading members of the Congress Alliance were charged with sabotage and faced the death penalty. Named after the suburb of Rivonia, Johannesburg, where six members of the MK High Command were arrested at their hideout, Liliesleaf Farm, on 11 July 1963. Incriminating documents, including a proposal for a guerrilla insurgency named Operation Mayibuye, were seized. Mandela, who was already serving a sentence for incitement and leaving South Africa illegally, was implicated, and his notes on guerrilla warfare and his diary from his trip through Africa in 1962 were also seized. Rather than being cross-examined as a witness, Mandela made a statement from the dock on 20 April 1964. This became his famous 'I am prepared to die' speech. On 11 June 1964 eight of the accused were convicted by Justice Qartus de Wet at the Palace of Justice in Pretoria, and the next day were sentenced to life imprisonment.

Robben Island

Island situated in Table Bay, 7 kilometres off the coast of Cape Town, measuring approximately 3.3 kilometres long and 1.9 kilometres wide. Has predominantly been used as a place of banishment and imprisonment, particularly for political prisoners, since Dutch settlement in the seventeenth century. Three men who later became South African presidents have been imprisoned there: Nelson Mandela (1964–82), Kgalema Motlanthe (1977–87) and Jacob Zuma (1963–73). Now a World Heritage Site and museum.

Sekhukhune

(1814–82). King of the Marota people (commonly called Bapedi). Illegitimate ruler who came to power using military force. As a result, his half-brother, and the legitimate heir, Mampuru, was forced to flee from the kingdom. He built his power by entering into diplomatic marriages with various royal dynasties, by incorporating other societies into his empire and by military conquest. This increased his support base and gave him legitimacy.

Seme, Pixley ka Isaka
(1881–1951). Political activist. Received his English name from American missionary Reverend S. C. Pixley who sent him to high school in the USA. Returned to South Africa after studying at both Columbia University and Oxford University. Co-founded the ANC, 8 January 1912 (through the South African Native National Congress) and was its president, 1930–37.

Sharpeville Massacre
Confrontation in the township of Sharpeville, Gauteng Province. On 21 March 1960, sixty-nine unarmed anti-pass protesters were shot dead by police and over 180 were injured. The PAC-organised demonstration attracted between 5,000 and 7,000 protesters. This day is now commemorated annually in South Africa as a public holiday: Human Rights Day.

Sisulu (née Thethiwe), Nontsikelelo (Ntsiki) Albertina
(1918–2011). Nurse, midwife, anti-apartheid and women's rights activist, and MP. Leading ANC member. Married Walter Sisulu, whom she met through her nursing friend,

Evelyn Mase (Mandela's first wife), 1944. Member of the ANCWL and Federation of South African Women (FEDSAW). Played a leading role in the 1956 women's anti-pass protest. The first woman to be arrested under the General Laws Amendment Act, 1963, during which time she was held in solitary confinement for ninety days. Continually subjected to banning orders and police harassment from 1963. She was elected as one of the three presidents of the UDF at its formation in August 1983. In 1985 she was charged with fifteen other UDF and trade union leaders for treason in what became known as the Pietermaritzburg Treason Trial. MP from 1994 until she retired in 1999. President of the World Peace Council, 1993–96. Recipient of the South African Women for Women Woman of Distinction Award 2003, in recognition of her courageous lifelong struggle for human rights and dignity.

Sisulu, Walter Ulyate Max (clan names, Xhamela and Tyhopho)

(1912–2003). Anti-apartheid activist and political prisoner. Husband of Albertina Sisulu. Met Mandela in 1941 and introduced him to Lazar Sidelsky who employed him as an articled clerk. Leader of the ANC, and generally considered to be the 'father of the struggle'. Co-founder of the ANCYL in 1944. Arrested and charged under the Suppression of Communism Act for playing a leading role in the 1952 Defiance Campaign. Arrested and later acquitted in the 1956 Treason Trial. Continually served with banning orders and placed under house arrest following the banning of the ANC and PAC. Helped established MK, and served on its High Command. Went underground in 1963 and hid at Liliesleaf Farm, in Rivonia, where he was arrested on 11 July 1963. Found guilty of sabotage at the Rivonia Trial, and sentenced to life imprisonment on 12 June 1964. He served his sentence on Robben Island and at Pollsmoor Prison. Released on 15 October 1989. One of the ANC team negotiating with the apartheid government to end white rule. Awarded the ANC's highest honour, Isitwalandwe Seaparankoe, in 1992.

Slovo, Joe
(1926–95). Anti-apartheid activist. Married Ruth First, 1949. Leading member of the ANC and the Communist Party of South Africa (CPSA). Commander of MK. Joined the CPSA in 1942 and studied law at the University of the Witwatersrand where he met Mandela and was active in student politics. He helped establish the Congress of Democrats (COD), and was accused in the 1956 Treason Trial. Detained for six months during the 1960 State of Emergency. He assisted in setting up MK. Went into exile from 1963

to 1990 and lived in the UK, Angola, Mozambique and Zambia. General secretary of the SACP, 1986. Chief of staff of MK. Participated in the multiparty negotiations to end white rule. Minister of housing in Mandela's government from 1994. Awarded the ANC's highest honour, Isitwalandwe Seaparankoe, in 1994.

Sobukwe, Robert Mangaliso

(1924–78). Lawyer, anti-apartheid activist and political prisoner. Member of the ANCYL and the ANC until he formed the PAC based on the vision of 'Africa for Africans'. Editor of *The Africanist* newspaper. Arrested and detained following the Sharpeville Massacre in 1960. Convicted of incitement and sentenced to three years' imprisonment. Before he was released, the General Law Amendment Act No. 37 of 1963 was passed, which allowed for people already convicted of political offences to have their imprisonment renewed — this later became known as the 'Sobukwe Clause' — which resulted in him spending another six years on Robben Island. He was released in 1969 and joined his family in Kimberley, where he remained under twelve-hour house arrest and was restricted from participating in any political activity as a result of a banning order that had been imposed on the PAC. While in prison he studied law, and he established his own law firm in 1975.

South African Communist Party (SACP)

Established in 1921 as the Communist Party of South Africa (CPSA), to oppose imperialism and racist domination. Changed its name to the South African Communist Party (SACP) in 1953 following its banning in 1950. The SACP was only legalised in 1990. The SACP forms the Tripartite Alliance with the ANC and COSATU.

Southern African Development Community (SADC)

An intergovernmental organisation of fifteen Southern African states, established on 17 August 1992, which aims to further socio-economic cooperation and integration of its members. It was a successor to the Southern African Development Coordination Conference (SADCC), which was established on 1 April 1980 when nine majority-ruled southern African countries signed the Lusaka Declaration 'Towards Economic Liberation'.

State of Emergency, 1960

Declared on 30 March 1960 as a response to the Sharpeville Massacre. Characterised by mass arrests and the imprisonment of most African leaders. On 8 April 1960 the ANC and PAC were banned under the Unlawful Organisations Act.

Stengel, Richard

Editor and author. Collaborated with Mandela on his autobiography, *Long Walk to Freedom* (published 1994). Co-producer of the documentary *Mandela,* 1996. Editor of *TIME* magazine.

Suppression of Communism Act, No. 44, 1950

Act passed 26 June 1950, in which the state banned the SACP and any activities it deemed communist, defining 'communism' in such broad terms that anyone protesting against apartheid would be in breach of the act.

Tambo, Oliver Reginald (OR)

(1917–93). Lawyer, politician and anti-apartheid activist. Leading member of the ANC and founder member of the ANCYL. Co-founder, with Mandela, of South Africa's first African legal practice. Became secretary general of the ANC after Walter Sisulu was banned, and deputy president of the ANC, 1958. Served with a five-year banning order, 1959. Left South Africa during the 1960s to manage the external activities of the ANC and to mobilise opposition against apartheid. Established military training camps outside South Africa. Initiated the Free Mandela Campaign in the 1980s. Lived in exile in London, UK, until 1990. Acting president of the ANC, 1967, after the death of Chief Albert Luthuli. Was elected president in 1969 at the Morogoro Conference, a post he held until 1991 when he became the ANC's national chairperson. Awarded the ANC's highest honour, Isitwalandwe Seaparankoe, in 1992.

Terre'Blanche, Eugene

(1941–2010).White supremacist, policeman, farmer and unsuccessful politician. Founder and leader of the Afrikaner Resistance Movement (Afrikaner Weerstandsbeweging — AWB) which swore to use violence to preserve white minority rule and stormed the World Trade Centre in Johannesburg while the negotiations for white minority rule were under way. Served three years in prison for assaulting a petrol station attendant and for attempting to murder a security guard. He was released in June 2004 and on 3 April 2010 he was murdered.

Transitional Executive Council (TEC)

In 1993, during the negotiations to end white minority rule, the ANC suggested a Transitional Executive Council which would 'promote the preparation for and transition to a democratic order in South Africa'. The ANC had argued that the white-dominated government of the time could not act both as referee and player in the elections. The TEC was to level the playing field and create a climate for free political activity in the run-up to the elections in April 1994. The TEC was made up of seven sub-councils: law and order — stability and security; defence; intelligence; foreign affairs; status of women; finance; and regional and local government and traditional authorities.

Treason Trial

(1956–61). The Treason Trial was the apartheid government's attempt to quell the power of the Congress Alliance. In early morning raids on 5 December 1956, 156 individuals were arrested and charged with high treason. By the end of the trial in March 1961 all the accused either had the charges withdrawn or, in the case of the last twenty-eight accused including Mandela, were acquitted.

Trew, Tony

(1941–). Anti-apartheid and ANC activist. Imprisoned, 1964–65. Left South Africa for exile in the United Kingdom. Appointed director of research at the International Defence and Aid Fund, 1980. Returned to South Africa in 1991 to work as a researcher for the ANC. Worked in communications research in President Nelson Mandela's office, 1994–99.

Truth and Reconciliation Commission (TRC)

Established by Mandela in 1995 as a way for South Africa to heal after decades of brutal abuse in the apartheid era, the TRC investigated human rights abuses at televised hearings which took place between 1960 and 1994. Perpetrators could apply for amnesty from prosecution for such abuses. They were obliged to testify about what they did and would receive amnesty should it be decided that their testimony was true and that their actions were committed for political motives.

Tshwete, Steve Vukile

(1938–2002). Anti-apartheid activist, political prisoner, politician and MP. Member of the ANC and MK. Imprisoned on Robben Island, 1964–78, for being a member of a banned organisation. Served on the ANC Executive Committee, 1988, and participated in the talks about talks between the government and the ANC to discuss conditions about beginning formal negotiations at Groote Schuur in 1990. Minister of sport and recreation, 1994–99. Promoted the de-racialisation of South African sport. Minister of safety and security, 1999–2002.

Tutu, Archbishop Desmond

(1931–). Archbishop Emeritus and anti-apartheid and human rights activist. Bishop of Lesotho, 1976–78. First black general secretary of the South African Council of Churches, 1978. Following the 1994 election, he chaired the Truth and Reconciliation Commission to investigate apartheid-era crimes. Recipient of the 1984 Nobel Peace Prize for seeking a non-violent end to apartheid; the Albert Schweitzer Prize for Humanitarianism, 1986; and the Gandhi Peace Prize, 2005.

Umkhonto weSizwe (MK)

Umkhonto weSizwe, meaning 'spear of the nation', was founded in 1961 and is commonly known by the abbreviation MK. Nelson Mandela was its first commander-in-chief. It became the military wing of the ANC. On the eve of the 1994 elections MK was disbanded and its soldiers incorporated into the newly formed South African National Defence Force (SANDF) with soldiers from the apartheid South African Defence Force, Bantustan defence forces, IFP's self-protection units and Azanian People's Liberation Army (APLA), the military wing of the PAC.

van der Merwe, Johan

(1950–2012). Police officer. Joined the South African Police Force in 1953. Commanded the security branch of the police from January 1986 until October 1989 when he was promoted to deputy commissioner of the

South African Police. Became a general in January 1990 when he became commissioner of the South African Police. Retired in March 1995.

Verwoerd, Dr Hendrik Frensch

(1901–66). Prime minister of South Africa, 1958–66. Minister of native affairs, 1950–58. National Party politician. Widely considered the architect of apartheid, he advocated a system of 'separate development'. Under his leadership South Africa became a republic on 31 May 1961. Assassinated in Parliament by Dimitri Tsafendas.

Victor Verster Prison

Low-security prison located between Paarl and Franschhoek in the Western Cape. Mandela was transferred there in 1988 from Pollsmoor Prison, and lived in a private house inside the prison compound. There is a statue of Mandela just outside the prison gates. Now named Drakenstein Correctional Centre.

Viljoen, Constand

(1933–). Politician and military commander. Joined the Union Defence Force in 1956 and by 1977 was chief of the army in South Africa. Along with fellow retired army generals, he formed the Afrikaner Volksfront in 1993. Before South Africa's first democratic elections he was thought to have amassed a force of between 50,000 and 60,000 to prepare for war to stop the democratic transition. In March 1994 he led a military effort to protect the head of the Bophuthatswana homeland against a popular coup. He then split from the Volksfront and co-founded the Freedom Front of which he became leader. His decision to participate in South Africa's first democratic elections in 1994 is credited with the prevention of loss of life. Retired in 2001 and handed over leadership of the Freedom Front to Pieter Mulder.

Xhamela
(See Sisulu, Walter.)

Zuma, Jacob Gedleyihlekisa
(1942–). Politician and anti-apartheid activist. Joined the ANC in 1959 and its armed wing, MK, in 1962. Convicted of conspiring to overthrow the apartheid government in 1963 and sentenced to ten years in prison. On his release, he continued to work for the ANC and rose to the position of chief of intelligence. Became a member of the ANC's National Executive Committee in 1977. Returned to South Africa in 1990 after the legalisation of the ANC. After the 1994 election, he served as provincial minister of economic affairs and tourism in his home province of KwaZulu-Natal. Elected deputy

president of the ANC in December 1997 and deputy president of South Africa in June 1999. On 14 June 2005, President Mbeki removed Zuma from his post as deputy president due to allegations of corruption and fraud. Sworn in as president of South Africa, May 2009.

APPENDIX C:
TIMELINE: 1990–99

11 February 1990:	Nelson Mandela is released from Victor Verster Prison, near Paarl.
27 February 1990:	Arrives in Lusaka, Zambia, on his first trip out of South Africa since 1962.
4 May 1990:	He and President F. W. de Klerk sign the Groote Schuur Minute agreeing on a common commitment towards the resolution of the political conflict, peaceful negotiations, the return of exiles, release of political prisoners and to lifting the State of Emergency.

6 August 1990:	Signs the Pretoria Minute suspending the armed struggle and concerning the release of political prisoners, the return of exiles and obstacles in the Internal Security Act.
12 February 1991:	Signs the D. F. Malan Accord with President de Klerk in an attempt to resolve deadlock between the ANC and the government over details of the Pretoria Minute, including what the ANC's suspension of armed conflict entailed and the ongoing release of political prisoners. It is agreed that MK will stop training in South Africa.
14 September 1991:	Signs the National Peace Accord, which attempted to curb political violence by specifying codes of conduct for all political parties. It was signed by twenty-seven political, trade union and government leaders.

20 December 1991:	Attends the opening of the multiparty negotiations, the Convention for a Democratic South Africa (CODESA), at the World Trade Centre, Kempton Park, near Johannesburg.
24 September 1993:	Addresses the United Nations in New York, asking for an end to sanctions against South Africa.
17 November 1993:	Attends the CODESA negotiations where the final pieces of the interim constitution are agreed upon.
10 December 1993:	Receives the Nobel Peace Prize in Oslo, Norway, with F. W. de Klerk.

18 December 1993:	Meets with the United Nations Special Representative over bringing the Freedom Alliance (white right-wing groups, the IFP and the Bophuthatswana and Ciskei Bantustan governments) into South Africa's peace process.
27 April 1994:	Votes for the first time in his life, in South Africa's first democratic elections, at Ohlange High School in KwaZulu-Natal.
6 May 1994:	South Africa's first democratic elections are declared free and fair by the Independent Electoral Commission.
10 May 1994:	Is inaugurated in Pretoria as South Africa's first democratically elected president.
24 May 1994:	Makes his first State of the Nation Address in Parliament as president of South Africa.

13 June 1994:	Addresses an Organisation of African Unity Summit in Tunisia.
18 August 1994:	Makes a speech in Parliament to mark his first hundred days as president.
17 November 1994:	Passes the Restitution of Land Rights Act into law, restoring the rights of those dispossessed by discriminatory land legislation dating back to the 1913 Land Act.
15 December 1994:	Launches his autobiography, *Long Walk to Freedom*.
17 December 1994:	Addresses the Forty-Ninth National Conference of the ANC in Bloemfontein.
10 February 1995:	Returns to Robben Island for a reunion with former political prisoners.
15 February 1995:	Announces that he will not run for re-election at the end of his term as president.

18 March 1995: Receives the Africa Peace Award in Durban, KwaZulu-Natal.

20 March 1995: Receives the Order of Merit from Queen Elizabeth II in Cape Town.

8 May 1995: Addresses the launch of the Nelson Mandela Children's Fund in Pretoria.

24 June 1995: Attends the final of the Rugby World Cup, which South Africa wins.

19 July 1995: Signs the Promotion of National Unity and Reconciliation Act to establish the Truth and Reconciliation Commission (TRC).

15 August 1995: Visits Betsie Verwoerd, the widow of Prime Minister H. F. Verwoerd, in the white enclave of Orania.

19 August 1995: Addresses a rally in Alexandra township, Johannesburg.

3 September 1995:	Holds talks with Suharto, president of Indonesia, on the conflict in East Timor.
23 October 1995:	Addresses the fiftieth anniversary meeting of the United Nations General Assembly, New York, USA.
9 November 1995:	Attends the Commonwealth Heads of Government Meeting in New Zealand.
23 November 1995:	Meets Rivonia Trial prosecutor Dr Percy Yutar at his official residence in Pretoria.
13 January 1996:	Speaks at the opening of the Africa Cup of Nations soccer tournament.
23 January 1996:	Meets with Mangosuthu Buthelezi in a bid to stop violence in KwaZulu-Natal.
1 February 1996:	Opens the Southern African Development Community Consultative Conference's Investment Forum, Johannesburg.

23 February 1996:	Speaks at the National Conference of Commitment: Gender and Women Empowerment, Johannesburg.
19 March 1996:	He and his wife Winnie Mandela (née Madikizela) are divorced.
8 May 1996:	Attends a dinner in Cape Town to celebrate the adoption of South Africa's new constitution.
9 May 1996:	Makes a statement on the withdrawal of the National Party from the Government of National Unity.
14 June 1996:	Makes a statement on the launch of South Africa's macroeconomic policy, Growth, Employment and Redistribution (GEAR).
23 June 1996:	Addresses a thanksgiving service upon the retirement of Archbishop Desmond Tutu, at St George's Cathedral, Cape Town.

11 July 1996:	Addresses the Joint Houses of Parliament of the United Kingdom, London, United Kingdom.
14 July 1996:	Accompanies French President Jacques Chirac at a military parade on the Champs-Élysées in Paris, France.
22 August 1996:	Meets the Dalai Lama in Cape Town.
1 September 1996:	His office confirms he is in a relationship with Graça Machel.
9 September 1996:	Begins three-year term as chair of SADC (South African Development Community).
2 November 1996:	Attends a reunion with his surviving law school classmates from the University of the Witwatersrand, Johannesburg.

27 November 1996:	Announces that South Africa will cut diplomatic ties with Taiwan and adopt diplomatic relations with the People's Republic of China.
7 December 1996:	Makes a speech to the International Olympic Committee Evaluation Commissions.
10 December 1996:	Signs South Africa's new constitution at Sharpeville.
3 February 1997:	Addresses the World Economic Forum at Davos, Switzerland.
2 May 1997:	Travels to Pointe-Noire in Zaire for peace talks aboard SAS *Outeniqua* between president of Zaire Mobutu Sese Seko and Congolese politician and rebel leader Laurent Kabila.
14 May 1997:	Arrives and leaves Pointe-Noire after the failure of a second round of peace talks between Zaire's Mobutu Sese Seko and Laurent Kabila.

21 May 1997:	Attends a World Economic Forum Southern Africa Economic Summit meeting in Harare, Zimbabwe.
2 June 1997:	Attends an Organisation of African Unity (OAU) Summit, Harare, Zimbabwe.
4 July 1997:	Hosts a party for more than 1,000 children affected with HIV/AIDS and other terminal illnesses.
25 July 1997:	Meets with the imprisoned leader of the East Timor Resistance Movement, Xanana Gusmão, in Jakarta, Indonesia.
25 August 1997:	Meets with President Laurent Kabila of the Democratic Republic of the Congo.
26 August 1997:	Pays tribute to F.W. de Klerk on the day in which De Klerk announces his resignation from the leadership of the National Party.

8 September 1997:	Attends a Southern African Development Community Summit in Blantyre, Malawi.
24 September 1997:	Declares Robben Island a national heritage site.
25 October 1997:	Attends the Commonwealth Heads of Government meeting in Edinburgh, Scotland.
29 October 1997:	Visits Libya to present Colonel Muammar Gaddafi with South Africa's highest award, the Order of Good Hope, in recognition of Libya's support of South Africa during the apartheid struggle.
31 October 1997:	Attends the coronation of King Letsie III in Maseru, Lesotho.
22 November 1997:	Addresses the National Men's March against rape, domestic violence and child abuse in Pretoria.

4 December 1997:	Meets with former Robben Island prison commander Colonel Prinsloo at a retirement home in Pretoria.
20 December 1997:	Hands over the reins of the ANC to Thabo Mbeki.
19 March 1998:	Attends the court case brought against him by the South African Rugby Football Union, Pretoria.
27 March 1998:	Visits Robben Island with US President Bill Clinton.
28 April 1998:	Holds discussions in Cape Town with the South African National Editors' Forum.
29 April 1998:	Addresses the Angolan National Assembly, Angola.
19 May 1998:	Attends the World Trade Organisation Summit in Geneva, Switzerland.

8 June 1998:	Addresses the summit of the Organisation of African Unity Heads of State and Government in Ouagadougou, Burkina Faso.
18 June 1998:	Meets Pope John Paul II at the Vatican.
3 July 1998:	Attends the Caribbean Community and Common Market conference in St Lucia.
12 July 1998:	Visits the site of a massacre in Richmond, KwaZulu-Natal.
18 July 1998:	Marries his third wife Graça Machel, on his eightieth birthday.
24 July 1998:	Attends the Mercosur (the Southern Common Market) Summit in Argentina.
13 September 1998:	Speaks at the opening of a Southern African Development Community Summit of Heads of State and Government in Mauritius.

21 September 1998:	Attends the fifty-third General Assembly of the United Nations in New York.
23 September 1998:	Receives the Congressional Gold Medal of the United States, Capitol Hill, Washington DC, USA.
24 September 1998:	Becomes the first foreign leader to receive the Companion of the Order of Canada, Ottawa, Canada.
8 October 1998:	Visits the Swazi royal family in Swaziland.
22 October 1998:	Opens the Morals Summit called by the National Religious Leaders Forum of South Africa in Johannesburg.
29 October 1998:	Receives the final report of the Truth and Reconciliation Commission in Pretoria.

30 October 1998:	Addresses a meeting of the Heads of State of the Economic Community of West African States, Abuja, Nigeria.
17 November 1998:	Addresses a rally in Dar es Salaam on a one-day official visit to Tanzania.
7 December 1998:	Attends the nineteenth summit of the Gulf Cooperation Council, Abu Dhabi, UAE.
13 December 1998:	Addresses the fiftieth anniversary of the World Council of Churches in Harare, Zimbabwe.
29 January 1999:	Addresses the World Economic Forum in Davos, Switzerland.
5 February 1999:	Gives his last State of the Nation Address in Parliament, Cape Town.
13 February 1999:	Makes a statement on his discussions with Colonel Muammar Gaddafi on the Lockerbie issue.

29 April 1999:	Meets Russian president Boris Yeltsin on a state visit to Moscow.
30 May 1999:	Attends the ANC's final election rally after participating in the campaign.
2 June 1999:	Votes in South Africa's second democratic elections.
9 June 1999:	Attends his last meeting of cabinet, Pretoria.
14 June 1999:	Attends the election and swearing-in of his successor, Thabo Mbeki, Parliament, Cape Town.
16 June 1999:	Attends the inauguration of his successor, President Thabo Mbeki, Parliament, Pretoria.

APPENDIX D: MAP OF SOUTH AFRICA, *c.* 1996

East Rand
Benoni
Germiston
Kempton Park

Johannesburg
Alexandra
Houghton
Naaroc
Rivonia

Soweto
Migtown
Orlando

Gazankulu

LIMPOPO

Lidoma

Nylstroom

White River

Zeerust

Mmabatho
Malileng

NORTH WEST

Nelspruit

Mabopane
PRETORIA
Witbank
GAUTENG

MPUMALANGA

MBABANE

SWAZILAND

Vryburg

Klerksdorp
Potchefstroom

Sharpeville Euston
Sebokeng

Bethal

Kuruman

Kroonstad

Standerton

Bethlehem

Vryheid

Upington

Welkom
Brandfort

Kimberley

FREE STATE

Bloemfontein

Botshabelo

MASERU

LESOTHO

KWAZULU-NATAL

Trust Feeds   Croctville Reserve
Howick   Cedanga

Pietermaritzburg

Durban

SOUTH
AFRICA

De Aar

NORTHERN CAPE

Port Shepstone

Calvinia

Victoria West

Middelburg

Engcobo Dutata Qusa
Mqhekerweni

Vanrhynsdorp

Queenstown

Gxinata

Mvezo Qunbu
Tsolo

Mqanduli

Beaufort West

Cradock

Fort Beaufort Alice Dialo

EASTERN CAPE

Robben Island
Table Bay

Paarl

Grahamstown

Peddle

East London

Cape Town
Bo-Kaap
Gugulethu
Langa
Matroosfontein
Mitchells Plain
Nyanga
Philippi
Rondebosch East
Sea Point

Stellenbosch

Simonstown

WESTERN CAPE

Oudtshoorn

Swellendam

Wildemess Sedgefield

Port Elizabeth

When South Africa's first democratically elected government came to power in 1994, the government reorganised its ten Bantustans, or homelands, and the four existing provinces into nine smaller fully integrated provinces as shown on this map.

The four provinces that existed from 1910–94 were reorganised into the new provinces as follows:

Old provinces	**New provinces**
Cape Province	Eastern Cape
	Northen Cape
	Western Cape
Natal	KwaZulu-Natal
Orange Free State	Free State
Transvaal	North West
	Limpopo
	Mpumalanga
	Gauteng

Of the ten Bantustans, only Ciskei and Qwaqwa had geographically coterminous areas of land. The other eight consisted of between three and forty-four scattered blocks.

Bantustan	Language grouping	New provinces
Bophutha-tswana★	Tswana	Free State Northern Cape North West Province
Ciskei★	Xhosa	Eastern Cape
Gazankulu	Tsonga	Limpopo Mpumalanga
KaNgwane	Swazi	Mpumalanga
KwaNdebele	Ndebele	Mpumalanga
KwaZulu	Zulu	KwaZulu-Natal
Lebowa	Sotho	Limpopo
QwaQwa	Sotho	Free State
Transkei★	Xhosa	Eastern Cape
Venda★	Venda	Limpopo

★ Four of the Bantustans had been declared 'independent' by the apartheid state between 1976 and 1981.

NOTES

Many of Nelson Mandela's speeches cited below can be viewed on the Nelson Mandela Foundation's website. Visit https://www.nelsonmandela.org/content/page/speeches.

All interviews conducted by Padraig O'Malley are from the O'Malley Archive and can be viewed on the Heart of Hope website, which is hosted by the Nelson Mandela Foundation. Visit https://www.nelsonmandela.org/omalley/index.php/site/q/03lv00017.htm.

Abbreviations
ANCLH: ANC Luthuli House
AP: Associated Press
NASA: National Archives of South Africa
NCOP: National Council of Provinces
NEC: National Executive Committee (of the ANC)
NM: Nelson Mandela
NMF: Nelson Mandela Foundation
NMPP: Nelson Mandela's Private Papers

SABC: South African Broadcasting Corporation
SAPA: South African Press Association
TRC: Truth and Reconciliation Commission

Preface

1 All quotations from NM's speech to the Fiftieth National Conference of the ANC, Mafikeng, 16 December 1997.

Chapter One: The Challenge of Freedom

1 Ralph Waldo Emerson, 'Self-Reliance', in *Essays* (Boston: 1841). Republished in 1847 as *Essays: First Series.*

2 'SA is Rendered Lawless and Ungovernable', *City Press,* 18 April 2015.

3 NM, *Long Walk to Freedom: The Autobiography of Nelson Mandela* (London: Abacus, 1994; citations from 2013 edition), p. 626.

4 C. L. R James, preface to *The Black Jacobins* (London: Secker & Warburg, 1938).

5 NM, 'The Presidential Years', p.1, NMF, Johannesburg, 1998.

6 NM, 'The Presidential Years', p. 1.

7 Niël Barnard, *Secret Revolution* (Cape Town: Tafelberg, 2015), p. 245.

8 NMF, press release, 'Ahmed Kathrada Remembers Reuniting With Madiba After His Release', 13 February 2015.

9 NM, 'The Presidential Years', p. 1.

10 NM, *Long Walk to Freedom,* p. 651.

11 NM, 'The Presidential Years', p. 1.

12 NM, 'The Presidential Years', pp. 1–2.

13 NM in conversation with Richard Stengel, Johannesburg, *c.* April/May 1993, CD 61, NMF, Johannesburg.

14 Valli Moosa, interview by Tony Trew, Cape Town, 8 September 2014.

15 NM, *Long Walk to Freedom,* p. 751.

16 Václav Havel, source unknown.

17 Barbara Masekela, interview by Tony Trew, Cape Town, 28 August 2014.

18 NM, 'The Presidential Years', p. 7.

19 NM, 'The Presidential Years', pp. 7–8.

20 Hugh Macmillan, *The Lusaka Years: The ANC in Exile in Zambia 1963–1994* (Johannesburg: Jacana Media, 2013), p. 258.

Chapter Two: Negotiating Democracy

1 Robin Denselow, *When the Music's Over: The Story of Political Pop* (London: Faber and Faber, 1990), p. 276.

2 NM, address to a rally in Cape Town on his release from prison, Cape Town City Hall, Cape Town, 11 February 1990.

3 Zoë Wicomb, 'Nelson Mandela', *New Yorker,* 16 December 2013.

4 NM, *Long Walk to Freedom,* p. 690.

5 Scott Kraft, 'ANC President Tambo Returns to SA After a 30-Year Exile', *Los Angeles Times,* 14 December 1990.

6 NM, interview by James Lorimer and Des Latham, Mandela's home, Vilakazi Street, Orlando West, Soweto, 15 February 1990, Paddi Clay collection.

7 NM, *Long Walk to Freedom,* p. 706.

8 NM, 'The Presidential Years', p. 2.

9 NM, 'The Presidential Years', p. 3.

10 Sydney Mufamadi, interview by Tony Trew, Johannesburg, 29 May 2015.

11 Ibid.

12 Ibid.

13 NM in conversation with Richard Stengel, Johannesburg, *c.* April/May 1993, CD 61, NMF, Johannesburg.

14 Ibid.

15 Ferdi Hartzenberg, interview by Padraig O'Malley, 25 August 1992, O'Malley Archive, Nelson Mandela Foundation.

16 Jessie Duarte interviewed by John Carlin, *Frontline,* PBS Frontline website.

17 NM, 'The Presidential Years', p. 3.

18 Ibid.

19 NM, televised address to the nation on the murder of Chris Hani, 13 April 1993.

20 Wilson Ngqose, interview by Mandla Langa, Johannesburg, 17 December 2016.

21 Agostinho Neto, 'Haste', *Sacred Hope,* translated by Marga Holness (Dar es Salaam: Tanzania Publishing House, 1974).

22 NM, speech to the Angolan National Assembly, Luanda, 29 April 1998.

23 Chris Hani, in *They Shaped Our Century:*

The Most Influential South Africans of the Twentieth Century (Cape Town: Human & Rousseau, 1999), in NM, 'The Presidential Years', p. 3.

24 One such poll was Markinor's November 1992 survey sampling African, coloured and Indian communities in metropolitan areas and whites nationally.

25 NM, 'The Presidential Years', p. 4.

26 NM, 'The Presidential Years', p. 8.

27 *Weekly Mail,* 30 April 1993.

28 NM, 'The Presidential Years', p. 9.

29 Hermann Giliomee, *The Afrikaners: Biography of a People* (London: C. Hurst & Co, 2003), p. 646.

30 Georg Meiring, interview with Hermann Giliomee, 11 November 2002, in Hermann Giliomee, *The Afrikaners: Biography of a People,* p. 646.

31 Martin Luther King, Jr, 'Nobel Lecture: The Quest for Peace and Justice', 11 December 1964.

32 NM, 'The Presidential Years', p. 9.

33 Ibid.

34 Joseph R. Gregory, 'P. W. Botha, Defender of Apartheid, is Dead at 90', *New York Times,* 1 November 2006.

35 Hugh Robertson, 'Intrigue Over *"New"* Offer to the Alliance', *Daily News,* 2 March 1994.

36 NM, 'The Presidential Years', p. 9.

37 Scott MacLeod, 'Nelson Mandela: I Am No Prophet', *TIME,* 26 February 1990.

38 NM, 'The Presidential Years', pp. 8–9.

39 NM, 'The Presidential Years', p. 9.

40 NM, 'The Presidential Years', pp. 9–10.

41 NM to Winnie Mandela in Kroonstad Prison, 1 February 1975, in *Conversations With Myself* (London: Macmillan, 2010), p. 212.

42 Niël Barnard, *Secret Revolution,* pp. 24–5.

43 NM, 'The Presidential Years', p.10.

44 Carl von Clausewitz, *On War* (Berlin, 1832).

45 Jonathan Hyslop, 'Mandela on War', in *The Cambridge Companion to Nelson Mandela,* edited by Rita Barnard (Cambridge: Cambridge University Press, 2014), p. 179.

46 NM, 'The Presidential Years', p. 10.

47 Constand Viljoen, interview by Tony Trew, Pretoria, 19 September 2015.

48 Martin Challenor, 'Victory for Alliance', *Daily News,* 22 February 1994.

49 Princeton Lyman, *Partner to History: The US Role in South Africa's Transition* (Washington, DC: United States Institute of Peace, 2002) pp. 171–9; Accord on Afrikaner Self-Determination, 23 April 1994, O'Malley Archive.

50 NM, 'The Presidential Years', p. 10.

51 Bill Keller, 'The South African Vote: The Overview; More Bombings Rattle South

Africans', *New York Times,* 26 April 1994.

52 James Baldwin, *No Name in the Street,* (London: Michael Joseph, 1972), p. 82.

Chapter Three: A Free and Fair Election

1 David Yutar, 'No-show Troopies may face prosecution', *The Argus,* 12 May 1994.

2 Johann Kriegler, interview by Tony Trew, Johannesburg, 2 February 2016.

3 Ibid.

4 Ibid.

5 S. Mbiti, *African Religions and Philosophy* (London: Heinemann, 1969).

6 NM, 'The Presidential Years', pp. 12–13.

7 Robert Mattes, Hermann Giliomee and Wilmot James, *Launching Democracy in South Africa: The First Open Election, April 1994,* edited by R. W. Johnson and Lawrence Schlemmer, April 1994 (New Haven, CT: Yale University Press, 1996), p. 129.

8 Johannes Rantete, *The African National Congress and Negotiated Settlement in South Africa* (Pretoria: J. L. Van Schaik, 1998), p. 243.

9 NM, 'The Presidential Years', pp. 13–14.

10 ' "Dirty Tricks" Election Row', *The Argus,* 8 April 1994.

11 Ibid.

12 Thabo Mbeki, interview by Joel Netshitenzhe and Tony Trew, Johannesburg, 17 December 2014.

13 NM, 'The Presidential Years', pp. 14–15.

14 NM, 'The Presidential Years', p. 15.

15 Charles Oulton, 'South African Elections: Huddleston Casts His Vote and Rejoices', *Independent,* 26 April 1994.

16 Paul Taylor, 'Historic Election Begins in South Africa,' *Washington Post,* 27 April 1994.

17 NM, *Long Walk to Freedom,* p. 742.

18 NM, 'The Presidential Years', pp. 15–16.

19 NM, 'The Presidential Years', p. 15.

20 This was said by Judge Johann Kriegler as chair of the Independent Electoral Commission; Peter Harris, *Birth: The Conspiracy to Stop the '94 Election* (Cape Town: Umuzi, 2010), pp. 267–75.

21 F. W. de Klerk, *The Last Trek — A New Beginning: The Autobiography* (New York: St Martin's Press, 1999), p. 336.

22 NM, victory speech upon the ANC winning the 1994 election, Carlton Hotel, Johannesburg, 2 May 1994.

23 NM, addressing guests during celebrations following the ANC election victory, Carlton Hotel, Johannesburg, 2 May 1994.

24 Jessie Duarte, interview by Tony Trew, Johannesburg, 15 July 2014.

25 Chris Streeter, interview by Tony Trew, Pretoria, 21 January 2015.

26 'Time Now to Begin Anew: Mandela Joins Peace Prayers', *Cape Times,* 9 May 1994.

27 Jessie Duarte, interview by Tony Trew, Johannesburg, 15 July 2014.

28 NM, *Long Walk to Freedom,* pp. 401–2.

29 Walter Sisulu, 'We Shall Overcome!', *Reflections in Prison,* edited by Mac Maharaj (Cape Town: Zebra Press and Robben Island Museum, 2001), p. 85.

30 Pixley ka Isaka Seme, 'Native Union', *Imvo Zabantsundu,* 24 October 1911, in Sheridan Johns III, *Protest and Hope 1882–1934,* vol. 1 of *From Protest to Challenge: A Documentary History of African Politics in South Africa 1882–1964,* edited by Thomas Karis and Gwendolen M. Carter (Stanford, CA: Hoover Institution Press, 1972), p. 71.

31 NM, 'The Presidential Years', p. 40.

32 Sydney Mufamadi, interview by Tony Trew, Johannesburg, 30 April 2015.

33 Ibid.

34 Ibid.

35 Ibid.

36 Barbara Masekela, interview by Tony Trew, Cape Town, 28 August 2014.

37 NM, address to the people of Cape Town on his election as president of South Africa, City Hall, Cape Town, 9 May 1994.

38 Jessie Duarte, interview by Tony Trew, Johannesburg, 15 July 2014.

39 NM, statement at his inauguration as president of the democratic Republic of South Africa, Union Buildings, Pretoria, 10

May 1994.

40 Adrian Hadland, 'Let's Build a Great SA', *Business Day,* Wednesday, 11 May 1994.

41 'F. W. de Klerk: Mandela Held My Hand for All to See', *City Press,* 6 December 2013.

42 Adrian Hadland, 'Let's Build a Great SA', *Business Day,* Wednesday, 11 May 1994.

43 NM, speech at the luncheon following his inauguration, Cape Town, 10 May 1994, SABC, SABC Archive, SABC Information Library, Johannesburg.

Chapter Four: Getting into the Union Buildings

1 Jessie Duarte, interview by Tony Trew, Johannesburg, 15 July 2014.

2 Fanie Pretorius, interview by Tony Trew, Pretoria, 11 July 2014.

3 President's office staff, interviews by Sahm Venter, October 1994.

4 William Ernest Henley, 'Invictus', *A Book of Verses* (London, 1888).

5 NM, 'The Presidential Years', pp. 27–9.

6 NM, 'The Presidential Years', pp. 22–3.

7 Barbara Masekela, interview by Tony Trew, Cape Town, 28 August 2014.

8 Ahmed Kathrada in conversation with Tony Trew and Joel Netshitenzhe, Johannesburg, 2 December 2014.

9 Jakes Gerwel, president's office submission

to the Presidential Review Commission, 25 September 1997.

10 NM, 'The Presidential Years', p. 19.

11 NM, 'The Presidential Years', pp. 19–20.

12 Jakes Gerwel, interview by Aziz Pahad, 21 July 2010.

13 Memo from director general, Office of the President, state expenditure, November 1997, Gerwel Papers (private collection).

14 Jan-Jan Joubert, 'He Could See the Essential Core', City Press, 8 December 2013.

15 Walter Sisulu, interview by Sahm Venter, Cape Town, October 1994.

16 Trevor Manuel, interview by Tony Trew, Johannesburg, 10 September 2014.

17 Nkosazana Dlamini-Zuma, interview by Tony Trew, Durban, 26 February 2016.

18 Mary Mxadana, interview by Sahm Venter, Cape Town, October 1994.

19 NM, interview by Charlayne Hunter-Gault, MacNeil/Lehrer NewsHour, PBS, 6 May 1994, from 'South Africa: Pres Elect Interview', AP Archive, story no. W066632.

20 NM, 'The Presidential Years', pp. 4–5.

21 Neal Chapman and Peter Wrighton, 'Civil society: The Role of Business and the Churches in Facilitating Transition', in South Africa at 10: Perspectives by Political, Business and Civil Leaders (Cape Town: Human & Rousseau, 2004), p. 29.

22 Tito Mboweni, interview by Tony Trew, Johannesburg, 12 September 2014.

23 NM, 'The Presidential Years', pp. 17–18.

24 NM, 'The Presidential Years', p. 18.

25 Thabo Mbeki, interview by Tony Trew and Joel Netshitenzhe, Johannesburg, 17 December 2014.

26 NM, 'The Presidential Years', p. 18.

27 F. W. de Klerk, *The Last Trek,* in NM, 'The Presidential Years', p. 238.

28 NM, 'The Presidential Years', pp. 18–19.

29 Trevor Manuel, interview by Tony Trew, Johannesburg, 10 September 2014.

30 Ibid.

31 Ibid.

32 Ibid.

33 F. W. de Klerk, email interview by Tony Trew, 13 March 2015.

34 Valli Moosa, interview by Tony Trew, Cape Town, 8 September 2014; Jessie Duarte, interview by Tony Trew, Johannesburg, 15 July 2014; Trevor Manuel, interview with Tony Trew, Johannesburg, 10 September 2014.

35 F. W. de Klerk, *The Last Trek,* pp. 342–4; David Welsh, 'Coalition Government, An Unwilling Marriage', in *State of the Nation,* 1997/98, Bertus De Villiers (editor) (Pretoria: HSRC), pp. 37.

36 Tim Cohen, 'Mandela's Saintly Reign a Case of Hit or Myth', *Business Day,* 11 May 1994.

37 Kader Asmal and Adrian Hadland with Moira Levy, *Politics in my Blood: A Memoir*

(Johannesburg: Jacana Media, 2011), p.193.

38 NM, 'The Presidential Years', p. 23.

Chapter Five: National Unity

1 Andries Nel, notes made on the day, 9 May 1994, private collection.

2 Trevor Manuel, interview by Tony Trew, Johannesburg, 10 September 2014.

3 Ibid.

4 Tito Mboweni, interview by Tony Trew, Johannesburg, 12 September 2014.

5 *Rapport,* 31 July 1994, in David Welsh, 'Coalition Government', in *State of the Nation,* p. 46.

6 Nelson Mandela, interview by BBC, October 1993, NMF tapes, BBC Tape M8, NMF, Johannesburg.

7 Padraig O'Malley, *Shades of Difference: Mac Maharaj and the Struggle for South Africa* (New York: Viking Penguin, 2007), pp. 400–402.

8 Constitution of the Republic of South Africa, 1996, chapter six: The National Executive, clause 89 (2).

9 Jakes Gerwel, interview by Padraig O'Malley, 8 November 1994, O'Malley Archive.

10 Kader Asmal and Adrian Hadland with Moira Levy, *Politics in my Blood,* p. 197.

11 Mangosuthu Buthelezi, interview by Padraig O'Malley, 3 October 1995, O'Malley Archive.

12 NM, interview by Patti Waldmeier, Union
Buildings, Pretoria, 1 July 1994, Patti Waldmeier interviews, Historical Papers Research Archive, William Cullen Library,
University of the Witwatersrand, Johannesburg.

13 Thabo Mbeki, interview by Joel Netshitenzhe and Tony Trew, Johannesburg, 17
December 2014.

14 SAPA, 'NP to Fare Worse than in 1994
Poll, Says Mandela', *The Citizen,* 26 June
1995.

15 F. W. de Klerk, *The Last Trek,* p. 357.

16 F. W. de Klerk, email interview by Tony
Trew, 13 March 2015.

17 Tony Leon, *Opposite Mandela: Encounters
with South Africa's Icon* (Johannesburg:
Jonathan Ball Publishers, 2014), p. 97.

18 AP Archive, 'South Africa — de Klerk and
Mandela Make Up', story no. W019071, 20
January 1995.

19 AP Archive, 'Mandela Denies Rumours of
de Klerk's Resignation', story no. 15992,
13 October 1995.

20 F. W. de Klerk, *The Last Trek,* p. 353.

21 NM to F. W. de Klerk, 26 September
1995, Gerwel Papers (private collection).

22 Graça Machel, interview by Mandla
Langa, Johannesburg, 22 September 2016.

23 F. W. de Klerk, *The Last Trek,* p. 353.

24 F. W. de Klerk, email interview by Tony
Trew, 13 March 2015.

25 Thabo Mbeki, interview by Joel Netshi-tenzhe and Tony Trew, Johannesburg, 17 December 2014.

26 NM, address on the occasion of the President's Budget Debate in the Senate, Houses of Parliament, Cape Town, 18 June 1996.

27 Jeremy Seekings, 'Partisan Realignment in Cape Town, 1994–2004', CSIR Working Paper, no. 111, December 2005.

28 Mangosuthu Buthelezi, interview by Tony Trew, Durban, 28 November 2014.

29 Jakes Gerwel, interview by Jan-Jan Joubert drawing on a 2010 interview, 'Jakes Gerwel: Mandela Could See the Essential Core', *City Press,* 10 December 2013.

30 Mangosuthu Buthelezi, interview by Padraig O'Malley, 3 October 1995, O'Malley Archive.

31 Mangosuthu Buthelezi, interview by Tony Trew, Durban, 28 November 2014.

32 Mangosuthu Buthelezi, interview with Tony Trew, Durban, 28 November 2014; NM to Irene Buthelezi, 3 August 1979, in NM, *Conversations with Myself,* pp. 170–2; NM to Chief Mangosuthu Buthelezi, 3 February 1989, in NM, *Conversations with Myself,* p. 255.

33 Anthony Lewis, 'Mandela the Pol', *New York Times Magazine,* 23 March 1997.

34 NM, 'The Presidential Years', p. 36.

35 Mangosuthu Buthelezi, interview by Padraig O'Malley, 3 October 1995, O'Malley Archive.

36 Statement by President Nelson Mandela on the NP's withdrawal from the Government of National Unity (GNU), 9 May 1996.

37 SAPA, 'Government Failed SA Says Winnie', *Citizen,* 6 February 1995.

38 Statement on Deputy Minister Winnie Mandela's apology, issued by the President's Office, 14 February 1995.

39 Statement by President Nelson Mandela on changes in the Ministry of Arts, Culture, Science and Technology, 27 March 1995.

40 AP Archive, 'South Africa: Winnie Mandela Resigns From Government', story no. 6108, APTV, 17 April 1995.

41 Statement on the reinstatement of Mrs Winnie Mandela, issued by the acting president, 12 April 1995.

42 Statement by President Nelson Mandela on changes in the Ministry of Arts, Culture, Science and Technology, 14 April 1995.

43 Bob Drogin, 'Winnie Mandela Quits Post, Criticizes Estranged Husband', *Los Angeles Times,* 18 April 1995.

44 *Sunday Telegraph,* 1 May 1994.

45 NM, 'The Presidential Years', pp. 23–4.

46 Khulu Sibiya, 'Truly, Truly Unforgettable', *City Press,* 15 May 1994, in NM, 'The Presidential Years', p. 24.

47 Ibid.

48 Jerry Zremski, 'Mandela Inauguration, Spirit of Reconciliation Thrills Houghton', *Buffalo News,* 11 May 1994.

49 Marga Ley, *'Wit, Swart Neem Mekaar as Gesinslede aan'* [White and Black Accept Each Other as Family], *Beeld,* 11 May 1994, in NM, 'The Presidential Years', p. 31.

50 Sarel van der Walt, 'Goeie SA "kan kom uit wittebroodstyd" ' [Good South Africa "can emerge from the honeymoon period"], *Beeld,* 11 May 1994, in NM, 'The Presidential Years', p. 31.

51 Themba Khumalo, 'Madiba's World Coup: Leaders Flock to Pretoria', *City Press,* 15 May 1994, in NM, 'The Presidential Years', p. 31.

52 'Sowetan Comment', *The Sowetan,* 11 May 1994.

53 Ibid.

54 Ken Owen, 'To Our Rainbow Nation Finally United in Peace', *Sunday Times,* 15 May 1994, in NM, 'The Presidential Years', p. 32.

55 NM, 'The Presidential Years', pp. 31–3.

56 NM, note, NMPP 2009/8, Box 7, file 11, p. 112 48, NMF, Johannesburg.

57 NM, notes for opening remarks at NEC meeting, box 4, folder 38, ANCLH, Johannesburg.

58 Yusuf Mohamed Dadoo, 'Why the South

Africa United Front Failed: Disruptive Role of the Pan Africanist Congress of Azania', March 1962, in *South Africa's Freedom Struggle: Statements, Speeches and Articles Including Correspondence with Mahatma Gandhi* (London: Kliptown Books, 1990).

59 NM, *Long Walk to Freedom,* p. 580.

60 Graça Machel, interview by Mandla Langa, Johannesburg, 22 September 2016.

61 NM, address at birthday celebration for veterans, Pretoria, 20 July 1996.

62 NM, address to veterans at banquet, State House, Pretoria, 23 July 1994.

63 Jay Naidoo, *Fighting for Justice: A Lifetime of Political and Social Activism* (Johannesburg: Picador Africa, 2010), p. 227.

64 Sydney Mufamadi, interview by Tony Trew, Johannesburg, 30 April 2015.

65 Jay Naidoo, interview by Padraig O'Malley, 14 April 2003, O'Malley Archive.

66 NM, address to veterans at banquet, State House, Pretoria, 23 July 1994.

67 NM, statement in the National Assembly, Houses of Parliament, Cape Town, 28 March 1996.

68 Ibid.

69 Chris Liebenberg, interview by Tony Trew, Somerset West, 1 December 2015.

70 Alan Hirsch, *Season of Hope: Economic Reform Under Mandela and Mbeki* (Scottsville: University of KwaZulu-Natal Press

jointly with Ottawa: International Development Research Centre, 2005), p. 93.

71 Trevor Manuel, interview by Tony Trew, Johannesburg, 10 September 2014.

72 Graça Machel, interview by Mandla Langa, 22 September 2016.

73 NM, reply to the NCOP debate on the President's Budget, Houses of Parliament, Cape Town, 29 August 1997, Hansard, cols. 1551–2.

74 Sue van der Merwe, interview by Tony Trew, Cape Town, 8 April 2015.

75 NM, notes prepared for a meeting of the NEC, 19 February 1996, NMPP 2009/8, box 7, file 11, African Bank 1995, pp. 1–7, NMF, Johannesburg.

76 NM, reply to the NCOP debate on the President's Budget, 7 August 1998, Debates of the National Council of Provinces, Hansard, 3 March to 12 November 1998, cols. 1807–15.

77 Trevor Manuel, interview by Tony Trew, Johannesburg, 10 September 2014.

78 Ibid.

79 Ibid.

80 Ibid.

81 Ahmed Kathrada in conversation with Joel Netshitenzhe and Tony Trew, Johannesburg, 2 December 2014.

82 Sydney Mufamadi, interview with Tony Trew, Johannesburg, 30 April 2015.

83 John Higgins, 'Living out our differences:

Reflections on Mandela, Marx and My Country: An interview with Jakes Gerwel', *Thesis Eleven,* vol. 115, no.1, Sage Publications, 2013.

84 ' "Unpredictable" Madiba Kept Bodyguards on Their Toes', *City Press,* 8 December 2013.

85 Toine Eggenhuizen, interview by Mandla Langa, Johannesburg, 10 February 2017.

Chapter Six: The Presidency and the Constitution

1 NM, speech from the dock at the opening of the defence case, Rivonia Trial, Pretoria Supreme Court, Pretoria, 20 April 1964.

2 NM, 'The Presidential Years', p. 30.

3 Johann Kriegler, interview by Tony Trew, Johannesburg, 2 February 2016; NM interviewed by David Dimbleby, Oxford, 2002, NMF Tapes, NMF, Johannesburg.

4 NM, 'The Presidential Years', p. 29.

5 Frene Ginwala, interview by Tony Trew, Johannesburg, 12 September 2014.

6 AP Archive, 'South Africa: Constitutional Court Ruling on Election Boundaries', story no. 14965, 22 September 1995.

7 Statement by the President's Office on the Browde Commission into South African Rugby Union, 26 September 1997.

8 AP Archive, 'South Africa: Mandela Testifies in Court', 19 March 1998.

9 NM, 'The Presidential Years', pp. 29–30.

10 Statement by the Office of the President on the SARFU Case, 17 April 1998.

11 NM, opening address in the President's Budget Debate in the National Assembly, Houses of Parliament, Cape Town, 21 April 1998.

12 Ibid.

13 Andy Capostangno, 'Black President for Rugby', *Mail & Guardian,* 22 May 1988.

14 NM, Bram Fischer Memorial Lecture, 9 June 1995.

15 Kader Asmal and Adrian Hadland with Moira Levy, *Politics in my Blood,* pp. 108–9.

16 Ibid, pp. 110, 125.

17 George Bizos, *Odyssey to Freedom* (Houghton: Random House, 2007), p. 487.

18 Nicholas Haysom, 'Negotiating a Sustainable Political Settlement: Part 2 Legitimation — Lessons from the South African Transition' (paper presented at Toward Inclusive and Participatory Constitution Making, 3–5 August, 2004, Kathmandu (Nagarkot)), p.9; Hassen Ebrahim, *The Soul of a Nation: Constitution-making in South Africa* (Cape Town: Oxford University Press, 1998), pp. 134ff.

19 Valli Moosa, interview by Tony Trew, Cape Town, 8 September 2014.

20 Thabo Mbeki, interview by Joel Netshitenzhe and Tony Trew, Johannesburg, 17 December 2014.

21 Cyril Ramaphosa, interview by Tony Trew, Johannesburg, 6 October 2014.

22 George Bizos, *Odyssey to Freedom,* p. 508.

23 NM, notes for an address to the NEC, 23 February 1995, box 3, folder 29, ANCLH, Johannesburg.

24 NM, reply to the debate on the State of the Nation Address, 24 February 1995.

25 Hassen Ebrahim, *The Soul of a Nation,* p. 132; *Cape Times,* 29 April 1996; *Mail & Guardian,* 4 April 1996 and 10 May 1996.

26 NM, address to the Constitutional Assembly on the adoption of the new Constitution, Houses of Parliament, Cape Town, 8 May 1996, Hansard, cols. 452–62.

27 George Bizos, *Odyssey to Freedom,* p. 518.

28 Langston Hughes, 'Justice', *The Panther and the Lash* (New York: Knopf, 1967).

29 George Bizos, *Odyssey to Freedom,* p. 518.

30 Constitution of the Republic of South Africa, 1996, chapter 8: Courts and the Administration of Justice, clause 174 (2).

31 George Bizos, *Odyssey to Freedom,* p. 519.

32 NM, speech at the inauguration of the Constitutional Court, 14 February 1995.

33 NM, speech at a state banquet in honour of Chief Justice Corbett, 11 December 1996.

34 NM, speech delivered on his behalf by the minister of justice at the Johannesburg Bar Council dinner in honour of Chief Justice

Mohamed, 25 June 1997.

35 NM, 'The Presidential Years', p. 29.

36 NM, speech at a banquet of the General Council of the Bar of South Africa, 28 July 2000.

37 Albie Sachs, *We, the People: Insights of an Activist Judge* (Johannesburg: Wits University Press, 2016), p. 303.

Chapter Seven: Parliament

1 Ingrid Jonker, 'The Child Who Was Shot Dead by Soldiers in Nyanga', *The Heinemann Book of African Women's Poetry,* edited by Stella and Frank Chipasula (London: Heinemann, 1995), p. 151, quoted by NM, during his State of the Nation Address, Houses of Parliament, Cape Town, 24 May 1994.

2 NM, State of the Nation Address, Houses of Parliament, Cape Town, 24 May 1994.

3 Frene Ginwala, interview by Tony Trew, Johannesburg, 12 September 2014.

4 Essop Pahad, interview by Joel Netshitenzhe and Tony Trew, Johannesburg, 11 September 2014.

5 NM, 'The Presidential Years', pp. 20–1.

6 NM, address on the occasion of the opening of the second session of the democratic Parliament, Houses of Parliament, Cape Town, 17 February 1995.

7 Statement by President Nelson Mandela

on portraits and works of art in Parliament, 30 January 1996.

8 Graça Machel, interview by Mandla Langa, Johannesburg, 22 September 2016.

9 Frene Ginwala, interview by Tony Trew, Johannesburg, 12 September 2014.

10 Max Sisulu, interview by Tony Trew, Johannesburg, 15 April 2015.

11 Frene Ginwala, interview by Tony Trew, Johannesburg, 12 September 2014.

12 Ibid; Max Sisulu, interview by Tony Trew, Johannesburg, 15 April 2015.

13 Max Sisulu, interview by Tony Trew, Johannesburg, 15 April 2015; Ben Turok, interview by Tony Trew, Cape Town, 17 March 2015; Sue van der Merwe, interview by Tony Trew, Cape Town, 8 April 2015.

14 NEC Minutes, 24 April 1995, box 5, folder 23, ANCLH, Johannesburg.

15 Mangosuthu Buthelezi, interview by Padraig O'Malley, 27 November 1996, O'Malley Archive.

16 NM, notes for a meeting with the ANC Caucus, NMPP 2009/8, box 3, notebook 12, pp. 20–1, NMF, Johannesburg.

17 NM, personal note, NMPP, box 4, file2, 011–12, NMF, Johannesburg.

18 NM, notes for a meeting with caucus, 18 August 1996, NMPP 2009/8, box 4, file 2, pp. 1–2, NMF, Johannesburg.

19 Richard Calland, *Anatomy of South Africa: Who Holds the Power?* (Cape Town, Zebra

Press, 2006), p. 89.

20 Andries Nel, interview by Tony Trew, Cape Town, 28 March 2015; SAPA, 'Decision on Afrikaans in Army Slated', *Star,* 1 February 1996.

21 Sophocles, *Fragments,* edited and translated by Hugh Lloyd Jones (Cambridge, MA: Harvard University Press, 1996), p. 37.

22 André Brink, 'Mandela a Tiger for Our Time,' *The Guardian,* 22 May 1999.

23 'The Day the Truth Hit Home', *Sunday Times* Heritage Project.

24 George Bizos, interview by Tony Trew, Johannesburg, 30 April 2015.

25 NM, reply to the Senate Debate on the President's Budget, 1 June 1995, Hansard, col. 1341.

26 Sydney Mufamadi, interview by Tony Trew, Johannesburg, 30 April 2015.

27 NM, notes for a meeting with ANC officials after his remarks on Shell House in the Senate, NMPP 2009/8, box 4, folder 1, NMF, Johannesburg.

28 NM, opening the National Assembly snap debate on events surrounding the shooting at Shell House, Houses of Parliament, Cape Town, 7 June 1995.

29 NM, closing address to the National Assembly in the snap debate on the Shell House incident, Houses of Parliament, Cape Town, 7 June 1995.

30 NM, speech at the final sitting of the first democratically elected parliament, Houses of Parliament, Cape Town, 26 March 1999.

31 Joseph Chiole, Second Reading Debate on the Commission on the Remuneration of Representatives Bill, 14 November 1994, Hansard, cols. 4256 and 4259.

32 NM, speech at the final sitting of the first democratically elected parliament, Houses of Parliament, Cape Town, 26 March 1999.

Chapter Eight: Traditional Leadership and Democracy

1 Pixley ka Isaka Seme, speech at the founding conference of the ANC, Bloemfontein, 8 January 1912.

2 NM, 'Clear the Obstacles and Confront the Enemy', *Reflections in Prison,* p. 12.

3 Christopher S. Wren, 'Foes of Apartheid Hold Unity Talks', *New York Times,* 10 December 1989.

4 NM, note to Walter Sisulu, NMPP 2009/8, box 5, file 5, NMF, Johannesburg.

5 NM, Participation of Traditional Leaders at CODESA, statement issued by the ANC, 17 December 1991.

6 NM, address to the youth, KaNyamazane Stadium, Mpumalanga, 13 April 1994

7 NM, 'The Presidential Years', pp. 34–8.

8 Allister Sparks, *Beyond the Miracle: Inside the New South Africa* (Chicago, IL: Univer-

sity of Chicago Press, 2003), p. 18.

9 Local Elections Task Group, *Local Government Elections in South Africa 1995/1996* (Pretoria: ABC Press, 1997).

10 Valli Moosa, interview by Tony Trew, Cape Town, 8 September 2014.

11 NM, 'The Presidential Years', pp. 38–9.

12 NM, address to rally in Durban, 25 February 1990.

13 South African Institute of Race Relations, *Fast Facts*, March 1997.

14 See the evidence to the TRC by Daluxolo Luthuli, a former member of MK who became a commander of Inkatha hit squads in KwaZulu-Natal after being trained by apartheid security forces, in *TRC Final Report*, vol. 6, section 3, chapter 3, p. 351, presented to President Nelson Mandela, 29 October 1998: Thula Bophela and Daluxolo Luthuli, *Umkhonto weSizwe: Fighting for a Divided People* (Johannesburg: Galago, 2005); see also Eugene de Kock's submission to the TRC, Amnesty Hearings, Port Elizabeth, 29 September–3 October 1997; and *TRC Final Report*, vol. 6, section 4, appendix, p. 583, presented to President Nelson Mandela, 29 October 1998.

15 Sydney Mufamadi, interview by Tony Trew, Johannesburg, 29 May 2015.

16 NM, 'The Presidential Years', pp. 36–7.

17 NM, address to rally in Durban, 25

February 1990.

18 NM, in conversation with Richard Stengel, Johannesburg, *c.* 26 April and 3 May 1993, CD 61, NMF, Johannesburg.

19 John Nkadimeng, Radio Freedom broadcast from Addis Ababa, Ethiopia, 18 November 1986.

20 Mzala, *Gatsha Buthelezi: Chief with A Double Agenda* (London: Zed Press, 1988), p. 64.

21 NM, in conversation with Richard Stengel, Johannesburg, *c.* 26 April and 3 May 1993, CD 61, NMF, Johannesburg.

22 NM, address at the launch of the South African Democratic Teachers Union, 6 October 1990, Shareworld, Shaft 17, Johannesburg.

23 NM, notes for an address to the NEC meeting, 21 January 1995, NMPP 2009/8, box 4, file 2, pp. 174–5, NMF, Johannesburg.

24 NM, *Long Walk to Freedom,* p. 689.

25 Walter Sisulu, interviewed on the sidelines of an Albertina Sisulu Foundation function, NMF Tapes, BBC TV Collection, M18A, NMF, Johannesburg.

26 'Under Fire in an Inkatha Stronghold', *Mail & Guardian,* 5 May 1995.

27 Ibid.

28 NM, closing address in the National Assembly Debate on the President's Budget, Houses of Parliament, Cape Town, 3 May

1995, Hansard, cols. 818–20.

29 Ibid.

30 Ibid.

31 Ibid.

32 Ibid.

33 NM, Senate debate on the President's Budget, Houses of Parliament, Cape Town, 1 June 1995, Hansard, cols. 1139–42.

34 7 June 1995, NMPP 2009/8, box 5, folder 4; 'Can 1000 Troops Stop the Carnage?', *Mail & Guardian,* 25 August 1995.

35 Sydney Mufamadi, interview by Tony Trew, Johannesburg, 29 May 2015.

36 NM, Two and a half years of democratic government: prepared by President Nelson Mandela for the NEC, November 1996, box 6, folder 58, ANCLH, Johannesburg.

Chapter Nine: Transformation of the State

1 One example of NM saying he had been on 'a long holiday for twenty-seven years' was when he revisited the site of his 5 August 1962 arrest in Howick on 15 November 1993.

2 Howard Fast, *Spartacus* (self-published, 1951); Leo Tolstoy, *War and Peace* (1869); Dee Brown, *Bury My Heart at Wounded Knee: An Indian History of the American West* (New York: Holt, Rinehart & Winston, 1970); Edgar Snow, *Red Star Over China* (London: Victor Gollancz, 1937).

3 Luis Taruc, *Born of the People* (New York: International Publishers, 1953).

4 Allister Sparks, *Beyond the Miracle,* p.18.

5 NM interviewed by the BBC, October 1993, NMF Tapes, BBC M8, NMF, Johannesburg.

6 Zola Skweyiya, interviewed by Padraig O'Malley, 30 November 1995, O'Malley Archive.

7 NM, note regarding an interview with Nomavenda Mathiane, NMPP 2009/8, box 7, file 11, p. 39, NMF, Johannesburg.

8 Transitional Executive Council Act, 1993; Barry Gilder, *Songs and Secrets: South Africa from Liberation to Governance* (New York, NY: Colombia University Press, 2012), pp. 156–7; Sydney Mufamadi, interview with Tony Trew, Johannesburg, 30 April 2015; Barry Gilder, interview by Tony Trew, Johannesburg, 24 November 2015; Siphiwe Nyanda, interview by Tony Trew, Johannesburg, 5 November 2015.

9 Graça Machel, interview by Mandla Langa, Johannesburg, 22 September 2016.

10 NM, notes edited for a speech prior to a meeting with SAPS generals, NMPP 2009/8, box 3, notebook 12, pp. 25–30, NMF, Johannesburg.

11 Ibid.

12 Ibid.

13 Ibid.

14 Sydney Mufamadi, interview by Tony

Trew, Johannesburg, 30 April 2015.

15 NM, notes for a meeting with SAPS officers, 30 November 1996, NMPP/8, box 7, file 11, African Bank 1995, pp. 89–93, NMF, Johannesburg.

16 Ibid.

17 NM, 'The Presidential Years', p. 40.

18 Stephane Botha, 'Commissioner of Police to Retire', *Business Day,* 11 January 1995; Sydney Mufamadi, interview by Tony Trew, Johannesburg, 30 April 2015.

19 NM, 'The Presidential Years', pp. 40–2.

20 Research staff, South African Institute of Race Relations, *Race Relations Survey 1993/ 1994,* South African Institute of Race Relations, Johannesburg, 1994, in NM, 'The Presidential Years', p. 42.

21 NM, 'The Presidential Years', pp. 40–3.

22 NM, 'The Presidential Years', p. 45.

23 Ian van der Waag, *A Military History of Modern South Africa* (Johannesburg and Cape Town: Jonathan Ball Publishers, 2015), p. 287; Princeton Lyman, *Partner to History,* p. 163.

24 Siphiwe Nyanda, interview by Tony Trew, Johannesburg, 25 November 2015.

25 Greg Mills, 'The South African National Defence Force: Between Downsizing and New Capabilities', *Naval War College Review,* vol. 52, no. 1, winter 1999, pp. 79–98.

26 Siphiwe Nyanda, interview by Tony Trew, Johannesburg, 25 November 2015.

27 AP Archive, 11 September 1994; Beeld archive, 10 September to 4 November 1994.

28 NM, NMPP 2009/8, box 3, notebook 12, NMF, Johannesburg.

29 NM, NMPP 2009/8, box 3, notebook 12, NMF, Johannesburg; AP Archive, 11 September 1994; Beeld Archive, 10 September to 4 November 1994.

30 Telex to Parks Mankahlana, Office of the President, from Amrit Manga of the *New Nation* containing his transcript of an interview with President Mandela, Speeches: Youth Day 1996, President Mandela Communication, NASA, Pretoria.

31 NM, note for a meeting of the NEC, 8–9 December 1995, NMPP 2009/8, box 4, file 1, pp. 159ff, NMF, Johannesburg.

32 Siphiwe Nyanda, interview by Tony Trew, Johannesburg, 25 November 2015.

33 Gert van der Westhuizen, *'Mandela kap voorstel teen Afrikaans',* [Mandela refuses proposal against Afrikaans] *Beeld,* 1 February 1996.

34 *Defence in a Democracy: White Paper on National Defence for the Republic of South Africa,* May 1996, section 51.

35 Louise Flanagan and Chandre Gould, 'What Modise Didn't Know About DCC',

Weekly Mail, 17 June 1994.

36 NM, opening address in the President's Budget Debate in the National Assembly, Cape Town, 21 April 1998.

37 'Mandela Speaks to the Nation', *The Sowetan,* 11 November 1996.

38 AP Archive, 'South Africa: President Mandela Praises Outgoing Military Chief', story no. 76476, 7 April 1998.

39 Trevor Manuel, interview by Tony Trew, Johannesburg, 10 September 2014.

40 Thabo Mbeki, interview by Joel Netshitenzhe and Tony Trew, Johannesburg, 17 December 2014.

41 NM, State of the Nation Address, Houses of Parliament, Cape Town, 9 February 1996.

42 Defence Review Committee, *South African Defence Review 1998* (Pretoria: Department of Defence, 1998); Public protector, auditor general and national director of public prosecutions, *Report to Parliament on the Joint Investigation into the Strategic Defence Procurement Packages Undertaken by the Public Protector, Auditor-General and National Director of Public Prosecutions,* 13 November 2001.

43 South African Department of Defence, *Department of Defence Annual Report 2001/ 2002* (Pretoria: Department of Defence, 2002), p. 62.

44 Yvonne Muthien, 'Democratic Consolidation in South Africa, 1994–1999', *Democracy South Africa: Evaluating the 1999 Election* (Pretoria: HSRC Publishers, 1999).

45 Charles Baudelaire, 'The Generous Gambler', *Figaro,* 1864.

46 NM, the text at the beginning of the note reads: 'The President and two Deputy-Presidents, the Ministers of Defence and of Safety and Security, Generals Georg Meiring and Van der Merwe should be briefed by the National Intelligence Service at the earliest possible convenience on the following issues.' NMPP 2009/8, NMF, Johannesburg.

47 Constitution of the Republic of South Africa, 1996, chapter 11: Security Services, clause 198 (a).

48 Sandy Africa, 'The Policy Evolution of the South African Civilian Intelligence Services: 1994-2009 and Beyond', *Strategic Review for Southern Africa,* vol. 34, no. 1, May 2012, p. 103.

49 Barry Gilder, interview by Tony Trew, Johannesburg, 24 November 2015.

50 A former staff member of Jakes Gerwel's office, in conversation with Tony Trew, Cape Town, 8 August 2015.

51 Barry Gilder, *Songs and Secrets,* p. 177.

52 Ibid.

53 Siphiwe Nyanda, interview by Tony Trew,

Johannesburg, 25 November 2015.

54 Lansana Gberie, 'Mandela's Struggles for Peace and Justice in Africa', *Africa Renewal Online,* December 2013.

55 Barry Gilder, interview by Tony Trew, Johannesburg, 24 November 2015.

56 NM, speech at the official opening of Intelligence headquarters, 5 December 1997.

57 Zola Skweyiya, interviewed by Padraig O'Malley, 30 November 1995, O'Malley Archive.

58 Niël Barnard, interview by Tony Trew, Overberg, 17 November 2015.

59 Jessie Duarte, interview by Tony Trew, Johannesburg, 15 July 2014.

60 Allister Sparks, *Beyond the Miracle,* p. 37.

61 Zola Skweyiya, O'Malley interview, 30 November 1995.

62 National Planning Commission, *Institutions and Governance Diagnostic* (Pretoria: National Planning Commission, 2015), p. 11; and Geraldine Fraser-Molekei, telephone interview by Tony True, 29 July 2016.

63 Public Service Commission, *State of Representivity in the Public Service — Findings;* Department of Public Service and Administration, *A Strategic Framework for Gender Equality Within the Public Service (2006–2015): Consultation Document* (Pretoria:

Department of Public Service and Administration, 24 November 2006).

64 NM to Thabo Mbeki, 6 June 1994, DP Pres Mbeki, box 002, folder 11/1/1 — President, closed, NASA, Pretoria.

65 Zola Skweyiya, O'Malley interview, 30 November 1995.

66 National Planning Commission, *Institutions and Governance Diagnostic,* pp. 22–3.

67 NM, State of the Nation Address, Houses of Parliament, Cape Town, 24 May 1994; NM, debate on the President's Budget ('100 Days Speech'), Houses of Parliament, Cape Town, South Africa, 18 August 1994.

68 NM, State of the Nation Address, Houses of Parliament, Cape Town, 17 February 1995.

69 NM, State of the Nation Address, Houses of Parliament, Cape Town, 9 February 1996.

70 Marion Edmunds, 'Skills Crisis Knocks Public Service', *Mail & Guardian,* 15 August 1997.

71 NM, opening address to the third session of Parliament, Houses of Parliament, Cape Town, 9 February 1996.

Chapter Ten: Reconciliation

1 NMF tapes, BBC Collection M2, NMF, Johannesburg.

2 James Baldwin, *No Name in the Street,* p. 130.

3 Indres Naidoo, *Island in Chains: Ten Years on Robben Island* (Harmondsworth: Penguin Group, 1982).

4 Michael Dingake, 'Comrade Madiba', *Nelson Mandela: The Struggle is My Life* (London: International Defence and Aid Fund for Southern Africa, 1978), p. 223.

5 Mac Maharaj, 'Profile', *Reflections in Prison,* p. 5.

6 Nkosazana Dlamini-Zuma describes how 'After the rendition by the ANC choir with Tambo conducting, there was a tumultuous standing ovation with Zambian President Kenneth Kaunda insisting on an encore', in *ANC Today,* vol. 6, no. 43, 3 November 2006.

7 'Mandela: The Man, the Image, the Brand', *City Press,* 18 July 2012.

8 'What Mandela's Critics Could Learn From Him', by Obadias Ndaba, *Huffington Post,* December 2013.

9 George Bizos, *Odyssey to Freedom,* p. 278.

10 NM, *Long Walk to Freedom,* p. 441.

11 NM, meeting with the Afrikaner community in Pretoria, 15 April 1999.

12 The Freedom Charter, adopted at the Congress of the People, Kliptown, Johannnesburg, 25–6 June 1955.

13 Zanele Mbeki in conversation with Man-

dla Langa, *c.* 1996.

14 NM, interview by Oprah Winfrey, *The Oprah Winfrey Show,* Harpo Productions, 2000.

15 NM, address on the Senate President's Budget debate, Houses of Parliament, Cape Town, 1 June 1995.

16 NM, closing address in the Senate Debate on the President's Budget, 1 June 1995, Hansard, col. 1279.

17 AP Archive, 'South Africa: President Mandela Issues Stern Warning to Leaders', story no. 23868, 8 March 1996.

18 Alex Marshall, *Republic or Death! Travels in Search of National Anthems* (London: Windmill Books, 2015), pp. 259–60.

19 Minutes of extended NWC, 7 September 1995, ANCLHM, box 14, folder 111, NMF, Johannesburg.

20 NM, address to a rally in Cape Town on his release from prison, Cape Town City Hall, Cape Town, 11 February 1990.

21 Saths Cooper, 'The Mandela I Knew: Prof. Saths Cooper', Tributes for Madiba, Nelson Mandela Foundation, 12 September 2013.

22 NM, Reply in Senate Debate on the President's Budget, 14 September 1994, Houses of Parliament, Cape Town.

23 NM, *Toespraak van president by geleent-heid van 'n onthaal deur die Burgemeester*

van Pretoria [Speech by the president at the occasion of a reception by the mayor of Pretoria], 26 August 1994.

24 Gert van der Westhuizen, *'Mandela praat met Afrikaners "Om kommunikasie oop te hou"'* [Mandela talks to Afrikaners to 'keep communications open'], *Beeld,* 29 June 1995; Kevin O'Grady, 'Volk Meet Mandela', *Business Day,* 29 June 1995.

25 NM, *Tydens 'n besoek aan die Afrikaanse Taal en Kultuur Vereninging (ATKV)* [During a visit to the Afrikaans Language and Cultural Union], 17 August 1995; *Beeld,* 18 August 1995.

26 NM, *Tydens 'n besoek aan die Ruiterwag-Saamtrek vir jong Afrikaner-Leiers* [During a visit to the Ruiterwag rally for young Afrikaner leaders], 13 January 1996; Willem Pretorius, *'Kies SA óf Afrikaner-Nelson',* *Beeld,* 15 January 1996.

27 NM, opening remarks at a meeting with Afrikaner organisations, 29 March 1996.

28 Ibid.

29 Constand Viljoen, interview by Tony Trew, Pretoria, 19 September 2015.

30 Constitution of the Republic of South Africa, 1996, chapter 14, schedule 6: Transitional Arrangements, section 20, clause 5.

31 Peet Kruger, *'Geheime gesprek lei tot deurbraak Onderhandelinge oor nuwe grondwet op koers'* [Secret talks lead to a break-

through. Negotiations about new constitution on course], *Beeld,* 20 April 1996; Peet Kruger, *'NP en VF se pogings het saam tot toegewing oor kultuurkommissie gelei'* [NP and VF's attempts have led to concessions over culture commission], 24 April 1996.

32 Thabo Mbeki, discussions with Afrikaner community, National Assembly, Houses of Parliament, Cape Town, 24 March 1999.

33 NM, 'Clear the Obstacles and Confront the Enemy', *Reflections in Prison,* p. 17.

34 Ibid.

35 Mandla Langa in conversation with Antjie Krog during the writers' conference Cité de Livre, Aix-en-Provence, 1997.

36 *SA Times,* London, 19 July 1995.

37 Constand Viljoen, interview by Tony Trew, Pretoria, 19 September 2015.

38 Ibid.

39 SAPA, 13 December 1996.

40 Niël Barnard, interview by Tony Trew, Overberg, 17 November 2015.

41 NM, televised interview on *Face the Media,* 14 December 1997, SABC, tape 66676MT, SABC Archive, SABC Information Library, Johannesburg.

42 Niël Barnard, interview by Tony Trew, Overberg, 17 November 2015.

43 *TRC Final Report,* volume 2, chapter 1, preface, presented to President Nelson Mandela, 29 October 1998.

44 Ibid.

45 NM, opening address in the Special Debate on the Report of the TRC, Houses of Parliament, Cape Town, 25 February 1999.

46 Ibid.

47 Human Sciences Research Council, *Public Opinion on National Priority Issues* (Pretoria, May 1999), p. 55.

48 NM, opening address in the President's Budget Debate in the National Assembly, Houses of Parliament, Cape Town, 15 April 1997.

Chapter Eleven: Social and Economic Transformation

1 The Reconstruction and Development Programme (RDP), 'Building the Economy', clause 4.1.1, 1994.

2 Ibid.

3 Layashi Yaker, *Preliminary Assessment on the Performance of the African Economy in 1994 and Prospects for 1995 — End of Year Statement,* presented to the United Nations Economic Commission for Africa, Addis Ababa, 15 December 1994.

4 Cabinet minutes, 11 May 1994.

5 ANC National Conference, *Ready to Govern: ANC Policy Guidelines for a Democratic South Africa Adopted at the National Confer-*

ence, 28–31 May, 1992 (Johannesburg: Policy Unit of the ANC, 1992).

6 NM, address at the seventy-fifth anniversary of the South African Communist Party, 28 July 1996, SABC, SABC Archive, SABC Information Library, Johannesburg.

7 ANC National Working Committee discussion document: TEC Sub-council on Finance, 27 April 1993, box 14, 112, ANCLH, Johannesburg.

8 William Smith, interview by Tony Trew, Pretoria, 11 July 2014.

9 NM, address at the National Assembly, Cape Town, 28 March 1996.

10 NM, State of the Nation Address, Houses of Parliament, Cape Town, 24 May 1994.

11 NM, 'The Presidential Years', p. 52.

12 Ibid.

13 *Native Life in South Africa Before and Since the European War and the Boer Rebellion* (1916) (Johannesburg: Raven's Press, 1982), p. 21.

14 NM, 'The Presidential Years', p. 52.

15 NM, preamble to the *White Paper on Reconstruction and Development, Government Gazette,* notice no. 1954 of 1994, 23 November 1994.

16 Ibid.

17 NM, address to Parliament, Houses of Parliament, Cape Town, May 1994.

18 Trevor Manuel, 'Twenty Years of Eco-

nomic Policymaking — Putting People First', *The Oxford Companion to the Economics of South Africa,* edited by Haroon Bhorat, Alan Hirsch, Ravi Kanbur and Mthuli Ncube (Oxford: Oxford University Press, 2014), p. 29; Alan Hirsch, *Season of Hope,* p. 69.

19 NM, interview by the BBC, NMF tapes, Iqbal Meer Collection, #1, NMF, Johannesburg.

20 Cabinet minutes, 26 October 1994, Transforming the Public Sector: The GNU's Contribution to the RDP, minute 7.4.2, item 1.3

21 Ibid.

22 NM, preamble to the *White Paper on Reconstruction and Development, Government Gazette,* notice no. 1954 of 1994, 23 November 1994.

23 Patti Waldmeir, *Anatomy of a Miracle: The End of Apartheid and the Birth of the New South Africa* (New York and London: W. W. Norton and Company, 1997), p. 213.

24 NM, election campaign, Lenasia, 19 April 1999, tape 66772MT, SABC, SABC Archive, SABC Information Library, Johannesburg.

25 Cabinet minutes, 26 October 1994, Transforming the Public Sector: The GNU's Contribution to the RDP, minute 7.4.2.

26 Christo Volschenk, *'Nuwe komitee kom*

vandeesweek byeen oor mandate vir groeiplan' [New committee will meet over the mandate on growth], *Beeld,* 3 August 1995.

27 Cabinet minutes, 6 December 1995, Towards a National Growth and Development Strategy, 7.1.

28 Sagie Narsiah, 'Neoliberalism and Privatisation in South Africa', *GeoJournal,* vol. 57, no. 1, May 2002, p. 3.

29 ANC, Fiftieth National Conference: Resolutions, Economic Transformation, Mafikeng, December 16–20 1997, clause 3.2.2.

30 NM, *Southern Africa Into the Next Century,* Sixteenth Singapore Lecture, 6 March 1997, Institute of Southeast Asian Studies, Singapore, 1997.

31 NM, 'The Presidential Years', pp. 47–9.

32 Richard Calland (editor), *The First Five Years: A Review of South Africa's Democratic Parliament* (Cape Town: IDASA, 1999).

33 NM, 'The Presidential Years', pp. 52–3.

34 NM, 'The Presidential Years', pp. 50–1.

35 *South Africa in Transition, Findings Regarding Households,* figure 6.1: 'Changes in type of housing in which households live between October 1995 and October 1999' (Pretoria: Statistics South Africa, 2001).

36 Jessie Duarte, interview by Tony Trew, Johannesburg, 15 July 2014.

37 Mandla Langa in conversation with Stephen Laufer, Johannesburg, 16 July 2016.

38 John Carlin, 'ANC Boards the Gravy Train: John Carlin in Johannesburg on the Underdogs Who Have Become Fat Cats in a Few Months', *Independent,* 27 August 1994.

39 NM, address on the anniversary of the Soweto Uprising, 16 June 1994.

40 NM, speech at the official opening of The Mandela Rhodes Foundation's offices, Oxford, 13 April 2000, NMF Tapes, Iqbal Meer Collection, Oxford 1 and 2, NMF, Johannesburg.

41 NM, address at AIDS conference, Barcelona, 12 July 2002, NMF Tapes, Iqbal Meer Collection #8, NMF, Johannesburg.

42 NM, briefing editors, 9 May 1999, NMF Tapes, BBC collection, NMF, Johannesburg.

43 President Mbeki used the phrase in a funeral oration for the late Alfred Nzo, 22 January 2000.

44 NM, State of the Nation Address, National Assembly, Houses of Parliament, Cape Town, 5 February 1999.

45 Anne Kriegler and Mark Shaw, 'Facts Show South Africa Has Not Become More Violent Since Democracy', *The Conversation,* 22 July 2016.

46 Francois Lötter, ' *"Wit koerante" ignorer*

misdaadstatistieke — president' ["White newspapers" ignoring the crime statistics — president], *Beeld,* 14 September 1998.

47 NM, 'The Presidential Years', p. 62.

48 NM, opening the Morals Summit called by the National Religious Leaders Forum, 23 October 1998.

49 Ibid.

50 Allister Sparks, *Beyond the Miracle,* p. 16.

51 NM, addressing the fifth national congress of COSATU, 7 September 1994, SABC, SABC Archive, SABC Information Library, Johannesburg.

52 NM, State of the Nation Address, National Assembly, Cape Town, 5 February 1999.

53 Ibid.

54 NM, speech at the final sitting of the first democratically elected parliament, Houses of Parliament, Cape Town, 26 March 1999.

Chapter Twelve: Negotiating the Media

1 Cameron J, *Holomisa v. Argus Newspapers Ltd.* 1996 (2) S.A. 588 (W).

2 NM, NMPP 2009/8, box 1, notebook 5, p. 17, NMF, Johannesburg.

3 Thami Mazwai, interview by Tony Trew, Johannesburg, 7 October 2015.

4 André Odendaal, *The Founders: The Origins of the African National Congress and the Struggle for Democracy* (Johannesburg: Ja-

cana Media, 2012), p. 147.

5 NM, *Long Walk to Freedom,* p. 208.

6 Ibid, p. 316.

7 Anthony Sampson, *Mandela: The Authorised Biography* (London: HarperCollins, 1999), p. 147.

8 NM, *Long Walk to Freedom,* p. 492 and p. 502.

9 NM, briefing editors and opinion makers, Pretoria, 10 May 1999, NMF Tapes, BBC, NMF, Johannesburg.

10 NM, address to the International Press Institute Congress, Cape Town, 14 February 1994.

11 Rehana Rossouw, 'Everyone Wants a Piece of the President', *Mail & Guardian,* 15 March 1996.

12 NM, notes for a meeting with editors of KwaZulu-Natal newspapers, Cape Town, 2 March 1995, South Africa National Archive, Nelson Mandela Communication/ Speeches: March, April, May 1995, NASA, Pretoria; Wyndham Hartley, ' "Crackdown" is No Idle Threat', *Natal Witness,* 3 March 1995.

13 Pamela Dube, 'It Takes Two to Tango and Government is Learning the Communication Steps', *Sunday Independent,* 8 July 2001.

14 Thami Mazwai, interview by Tony Trew, Johannesburg, 7 October 2015.

15 NM, note on an off-the-record conversa-

tion with the editor of *Die Burger,* NMPP 2009/8, box 4, folder 1, pp. 1–2, NMF, Johannesburg.

16 Mandla Langa in conversation with Khulu Sibiya, June 2017.

17 Jakes Gerwel, 'The Day Mandela Was in Hustler', *Rapport,* 9 June 2012.

18 NM, speech at the launch of the Canadian Friends of the Nelson Mandela Children's Fund, SkyDome, Toronto, 25 September 1998.

19 NM, address to the International Press Institute Congress, Cape Town, 14 February 1994.

20 Khaba Mkhize, 'Breakfast with Nelson Mandela', *Natal Witness,* 19 August 1994; Ray Hartley, 'ANC Broadsides Against Press', *Sunday Times,* 4 September 1994; Thami Mazwai, interview by Tony Trew, Johannesburg, 7 October 2015.

21 The television interview is referenced in 'Some Black Newsmen Rapped for Secret Agenda', *Business Day,* 3 November 1996.

22 Guy Berger, 'Media and Racism in Mandela's Rainbow Nation', Prime Time for Tolerance: Journalism and the Challenge of Racism: International Federation of Journalists World Conference, Bilbao, Spain, 2–4 May 1997.

23 NM television interview, 11 November 1996, SABC, SABC Archive, SABC Information Library, Johannesburg; 'Some Black

Newsmen Rapped for Secret Agenda', *Business Day,* 3 November 1996; 'Mandela Slams Some Black Journalists', *Citizen,* 13 November 1996.

24 NM, note, NMPP 2009/8, box 4, file 1, 128–9.

25 NM, speech to the Fiftieth National Conference of the ANC, Mafikeng, 16 December 1997.

26 NM, note, NMPP 2009/8, box 4, p. 4, NMF, Johannesburg.

27 NM, note on response to the political report to the Fiftieth ANC Congress, December 1997, NMPP 2009/8, box 4, folder 1, pp. 1–2, NMF, Johannesburg.

28 Ibid.

29 Ibid.

30 NM, address to the closing session of the Fiftieth National Conference of the ANC, 20 December 1997, Mafikeng.

31 *The Sowetan,* 20 November 1996; *Financial Mail,* 22 November 1996.

32 NM, 'The Presidential Years', p. 33.

Chapter Thirteen: On the African and World Stages

1 Harriet Beecher Stowe, *Uncle Tom's Cabin* (Washington, DC, 1852); Booker T. Washington, *Up from Slavery: An Autobiography* (New York: Doubleday and Company, 1901).

2 OAU Assembly of Heads of State and Government, Declaration on the Political and Socio-economic Situation in Africa and the Fundamental Changes Taking Place in the World, 9–11 July 1990, Addis Ababa.

3 OAU, Assembly of Heads of State and Government, Declaration on the Establishment Within the OAU of a Mechanism for Conflict Prevention, Management and Resolution, 28–30 June 1993.

4 NM, statement at the OAU meeting of heads of state and government, Tunis, 13 June 1994.

5 Nkosazana Dlamini-Zuma, interview by Tony Trew, Durban, 26 February 2016.

6 NM, statement as chairperson of SADC at the official opening of the summit of SADC heads of state and government, Blantyre, 8 September 1997.

7 Ibid.

8 SADC Heads of State and Government, Summit, Gaborone, 28 June 1996.

9 NM, SADC Organ, 7 September 1997, NMPP notes, box 5, file 3, 074–86, NMF, Johannesburg.

10 NM, notes on SADC summit in Maputo, 2 March 1998, NMPP notes, box 4, file 2, 055–60, NMF, Johannesburg.

11 Quett Ketumile Joni Masire, *Very Brave or Very Foolish?: Memoirs of an African Democrat* (Botswana: Macmillan Botswana, 2006), p.279.

12 Deputy President Thabo Mbeki, statement to the National Assembly on the situation in the Democratic Republic of the Congo, Houses of Parliament, Cape Town, 21 May 1997.

13 Ibid; Aziz Pahad, interview by Tony Trew, Johannesburg, 1 February 2016.

14 NM, notes following a meeting with Comrade Kabila, Genadendal, 15 May 1997, NMPP 2009/8, box4, file2, pp.1–4, NMF, Johannesburg.

15 Acting President Buthelezi, Developments in Lesotho, Statements to the National Assembly, 22 September 1998, Hansard, cols. 6763–6778.

16 Cabinet minutes, 23 September 1998.

17 AP Archive, 'South Africa: President Mandela Calms Concern Over his Health', 27 September 1998, story no. 89970.

18 NM, State of the Nation Address, National Assembly, Houses of Parliament, Cape Town, 5 February 1999.

19 NM at the World Economic Forum Southern Africa Economic Summit, Harare, 21 May 1997, tape 71942MT, SABC, SABC Archive, SABC Information Library, Johannesburg.

20 NM, address to the Mercosur Heads of State Summit, Ushuaia, Argentina, 24 July 1998.

21 NM, address at the Forty-ninth Session of the General Assembly of the UN, New

York, 10 October 1994.

22 Ibid.

23 NM, address at the inaugural session of the Twelfth Conference of Heads of State or Government of Non-Aligned Countries, Durban, 2 September 1998.

24 Ibid.

25 NM, address to the Joint Houses of Congress of the USA, Washington, DC, 6 October 1994.

26 NM, address to the Swedish Parliament, Stockholm, 18 March 1999.

27 'Mandela praises Gaddafi', *Sunday Times* Foreign Desk, 20 May 1990; Fritz Joubert *'Mense in VSA vies vir Mandela'* [People in the USA are angry with Mandela], *Beeld,* 24 May 1990.

28 Khalil I. Matar and Robert W. Thabit, *Lockerbie and Libya: A study in International Relations* (London: McFarland & Company, Inc, 2004).

29 NM, Statement on Lockerbie drafted and released in Tunis, NMPP 2009/8, box 6, file 8a, NMF, Johannesburg.

30 'SA Calls for Lifting of Sanctions on Libya', *The Star,* 22 October 1997.

31 OAU, Declarations and Decisions adopted by the Thirty-Third OAU Assembly of Heads of State and Government, Harare, 2–4 June 1997.

32 NM visits Libya, October 1997, tape 66786, MT22, SABC, SABC TV Archive,

SABC Information Library, Johannesburg.

33 Ibid.

34 Lyn Boyd-Judson, *Strategic Moral Diplomacy: Understanding the Enemy's Moral Universe* (West Hartford, CT: Kumarian Press, 2011); Khalil I. Matar, Robert W. Thabit, *Lockerbie and Libya.*

35 Lyn Boyd-Judson, *Strategic Moral Diplomacy.*

36 NM, address to the Congress of the People, Libya, 19 March 1999.

37 Jakes Gerwel, interview by Aziz Pahad, 21 July 2010.

38 NM, statement on South Africa's relations with the Greater Chinese Region, 27 November 1996, SABC, SABC TV Archive, tape 25459MT, SABC Information Library, Johannesburg.

39 'Taiwan's Minister Fails with Mandela', United Press International Archive, 4 December 1996.

40 NM, address at Beijing University, Beijing, 6 May 1999.

41 NM, interview by Phil Molefe and Antjie Krog, 'Farewell Interview With the SABC', broadcast live from Qunu, SABC, 20 May 1999.

Epilogue

1 Graça Machel, interview by Mandla Langa, 22 September 2016.

2 NM to Winnie Mandela in Kroonstad Prison, 1 February 1975.
3 Zelda la Grange, *Good Morning Mr Mandela: A Memoir* (New York: Plume, 2015), p. 128.
4 While being interviewed by a panel, this was Mandela's answer to a question by Phil Molefe who asks about his feelings as he prepares to step down as president of the ANC. NM, televised interview on *Face the Media,* 14 December 1997, SABC, tape 66676MT, SABC Archive, SABC Information Library, Johannesburg.
5 NM, closing the ANC's Fiftieth National Conference, Mafikeng, 20 December 1997.
6 NM, election campaign, 31 May 1999, tape 66717MT, SABC, SABC Archive, SABC Information Library, Johannesburg.
7 NM, speech at the final sitting of the first democratically elected parliament, Houses of Parliament, Cape Town, 26 March 1999.

ACKNOWLEDGEMENTS

In 1971 Nelson Mandela wrote a letter from Robben Island to his old friend Fatima Meer, in which he expressed doubt about memoirs — 'What a sweet euphemism for self-praise the English language has evolved! Autobiography.' And yet just four years later he had embarked on the first draft of what was to become his bestselling memoir *Long Walk to Freedom*.

As Mum Graça Machel indicates in the prologue to this book, the contingencies of time and struggle informed his decisions to write both *Long Walk* and the early sections of what has become this volume. The same contingencies ensured lengthy gestation periods for both books — each book took almost twenty years to get published.

Given the length of its gestation and the complexity of its provenance, *Dare Not Linger* demands multiple acknowledgements. Mum Machel's determination to see it through, and her constant presence through the process, inspired us. Mandla Langa was almost too good to be true as a writer willing to work with a demanding collective. Joel Netshitenzhe and Tony Trew provided extraordinary research and analysis capacity, as well as generating the first narrativisation, drawing on both Mr Mandela's writing and the contents of 'the archive'. Tony was tireless in trawling multiple archival repositories. In this he was ably assisted by Janet Levy and the Nelson Mandela Foundation archives team — Razia Saleh, Zanele Riba, Lucia Raadschelders and Sahm Venter. As always, Sahm, the team's senior researcher, provided authority of first and last resort on our founder's life and times. Our chief executive, Sello Hatang, was the glue holding the whole process together — he both opened doors and held them open. The support given to us by the executors of Mr Mandela's estate was indispensable. Special thanks are due to Judge Dikgang Moseneke.

In the early phases of the project, as Mr Mandela toiled with pen in hand, Zelda la Grange was the dynamo maintaining its momentum. She was supported devotedly by Vimla Naidoo, Maretha Slabbert and Thoko Mavuso. Zelda also became critical to its being revived under the auspices of the Nelson Mandela Foundation after Madiba's passing, and remained available for queries of all kinds until the end. Also playing a role in the early phases was research assistant Thembeka Mafumadi.

Our publishing partners have been a joy to work with. Special thanks to Geoff Blackwell, Rachel Clare, Kate Cooper, Jonny Geller, Cameron Gibb, Benjamin Harris, Sloan Harris, Ruth Hobday, Jenny Moore, Georgina Morley, Terry Morris and Andrea Nattrass. Among other things, Andrea provided deep understanding of Mandla's writing processes.

The Industrial Development Corporation was a generous and supportive funding partner.

We are indebted to the many individuals (some referenced, some not) who generously gave of their time and knowledge in interviews. Builders and managers of websites that ease access to historical records should also be acknowledged, as should archivists, who quietly go about preserving records and making them available without fuss or favour. And thanks also go to Chris Williams for sharing his knowledge of sources.

In terms of the archival work underpinning this project, certain institutions and the individuals working in them require special mention:

- Parliamentary Library, Parliament, Republic of South Africa (Sadeck Casoojee)
- The Presidency, Republic of South

Africa (Cassius Lubisi, Lusanda Mxenge, William Smith, Busani Ngcaweni, Bongani Ngqulunga, Anande Nothling and Daphne Mhlongo)
- ANC Archives, Luthuli House (Zolile Mvunelo and Mandla Khumalo)
- ANC Archives, National Heritage and Cultural Studies Centre, University of Fort Hare (Mosanku Maamoe)
- National Archives of South Africa (Natalie Skomolo, Zahira Adams and Gerrit Wagener)
- National Library, Cape Town
- ANC Parliamentary Caucus Research and Development Unit (Mark Sweet)
- University of Cape Town Library, African Studies Collection
- South African Broadcasting Corporation (Sias Scott and Moloko Maserumule)
- Historical Papers, William Cullen Library, University of the Witwatersrand Gabriele Mohale)
- Statistics South Africa (Pali Lehohla and Faizel Mohammed)
- Ipsos library (Mari Harris)

Ultimately, of course, this book belongs to Nelson Mandela. Without the abiding inspiration of his life and work it would not have been worth making. I have no doubt that he would have been pleased with Mandla's craft as a storyteller.

Verne Harris
Nelson Mandela Foundation

PERMISSIONS ACKNOWLEDGEMENTS

Grateful acknowledgement is made for permission to reprint the following material:

Page 78: Extract from the poem 'Haste', taken from *Sacred Hope* by Agostinho Neto, copyright © 1974 Tanzania Publishing House. Translation by Marga Holness. Page 293: Extract from the poem 'Justice', taken from *Scottsboro Limited: Four Poems and a Play in Verse* by Langston Hughes, copyright © 1932 Golden Stair Press. Reproduced by permission of David Higham Associates. Pages 306–7: Extract from the poem 'Die Kind' by Ingrid Jonker.

Page 6: Nelson Mandela Foundation, photograph by Ardon Bar-Hama; page 7: Nelson Mandela Foundation, photograph by Ardon Bar-Hama; plate 1: Nelson Mandela Foundation, photograph by Ardon Bar-Hama; plate 2: Chris Ledochowski (top); Louise Gubb courtesy Nelson Mandela Foundation (bottom); plate 3: AFP/Getty Images; plate 4:

Frans Esterhuyse (top); Tom Stoddart Archive/Getty Images (bottom); plate 5: Denis Farrell/AP (top); David Brauchli/AP (bottom); plate 6: Peter Turnley/Getty Images (top left); Paul Weinberg/South Photographs/ Africa Media Online (top right); Nanda Soobben/Africa Media Online (bottom); plate 7: Lewis Horwitz courtesy Nelson Mandela Foundation (top); Alexander Joe/ AFP/Getty Images (bottom); plate 8: Foto24/ Gallo Images/Getty Images (top); unknown courtesy Nelson Mandela Foundation (bottom); plate 9: Nelson Mandela Foundation, photograph by Ardon Bar-Hama; plate 10: Paul Weinberg/South Photographs/Africa Media Online (top left); Oryx Media Archive/ Gallo Images/Getty Images (top right and middle left); Obed Zilwa/AP (middle right); Mike Hutchings/Reuters (bottom); plate 11: Nelson Mandela Foundation, photograph by Ardon Bar-Hama; plate 12: Walter Dhladhla/ Getty Images (top); Henner Frankenfeld/ Picturenet Africa (bottom left); Adil Bradlow/ Africa Media Online (bottom right); plate 13: David Goldblatt/South Photographs/ Africa Media Online (top left); Guy Tillim/ AFP/Getty Images (top right); Clinton Presidential Library (bottom left); Yoav Lemmer/ Getty Images (bottom right); plate 14: Nelson Mandela Foundation, photograph by Ardon Bar-Hama; plate 15: Pool BASSIGNAC/ BUU/HIRES/Getty Images (top); Eric Miller courtesy Nelson Mandela Foundation (middle left); Julian Parker/Getty Images (middle right and bottom left); Amr Nabil/ Getty Images (bottom right); plate 16: Str Old/Reuters; plate 17: Media24/Gallo Images/Getty Images; plate 18: Nelson Mandela Foundation, photograph by Ardon Bar-Hama; plate 19: Juda Ngwenya (top); Paul Grendon/Alamy (bottom); plate 20: Ross Kinnaird/EMPICS/Getty Images; plate 21: Oryx Media Archive/Gallo Images/Getty Images (top); Walter Dhladhla/Getty Images (bottom); plate 22: Adil Bradlow/Africa Media Online (top); Louise Gubb/ lugubb@iafrica.com (bottom); plate 23: Louise Gubb/lugubb@iafrica.com (top); Benny Gool (bottom left); Eric Miller courtesy Nelson Mandela Foundation (bottom right); plate 24: Eric Miller courtesy Nelson Mandela Foundation (top); Zapiro (bottom).

Page 6: From chapter six of Mandela's memoir on his presidential years, he reflects on being brought before the Constitutional Court. A staunch advocate of the democracy's new laws under its Constitution, he writes: 'In the new South Africa there is nobody, not even the President, who is above the law, that the rule of law generally and, in particular, the independence of the judiciary should be respected.' (See page 269.)

Page 7: From an early draft of Mandela's

memoir of his presidential years, he describes the world's reaction to South Africa's first democratic elections in April 1994: 'The world, aware of the formidable challenges facing the first democratically elected government, hailed us as a miracle nation and threw open its previously closed doors to all South Africans, irrespective of their ethnicity and background.'

ABOUT THE AUTHORS

Nelson Mandela was born in the Transkei, South Africa, on July 18, 1918. He joined the African National Congress in 1944 and was engaged in resistance against the ruling National Party's apartheid policies for many years before being arrested in August 1962. Mandela was incarcerated for more than twenty-seven years, during which time his status as a potent symbol of resistance to apartheid grew steadily. Released from prison in 1990, Mandela won the Nobel Peace Prize in 1993 and was inaugurated as the first democratically elected president of South Africa in 1994. He is the author of the international bestseller *Long Walk to Freedom*. He died on December 5, 2013, at age ninety-five.

Mandla Langa was born in 1950 in Durban, South Africa. After being arrested in 1976, he went into exile and has lived in Botswana, Mozambique, and Angola — where he did his Umkhonto weSizwe (the armed wing of the African National Congress) military training — as well as in Hungary, Zambia, and the United Kingdom, where he was the African National Congress's cultural representative. A writer and journalist, he was the first South African to be awarded the Arts Council of Great Britain bursary for creative writing, and he has been a columnist for the *Sunday Independent* and *The New Nation*. In 2007 he was the recipient of the presidential Order of Ikhamanga in Silver for his literary and journalistic contribution to democracy in South Africa. He is also the author of several acclaimed novels, including *The Lost Colours of the Chameleon*, which won the 2009 Commonwealth Writers' Prize for Best Book in the African region.

Graça Machel was born in Gaza, Mozambique, in 1945. She was a member of the Mozambique Liberation Front (FRELIMO), which fought for and won independence from Portugal in 1975. A teacher, a human rights activist, an international advocate for women's and children's rights, and a politician, she was — from 1975 until his death in 1986 — married to Samora Machel, the first president of Mozambique. She married Nelson Mandela on his eightieth birthday, in July 1998. Among numerous awards for her humanitarian work, she was a recipient of the

United Nations Nansen Medal in 1995, and in 2007 she was made an honorary Dame Commander of the Order of the British Empire.

The employees of Thorndike Press hope you have enjoyed this Large Print book. All our Thorndike, Wheeler, and Kennebec Large Print titles are designed for easy reading, and all our books are made to last. Other Thorndike Press Large Print books are available at your library, through selected bookstores, or directly from us.

For information about titles, please call:
(800) 223-1244

or visit our website at:
gale.com/thorndike

To share your comments, please write:
Publisher
Thorndike Press
10 Water St., Suite 310
Waterville, ME 04901

2·20·18